This book is a non-geographic and timeless gem! Its analysis of ideas, themes and slogans goes beyond specific times and geographical boundaries. Evangelicals may not always be precise in discerning the direction or time of a powerful revival movement, given that God's ways are not our ways (Isa 55:8). Yet here Dr. Mwangi has been able to link a relationship of several exchanges of concepts with intercontinental and timeless sociological impacts. He has reestablished the centrality of sanctification in the Keswick revival. The link Mwangi has established of the Keswick revival through the vein of "walking in the light" to the East African Revival Movement is very powerful. This theme has, with time, gone through a metamorphosis without changing the core and while spreading its aroma, it has now been lifted by the GAFCON movement as a central feature. Just like what GAFCON is to the future of Anglicans in the world, this book at hand has the potential and synergy to call the church in Africa to not lose the saltiness that enabled it to sail through trying moments of history. I highly rate this book.

Rt. Rev. Joseph Kibucwa, DD
Diocese of Kirinyaga, Kenya

This is a clearly written, historical introduction to, and influence of the Keswick theology and teachings, within the East African Revival Movement (EARM). The author is from the Anglican Church of Kenya and investigates the East African sociological worldview to have some significant exchange of concepts and meanings primarily from the viewpoints of exclusion and inclusion. He challenges the "walking in the light" fundamentals and motivates Brethren's participation in the *missio Dei*, from exclusive to the inclusive predisposition of mutual Christian coexistence.

Johannes Knoetze, PhD
Professor, Department of Practical Theology and Mission Studies,
University of Pretoria, South Africa

The story of the East African Revival Movement (EARM) continues to intrigue the world of scholarship. Each book that is written about the EARM brings to light new aspects and interpretations of both Scripture and theological themes. In this book, Mwangi has creatively examined the theology of sanctification among members of the EARM from a specific region and has offered an alternative perspective of sanctification by the people. Using lived experiences of the people, Mwangi shows how sanctification permeates other aspects of life and influences the totality of the Christian life. He explores and brings to light the patterns and processes of sanctification in Christian living. Integrating Scripture, practical theology and pastoral practice, this book will be of great importance to students of theology, especially lived Christianity, as sanctification is not an abstract concept but an integral part of the Christian life.

Esther Mombo, PhD
Professor, School of Theology,
St. Paul's University, Limuru, Kenya

Dr. Mwangi's analysis of the biblical roots of revival, as well as his insights into the challenges for mission and evangelism, lead him to argue that the East Africa Revival Movement needs to be more socially engaged, less focused on its own community and more responsive to variety and flexibility, while still maintaining a strong witness to the cost of discipleship. Mwangi does not speculate about the future of the Revival movement in Kenya, but he does point to its weaknesses in speaking to a new generation, and the simple fact that its membership is growing old. Mwangi's deep knowledge of biblical exegesis and mission theology provide much valuable material to inform a renewal of evangelism in the years to come, whether this involves the existing Revival movement or some new way. The Revival movement has shown remarkable persistence over the last hundred years. If God chooses to initiate a new revival, the *Balokole* will not complain. In the words of one of their favorite passages, they will simply "give thanks to God the Father at all times and for everything in the name of our Lord Jesus Christ" (Eph 5:20).

Kevin Ward, PhD
Former Senior Lecturer of African Religious Studies,
University of Leeds, UK

The Influence of Early Keswick Theology of Sanctification in the Socio-ethical Life of the East African Revival Movement

A Missional Perspective

Robinson Kariuki Mwangi

ACADEMIC

© 2025 Robinson Kariuki Mwangi

Published 2025 by Langham Academic
An imprint of Langham Publishing
www.langhampublishing.org

Langham Publishing and its imprints are a ministry of Langham Partnership

Langham Partnership
PO Box 296, Carlisle, Cumbria, CA3 9WZ, UK
www.langham.org

ISBNs:
978-1-83973-227-0 Print
978-1-78641-142-6 ePub
978-1-78641-143-3 PDF

Robinson Kariuki Mwangi has asserted his right under the Copyright, Designs and Patents Act, 1988 to be identified as the Author of this work.

All rights reserved. No part of this publication may be reproduced, stored in a retrieval system or transmitted, in any form or by any means, electronic, mechanical, photocopying, recording or otherwise, without the prior written permission of the publisher or the Copyright Licensing Agency.

Requests to reuse content from Langham Publishing are processed through PLSclear. Please visit www.plsclear.com to complete your request.

All Scripture quotations, unless otherwise indicated, are taken from the Holy Bible, New International Version®, NIV®. Copyright ©1973, 1978, 1984, 2011 by Biblica, Inc.™ Used by permission of Zondervan.

Scripture quotations marked (ESV) are taken from The Holy Bible, English Standard Version® (ESV®), copyright © 2001 by Crossway, a publishing ministry of Good News Publishers. Used by permission. All rights reserved.

British Library Cataloguing-in-Publication Data
A catalogue record for this book is available from the British Library

ISBN: 978-1-83973-227-0

Cover & Book Design: projectluz.com

Langham Partnership actively supports theological dialogue and an author's right to publish but does not necessarily endorse the views and opinions set forth here or in works referenced within this publication, nor can we guarantee technical and grammatical correctness. Langham Partnership does not accept any responsibility or liability to persons or property as a consequence of the reading, use or interpretation of its published content.

Contents

Acknowledgements xiii

Abstract xv
    Key Terms xvi

Foreword xvii
    When We Walk with the Lord

Preface xxv

Chapter 1 1
Background and Problem Statement
    Introduction 1
    Research Background and the Problem Statement 1
        Background 1
        Historical Overview of the Prevailing Situation 2
        Definition of Concepts 3
        Problem Statement 4
        Main Research Question 12
        Rationale 13
        Theoretical Framework 14
        Paradigm Based on the *Missio Dei* 15
        Research Methods 15
    Conclusion 27

Chapter 2 29
Keswick Theology of Sanctification: Socio-historical Background for Walking in the Light
    Introduction 29
    Walking in the Light 29
        Contextual Definition 30
        Contextual Description 30
        Walking in the Light in the *Missio Dei* 32
    A Historical View of Keswick Theology 52
        Keswick Antecedents 52
        Keswick Views of Sanctification Theology 58
    Affinity Between Sociological Circumstances and Keswick
        Theology 72
        Affinity on the Segregation of Human Beings 73

    Affinity with Faith in the Supernatural 75
    Affinity with Community Ethics 76
    Affinity with Rites of Passage 76
    Affinity with Blood Symbolism..77
    Affinity with a Seclusion Period 78
  Evaluation of the EARM against *Missio Dei* 79
    Exposition of the Scripture..80
    Centrality of the Cross 81
    Public Confession 82
    Legalism 83
  Conclusion...85

Chapter 3 87
Anglican Scholarship on Keswick Theology of Sanctification and Walking in the Light in the EARM
  Introduction 87
  A Historical Overview of Anglican Church Scholarship
    on EARM..88
    A Brief Overview of Anglican Scholarship on EARM.................89
    A Brief Overview of the Genesis of EARM...................................93
    EARM's Heritage of Keswick Theology 111
  Nature and Current Trends Regarding Anglican Church
    Scholarship on Keswick Theology's Influence on EARM's
    Walking in the Light: Findings and Analyses of the
    Prevailing Situation 128
    Data Construction 128
    Demographic Data: Distribution of Respondents
      According to Their Categories 134
    Constructing Themes 136
  Conclusion...158

Chapter 4 161
Prevailing Basic Missiological Tenets and Practices of Walking in Light
  Introduction 161
  Basic Missiological Tenets That Provide A Platform to
    Analyze the Prevailing Practices of Walking in the Light 162
    Incarnational Principle 162
    Cross-centered Principle...165
    Centripetal-centrifugal Principle..168
    Missio Logoi Principle 171

Missio Dei Principle 175
Interpretation of the Main Biblical Texts to Give Missiological
    Perspectives on the Prevailing Situation 177
    Historical Development of the Interpretation of Ephesians 178
    Historical Development of the Interpretation of
        Ephesians 6:13 194
    Historical Development of Interpretation of
        1 Corinthians 11:13–15 208
    Historical Development of Interpretation of Daniel 1:8–16 224
Anglican Evangelical Tradition Framework for Walking in
    the Light 239
    Supremacy of Scripture 240
    Reformed Doctrine Ecclesiology 246
    Engaging the Prayer Book 251
A New EARM Model of the Theology of Sanctification 256
    Prevailing Theology of Sanctification and Holiness 256
    Preferred Theology of Sanctification and Holiness 259
Brethren's Lifestyle in the Anglican Evangelical Tradition;
    Faithful Participants in the *Missio Dei* 262
    Born-again Testimony 262
    Worship Styles 263
    Moral Codes 264
Conclusion 266

Chapter 5 267
Missiological Foundations to Critique Particular Tenets of
    Walking in the Light
Introduction 267
Missiological Foundations 268
    Historical Perspective of Missiology on Brethren Beliefs
        and Practices of Walking in the Light 269
    Theological Perspective of Missiology on Brethren Beliefs
        and Practices of Walking in the Light 297
    Anthropological Perspective of Missiology on Brethren
        Beliefs and Practices of Walking in the Light 314
Summary of the Prevailing Situation As It is Today Using
    Historical and Empirical Analyses. 327
    Historical Analysis 329
    Empirical Analyses 331
    Analysis of Affinity Between Historical and
        Empirical Trends 336

    Anglican Church Mission Statement Perspective to
        Summarize the Current Situation As It Should Be..........................339
            Mental Transformation...340
            Physical Transformation...342
            Spiritual Transformation..343
            Social Transformation..344
        A Summary of the Situation (of Walking In the Light) as
            It Should Be 345
    Viable Biblically Based Model of *Missio Dei* 348
        Self-directed Lifestyle (Brethren's Old Model).............................349
        Christ Directed Lifestyle (Brethren's New Model) 351
        The Great Commission: The Basis for the Changed World
            Model of Walking in the Light..353
    Conclusion..357

Chapter 6 359

    Conclusion and Way Forward
        Summary of Viewpoints 359
        Synthesis of Own Insights of Moving from the Current to
            Preferred Scenario 360
            Synthesis of Insights on Current Scenarios; Exclusive
                Beliefs and Practices of Walking in the Light.......................361
            Synthesis of Insights on Preferred Scenario; Inclusive
                Beliefs and Practices of Walking in the Light.......................363
        Gaps in the Literature...366
            EARM Convention...366
            Doctrine of Justification...367
            Born-again Testimony..367
            Eschatological Undertones 368
        Research Objectives..368
        Recommendations for Further Research.....................................370

Bibliography 373

Appendix 1 397
    Factions in the EARM

Appendix 2 399
    Interview Guide for the Focus Groups and the One-on-One,
    EARM's Leaders

Appendix 3 401
    Interview Guide for Theological Students, Clergy, Bishops and the Main Stakeholders

Appendix 4 403
    Inductive and Comparative Data Analysis in the Seven Centers in the ACK Diocese of Mbeere

Appendix 5 411
    Nature and Current Trends Regarding Anglican Church Scholarship on Keswick Theology's Influence on EARM's Walking in the Light: Findings and Analyses of the Prevailing Situation

List of Tables

Table 1: Target Population 20
Table 2: Demographic 135
Table 3: Data by Categories 136
Table 4: Respondents Never Heard of Keswick Theology 139
Table 5: Interpretation of Biblical Texts by Brethren 143
Table 6: Influence of Keswick Theology 328

List of Figures

Figure 1: Factions within Brethren fellowship 257

Figure 2: Brethren at local fellowship 258

Figure 3: Sharing ethical codes 258

Figure 4: Generation gap dilemma 259

Figure 5: Mutual sharing with clergy 260

Figure 6: Sufficiency of the Cross 260

Figure 7: Convergent point 261

Acknowledgements

I am most grateful to my beloved wife Susan Wambui and my cherished children Franklin Mwangi, Gertrude Wanjeri and Grace Victoria Angela for your love, support, perseverance, encouragement and prayers during my constant absence.

I would like to express my sincere gratitude to GWC, South Africa, for providing a bursary to complete this project through Evangelical Research Fellowship. Also to Latimer Trust for partly funding my field research. I would like to express my sincere thanks to my colleagues and the lecturers at GWC for their excellent contribution to this study. For instance, the constructive criticisms of Dr. Robert Dole and Dr. Ben Dean in the formative stages of this study were insightful and beneficial, and the GWC Chief Librarian, Mr. Colin Majackie, allowed a particular arrangement of study hours. To all of you, I say thank you very much.

Sincere thanks go to the retired principal of the St. Andrew's College of Theology and Development, Kabare, Rev. Canon Dr. Moses Mwangi Njoroge and the retired Archbishop of the ACK, His Grace the Most Rev. Dr. Eliud Wabukala who recommended me for sponsorship. Thank you for finding me worthy to enroll for a PhD. I salute you for your confidence in me.

I wish to salute my supervisor Prof. Johannes Knoetze; without his dedicated supervision, this study would not have come to completion. Equally, the administration of Potchefstroom Campus of North-West University for patience throughout my studies. I would also like to thank Nico Nel for language editing this study. Your conscious attention to language matters is commendable.

Sincere thanks also go to the bishops of the ACK Kirinyaga, Embu, Mount Kenya Central, Mount Kenya West and Mbeere for not only inspiring profound insights for reflection but also allowing me to do field research in your jurisdictions. Accolades also go to all my research assistants and field research respondents without whom I would have missed some significant socio-ethical concerns of this study.

I also wish to express my thanks to Bishop Joseph Karimi Kibucwa of ACK Kirinyaga Diocese for praying with me from beginning to the end of this study, giving it the blessings it now enjoys. Likewise, a vote of gratitude to the staff and students of St. Andrew's College, Kabare, for your understanding, inspiration and prayers. Finally, I owe immeasurable thanks to all those who have assisted me in one way or another in shaping my life.

Abstract

The thesis investigates the influence of early Keswick theology of sanctification in the socio-ethical life of the East African Revival Movement (EARM), 1930–2015, in the Anglican Church, Mount Kenya Region within the framework of *missio Dei*. It starts with the proposition that early Keswick theology of sanctification is behind the beliefs and practices of "walking in the light" leading to splits within the EARM that affect church mission.

This study poses one primary question, namely, does the Keswick theology of sanctification contribute to the socio-ethical understanding of walking in the light in the EARM and thus influence the mission of the Anglican Church, Mount Kenya region? Following historical and empirical analysis, it has been claimed that "walking in the light" has led to a split in EARM. The study mainly uses qualitative research to document information from primary and secondary sources to analyze historical and empirical data of the current phenomenon. The principal data collection method is focused group discussion and one-on-one interview. The research employs guided questions to elicit perspectives of respondents' view of the prevailing situation. The data reveals six themes which are compared with historical themes to culminate in three clusters of conversion, worship style, and moral codes. Following this an analytical summary of the current historical and empirical situation is structured around these three clusters which then informs an analysis of the trend of "walking in the light" in EARM.

The study has established that Keswick theology of sanctification finds affinity with East African socio-historical circumstances which enabled Keswick theology and East Africa sociological worldview to have a significant exchange of concepts and meanings primarily from the viewpoints of exclusion and inclusion. However, the study found that Anglican Church scholarship mainly explores EARM from historical, cultural and theological perspectives and thus has not documented its influence of "walking in the light" on the involvement of EARM in the mission of God, particularly in the Mount Kenya region. Indeed most respondents, except main stakeholders, showed ignorance of Keswick *theology*. As a result, the missiological tenets challenges walking in the light fundamentals and motivates Brethren's participation in the mission of God. (Note: "Brethren" is used in Kenya to refer to members of the EARM.) Thus when walking in the light is critiqued against the missiological foundations it falls short of the mandate of involvement in the *missio Dei* due to its exclusive disposition. Consequently, when the current trend is compared to the mission statement, the prevailing situation of walking in the light has hindered mission in the Anglican Church Kenya (ACK). Thus, ACK mission demonstrates the preferred scenario: A shift on the part of Brethren from exclusivity to inclusivity in the way Christians coexist.

Key Terms

East African Revival Movement (EARM), Keswick theology/teachings, sanctification, socio-ethical life, walking in the light, fellowship, saved, *missio Dei* (mission of God), missiology, Anglican Church Kenya (ACK).

Foreword

When We Walk with the Lord

The East African Revival Movement is a truly remarkable movement of impressive influence. It is far reaching in its scope with deep ecclesiastical, sociological and theological influences. Since its formative years in the late 1920s, and eventual spread to every part of Eastern Africa and beyond, the movement has continued to capture imaginations, impact communities, inspire scholarship and shape theological views and social-ethical behaviour as it resolutely continues to endure the passage of time.

The movement's provenance straddles two worlds – one deeply steeped in the history of evangelical missionary movement and the other, a world of African traditional spirituality. Born out of the cross fertilization of these two worlds, the East African Revival Movement is a holiness movement of its own kind. It is as much African as it is Christian. The movement resolutely emphasises the necessity of a conversion experience and conscious "personal salvation," thereby shaping a vision of a new community of born-again Brethren bound together by shared testimony and regular fellowships. The Brethren are distinct and set apart by their experience of new birth. Their verbalized personal testimonies and the commitment to walk daily with the Lord, a way of life popularly tagged, "walking in the light," provide a window into the Brethren's moral universe. The "saved" or the "born-again" distinguish themselves by their obligation to the fellowship of the Brethren, appropriation of biblical faith as they understand it and adherence to moral and ethical codes as they sacrificially lead a life worthy of a Christian's calling.

Ironically, the movement to date has by and large remained part of the larger communities of faith despite their uncompromising stance on the need for a conversion experience, which is potentially divisive. The Brethren's logic for continued adherence to particular denominations is not hard to understand. The fellowship of the "saved Brethren" within the larger church provides a kind of church within the church. Short of schism, a "saved" believer is in every sense separate and must live above the indulgences of the worldly church. This is sustained through faithful commitment to a higher calling of moral and ethical purity. The outward marks of the members are evidenced by attending regular fellowships, confession of sin, regular repentance and a devotion to the way of the cross characterised by a life of spiritual fervour and change in social behaviour.

An exploration of the background source of a theology of sanctification, encapsulated in the phrase "walking in the light," and how this informs the Brethren's response to the mission of God is the subject of this book. The central thesis is that there is an observable influence of early Keswick theology of sanctification which underpins the East African Revival Movement's theology of "walking in the light," and the resultant social and ethical practices. The reason for the easy embrace of such a theology by the African converts is seemingly aided by existing African social-cultural practices. Admittedly, most African communities would mark important rites of passage with rituals of separation followed by restoration and inclusion.[1] Liminal boundaries serve to create hierarchies of sacredness and to define status and identity. If the conceptual framing of the Brethren's views of "separation," are cultural, their theological nuances are, nevertheless, thoroughly biblical. The contention here is not so much with their source of theological inspiration but perhaps with how biblical references are selected, interpreted and applied. They introduced no doctrinal novelty. More than any other teaching, their understanding of select scriptures is directly responsible for the subsequent theology of justification and sanctification, the emergence of specific moral

---

1. For example, as Brian Stanley citing a study of the Bahima of North-Eastern Ankole by D. J. Stenning observes, "that the use of public confession as an institutional means of initiation into the Revival fellowship was a reflection of traditional religious practice." Brian Stanley, "The East African Revival: African Initiative within a European Tradition," in *Churchman* 92, no. 1 (1978): 11; compare D. J. Stenning, "Salvation in Ankole," in *African Systems of Thought*, eds. M. Fortes and G. Dieterlein (OUP for the International African Institute: London, 1965), 258–275.

and ethical codes and their attitude towards the larger church and involvement in mission. It is important to note, for example, how the interpretations of the scriptures identified in this book are exegetically analysed and their impact on the socio-ethical choices of the Brethren are explored. The most influential of these biblical data include, but not limited to Genesis 12:1; Psalms 127:1; Daniel 1:8–16; Matthew 5:14; Romans 13:8; 1 Corinthians 11:14–16; 2 Corinthians 6:14–18; Ephesians 5:14, 6:14–20; and 1 John 2:9–11, but such texts as Proverbs 28:13; Matthew 16:24–26; Luke 9:23; John 3:20; Acts 19:18; and Romans 10:9, among others, could be added as equally influential. Believing that the scriptures will always and literally mean what it says, the Brethren endeavour to put to practice the demands of these teachings in obedience to the word of God.

Observable discontinuities between the East African and the Keswick revival movements beg at least one important question: To what extent is the change in social and ethical behaviours to be attributed solely to the influence of the Keswick's theology of sanctification? There are other likely sources of influence. The revival was most likely as a result of a general response to a worrying nominalism that was prevalent at the time. Frustrations from general laxity and worldliness of the church, including morally corrupting practices such as drunkenness, sexual indiscretions and witchcraft featured recurrently in most missionary reports.[2] Joe Church himself, one of the missionary founders of the movement contends that, "the revival came as a result of spiritual hunger and a desire for the fullness of the Holy Spirit."[3] Most converts lived unchanged lives embracing ecclesial membership, professing a form of religiosity but by their way of life "denying its power thereof" (2 Tim 3:5 KJV).[4] This must have motivated a quest for a meaningful and transformative "salvation." It cannot be ignored, also, that the revival is genuinely

---

2. See for example, Gordon Hewitt, *The Problem of Success: A History of the Church Missionary Society. Volume 1, 1910–1942* (London: SCM Press, 1971), 239; Stanley, "The East African Revival," 1–3.

3. Cited in Hazel Ony'ayo Avanga, "Internal Movements in the Anglican Diocese of Maseno North: With Special Reference to the East African Revival Movement," (MA Thesis submitted to University of Nairobi, 1986), 17, https//www.erepository.uonbi.ac.ke; See also Stanley, "The East African Revival," 5.

4. Compare, for example, Avanga, *Internal Movements in the Anglican Diocese of Maseno North*, iv, 62–68.

the work of the Holy Spirit, unique and specific to this context and time in accordance with God's purpose.[5]

The movement, at least in its early stages, was thoroughly missional and evangelistic in intent and passion. The church was seen as a fertile mission field in dire need of the gospel to truly receive and enjoy the kingdom of God. The movement's desire was to revive and renew the church and not to break away. This could explain why the Brethren remained in the church despite differences with some missionary leaders, clergy or the bishop. As Brian Stanley so aptly articulates, "the mission which had insisted, despite doctrinal differences, on remaining within the [church] should give birth to an African spiritual awakening which refused, despite the tensions it created in the ecclesiastical structure, to countenance the possibility of schism."[6]

The sole quest to renew the whole church exonerates the movement from any accusation of being cultic or schismatic.[7] The internal splitters of the later years reflect a more inward-looking settlement phase, one more preoccupied with internal dynamics and differences than outreach or evangelism. The few breakaways, more common in Western Kenya than Central, such as the *kuhama* or the Johera/Joremo schismatics were rather an exemption than a reflection of a specific pattern within the movement. In general, the internal divisions, as conspicuous as this may be, were neither the direct cause of an all-out schism nor any serious fallouts with the church.

As rightly identified in this book, the different groups, among them the *kufufuka, kutembea, kupaa* and *kusimama,* are distinct yet streams of the same larger fellowship of the Brethren. Just as the larger movement remained within the church, so are the varied strands of the movement, differing on a number of issues yet "belonging" to the same larger communities of faith. It is the theological, missiological and sociological emphases and nuances that sets each apart from the other, as they co-exist within the larger whole. It must be admitted, however, that their differences were always a threat to

---

5. C. P. Groves. *The Planting of Christianity in Africa. Volume 4, 1914–54* (London: Lutterworth Press, 223.

6. Stanley, "The East African Revival," 17.

7. See, for example, Neville Langford Smith, *International Review of Missions*, no. 43 (1954): 78; and "Come as the fire: Revival in the Church in East Africa," *Kenya Church Review*, (1957): 40.

the unity and effective witness of the church as a whole.[8] Separate annual conventions or weekly fellowships often reveal their sharp differences and display bad witness. In this regard, the power of the church as the light of the world and thereby a liberating mission force was generally undermined, ironically by the witness of those who "walk in the light."

The phrase "walking in the light" as well as the names of the different groups within the larger movement gives a good idea of the kind of theological views the movement held. Strictly speaking, the movement neither developed any theology nor preached any new doctrine different from that of the mother church. Their emphases on "walking in the light," by modelling a victorious and sanctified Christian life drew attention to the need for a practical commitment to what already is professed in faith but lacking in practice. The scripture remained the uncontested source of theology and doctrine, safe for often literal interpretations, which ominously tended to impose extra-biblical demands on the Brethren.

Aspects of theology of the cross and specifically the cleansing power of the blood of Christ was commonly emphasised. In practice, this involved repentance and confession of sin, forgiveness of the same and a spiritual reawakening demonstrable in changed social morality, as well as integrity in matters of ethics. Brethren are expected to show forth marks of being "saved" as evidence of a "new birth." They were distinct or set apart, not by any measure of adherence to distinct theological teachings, but by their testimony regarding their experiences of conversion, deliverance from sin, a call to holiness and a new vision of a victorious Christian life. Besides changed lives and testimonies, songs such as *tukutendereza yesu, tembea na yesu, nimeoshwa na damu*, etc. afford insight into the Brethren's theological understandings. These were commonly sung during fellowship gatherings at which testimonies and public confessions of sins are received. Shying away from confessing any sin, ungodly desires and thoughts, or holding back disclosure of any moral laxity is deemed a work of darkness and the "saved," having nothing to fear, must walk in the light regarding these things. Out of practical commitment to live a victorious life on a daily basis, was born ethical and moral codes, which directed daily "walk with Jesus." Some of the practices born out of

---

8. Avanga, "Internal Movements in the Anglican Diocese of Maseno North," iv.

literal interpretations of some scripture references tended to be legalistic, unwittingly becoming counter missional.

The practice of "walking in the light" sharply polarised the "saved" and the "unsaved," exposing, at least in the eyes of the Brethren, the wheat and the tare in the church. The Brethren's spiritual awakening and especially the acute awareness that every believer is a sinner standing in need of forgiveness, reconciliation to God and humanity, and spiritual deliverance lent urgency to the missional and evangelistic zeal to share the story of their encounter with Jesus Christ. This was typically done through confession of Jesus as Lord and personal saviour, shared as a testimony with anyone who would listen. This practice, driven by a deep-seated conviction is not without practical missiological and evangelistic implications. The practice of sharing testimonies expressing the joy of encounter with Jesus and the sweet experience of salvation thereby, fanned the fervour to witness. As Hazel Avanga observes,

> All Brethren feel the obligation of sharing their faith and experiences with others especially those believed to be outside of the group. [In any case] it is, . . . the duty of every member of the revival movement to share his faith everywhere and with anybody with whom he comes in contact.[9]

In this regard, the revival movement may have had a significant role in evangelism although this may not have received the recognition it deserves. With appropriate guidance and oversight, the church could evolve a rich mission strategy, if only the Brethren's passion for witnessing is tapped and utilized in the service of a structured evangelism.

The significance and continued impact of the movement in the mainline churches of East Africa cannot be ignored. From the culture of a contextualized Christian greetings, the practice of extempore prayers and testimonies, informal or non-liturgical worship and expressions of gratitude acknowledging God's blessings, which has become part and parcel of the social landscape to serious theological topics of sin, the cross, and redemption through the cleansing power of the blood of Christ, we see evidence of the continued impact of the revival movement. The movement's fearless stand on the word of God as they understood it, has often afforded an inspirational model of faith

---

9. Avanga, 89.

even in such difficult times as during the Mau Mau uprising or the church of Uganda's standing up to Idi Amin.[10]

Despite annual conventions and weekly meetings, which are still commonplace and as strong as ever, the overall visibility of the revival movement does not seem as prominent as it used to be. As the longest running revival movement, however, it seems the movement's continued presence is here to stay, and perhaps a reawakening similar to the early days of the movement is likely to recur again. The Brethren's emphases on the seriousness of human sin, the need for repentance and a daily walk with Christ should challenge our faith. It should call us to action in showing what our faith stands for, and what practical implications a genuine commitment to "walking in the light" means for peace of the world, regeneration of the environment, reduction of poverty and violence and the enjoyment of "life in all its fullness" (John 10:10) as God intends for humanity in Christ Jesus.

Joseph D. Galgalo, PhD
Provincial Secretary, Anglican Church of Kenya
Assistant Bishop, ACK Diocese of All Saints
Former Vice Chancellor, St Paul's University, Limuru, Kenya

---

10. Stanley, "The East African Revival," 17.

Preface

In the intricate tapestry of Christian thought and practice, certain theological engagements or trends have left indelible marks on the fabric of faith. Among these, the Keswick theology of sanctification emerges as a luminous strand, illuminating the socio-ethical life of the East African Revival Movement (EARM) from 1930 to 2015. Our journey through these pages explores this theological current within the context of the Anglican Church in the Mount Kenya Region – a journey transcending mere historical analysis and beckons us toward missional reflection.

In this historical, theological and missional exploration, we delve into the intricate interplay between Keswick's theology and the EARM. Our journey traverses historical backgrounds, theological delineations and the lived experiences of believers. We seek to understand how Keswick's teachings on sanctification resonated with the socio-cultural context of East Africa – a context influenced by both internal dynamics and external forces.

Our investigation begins by defining key concepts. What does it mean to walk in the light individually and collectively? How did Keswick's theology intersect with the EARM's commitment to social ethics? These questions propel us forward, inviting us to explore the nuances of obedience, holiness and mission.

As we turn the pages, we encounter pioneers – proponents and teachers – who propagated Keswick theology. They distinguished between the saved and those who had surrendered, shaping the spiritual landscape of East Africa. Their influence extended beyond doctrinal debates; it soaked into the very fabric of community socio-ethical life, affecting relationships, ethics and mission.

Yet, gaps remain. What remains unknown about this intersection? How can this study build upon existing knowledge? These questions beckon us to tread new ground, to illuminate unexplored corners of history and theology. Our aim is not mere academic curiosity; it is missional, i.e., to discern how sanctification impacts the collective witness of the Anglican Church in the Mount Kenya Region and beyond.

In the following chapters, we dig deeper, guided by inquisitiveness and reverence. We disentangle threads of influence, trace footprints across time, and seek wisdom from the past which informs the present and the future. As we do so, we honor the legacy of Keswick theology, recognizing its enduring impact on the socio-ethical beliefs and practices of the EARM.

Firstly, the book focuses on the birth of the Keswick movement, in the late 19th century, and emphasizes the "higher life" experience; a deeper sanctification marked by surrender and empowerment over sin principle. Its roots are intertwined with revivalism, holiness teaching and global missionary fervor. Within the socio-historical landscape of East Africa, Keswick's teachings found fertile ground. As we explore this background, we encounter pioneers who hungered for holiness, grappled with sin's power and sought the radiant path of sanctification. Their journey was not intangible; it intersected with daily life, i.e., the rhythms of family, community and church. Certainly, Keswick's call to "walk in the light" resonated with the EARM's longing for change.

Secondly, it demonstrates how Anglican scholars engaged with Keswick theology, wrestling with its teachings and implications. The questions on how they interpreted sanctification and the way they bridged the gap between theological discourse and lived experience were paramount. We thus explore historical literature, documents and pastoral letters to acknowledge voices that shaped the EARM's understanding. These scholars stood at the crossroads of tradition and renewal, seeking to harmonize Keswick's fire with Anglican liturgy.

Thirdly, it affirms that "walking in the light" was more than a theological theory; it was a lived reality. Brethren gathered in fellowship meetings, singing Tukutenderezza (we praise) hymns, confessing sins and seeking purity. Here you will find that the EARM's ethos informed by simplicity, confession and accountability mirrored Keswick's teachings. This walk illuminated the key biblical texts to give a historical missiological perspective on the current situation – a path toward evangelism. Thus, holiness was not an isolated pursuit as it propelled the mission. The transformed life became an inspiration, drawing others to the light.

Fourthly, as we critique, we tread carefully, because Keswick's individualistic focus sometimes clashes with communal realities. Questions of whether sanctification empowers believers for service beyond personal piety are critical. Thus, a missiological lens helps us discern how "walking in the light" impacts relationships, justice and cross-cultural witness.

May this study inspire both scholars and practitioners to work together as a missional masterpiece echoing across generations, harmonizing faith, ethics and the mission of God. We are therefore invited to "walk in the light," not as isolated pilgrims, but as a missional community, reflecting the radiance of Christ.

CHAPTER 1

Background and Problem Statement

Introduction

This study examines the extent to which the early Keswick theology of sanctification influenced the socio-ethical model for "walking in the light" in the Anglican Church, Mount Kenya region. As suggested by the acronym EARM, the revival fellowship permeates the Eastern Africa countries mostly within the mainstream Protestant churches. The scope of the study was, however, confined within four selected Anglican Dioceses in the Mount Kenya region.[1] Although it seemed wide, this is a local area on the slopes of Mount Kenya. The researcher used a historic-analytical design to address the research objectives, which involved both primary and secondary methods of data collection.

Research Background and the Problem Statement
Background

The word "Mission" is a key term in this study. It is a complex term, Richebächer advises Christians to treat the mission of a triune God as an aspect they cannot bring to people of other faiths because God, their creator, is already at work in them.[2] The researcher will, therefore, seek to contextualize

---

1. The Mount Kenya region comprises nine Dioceses: Kirinyaga, Embu, Mbeere, Meru, Mt Kenya Central, Mt Kenya West, Mt Kenya South, Murang'a South and Thika.
2. Richebächer, "*Missio Dei*," 596.

the concept of mission from the Christian viewpoint to avoid misrepresentation in substance, application, and outcome.

This study sought to assess the influence of Keswick theology of sanctification for the socio-ethical life of *walking in the light*[3] in the EARM, Anglican dioceses of Mount Kenya region. The focus was the Anglican Dioceses of Mount Kenya region, in the light of God's mission, in the four selected Dioceses of Mt Kenya central, Kirinyaga, Embu and Mt Kenya West.

Historical Overview of the Prevailing Situation

Revival in East Africa was first preached mainly to people who were Christians in the sense that they were already baptized, confirmed and in church activities. Gitari observes that EARM professes that baptism and confirmation are not enough for salvation.[4] To be assured of salvation one needs to accept Jesus Christ as a personal savior. The way to salvation is to realize that one is a sinner, and is convicted of his or her sins. One realizes sins are taken away at the cross of Christ. It is by surrendering to Jesus and publicly confessing sins that one is received into the revival fellowship by singing the *Tukutendereza*[5] chorus.

The revival teaches that a saved person needs daily sanctification. This is attained by a life of daily walk with the Lord,[6] regular examination of one's heart and repentance. Barrington-Ward at Birmingham confessed to a challenging encounter with an English lady who had arrived from Uganda and asked if she could be "in the light," because he did not know how he should respond to this phrase.[7] On the other hand the Brethren[8] know that one is living a sanctified life when one "walks in the light," i.e. regularly attends a fellowship meeting and gives a testimony as opposed to spiritually cold Christians.

---

3. Ward and Wild-Wood, *East African Revival*, 215.
4. Gitari, "A Paper," 1.
5. *Tukutendereza* is a Luganda name for "we praise" and is used as a greeting and signature song of all members of EARM.
6. Used interchangeably with "walking in the light."
7. Barrington-Ward, "Revival Through CMS Eyes," 53.
8. A member of EARM.

A weekly fellowship gives each person an opportunity to share with the Brethren[9] the kind of life he has lived since the last fellowship meeting. A Christian who neither attends the fellowship meetings nor walks in the light is thought to be lukewarm or, as Ward and Wild-Wood observe, is considered not saved.[10] This scenario led to a split in the revival following the reading of Ephesians 5:14.[11] A section of EARM interpreted this text to mean anyone involved in socio-ethical activities is spiritually dead and needs to arise from the dead. Thus, spiritually dead Christians are not sanctified and therefore not walking in the light.[12] This resulted in the two prevailing factions of EARM in the Anglican Church, Mount Kenya region.

Definition of Concepts

It is now necessary to define some of the key terms that we will use in this study.

Socio-Ethical Life

The phrase "socio-ethical life" will be used to refer to the day-to-day life of the community. Wright imagines ethical obedience from the perspective of walking in the way(s) of the Lord. He works with moral obedience in the light of the covenant relationship with God that influences the relationship with the community, thus a social-ethical life.[13] Bosch adds a concept of justice alongside evangelism and social responsibility in what he terms a second credibility test.[14]

---

9. The other members of EARM, who call themselves "Brethren."
10. Ward and Wild-Wood, *East African Revival*, 215.
11. Nthamburi, *From Mission to Church*, 117.
12. Kamau, "Critical Analysis," 33.
13. Wright, *Mission of God*, 364.
14. Bosch, *Transforming Mission*, 418, notes:
    "A proclamation that does not hold forth the promises of the justice of the kingdom to the poor of the earth is a caricature of the Gospel: but Christian participations in the struggles for justice which does not point towards the promises of the kingdom also makes a caricature of a Christian understanding of justice."

Keswick Theology

According to Naselli, this phrase denotes five days of progressive teaching commonly referred to as a spiritual clinic, moving from conviction of sin, to God's provision of a cure that frees from sins power, to a crisis experience of consecration, to the filling of the Spirit, to finally a call to mission and Christian service.[15] Naselli further contends that this teaching characterized early Keswick[16] conventions (1875–1920) that had a stereotyped sequence.[17] This early Keswick theology will be the lens through which the prevalent model of walking in the light that has led to discord in the revival in Kenya will be assessed.

Missio Dei (Mission of God)

This concept is not only generative, but its Trinitarian perspective further compounds its intricacy. In the light of *missio Dei's* generative character, this researcher might have to agree with Moreau's sentiments, "Thus, at least for now among evangelical writers, knowing how a particular person uses a term is more important than knowing what the term means in the larger discipline of missiology."[18] This is because the term *missio Dei* is bedeviled by multiple meanings informed by contextual viewpoints. It seems there is not a commonly agreed definition. However, Bosch provides a working definition that guides this study. He defines the *missio Dei* as "God's self-revelation as the one who loves the world, God's involvement in and with the world, the nature and activity of God, which embraces both the church and the world, and in which the church is privileged to participate."[19]

Problem Statement

At the core of this study is the socio-ethical influence of the concept and practice designated by the catch-cry "walking in the light" that is believed to have led to the split in EARM. The dynamics of this influence appear to resonate

---

15. Naselli, *Keswick Theology*, 29, 172–213.
16. Keswick is a town in the Lake District in northwest England where the first convention was held in 1875 (see Naselli, *Keswick Theology*, 17).
17. Naselli, 29.
18. Moreau, Corwin and McGee, *Introducing World Missions*, 73.
19. Bosch, *Transforming Mission*, 10.

with early Keswick theology[20] and hindered mission in the Anglican Church, Mount Kenya region. This study, therefore, was undertaken to systematically explore various facets that comprised the problem.

General Topic

Since the Triune God is actively involved in and with the world, the church is called to join in his mission to investigate and implement the mission mandate. This study falls in the field of missiology and thus will seek to bring to the fore the interaction of God, creating the world and the church. The understanding of sanctification from the perspective of Keswick teachings contribute to the prevailing situation in EARM and must be researched. The socio-ethical situation of walking in the light pervades EARM in Mount Kenya region impacting on community relationships. The ensuing "holier than thou" attitude segregates a section of Christians from fellowship who fail to live a transparent and open life.

How the Specific Topic is Relevant to the General Topic

The eighteenth and nineteenth-century revivals and awakenings have a bearing on the mission trend that saw the beginning of the Keswick movement in England in 1875. The ensuing Keswick teachings are viewed by scholars like Stanley[21] and Ward[22] as influencing social-ethical behavior observed in EARM today.

Furthermore, the student movements in the early twentieth-century England, reckoned to have been propelled by faith missions of the day were to a great extent influenced by the Keswick teachings.[23] These teachings were filtered to Eastern Africa, mainly through the British evangelical missions,[24]

---

20. Kevin De Young ("Andy Naselli," 4) recalls his high school days: "When I shared my Christian "testimony" in my high school and early college years, I would say something like this: "I was saved when I was eight years old, and I surrendered to Christ when I was thirteen. By 'saved' I meant that Jesus became my saviour and that I became a Christian. By 'surrendered' I meant that I finally gave full control of my life to Jesus as my Master and yielded to do whatever he wanted me to do." This description outlines two levels of Christians and thus affects mission.
21. Stanley, "East Africa Revival," 10–11.
22. Ward, "Revival, Mission, and Church," 19.
23. Reed, *Walking in the Light*, 57.
24. Stanley, "East Africa Revival," 10.

with little concern for the theological meaning of the term sanctification, and the result was a blurred understanding of church mission.

What is Already Known about the Topic?

A review of the available literature is vital as one commences research. Smith emphasizes the importance of isolating academic writings related to the topic to see what has been done and what questions remain unanswered. This helps to identify data sources that other researchers have used and thus contributes to bringing to the fore a research gap.[25]

In the proposed research topic no sufficient study seemed to have been done to address the issues in question. Scholars like Kevin Ward, Emma Wild-Wood, John Karanja and others have written widely on EARM from the historical, cultural and socio-theological perspectives. Most of the investigations done in the research area in Kenya had attempted to address the question of the socio-ethical implications of the EARM dictum, walking in the light. However, none of them had written specifically on the influence of Keswick theology on the socio-ethical model in relation to the *missio Dei*. The following overview of selected available literature is pivotal.

Social-ethical obedience: walking in the light in the early Keswick theology

Scholars such as Andrew Naselli,[26] Steve Barabas[27] and others have attempted to provide biblical-theological discourses on ethical obedience that are critical to understanding the influence of Keswick theology on EARM's socio-ethical life of walking in the light.

Naselli in his book, *Let Go and Let God? A Survey and Analysis of Keswick Theology*, observes that "let go and let God" teaching is not biblically sound because it creates two categories of Christians: on the one hand, saved and on the other hand, surrendered. Naselli's view sheds light on the understanding of the research topic from a biblical and theological perspective. He brings to the fore Keswick's erroneous monergestic perspective; let go and let God,

---

25. Smith, *Academic Writing*, 130.
26. Naselli, *Let Go and Let God?*
27. Barabas, *So Great Salvation*.

which could have led to the practice of socio-ethical obedience observable in EARM today.

Likewise, Barabas' book, *So Great Salvation: The History and Message of the Keswick Convention* (regarded as a standard interpretation of Keswick theology) examines erroneous views of Keswick theology of sanctification. However, his views on mortification and vivification seem to misrepresent biblical views.[28] This will be demonstrated later in this study. Furthermore, the doctrine of second blessing connected with a quietist idea of sanctification by faith alone is unscriptural, though it was a Keswick distinctive and was propagated by it.

EARM social ethics of walking in the light: impact on Christian missionaries and implications for social responsibility.

John Church,[29] [son to Joe Church] describes *Balokole*[30] as full of spiritual awareness that astounded even missionaries.

Barrington-Ward, once General Secretary of the Church Missionary Society (CMS) and later Bishop of Coventry, UK, provides a critical observation on the EARM ethical practice of walking in the light. He draws attention to the dangerous element of withdrawal from the real life of the church and society, particularly the tendency to withdraw from social responsibility. He contends that the revival fellowship could be an exclusive group when the experience of the power of the Holy Spirit is made the basis of fellowship among members of the group while those who do not qualify remain outside it.[31]

EARM social-ethics: walking in the light and its implications for the Anglican Church Mount Kenya region.

Jason Bruner examines key themes in the public confession of personal sin like stealing, sexual indiscretions and witchcraft. The paper argues that the Brethren developed a common moral discourse through their public confessions and testimonies. Bruner highlights how the Brethren interacted with

---

28. Barabas, *So Great Salvation*, 68–74.
29. Church, "Personal Experience," 41–51.
30. The revival movement came to be widely known in East Africa as the *Balokole*, which means the "saved ones" in the Luganda language. The word became synonymous with the East African Revival – one of the most significant Christian movements in modern history.
31. Barrington-Ward, "Revival Through CMS Eyes," 53–60.

traditional taboos and social values. His views on public confession of sin shed light on the understanding of our research topic from a socio-ethical perspective model of walking in the light. Bruner further contends that public confession of sin allowed the revivalists to name particular threats to their spiritual and temporal lives while connecting them through a new sense of fellowship. The new fellowship was only enjoyed by those who had confessed the sinfulness of their past ways and thereby broken down barriers between their public self and private self.[32]

In addition, John Karanja in his book, *Founding an African Faith*, while appreciating opposition to the practice of public confession by church leaders, observes that it suited the Kikuyu[33] religious consciousness. This is because the public confession was an integral part of the Kikuyu religion and culture. He asserts that EARM's public confession served to strengthen the Brethren's resolve to live by the demands of their new faith. He points out that revival contributed much towards moral transformation in the Protestant churches in central Kenya[34] (located within the Mount Kenya region).

David Gitari, Bishop Emeritus of the defunct Anglican Diocese of Mount Kenya East and later Archbishop of the Anglican Church of Kenya (1997–2002), in his paper "East African Revival," points out how the revival caused the church in central Kenya to survive and even to grow during the *Mau Mau*[35] uprising (1951–1955).[36] In his autobiography, *Troubled but not Destroyed*, Gitari recounts that many members of the EARM "had refused to take the *Mau Mau* oath because they could not mix the blood of Jesus that has washed their sins away with that of goats."[37] He observes that the greatest strength of revival is the fact that Christians are challenged to examine their lives every day and to seek inward sanctification.[38]

---

32. Bruner, "Public Confession," 254–268.
33. This is the dominant tribe in central Kenya.
34. Karanja, *Founding African Faith*.
35. Refers to a nationalist political movement that fought for Kenyan independence.
36. Gitari, "Paper on East African Revival," 1.
37. Tribal oathing that was administered to members of the "Gikuyu" tribe following the assassination of Tom Mboya (5 July 1969), a seasoned politician, supposedly to ensure the government of Kenya remained in the hands of "Gikuyu" (see Gitari, *Troubled but not Destroyed*, 184–185).
38. Gitari, *Troubled*, 185.

What is Not Yet Known about the Topic?

EARM had a rather focused mission since its arrival in Kenya in 1935–1936, with some places, as noted by Mambo[39] like Mombasa (1964) and Kikuyu (1970) realizing attendance of 20,000 and 30,000 people, respectively. This is impressive because it has been said that around this time some cracks had begun within the fellowship resulting in five distinctive schismatic groups: *Arahuka* (Arise), *Simama* (Stand), *Mtama na Maji* (Sorghum and Water), *Thama* (Exodus) and *Kupaa* (Rising Up).[40] The first two are still active while the rest are either defunct or inactive. The concern for this study will be Arise and Stand, not for comparative reasons but to understand the effect of Keswick theology on their conception of the socio-ethical life. Interpretation of the central biblical texts on sanctification particularly by Arise and Stand seem to have led to dissension. (See Annexure 1 for details on the particular hermeneutical and theological emphases that could have shaped EARM's theology, spirituality, and ethics in each group.)

The fundamental issue in this context had been the application of some biblical texts, for example, Ephesians 5:14 and Luke 22:45–46 that encouraged Brethren to arise from sleep.[41] As Peterson points out, "inadequate attention has been paid to the use of holiness terminology in the New Testament and to passages which deal specifically with the subject of sanctification."[42] The interpretation and application of the Ephesians text sparked serious division in 1971 leading to *Kufufuka*[43] and *Simama*[44] holding their meetings at St. Stephen's Church, Nairobi on the first Sunday and the second Sunday of each month, respectively. In the Mount Kenya region, *Kufufuka* and *Simama* held

---

39. Mambo, "Revival Fellowship," 113.
40. Gitari, "Paper on East African Revival", 4.
41. Gitari, 5.
42. Peterson, *Possessed by God*, 16.
43. *Kufufuka* or *Kuzuzuka* are Swahili names for *Arise* which originated from Blasio Kigozi when he challenged the sleeping church of Uganda to wake up (Nthamburi, *From Mission to Church*, 117).
44. *Simama* is a Swahili word for Stand. Its adherents are proud to be called *Simama* because of their firm faith and claim to be the original members of EARM. *Simama* is the biggest group in the Anglican Diocese of Kirinyaga.

their monthly meetings at Maragua and Murang'a cathedral, respectively.[45] Disparity in these factions was amplified in 2011[46] in central Kenya.

The fact that *Arise* and *Stand* rarely fellowship together baffles Christians who seek to protect the prevailing socio-ethical spirituality of walking in the light. Members of *Arise* accuse those within the revival of being spiritually dead because they keep dogs, accept dowries or receive loans. *Stand* disagrees with the interpretation of the Ephesian text and opposes *Arise* in almost everything. The wrong use of this verse impacted the EARM, shaking its long history of monolithic spirituality.

How Will This Study Build on What is Already Known and What Gap Will It Address?

There is arguably an underlying spirituality of *Kufufuka* that does, in fact, reflect the researcher's objective to explore an understanding of socio-ethical beliefs and practices that have characterized the EARM for over fifty years. This will be used to investigate how Keswick's theology of sanctification is connected to the emergence of EARM's socio-ethical concepts and practices of walking in the light in the Anglican Church, Mount Kenya region. Superficial use of key passages on sanctification and holiness seems to have been one of the leading causes of the current walking in the light model that appears to set apart members of EARM not only from themselves but other Christians too. This categorization paved the way for the so-called two types of Christian scenario that impacts the church negatively and distorts what it ought to be in the light of *missio Dei*.

The author contends that some scholars such as Kevin Ward, John Karanja, and Esther Mombo have failed to notice the effect of sanctification theology as taught, understood and applied by EARM. Its application appeared to have influenced the walking in the light model in the Anglican Diocese of Mount Kenya region. So, despite the growing interest in the twenty-first-century theological representation, no theologian had seriously examined the influence of Keswick theology of sanctification on EARM socio-ethical

---

45. Gitari, "Paper on East African Revival", 5.

46. *Stand* held its convention in August at *Kamuiru* Boys Secondary School while *Arise* held its own in December at Kabare Girls Secondary School attended by members from Rwanda, Uganda, Tanzania and Kenya. According to Mr. Stanley Nyaga, a key leader of *Arise*, *Stand* did not attend.

life of "walking in the light" in the context of *missio* Dei. It appeared Keswick theology of sanctification led to legalism and excesses which caused splits in the EARM.

The Specific Problem That Is the Focus of This Study

Reed[47] and Ward[48] observe that historians of EARM traced its early beginnings to 1929 when Joe Church and Simeon Nisibambi started meeting regularly for prayer in Gahini, Rwanda. They were revived and shared their experiences with Blasio Kigozi and Yosia Kinuka. The revival spread quickly to Uganda, arriving in central Kenya in 1936. It flourished, as previously mentioned, until 1971 when a great rift grew among the Brethren. An attempt at reconciliation has been futile to date.

The original message of *Kufufuka* was to encourage Brethren to arise from sleep (Eph 5:14) and to be renewed inwardly. There is nothing unbiblical about this emphasis. The *Kufufuka* Brethren erred by assuming that renewal means doing away with socio-ethical practices like acquiring loans, life insurance, paying and receiving a dowry and keeping dogs to guard homesteads. Legalism had spoiled a real message. They assumed that a Christian is awakened if he or she does not partake in these practices and instead relies wholly on God's providence.

These ideas resonate well with the Keswick teachings which Reed[49] observes emphasized utter reliance on God rather than on human effort. Human means of raising money for the mission, for example, were discounted, as were human means of advancing in the Christian life: trust was all. These Christians have not only been raised from sleep but are on the *glory train*[50] to heaven. This had consequences for church mission. The members of *Arise* detached themselves from social activities, claiming getting involved in them means one is spiritually dead, thus not in the light, while *Stand* members observed these activities. This resemblance between Keswick teachings and EARM's socio-ethical influence of *walking in the light* is no coincidence and must be investigated.

---

47. Reed, *Walking in Light*, 19.
48. Ward, "Introduction," 3.
49. Reed, *Walking in Light*, 57.
50. These are the Brethren who have not only been raised from sleep; they are on the road ascending to heaven.

This situation challenges the church today. Shall it continue with this rift which has caused two factions in the church, or shall it build a paradigm based on the *missio Dei* to give the correct way of walking with God and thus do mission? The church has closed its eyes to this problem for nearly fifty years resulting in some of its members not understanding what *walking in the light* means. What is to be done to shape and apply a correct theology of walking in the light from the perspective of God's mission?

Being challenged by this situation and related questions, the researcher was motivated to focus on the socio-ethical influence of walking in the light. The problem, therefore, is: What was the underlying phenomenon in the Keswick theology of sanctification that could have brought about the socio-ethical influence of *walking in the light* in EARM in the Anglican Church, Mount Kenya region? Why did this split begin? What motivated it? A paradigm shift from the current scenario to a preferred one was a key point of presentation and indigenization.

Main Research Question

Does the Keswick theology of sanctification contribute to the socio-ethical understanding of *walking in the light* in the EARM and thus influence the mission of the Anglican Church, Mount Kenya region?

Out of this, the following questions arose:

- What were the socio-historical circumstances that led to the influence of Keswick theology of sanctification on the EARM's understanding of walking in the light?
- How does current Anglican Church scholarship regard the Keswick theology of sanctification and walking in the light in the EARM?
- What, if any, were the basic missiological tenets and practices that had helped shape walking in the light in EARM?
- What were the missiological foundations needed to critique specific tenets of walking in the light in EARM?
- How has Keswick theology influenced walking in the light in the Anglican Church?
- What were the significant implications of walking in the light for the present-day mission in the Anglican Church of Kenya?

Aim

This study sought to investigate the contribution of the Keswick theology of sanctification to the socio-ethical understanding of walking in the light in the EARM, thus motivating the mission of the Anglican Church, Mount Kenya region.

Research Objectives

Therefore, the main objective of this study was to investigate the contribution of Keswick sanctification theology to the socio-ethical understanding of walking in the light in the EARM and influencing the mission of the Anglican Church, Mount Kenya region.

This involved the following specific objectives:

- To determine the socio-historical circumstances that led to the influence of Keswick theology of sanctification to the EARM's walking in the light.
- To investigate current Anglican Church scholarship regarding Keswick theology of sanctification and walking in the light in the EARM.
- To examine the basic missiological tenets and practices which shaped the walking in the light framework in EARM.
- To explore the missiological foundations needed to critique specific tenets of walking in the light in EARM.
- To explore how Keswick theology influenced walking in the light in the Anglican Church.
- To determine significant implications of walking in the light for the mission in the Anglican Church of Kenya.

Rationale

In this context, it is crucial to elucidate the four dioceses, address common challenges, explore the initiative "Arise and Stand," and emphasize the significance of "walking in the light."

The Four Anglican Dioceses

The rationale encompasses the reasons for choosing the four Anglican dioceses and the significance of this study. The four dioceses were selected for three reasons: first, they trace their origin from "the Diocese of Fort Hall which was created in 1961 with the Rt. Rev. Obadiah Kariuki as its first bishop. He had previously been Assistant Bishop of Mombasa and the Suffragan Bishop with special responsibility for central Kenya. The name of the Diocese was changed to Mount Kenya in December 1964."[51] Second, the founder of Mount Kenya Diocese[52] was an influential member of the revival movement and thus gave a good start to the growth of revival in Mount Kenya region. Third, they share the common socio-ethical phenomenon of walking in the light.

Common Challenges

EARM impacts everyday challenges in the selected dioceses, such as acceptable and unacceptable moral ethics and the inability to bridge the generation gap.

Arise and Stand

The difference between *Stand* and *Arise* has persisted with the two factions regularly holding their conventions separately. This development demonstrates that while Anglican dioceses sought to consolidate mission, the two most successful strands in EARM were busy advancing seeds of discord within the revival in Mount Kenya region.

Walking in the Light

This research was necessary because, on the one hand, it illuminated the walking in the light concept of promoting mission. On the other hand, it developed a socio-ethical model for the church with reference to issues concerning EARM that could be replicated by other mainstream Protestant churches in Kenya and beyond.

Theoretical Framework

The study was founded on a conceptual framework consisting of main assumptions and a central theoretical argument.

---

51. Church of Province of Kenya, *Rabai to Mumias*, 116.
52. Kariuki, *Bishop Facing Mount Kenya*, 47.

Main Assumptions
- *Missio Dei* is a multifaceted concept arising from Holy Scripture that demands close exegetical and theological analyses, as well as contextual definitions, interpretations, and applications to suit local situations and identify issues faced by EARM to advance mission in the Anglican Church successfully.
- An appropriate model would be required.

Central Theoretical Argument

The central theoretical argument of this work is that Keswick teaching on the sanctification theology has been the catalyst behind the current socio-ethical concepts and practices of walking in the light that pervade EARM. The thesis further suggests a viable model that exemplifies the tenets of *missio Dei*, capable of practical implementation of the preferred model of walking in the light.

Paradigm Based on the *Missio Dei*

The study proposes an incorporative model of walking in the light that will take into account a paradigm shift from the prevailing situation to the preferred scenario. An incorporative model of walking in the light would provide a valuable base for church activities where Arise and Stand would share common perspectives of church mission. This model may initiate more dialogue and research on walking in the light that is localized within the Anglican Church, Mount Kenya community in particular and in the East African region in general. This will enable the community to experience the socio-ethical influence of walking in the light that is deeply rooted in the evangelical Anglican tradition as a faithful participant in the *missio Dei*.

Research Methods

Introduction

The aim of this study has been to examine the extent to which the Keswick theology of sanctification had influenced the prevailing socio-ethical behavior demonstrated by walking in the light in EARM. This behavior appeared to promote an exclusive spirituality while catering to the revival's growth.

The researcher largely used qualitative research to document information from primary and secondary sources to analyze historical and empirical data of the present situation. The researcher worked out a synopsis of relevant biblical and theological resources to recommend a preferred socio-ethical scenario of walking in the light.

Since this is a contextual study, various approaches to methods of data collection were used to achieve research objectives.

Literature

The study of relevant literature was done to outline historical and theological perspectives of the mission in the Anglican Church, Mount Kenya region. Both published and unpublished documents relevant to the study were consulted.

Brief Exegesis

An exegetical and theological study of selected scriptural texts that form the basis of Keswick beliefs and practices in EARM were evaluated according to the grammatical-historical method.[53] This was done to ascertain the biblical author's original intended meaning in the text as a basis of engaging Keswick beliefs and practices of walking in the light in EARM. This was necessary for ascertaining biblical perspectives in the light of *missio Dei*.

Interviews

To identify and explore the prevailing situation, interviews were conducted with members of EARM in the four select dioceses. Particular attention was given to EARM leaders to get authoritative information regarding the emergence of socio-ethical beliefs and practices of walking in the light, and its subsequent impacts on a church mission. Findings from interviews and questionnaires were analyzed to identify an ideal model and draw appropriate conclusions.

General Design of the Study

Merriam observes that "the merits of a particular design are inherently related to the rationale for selecting it as the most appropriate plan for addressing the research problem."[54] On the one hand, it helps to identify data categories, and on the other, it helps to determine sources of information. It is also pivotal

---

53. Marshall, "Evangelicalism and Biblical Interpretation," 102.
54. Merriam, *Qualitative Research*, 50.

to clarify to the readers the research process because as Hofstee notes, by "explaining the research design, you provide the readers with a theoretical background to your method."[55] In other words, a good design informs the researcher's choice and arrangements of research instruments that eventually lead to a reasonable conclusion.[56]

The researcher used elective design to answer the research question adequately (what was the contribution of a Keswick theology of sanctification to the socio-ethical influence of walking in the light in the EARM as manifested in the Anglican Church today?). The crux of this question underlines a socio-historical and theological context in which the current standing of the revival is alleged to have evolved into over the years. It suffices, hypothetically, to state that the Keswick teaching on sanctification theology was the catalyst behind the prevailing walking in the light behavior in EARM. It seemed there was a phenomenon within the revival that propelled its doctrine and thus underpinned this study. The design was structured in the light of research objectives to test the thesis statement.

Thus, the working dynamics of the following research design were adapted, with some adjustment, from Smith.[57] His theological framework resonates well with concerns of this study. Furthermore, his "frame of reference comes from the South African Higher Education System,"[58] and is thus authentic and contextual.

Chapter 1: Research Proposal

This section captures the historical overview, background and problem statement that outlines the prevailing situation. The preliminary literature is also outlined in the light of what is already known about EARM's socio-ethical model of walking in the light. The main factions of EARM are described alongside the walking in the light model and consequently address the research gap. The chapter also discusses the main research question, rationale, theoretical framework, paradigm base and research methods.

---

55. Hofstee, *Constructing a Good Dissertation*, 120.
56. Hofstee, 116.
57. Smith, *Academic Writing*, 212.
58. Smith, 8.

Chapter 2: Keswick Theology of Sanctification: Socio-Historical Background for Walking in the Light.

This helped to conceptualize the term "sanctification" and to understand its role in the socio-ethical formation of EARM. To offer a critique from the perspective of Christian theology, it was necessary to formulate a paradigm to assist sound ethical obedience involving the *missio Dei*.

Chapter 3: The Anglican Church Scholarship on Keswick Theology of Sanctification and Walking in the Light Model in the EARM.

First, the researcher carried out a historical overview of the prevailing socio-ethical beliefs and practices of walking in the light in EARM.

Second, the researcher did a situational analysis to describe the current situation.

Chapter 4: Prevailing Basic Missiological Tenets and Practices of Walking in the Light.

A preferred scenario would not be possible without working on the basic missiological tenets and practices that shaped the framework of the prevailing socio-ethical influence of walking in the light in EARM. An exegetical study of the key biblical texts was interpreted to give missiological perspectives on the prevailing situation.

The author had a bias toward the Anglican evangelical tradition which held together the missiological foundations needed to critique specific tenets of the prevailing model of walking in the light in EARM. This informed the researcher's theoretical framework to analyze scriptural teachings related to sanctification and holiness to culminate in a new EARM model of the theology of sanctification.

Chapter 5: Missiological Foundations to Critique Specific Tenets of Walking in the Light.

The value of the prevailing socio-ethical beliefs and practices of walking in the light could not be understated as it had nurtured the majority of Christians in East Africa. Therefore, the researcher summarized the prevailing situation using historical and empirical analyses.

Next, the researcher summarized the prevailing socio-ethical situation as it should be in the perspective of the Anglican Church mission statement in Kenya. This study also suggests a viable biblically-based model of *missio Dei*.

Chapter 6: Conclusion
The researcher sought to conclude the study by offering practical suggestions for moving from the prevailing socio-ethical situation to the preferred mission ethic.

Why the Proposed Research Design and Methodology are Appropriate to Address the Research Aim and Questions
Historical analytical design
The proposed research design was generated by the research questions and is thus appropriate to address this study. The researcher used various techniques to discuss each objective. In respect to the historical nature of this study, the researcher employed historical analytical design. This design helped to get the background information of the prevailing phenomenon. However, it can be a challenge to connect the past and the present, therefore interpretation was required.[59]

To enhance the performance of historical events, the researcher employed survey-based research to elicit data from representatives of a larger group of people who were ready to divulge the information on people's views, needs and attitudes.[60] Care was taken in the type of questions to be asked, how to ask them, population sampling, representative sample and ethical concerns.[61] This approach was necessary to track the unfolding situation of the socio-ethical influence of walking in the light and showing what should be done to have biblically-sound ethics in EARM.

Methodology
Hofstee refers to methodology as "The nitty-gritty of the matter" that explicates the research design, clarifying and justifying its application and informing data collection and analysis procedure "appropriate to your thesis statement."[62] In a nutshell, the research process should not only convince the reader but serve as a guide manual.

---

59. Hofstee, *Constructing a Good Dissertation*, 126.
60. Hofstee, 122.
61. Hofstee, 122.
62. Hofstee, 115.

Population and sampling techniques:

A non-probability sampling technique, also referred to as purposeful sampling,[63] was used to obtain a sample of respondents to help gather information based on EARM's socio-ethical beliefs and practices. The target population was drawn from members of EARM in the four selected dioceses. To choose the sample for this study the researcher adopted a criterion-based selection to "create a list of the attributes essential" for study and then "proceed to find or locate a unit matching the list."[64] This criterion was important because it allowed getting responsible informants.

The population for the study was drawn from the four selected dioceses with a target population of 2500 members[65] of EARM. A sample size of about 400 respondents and committed members[66] sufficed to help gather information for the study. Focus groups were made of ordinary members of EARM and theological students; one-on-one in-depth interviews with EARM's leaders and clergy were conducted, while email questionnaires were sent to bishops and prominent stakeholders of EARM. They were spread as shown below.

Table 1: Target Population

Focus Group Interview	Twenty groups of 10–15 ordinary members	200–300	210–315
	One group of theological students	10–15	
One-on-one In-depth Interviews	Five groups of 5 – 10 EARM leaders per county	20–40	40–80
	Five groups of 5 – 10 clergy per county	20–40	
Self-administered Questionnaire via Email	A bishop per diocese	4	4
	Prominent stakeholders	5–10	5–10
Total respondents			259–405

---

63. Merriam, *Qualitative Research*, 73–83.

64. Lecompte, *Ethnography and Qualitative Design*, 70.

65. This is according to Mr. Stanley Nyaga (interview with author on 23 October 2013), a key member of EARM in Kirinyaga County.

66. Refers to the EARM members who attend Brethren fellowships on a regular basis.

Data collection:

The researcher conducted interviews in *Kikuyu, Kiswahili,* and English as was appropriate to the informants' context. Group interviews applied to the ordinary members of EARM and to theological students (St. Andrew's College students who were members of EARM). The one-on-one method was used to interview the district leaders of EARM and the clergy; these were voice-recorded. The researcher emailed a questionnaire to the bishops of the four selected dioceses and other stakeholders.

The investigator's Christian upbringing was influenced by EARM and well informed about its concepts and practices. To avoid influence on the data collection procedure, bracketing was used to avoid manipulating the description of the phenomenon under study. Tufford and Newman[67] observe that bracketing alleviates the potentially damaging effects of unacknowledged preconceptions related to the research. It ensures that pre-understanding information will not influence the data. Voice-recording and taking notes are pivotal to ensure a thorough data collection process.

The formatting of questions:

Good questions are a recipe for good and reliable data. Merriam argues that "the way in which questions are worded is a crucial consideration in extracting the type of information required."[68] Thus, care was taken in phrasing the questions to avoid any misunderstanding. Furthermore, Merriam recommends a careful review of questions to remove poorly formatted ones before the start of the interview.[69] This could call for the preliminary involvement of respondents to critique the questions and recommend those that might require modification. The questions were written to create an accurate record of the actual questions and answers.

Reliability of research instruments:

Reliability refers to the extent to which research findings can be replicated, i.e. if repeated will yield the same results.[70] The test of the reliability of the instrument was done by conducting a pilot study of at least one Anglican diocese

---

67. Tufford and Newman, *Qualitative Social Work*, 81.
68. Merriam, *Qualitative Research*, 95.
69. Merriam, 100.
70. Merriam, 220.

within Mount Kenya region that did not participate in the actual study. Thus, the collected data from the four select dioceses were evaluated and findings compared with this other diocese to ascertain consistency of the instrument.

The validity of the instrument:

Merriam argues that validity concerns the extent to which the findings of one study can be applied to other situations, i.e., how generalizable are the results of a research study?[71] The interview tool, as well as the answers, were scientifically evaluated by experts in the field to ensure that the questions put to the respondents would gather the required data to respond to the research objectives.

Data collection instruments and techniques:

The researcher used interviews and document analysis techniques to collect the relevant data for this study.

1. Interview: Interview[72] was the primary method of gathering information because it is the commonest way of eliciting data in qualitative research. DeMarrais defines interview as a conversation between a researcher and informant on questions related to the research study.[73] Merriam[74] adds that interview is essential when one cannot observe behavior, feelings or how people interpret a phenomenon. This helped to gather data on the present reality of the situation.

The researcher required five research assistants from every county in the selected Dioceses to help with the research planning process prior, during and after the interviews. They were comprised, but not exclusively, of former students at St. Andrew's College of Theology, Kabare, Kenya. The main selection criterion was membership in EARM, and the non-probability sampling technique was used as exemplified above. To ensure quality, the researcher brought all twenty research assistants (Annexure 2) together for a one-day seminar at St. Andrew's College of Theology, Kabare, Kenya before the start of the interviews. The proposed guest speaker was Prof. John Ndug'u Ikenye

---

71. Merriam, 223.
72. Interview instruments will be scientific.
73. DeMarrais, *Qualitative Interview Studies*, 55.
74. Merriam, *Qualitative Research*, 88.

(Annexure 3), the head of Pastoral Theology and Social Sciences Department at St. Paul's University, Limuru, Kenya. The topics to be covered were guided by the North-West University ethical code. Other items included selection and registration criteria of the informants, classification, coding of the data, and establishing rapport.

The following interview designs applied to focus groups, one-on-one, and e-mail.

Focus groups interview design. Merriam defines a focus group interview as "an interview on a topic with a group of people who have knowledge of the topic."[75] This design suits this study because groups of EARM's ordinary members and theological students[76] (Annexures 4 and 5), respectively were interviewed. This method is unique, says Chandran, "because it is less structured, more informal and interactive . . ."[77] The discussion questions were administered at different times in the selected counties. This design was semi-structured[78] to allow a mix of informal and formal questions, and thus friendly to all respondents.

Interviews[79] took place at local centers of worship across the four counties. Since it was not possible to visit every center due to logistic challenges, the researcher randomly selected about twenty centers, at least five from each county. The face-to-face method of interviewing was paramount. Since this study focused on the current situation, the research on Keswick theology was done within the Kenyan context.

The focus group discussion was comprised of ordinary members, five focus groups of ten to fifteen members per county, i.e., fifty to seventy-five members per county. Theological students formed one focus group of ten to fifteen members at St. Andrew's College, Kabare. The proposed questionnaire applied to the above respondents, respectively.

One-on-one in-depth interview guide. The EARM leadership (Annexure 4) and the clergy[80] (Annexure 5) were interviewed by five to ten members

---

75. Merriam, 93.
76. Members of EARM.
77. Chandran, *Research Methods*, 106.
78. All questions are either flexibly worded or a mix of more or less structured questions.
79. Interviews will include a scientifically-approved questionnaire.
80. Those who are members of EARM.

respectively, per county. That means the total respondents on a one-on-one in-depth interview in the four counties ranged from forty to eighty. The population sampling and data collection techniques used to describe focus group design applied. One-on-one interview, referred to by Merriam as the person-to-person encounter, is the commonest type of interview "in which one person elicits information from another."[81] It appeared to be the best tool to extract confidential information from a respondent though it may lack interrogation from other informants (focus groups) and thus can lead to questions about its objectivity and reliability. However, the research instruments were evaluated in the light of data findings from informants who did not participate in the actual research.

The researcher voice-recorded information during the interview, so as not to miss facts that might be substantial. As a non-participatory observer, the researcher also wrote observer's comments to capture non-verbal reactions. Research assistants were necessary to standardize the recording process.

Interview design for bishops and other prominent stakeholders (Annexure 5). This technique applied to both one-on-one and email interviews. Therefore, five to ten prominent stakeholders were randomly selected to inform areas that might be unclear from the existing written literature. The four bishops of the selected dioceses were also respondents.

First, the researcher needed an introduction to establish rapport, indicating what study he was undertaking, the purpose of the interview and an ethical declaration. Second, the respondents' identities were to be protected, and disclosed only if permitted in writing. Third, the researcher explained why the respondents' information was significant in this study.

2. Documents: This is the second technique that was used in this study. Merriam uses the term document "as an umbrella to refer to a wide range of written, visual, digital, and physical material relevant to the study at hand."[82] The explanation of the term "document" seems to go beyond secondary research and in essence shares in primary research. Primary sources, observes Merriam, "are those in which the originator of the document is recounting the first-hand experience with the phenomenon of interest. The best primary

---

81. Merriam, *Qualitative Research*, 88.
82. Merriam, 139.

sources are those recorded closest in time and place to the phenomenon by a qualified person."[83]

This technique, therefore, is used in regard to a distant past where individuals with knowledge may not be alive. In other perspectives, an indirect method of data collection seems to replace the term document as expressed by Chandran: "Indirect sources of data include hearsay narratives, written documents, and books. Historical research, for example, relies heavily on indirect sources of information such as individuals who have heard of history or events, records of events, activities in the form of hand-written notes, minutes and books."[84]

Documents, with this understanding, helped answer research questions concerning the emergence of the current socio-ethical lifestyle. This was best suited to interpret how the situation emerged and also set the pace to explain the preferred scenario.

The main limitations of this technique as outlined by Merriam[85] were:

a As documents are not produced for research purposes, the information they offer may not be in a form that is useful to the investigator.
b The authenticity and accuracy of documents are difficult to determine.

No doubt this technique requires a skillful approach. Merriam rightly notes, "Since the investigator is the primary instrument for gathering data, he or she relies on skills and intuition to find and interpret data from documents."[86] The researcher visited the Kenya National Archives and the Anglican Church of Kenya Archives in Nairobi. Also, learning institutional libraries in Kenya like St. Andrew's College of Theology, Kabare and St. Paul's University, Limuru were consulted. In South Africa, George Whitefield College (Cape Town), Stellenbosch University and North-West University (Potchefstroom) were a central source of library data.

---

83. Merriam, 152.
84. Chandran, *Research Methods*, 109.
85. Merriam, *Qualitative Research*, 153–154.
86. Merriam, *Qualitative Research*, 150.

Limitations

The study was done in the Anglican Church, Mount Kenya region. If the researcher was to expand the scope, the study would become too wide for proper research. According to documented records, the first revival convention was held at Kahuhia[87] in 1947.[88] In order to capture EARM's background, the study ranged from 1930 to 2015. The concentration was in the Anglican dioceses in the selected counties. It might be easy to generalize data findings to other Anglican dioceses influenced by the revival in Kenya and beyond. However, it might be a challenge to other churches influenced by the revival such as the Methodist Churches of Kenya and the Presbyterian Church of East Africa because of denominational differences. So, the researcher does not expect to make a definitive conclusion but offer a suggestive viable model.

The success of the data collecting instruments depended largely on the rapport the researcher developed with the respondents. Sometimes he relied on his research assistants who were expected to be in fellowship with the informants for efficient gathering of information.

Ethical Considerations

Identification of research respondents across the two dominant factions in the EARM was a challenge. The researcher avoided asking probing questions that might reveal their identity. Their identity was, therefore, stored in coded files to prevent potential risk to the research participants.[89] Meriam further argues that the informants have a right to "the protection from harm, the right to privacy, the notion of informed consent and the issue of deception all need to be considered ahead of time."[90] The North-West University manual for postgraduate students has described the vulnerable groups and the potential risk areas (see footnotes 7 and 8).[91] The researcher needed strategies put in place to ascertain that appropriate practices and safeguards were rigorously implemented. *Arise* and *Stand* are small communities who know each other, the members are in various power relations with each other, and the research

---

87. Kahuhia is a place in the Diocese of Mount Kenya Central in the Mount Kenya region.
88. Mambo, "Revival Fellowship", 113.
89. Hofstee, *Constructing a Good Dissertation*, 118.
90. Meriam, *Qualitative Research*, 230.
91. North-West University, *Manual for Postgraduate Studies*, 61.

involves questions about conflict; this is important to protect human subjects from harm.

As indicated earlier, the objective of this study was not to draw a comparison between *Arise* and *Stand* as this could lead to stigma and potential harm to the respondents. The gist of this work, therefore, was the understanding by the EARM of the socio-ethical concepts and practices of walking in the light. There were no questions specifically meant for any of the factions. Furthermore, they were to give informed consent (Annexure 6) whether to be interviewed in one group or separately. The experts checked the efficacy of the questionnaires as an appropriate tool for this study before the commencement of the survey. The ethical research code was enforced through an ethics committee of NWU (Annexure 7) and the oversight of the researcher's NWU supervisor.

As a member of Anglican Church of Kenya mostly influenced by EARM, the researcher was aware of moral boundaries and ethical practices, which he had to respect. This study took place within church-based institutions and required consent letters (Annexure 8) from church ministers to allow their parishioners to attend the interviews. Informed consent by members of EARM was seminal as research assistants had to register informants voluntarily in their local churches.

Conclusion

The researcher has shown how the Keswick theology of sanctification influenced the prevailing situation of EARM in the Anglican Church, Mount Kenya region, promoting an exclusive socio-ethical belief and practice of walking in the light while catering for the revival's growth. The researcher has also shown how qualitative research can be used to document information from primary and secondary sources to analyze historical and empirical data of the present situation and to work out a synopsis of relevant biblical and theological resources to recommend a preferred scenario. This study has also shown the unfolding gap in the existing literature that this study sought to fill. Despite the growing interest in the twenty-first-century theological representation, no theologian has yet seriously examined the influence of Keswick's theology of sanctification on the EARM socio-ethical representation of walking in the light in the context of *missio Dei* in the Anglican

Church, Mount Kenya region. This gap in the exisiting literature informs the thesis statement that Keswick teaching on the sanctification theology had been the catalyst behind the prevailing socio-ethical influence of walking in the light in EARM. Thus, the following chapter sought to explore the socio-historical context that could have attracted Keswick teachings in East Africa.

CHAPTER 2

Keswick Theology of Sanctification: Socio-historical Background for Walking in the Light

Introduction

This chapter discusses the socio-historical circumstances that led to the influence of Keswick's theology of sanctification in EARM's practice of walking in the light. A sixfold approach will be used to answer the question that guides this chapter. The first introduces the chapter as a whole; the second defines walking in the light, and since this is a mission study it is placed in the context of *missio Dei*, when the socio-historical context of East Africa is described; the third gives a historical view of Keswick Theology; the fourth explores the affinity between the sociological circumstances and Keswick theology; the fifth evaluates EARM against *missio Dei* and the sixth concludes the chapter. This will position the EARM's socio-historical concept and practice of walking in the light in its proper context.

Walking in the Light

An explanation of the relationship between the Anglican Church and EARM is necessary before working on the theme of this section. Though initially EARM had infiltrated the Anglican Church in East Africa in the early twentieth century, it nevertheless later was attracted to other mission churches such as Methodist and Presbyterian. The movement brought together a significant number of adherents from these churches. The fact that this study investigates EARM in the Anglican Church justifies its relationship as that of a daughter and a mother, respectively. Thus, "EARM" is not a synonym with the Anglican or any other church, but is a movement that cuts across the Protestant mission churches.

Following this, a contextual definition and description of walking in the light is necessary before situating it in the *missio Dei*. To place walking in the light into a manageable socio-historical context, the focus narrows mainly to Kenya, one of the East Africa countries[1] adversely influenced by the EARM.

Contextual Definition

The phrase "walking in the light" as used by the members of EARM refers to sanctification attained by a life of walking daily with the Lord and a regular examination of one's heart and repentance.[2] Ward & Wild-Wood concur with Gitari in their statement that walking in the light means being transparent and open with one another.[3] In spite of its somewhat erroneous theological background, walking in the light has had a profound influence on EARM's socio-ethical belief and practice. To grasp the strength of this force something more elaborate and descriptive than a definition is required.

Contextual Description

Bruner gives one of the most profound descriptions of the phrase "walking in the light" from the perspective of the EARM:

> the *Balokole*[4] believed that spiritual darkness shrouded sinful secrets, and they worked to bring these secrets to the light. They believed that sins must be exposed through public confession, and revivalists developed a lifestyle of making public those sins.

---

1. The countries that comprise East Africa are Sudan, South Sudan, Eretria, Ethiopia, Seychelles, Kenya, Uganda, Tanzania, Rwanda and Burundi. Among these, Kenya, Uganda, Tanzania, Rwanda and Burundi are the main focus of EARM because of their historical contact with the Keswick movement.

2. Gitari, "Paper on East African Revival", 2.

3. Ward and Wild-Wood, *East African Revival*, 215.

4. Refer to the saved ones in Luganda language and is synonymous to the Brethren, a term widely used in Kenya to insinuate members of EARM.

They called this way of life "walking in the light" (*okutambulira mu musana*).[5]

Gitari asserts that Brethren will know that one is living a sanctified life when one attends fellowship meetings regularly, testifies about his trials and temptations, and walks in the light.[6] The weekly fellowship meeting gives each person an opportunity to share with the Brethren the kind of life he has lived since the last fellowship meeting. Since they consider the devil to be always at war with believers, the testimony must include a statement of the temptations one has gone through and the way he has turned to Jesus for victory. This, in a nutshell, is what it means to walk in the light from the Brethren's point of view. If one's lifestyle is to the contrary, one may be declared as no longer saved. Furthermore, Brethren who have nothing to say during a fellowship meeting may cause concern and might even be declared lukewarm or spiritually cold.

As a result, public testimony and confession have become the most enduring, albeit sometimes contentious and confrontational, EARM phenomenon that achieves walking in the light. It is contentious because of a tendency to confess past misdeeds that might breed serious relational consequences with the aggrieved member of the community who hitherto had no knowledge of betrayal. It could also prove confrontational. For instance, the Principal of Crowther Hall, Birmingham, completely unaware of the revival practice, was accosted by an English lady back from Uganda. She asked whether she could be in the light with him, i.e., point out one or two of his shortcomings, after which he was fully reinstated to fellowship with her.[7] Though this practice of public confession is dying as noted by Karanja,[8] it is still one of the most cherished ways to explicate the principle of a daily walk in the light.

Indeed, walking in the light has become a catchphrase among the members of EARM. For example, in Kenya, they are referred to in the Kiswahili language as *watu wa nuru* (people of the light). In fact, a slot has always been given during weekly revival fellowships for members to shed light. That is to confess to one another the sins of the previous week. The phrase has also

---

5. Bruner, "Public Confession," 256.
6. Gitari, "Paper on East African Revival," 2.
7. Barrington-Ward, "Revival Through CMS Eyes," 54.
8. Karanja, *Founding the African Faith*, 146.

been used within EARM as a way of enlightening each other about coming events. However, the formal statement is what particularly describes the Brethren concerning the practice of a daily walk with the Lord, i.e., a life of daily sanctification. Such a life, in the eyes of Brethren, invariably describes a saved person.

Hooper states that EARM expects a saved person to daily yield to the Holy Spirit and Christ by faith.[9] This habit of yielding or brokenness in the daily walk with God, in the power of Jesus' cleansing blood and the mediation of the Holy Spirit, influences an abiding attitude of prayer and crying to God as "Abba, Father," in what looks like a real communion with God (Rom 8:15–16).[10]

Further, Senyonyi states that the revivalists have a dire need to unmask anything that could prejudice their freedom to share their walk with God. They believe that if they walk in the light as He is in the light, Jesus Christ's blood will cleanse them from all sin (1 John 1:7).[11] Indeed, Kariuki,[12] one of the early Anglican bishops in Kenya, recalls his interaction with Nisibambi that led to his understanding of Christ as his personal light and savior. Indeed, personal light arose out of the belief that the revival works in an individual before it could work in the Brethren fellowship. In consultation with the church, these fellowships sometimes become particularly significant in planning and executing the Brethren's mission among other agenda. The extent to which walking in the light has been buttressed in the mission of God might require unpacking.

Walking in the Light in the *Missio Dei*

The concept of "walking in the light" holds significance within the context of the East African Revival Movement (EARM) in the Anglican Church of Kenya and its relationship to the missio Dei. We will unpack this concept under the following headings:

---

9. Hooper, "Theology of Trans-Atlantic Evangelicalism," 87.
10. Hooper, 88.
11. Senyonyi, "GAFCON EA Revival Distinctives," 8.
12. Kariuki, *Bishop Facing Mount Kenya*, 52, 53.

Description of Missio Dei

The concept of *missio Dei* underpins all the socio-ethical teachings of the Bible as far as EARM's mission of walking in the light is concerned. Wright argues that the ethical challenge to God's people is twofold. On the one hand, the challenge is to recognize the mission of God as the heartbeat of their very existence and on the other, to respond in ways that express and facilitate it rather than deny and hinder it.[13] Wright further notes that the Bible's grand narrative is about the mission of God and demands an appropriate ethical response from humanity.[14] Abraham (Gen 22:16–18) serves as a model for the continuing education of his descendants who must walk in the way of the Lord in righteousness and justice so that God can accomplish the missional purpose of Abraham's election.[15] This is well articulated in Genesis 18:18–19 which expresses a moral agenda for the nations on earth.

Wright singles out Sodom as a model of the fallen world and demonstrates God's response (judgment) on evil doers, those who negate the way of the Lord.[16] Abraham is posited as a model of God's mission albeit in a context of the wickedness of Sodom.[17] Wright examines the ethical content of the phrases "the way of the Lord" and "doing righteousness and justice."[18] These two protracted phrases anchor ethical expressions in this section as per the teachings and expectations of the Israelites in relation to Yahweh. They will also provide insight into understanding the principal theme, walking in the light in the EARM.

On the one hand, the expressions "keeping the way of the Lord" or "walking in the way of the Lord," Wright argues, was a metaphor used in the Old Testament to contrast with the ways of other gods or the way of sinners – in this particular case, the way of Yahweh and the way of Sodom.[19] Wright notes that the expression walking in the way of the Lord is mostly used to construe

---

13. Wright, *Mission of God*, 357.
14. Wright, 358.
15. Wright, 358.
16. Wright, 359.
17. Wright, 360.
18. Wright, 363.
19. Wright, 363.

obeying God's command so as to reflect God in human life.[20] That is, doing for your neighbor what God has done for you.

On the other hand, the expression "righteousness and justice" speaks of conformity to what is right or expected, rightly expressed as social justice, actual things that you do.[21] This missional ethics concept could be further explicated in two ways. First, mission as an instrument to dispense release to the oppressed. This understanding arises from the belief that the way of the Lord is to do righteousness and justice for the oppressed, and is against the oppressor. While expressing the importance of ethics in God's mission to bless the nations, Wright[22] contends that ethics sandwich election and mission. This portrays the missional logic of Genesis 18:19 as effected through Abraham's election that was anticipated to bring out a community's dedication to the ethical reflection of God's character. Second, Wright asserts that God's aim to dispense blessings to the nations is tied to God's ethical demand on the people he has created to be the agent of that blessing.[23] This moral imperative has practical dimensions explicated by missional ethics of practical holiness because "being holy meant living lives of integrity, justice, and compassion in every area of life."[24]

Walking in the Light within a Mission of God's Framework

Since the people of God are called to be a light to the nations, they ought to walk in the light with the transformed lives of a holy people. Thus, the problem attended to in this context is that walking in the light has led to categorizing one group of Christians as saved while the other group is not. This has hampered the mission of the church. The Brethren appear to focus more on the outward conformity exemplified by socio-ethical beliefs and practices than inward conformity achieved through the power of the Holy Spirit. But a concept of walking in the light is needed that operates within a comprehensive mission framework, which helps the church participate fully in the *missio Dei*. Indeed, Daugherty argues that if the church's mission is to

---

20. Wright, 364, 365.
21. Wright, 365, 367.
22. Wright, 368.
23. Wright, 369.
24. Wright, 373.

extend the *missio Dei*, it can be nothing short of continuing that embodiment of God in Christ among the people of the world.[25]

However, the *missio Dei* concept is not primarily an activity of the church, but an attribute of a missionary God. Therefore, it is not the church that has a mission but the Triune God. Thus, the concept of walking in the light raises a critical question about its place in the Trinitarian God. This is because Brethren seem to emphasize the centrality of the cross [Christ] while the other members of the Trinity are relegated to the periphery. This anomaly shall be discussed during evaluation of EARM against *missio Dei* later in this chapter. Aagaard observes that mission ought to be seen as a movement from God to the world, and the church should be viewed as an instrument for that mission.[26] Certainly, there was no better way for God to exemplify His love for humanity than through the glorious incarnation of his Son and our Savior, Jesus Christ. Hence, as partakers of mission in God, Christians are bound to walk in His holiness (i.e., in His light).

Since the Bible is about the mission,[27] then walking with God is itself walking in the mission of God. Thus, the biblical concept of walking in the light is without a doubt synonymous with walking with God. This idea is postulated in both Testaments. Whereas Genesis 5:24 and 6:9 indicate Enoch and Noah had a righteous walk with God, 2 Peter 3:9 shows that believers are to walk in the light of the Lord's return, given the judgment that is coming on the world. So, the Genesis texts are indicative of the status of the walk which is in the Spirit and perfect. This suggests that God's mission is a way of life for the people of God. Also, Peter's text brings to the fore the imperative aspect of God's expectations towards humanity with regard to His mission. The declarations seem to indicate a calling of people of God to a particular vocation whose characteristics demand righteous disposition towards God and His mission. This confirms that God has not left His Great Commission at the mercy of humanity as He swore to build his missional church (Matt 16:18).[28]

---

25. Daugherty, "Mission Dei," 165.
26. Aagaard. "Trends in Missionary Thinking," 13.
27. Wright, *Mission of God*, 29.
28. Piper, *Let the Nations Be Glad*, 75.

The mission is therefore, as Bosch observes, a movement from God to the world and the church is a vessel for that mission.[29]

In addition, Wright argues that if mission should be biblically informed and authenticated, then it should underpin the church's committed participation as God's people, at God's invitation and command, in God's own mission within the history of God's world for the redemption of God's creation.[30] Therefore, God is the owner of the mission while the Church is a participant at the invitation and command of God. Moreover, Wright's mention of the purpose of God's mission as redemption of God's creation[31] fits well with John Piper's conception of the missionary text in John 10:16 that affirms God's missionary purpose of gathering His sheep, or building His church (Matt 16:18) from all the nations.[32] This resonates with Bosch's argument that the church is an instrument of God's love in the world because He is a fountain of sending love.[33] If this is the case, the church (through which EARM's operates) ought to champion practical holiness by positioning walking in the light in its right perspective in the mission of God. This positioning may be an exercise in futility when not placed in the socio-historical context.

Socio-historical Context of Kenya

As mentioned earlier, East Africa comprises ten countries, but among these only Rwanda, Uganda, Tanzania and Kenya could be said to have experienced the profound influence of EARM since its origin at Gahini, Rwanda in 1929.[34] The four countries provide a sufficient socio-historical background for EARM's beliefs and practices for walking in the light. To answer the research question exhaustively the focus has been narrowed onto Kenya,[35] the home country of the researcher, where the movement appeared in 1938.[36] The other

---

29. Bosch, *Transforming Mission*, 390.
30. Wright, *Mission of God*, 22–23.
31. Wright, 23.
32. Piper, *Let the Nations Be Glad*, 206.
33. Bosch, *Transforming Mission*, 390.
34. Ward, "Introduction," 3.
35. Since the author was born and raised in Kenya it seemed prudent to situate the study in the Kenyan context. Again, although he is not a member of EARM, he came to faith through the ministries of the Brethren in Kenya.
36. Langley and Kiggins, *Serving People*, 198.

three countries will prove useful for other critical and backup information. This is because the analogous socio-historical context of walking in the light has been found across the East African region, especially in the aforesaid nations. It is important therefore to establish the daily life circumstances and experiences that led to its acceptance, particularly by ordinary people. These circumstances and experiences were informed by both external and internal influences.

External Influences

The external influences, in this context, will refer to a situation that was inspired by events or forces from outside or beyond the powers of the East African people. We shall consider racial segregation, epidemics and diseases as the major threats that could have influenced Africans' livelihood at the beginning of the twentieth century.

Racial segregation

In 1905 the white settlers in Kenya, following the example of South Africa, made the British government enact racial laws to control and subjugate Africans. According to these laws, not only were African native reserves created but also the Masters and Servants Ordinance, poll tax and pass system were established.[37]. This denied Africans their tribal land and reduced them to servanthood under strict labor policies. Indeed, Odhiambo notes that the European demarcation of the Kenyan land was racist with the best land going to the Europeans, the so-called white highlands.[38] Furthermore, Odhiambo argues that the 1915 Crown Lands Ordinance made the reserves Crown land, and the Africans tenants could be evicted any time.[39]

This led to Africans feeling insecure in their own country, for they were subdued and subjected not only to harsh means of earning money but to poll taxes as well.[40] More hardship and suffering were in the offing when in 1919 the new governor, General Northey, issued a circular to increase the labor force.[41] This circular subjected Africans males over sixteen years of age

---

37. Muita, *Hewn from the Quarry*, 4.
38. Odhiambo, *History of East Africa*, 157.
39. Odhiambo, 157.
40. Odhiambo, 156.
41. Odhiambo, 156.

to carry a *kipande*.⁴² It was illegal to be found without it. In principle, the *kipande* became a badge of servitude. These abuses aroused national feelings culminating in social unrest. Harry Thuku, who received a mission education, became secretary of the Young Kikuyu Association, a mouthpiece for African grievances. He was arrested in 1922, leading to bloody violence in Nairobi that left many Kenyans dead.⁴³ This signaled the beginning of concerted pressure by Africans for complete independence from the white-dominated rule.

Africans felt let down even by missionaries who meticulously worked alongside the colonial officials such that there was little point in distinguishing one set of white people from another.⁴⁴ This observation resonates with a saying by the Gikuyu people of Kenya during the colonial era, *gutiri Muthungu na Mubia* (there is no difference between a priest and a colonial administrator). As Gatumu observes, many CMS missionaries of this period assumed their nationality was a crucial issue for them; but ironically, this negative appraisal of their status proved more significant, culminating in Africans' conclusion that European domination was equivalent to the spreading of the gospel.⁴⁵ Indeed, the CMS had to follow secularizing tendencies, despite reservations that these might betray the principles associated with the previous years of heroic evangelism⁴⁶ that as Walls notes, never regarded Africans as children.⁴⁷

Thus, both the European settlers and missionaries seemed to approach Africans from a racist point of view, where Africans' interests were considered inferior to that of the white people. This being the case, many Africans felt betrayed and sought ways to make their grievances heard primarily through the political outlet. The formation of a militant group led by Harry Thuku in 1922 was a high point of defiance against racism⁴⁸ and inspired Africans to protest openly (walking in the light) against colonialism in Kenya. Thus, entry of Keswick theology in East Africa could have found adherents who had already experienced segregation. It was not difficult therefore to accommodate

---

42. This was an identity (pass) card contained in a metal box.
43. Sagay and Wilson, *Africa: A Modern History*, 369.
44. Walls, *Cross-Cultural Process*, 103.
45. Gatumu, *Pauline Concept*, 30.
46. Beidelmann, *Colonial Evangelism*, 72.
47. Walls, *Cross-Cultural Process*, 98.
48. Odhiambo, *History of East Africa*, 155.

Keswick teachings of two sets of people, the saved and the surrendered Christians. This led to the beginning of the *abaka*, "those on fire, from the verb *kwaka*, to set light to."[49] This describes the wave of evangelistic zeal in those who were getting saved, leading to moral transformation exemplified by the changed life of being in the light with one another. This resulted in the formation of the Brethren, those who walk in light and share testimony with one another. Thus, the Brethren became a set of Christians in Kenya whose teachings set themselves apart from other Christians. Indeed, they exemplify a lifestyle pattern, akin to what could be regarded as socio-ethical racism. Let's now turn to the other continuum of circumstances beyond Africans' control.

Epidemics and diseases

At the beginning of the twentieth century, the Gikuyu of Kenya were burdened with diseases and famines such that these maladies were sometimes used to compute years or events.[50] Also, the famine year of 1917, says Wambugu,[51] came to be called famine of Kimotho (the Gikuyu name for left-handed; his real name was Lawford) who was the District Commissioner of Fort-Hall, Murang'a today. This naming proves the intensity of the occurrences and the impact left in its wake.

The phenomena were widespread even outside the borders of Kenya. For instance, Guillebaud records the intensity of the dreaded leprosy in Uganda and Rwanda, so that the first missionary doctors secured a special block at Kabale Hospital for leprosy sufferers.[52] The problem of this scourge was underlined by the proposal to build a leprosy hospital at Kabale, Uganda in 1928. This is not to suggest leprosy was the only challenge facing the East African countries, as other diseases were common too. In his Rwanda notes, Church recorded a unique malady:

> Now a word about yaws – this extraordinary disease hardly ever heard in Europe. It is somewhat like syphilis, but not spread in the same way; incurable, chronic, crippling, often ending in limb contractions and blindness, and even babies in arms came

---

49. Church, *Quest for the Highest*, 100.
50. Wambugu, Ngarariga, and Kariuki, *Agikuyu*, 139, 210–214.
51. Wambugu, Ngarariga, and Kariuki, 211.
52. Guillebaud, *Grain of Mustard Seed*, 35.

covered all over their bodies with the secondary infections stage and swarming with flies. But by the mercy of God . . . a rapid and dramatic cure [was found] called Sobita, a water-soluble white powder of sodium bismuth tartrate . . . We reckoned that about 90% of the people were or had been infected by yaws in Eastern Ruanda . . . [The] injections hurt, but the more they hurt the more the people liked them, and the name of the hospital went far and wide.[53]

Yaws, among other skin diseases, was also common in the Gikuyu land as observed by Wambugu:

> Very few of the *Agikuyu* escaped the disease called yaws (*muchari*).[54] This was usually contracted in childhood. After an incubation of from twelve to twenty days, the prodromic period begins, and the skin loses its brightness and becomes pale and discoloured. The patient feels indisposed, general relaxation sets in with pain at the lumbar region and at the joints, cephalea, gastric troubles, and fever. After some time there appears a cutaneous eruption, itching and painful at pressure. In less than one week the eruption becomes vascular and suppurates. Within about three weeks it is fully developed, and secondary groups appear elsewhere on the body. At this stage, fever disappears.[55]

In 1919 the Gikuyu land of Kenya was devastated by a plague that killed tens of thousands. Kariuki[56] underlines the intensity of this plague by the fact that his *rika* (age-set) came to be called *Rika ria kimiiri*[57] (the age-mate of the slayer).

Another unusual incident worth mentioning was the Ruanda note by Bert Jackson in August 1928 of a sickly baby receiving treatment. He wrote:

---

53. Church, *Quest for the Highest*, 35–36.

54. An infectious tropical disease marked initially by red skin eruptions and later by joint pains. It mainly affects children and is caused by the bacterium Treponema pertenue.

55. Wambugu, Ngarariga, and Kariuki, *Agikuyu*, 140.

56. Kariuki, *Bishop Facing Mount Kenya*, 22.

57. *Kimiri* is a kikuyu name which could variously be interpreted as destroyer or exterminator. It was a term used to refer to a machine used to crush sugarcane to produce juice in the Gikuyu land.

> I was walking across the country a few days ago when the cry of child faintly caught my ear. As I drew nearer the cry developed into one never-ending howl which I think I shall never forget. I found a poor little chap about five or six years old just covered with sores from head to foot so that he could neither lie, sit nor stand without pressing on some of them, and surrounded by a cloud of flies. A fond parent was in the process of picking off old mud from the sores and putting on fresh. This is the native idea of a healing dressing. It certainly does prevent the flies from eating the child alive and also hinders the spread of infection, but imagine what a comfortable dressing sunbaked mud makes on raw flesh! Now with an injection, all these sores soon heal up and a child takes an interest in life once more.[58]

Such were the circumstances and experiences meted out against East Africans by diseases they could hardly handle at times except through outside help. The coming of Europeans with conventional medicine that could do wonders in comparison with traditional alternatives must have led Africans to change side from traditional and cultural ways of treatment to modern medicine. No wonder Guillebaud notes that some of the first people to respond to the gospel messages were leprosy patients at Kabale.[59] Given this background of maladies, it could not have been difficult for Africans to see the light in the missionaries' method of dealing with diseases. This trust in the missionary ways of curing most of the physical ailments could have influenced Africans to accept salvific messages.[60] Consequently, many Africans left behind ways of darkness for the modes of light.

A recap of external influences at the dawn of Keswick theology in East Africa shows that, while racism brought to the fore preferential treatment of one person against the other, diseases and epidemics appeared to bring the races together. However, in both ways, a need to embrace a new way of life (a new light) was remarkably evident. They needed to move away from the dehumanizing forces that seemed to oppress and maim, to freedom and

---

58. Church, *Quest for the Highest*, 36.
59. Guillebaud, *Grain of Mustard Seed*, 35.
60. Church, *Quest for the Highest*, 35.

well-being. Since Africans lived in communities, this turnaround could not be hidden. Let's turn now to the internal influences.

Internal Influences

The other spectrum of influences was motivated by Africans themselves as a way to safeguard their culture and posterity. These are internal forces and include public confession, African sacrifice, rites of passage, age-sets marriage, and communal life. Each item is discussed in turn showing how their unique nature could have reinforced a need to walk in the light.

Public confession

Karanja[61] observes that confession played a significant role in African religion and culture. It was used among the Gikuyu to drive away effects of ritual defilement or taboo (*thahu*) to achieve healing. A symbolic vomiting (*gutahikio*) was done by a traditional healer to treat supernatural illnesses. A case in point is Kenyatta's[62] description of a healing ritual where the sick person is led to confess all evils.

> Before the magician proceeds with his actual work of healing, the sick man who is about to be treated is asked to spit on the healing magic or to lick it. In this way, a direct communication with the ancestral spirits is established through the medium of the magician. At this juncture, the magician starts to chant the healing ritual with a strong voice and unusual tone and rhythm, accompanied by the tinkling of the *rugambi*.[63] At the same time, he swings the magical horn over the head of his patient. Suddenly, in a mystical state of mind, he stops chanting and, looking the sick man straight in the face, he addresses a few words of a magical formula to him, saying:
>
> > "Sick man, I have come to chase away your illness. I will also chase away the evil spirits which have brought it.

---

61. Karanja, *Founding the African Faith*, 147.
62. Kenyatta, *Facing Mount Kenya*, 281–282.
63. This is a small hand bell which is part and parcel of the healing magic. It is easily recognized by its peculiar sound, which is believed to have the power of frightening the evil spirits.

Confess the evils which you know, and also those you do not know. Prepare yourself, for you are about to vomit all these evils."

The magician had dug a round hole in the ground into which he poured some water. At this point he dipped what was believed to be healing magic into the water to induce the evil spirits to come out. The sick man kneels, facing the water as if he was vomiting while the magician squats on the other end facing the sick man. The magician recites the following spell:

> This (pointing to the healing magic) is a root. I root out the evils which are in your body.
>
> This is clearing away. I clear away the evils which are in your body.
>
> This is a weakening. I weaken the evil spirits which are in your body.
>
> This is a calming. I calm the illness which is in your body.

After each sentence, the sick man licked the githitu (the healer's magical charm) and spat in the water. He pretended to vomit saying: "I vomit the illness and the evil spirits that are in my body."[64]

By the act of symbolic vomiting, the sick person was assured that he had received total healing and thus calming his psychological anxiety.

This vomiting gesture meant that the victim was now set free to walk and mingle with people as a clean person, a fact that was acclaimed and certified by the medicine man. The sick man was now declared righteous, no longer guilty of the charges that had been directed against him. Therefore, public confession of sin as taught by the Keswick movement may well have sounded familiar to those used to the East African practice of vomiting up evil spirits. Hence, the need to walk in the light could have made sense as a way to achieve a not guilty verdict – not guilty of sin. Indeed in East African practice, sometimes propitiation was done by performing a sacrifice to redeem the victim.

---

64. Kenyatta, *Facing Mount Kenya*, 283.

Ritual sacrifice

Wambugu state that a sacrifice was more of a public worship that would require a sacrifice of a goat by a medicine man to appease the spirits or avert a taboo.[65] Some Gikuyu people sprinkled blood while others sprinkled *tatha*[66] as exemplified by Wambugu:

> [First] Anyone who touched a corpse or was bereaved, he contracted a special impurity called *Gikuu* (death). If such a person drunk cow's milk or passed through cattle's herd, all the cattle became unclean. A medicine man had to be called to slaughter and sprinkle the herd with its *tatha*.
>
> [Second] If anyone was heard to whisper in the night near the hut, or a stick fell on the thatch or struck against the wall, it was believed it was poisoned by the enemy. A goat had to be slaughtered the next day. Enough sprinkling of blood was to be done in the direction where whispering was heard or where the sound of the stick was heard.[67]

The list of incidences that warranted sacrifice is endless, and Wambugu could only manage to record twenty-seven cases.[68] This shows that circumstances that led to the slaughter of an animal were frequent. The fear of the evil spirit was an ever-present phenomenon in the people's mind. The shedding of blood – to appease the spirit – was a significant gesture that assured the victim and the community of salvation from evil. Similarly, the shedding of Christ's blood on the cross to save humanity from the sin principle was one of the fundamental teachings of Keswick theology. Thus, Keswick teachings could have sounded similar in the East African circumstances to the shedding of sacrificial blood to appease the spirits. Again, these sacrifices were made in public, declaring salvation from evil spirits. The victim could now walk in the light, publicly acknowledging salvation from evil and taboo. He or she was welcomed back to full participation in the affairs of the communal life.

---

65. Wambugu, Ngarariga, and Kariuki, *Agikuyu*, 190, 191.
66. The contents of the stomach and intestines of the animal.
67. Wambugu, Ngarariga, and Kariuki, *Agikuyu*, 192.
68. Wambugu, Ngarariga, and Kariuki, *Agikuyu*, 191–194.

Communal life

Kunhiyop observes that the "we and us" concept is deeply rooted in Africans from childhood.[69] Mbiti's exposition of the concept of community cited in Kunhiyop is enlightening:

> In traditional life, the individual does not and cannot exist alone except corporately. He owes his existence to other people, including those of past generations and his contemporaries. He is simply part of the whole. The community must, therefore, make, create or produce the individual; for the individual depends on the corporate group . . . Only in terms of other people does the individual become conscious of his own being, his own duties, his privileges and responsibilities towards himself and towards other people. When he suffers, he does not suffer alone but with the corporate group; when he rejoices, he rejoices not alone but with his kinsmen, his neighbours and his relatives whether living or dead. When he gets married he is not alone, neither does the wife "belong" to him alone. So, also the children belong to the corporate body of kinsmen, even if they bear only their father's name. Whatever happens to the individual happens to the whole group, and whatever happens to the whole group happens to the individual. Therefore the individual can only say, "I am because we are, and since we are, therefore, I am.[70]

Hence the Gikuyu saying: *kamuingi koyaga ndiri*,[71] which means corporate activities make massive works easier. This fits well with relationships and community values. As Kenyatta contends, "an old man who has no children of his own is helped by his neighbour's children . . . his hut is built, his garden dug, firewood is cut and water is fetched for him."[72] This justifies another Gikuyu proverb, *rui runenehagio in tuthima* (a river is enlarged by its tributaries) and demonstrates the importance of the individual. At the same time, the person must not forget that he is an individual among others,

---

69. Kunhiyop, *African Christian Ethics*, 20.
70. Kunhiyop, *African Christian Ethics*, 21.
71. *Ndiri* is a heavy wooden mortar and requires many people to lift it.
72. Kenyatta, *Facing Mount Kenya*, 113.

and so must consider the rights of other people. So the daily expectations for human beings have been to live both as an individual and as a community.

This is better illustrated through the age-set system. A Gikuyu proverb *Nyumba na riika itiumanagwo* (a family- or /clan and an age group are inseparable) could be a case in point. The proverb cautions an individual that he cannot be separated from his clan and age group no matter what the individual may have done. The need to stay in tune with community norms could not thus be stressed more. It may not have been a surprise, therefore, that the seed of the Keswick beliefs and practices, which displayed community set up, found fertile ground in East Africa.

To be a full member of the community with rights and privileges, one had to pass through a rite of passage, as applicable in different African cultural systems. Rites of passage form an important community group dynamics that include the age-set system referred to above. These dynamics could have created the necessary channels for Keswick theology which also takes pride in community undercurrents.

Rites of passage

A rite of passage is the circumstance that more than any other favored Keswick spirituality in East Africa. It was performed on special occasions to indicate entry into a new stage of life such as birth, puberty, marriage, and death. When any of these rituals took place, it not only attracted the immediate family but the surrounding community. Puberty and marriage rites dynamics are community-centered and therefore seem to offer suitable socio-historical circumstances that could have favored Keswick theology in East Africa. We begin with puberty rites.

Puberty rituals have been practiced for centuries on young men and women across Africa and beyond. In Kenya, circumcision is common except among the Luo and Turkana societies. In the past, it was usually performed in a public ceremony.

The significance of it being held publicly had implications to the initiate and the community. First, as Magesa observes, the initiation confirmed the initiate's connection with the ancestors through formal induction into the ethnic group.[73] It was a mark of unity with the people. Second, it was intended

---

73. Magesa, *African Religion*, 101.

to instill courage. Magesa argues, "Without courage among the youth, the life-force of the clan withers and will eventually die. For if the young men of the community are cowards, who will then defend the people? Similarly, will there be live births if the mothers-to-be cannot bear pain, namely, the pain of childbirth?"[74] Kenyatta observes that "the parents would sing for joy saying our children are brave, *ee-ho* (hurrah). Did anyone cry? No one cried - hurrah!" It was bad news for the community to hear of a cowardly gesture from an initiate, more so a male. Each community expected to raise strong and bold young men to defend the tribe from outside aggression, which is not possible with a weakhearted person. Third, it was a public recognition that one has passed from childhood to adulthood, and thus one could now marry. Fourth, one was ushered into tribal secrets.[75] Mbiti[76] states that during seclusion the young people underwent a period of education in tribal life to overcome difficulties and equip them mentally, emotionally and morally. Thus, no single member, say of the Gikuyu tribe, could have remained uncut. Finally, every young person who is circumcised at a particular time entered a special age-group commonly known as *Rika* or age-mate.

Rika argues Magesa was the most reputable group relation established by the very act of initiation.[77] Magesa further contends that such people enjoy a unique social and moral tie of loyalty and devotion with one another. They stood in the very closest relationship with each other, in spite of their geographical distance regarding where age-set members were initiated or presently living.[78] Kenyatta observes, "If one member of an age-group is insulted and is physically unable to avenge the injury, the other members of his age-group will cooperate with him in attaining satisfaction. For an insult to one member of an age-group is regarded as an insult to the entire age-group . . . in the matter of paying off a fine . . . age-group, rika, will contribute toward the payment . . ."[79] Magesa concurs with Kenyatta and shows the unique oneness validated by the simultaneous spilling of their blood. Thus, they referred to each other as brothers, and to the parents of each one of

---

74. Magesa, 9.
75. Kenyatta, *Facing Mount Kenya*, p.141.
76. Mbiti, *Introduction to African Religion*, 96.
77. Magesa, *African Religion*, 101.
78. Magesa, 102.
79. Kenyatta, *Facing Mount Kenya*, p. 114.

them as father and mother and their female siblings as sisters, who deserve respect.[80] This practice, Magesa argues, is replicated by the Nuer people, a Nilotic ethnic group of South Sudan.[81]

The importance of age-sets was further amplified by the fact that they marked seasons. Thus, Kariuki,[82] Bishop of Mount Kenya South (1975–1976) gives a vivid description of the 1918 global influenza pandemic that killed 40 million people across the globe. Those circumcised in 1919 when this pandemic was sweeping through the Kikuyu land killing tens of thousands came to be known as the *Rika ria kimiri*[83] (age-group). Kariuki[84] and Magesa[85] further contend that the bond that was established by the *Rika* was often stronger than blood relationships, perhaps equated to blood-brotherhood.[86] Kariuki explains his argument:

> Age-mates have an abiding confidence in one another, because of their common experiences during the entire process of initiation. It does not matter if a member of my age-group happens to come from as far afield as Nyeri, Murang'a, or Rift Valley. Once he enters my homestead and identifies himself as a member of my age-group, even before I have discovered his name, I welcome him wholeheartedly. I would not hesitate to slaughter a ram or a he-goat (*Thenge*) for my *wakini* [my true friend] if my personal wealth at that time allowed it. For indeed we Gikuyu still regard it as the highest honour to slaughter an animal for one's fellow *wakini*.[87]

This public acknowledgment and acceptance of one's age-mate depict strong ties of the *Rika* so as to slaughter an animal for him. This gesture would be brought to light to fellow members of the *Rika* in the vicinity. They

---

80. Magesa, *African Religion*, 103.
81. Magesa, 103.
82. Kariuki, *Bishop Facing Mount Kenya*, 22.
83. *Rika ria kimiri* insinuates those circumcised when the destroyer struck the kikuyu land.
84. Kariuki, *Bishop Facing Mount Kenya*, 23.
85. Magesa, *African Religion*, p.103.
86. A blood brotherhood or blood pact was an initiation ritual where blood was exchanged, "either by mixing it with food and eating it or by sucking one another's blood from an incision" (Magesa, 106).
87. Kariuki, *Bishop Facing Mount Kenya*, 23–24.

were bound together by their common experiences through the entire initiation process and would call one another *wanyua wakini* (your real friend). This demonstrated togetherness and trust that not only defined respect for senior age-groups but very importantly structured and knitted the community together openly and transparently.

Marriage, argues Magesa, is a journey to attain full humanity and begins with rituals and ceremonies to establish and solidify ties of common knowledge and understanding necessary for kinship.[88] For example, Kenyatta illustrates how a girl was seemingly abducted by the young man's female relatives and carried "shoulder-high. The girl struggles and refuses to go with them and even to seem to shed tears, while the women giggle joyously and cheer her with songs and dances. The cries and cheers can be heard for miles around, and the Gikuyu people will know that the son of so-and-so has taken the daughter of so-and-so in marriage."[89] Sometimes parents would arrange the marriage of their child into a particular family from a young age. However, Nyaga of the Meru of Eastern Kenya argues that this pre-arranged marriage could not materialize if the young man or lady chose to marry elsewhere.[90]

This rite of passage was crucial to the sustenance of kinship structure and had social-ethical implications as described by Kisembo when he quoted an address by a Zulu pastor to a newly married couple. The pastor says to the bride: "Mapule, you should bear in mind . . . that you are married not to your husband Paul, but to his family. That means you have to identify completely with all his relatives, look after them, care for them, go out of your way to make them happy. If you do that, you will have no cause for regret." And to the groom, he says: "you, Paul, will have to do likewise with Mapule's relatives. Her people are your people and vice versa. Both of you will notice that old people in the community will tend to visit you, even for a brief moment . . . to show their interest in your welfare."[91]

The social ties thus established unify and solidify the tribe as one organic whole such that the community could be mobilized quickly for a corporate activity like digging or building bridges. It was not a private affair but a family.

---

88. Magesa, *African Religion*, 121.
89. Kenyatta, *Facing Mount Kenya*, 165.
90. Nyaga, *Customs and Traditions*, 108.
91. Kisembo, Magesa and Shorter, *African Christian Marriage*, 182.

The study looked at external and internal influences that could have played a part in the establishment of EARM. The external circumstances were unwelcome phenomena that Africans loathed and fought against. The experiences of being prejudiced against and the dilapidating diseases forced many East Africans, particularly in Kenya, to seek for socio-political solutions: the Young Kikuyu Association (YKA) aired grievances, *Mau Mau* expressed solidarity to take back their land and rights, and hospitals were built to deal with marauding pandemics. Africans needed to speak their concerns through social-political organizations like YKA while medically, missionary doctors were able to provide the necessary injections. On the one hand, Africans had to physically take up arms to defend their human rights which had been grossly violated by colonial masters. On the other hand, they had to acknowledge the power of western medicine over that of the African medicine man. In both ways, they had to make a paradigm shift to regain their full humanity.

Internal influences emanated from internal circumstances and experiences that were fostered and reinforced by African cultural systems. They were public and communal, enhancing collective responsibility and belonging in line with John Mbiti's dictum, "I am because we are, and since we are, therefore I am."[92] The involvement of the entire community in the affairs of an individual shows the strength of kinship and another relatedness that must be woven together into the moral fabric through various initiations.

Given the above discussion, the researcher shall make a few observations as to why East Africans found it necessary to walk in the light with each other in their daily life. This walking in the light had a twofold meaning. First, it meant that if they are together in their belief and practice they are thus in the light with one other. Second, conversely, if they are not together they are thus not in the light with each other. So the following observations are made from the perspective of the two mentioned scenarios:

- Africans were exposed to a color bar and discrimination by the colonial masters. This set boundaries between blacks and whites, and could have influenced East Africans to readily associate with Keswick theology that divided Christians into saved and surrendered. This may have led to the rise of the *abaka*, those on

---

92. Mbiti, *African Religion and Philosophy*, 108–109.

fire – the ones who have surrendered their lives to Jesus as their Lord and Savior.[93]
- Africans found European missionaries to have medicine that worked wonders, so they associated themselves with missionary doctors who not only provided a solution for physical healing but also led them to spiritual healing. This transition could not be hidden and might have provided an avenue for second-blessing teaching. This teaching divided Christians into those who had received the blessing and those who had not.
- The practice of publicly vomiting of evil through a process of psychological manipulation resonates with Keswick teaching about the public confession of sin. Public confession of evil was by far the most profound circumstance that could have found a parallel with Keswick theology. Thus, those who confessed their sins were thought to be in the light with one another and vice versa.
- Rites of passage were by nature steps towards full community integration. That is why one had to undergo the ritual in the full view of the entire community. This was important because recognition by one's juniors or seniors avoided misrepresentation in various settings which could lead to taboo warranting a sacrifice to thwart danger in the community. Africans' rites of passage may well have seemed to have parallels with the sanctification process as taught by Keswick theologians. The process required step by step movement towards spiritual maturity in what was called Spirit-filled life. This rendered a Christian able to live a victorious life without which one became a spiritual casualty. Thus, there was a real need to pass through the established process or suffer condemnation. A circumcision candidate who cried or showed signs of cowardice during the actual operation was a great let-down to the community and will have to live with stigma.

---

93. Franklin, "TRUTH."

All these factors required public display because the community was one unit and anything affecting its stability needed the attention of everybody. In other words, all had the right to know what is happening within the community. So everything, as much as possible, had to be brought into the public scrutiny – into the light. As Mbiti rightly says, community awareness has been critical to the security and peace of its members because an individual exists only because others exist.[94]

Having discussed walking in the light in the *missio Dei* and the Kenyan socio-historical context, an exploration of the historical background of Keswick theology is vital.

A Historical View of Keswick Theology

Naselli observes that Keswick theology is not easy to describe due to its lack of structure and different doctrinal positions.[95] But in essence, it refers to the shared views of the doctrine of sanctification and personal holiness held by the prominent proponents of the early Keswick movement.[96] Before the views on Keswick theology can be explored, it is important to briefly assess the main Keswick antecedents.

Keswick Antecedents

The genesis of the holiness tradition in America begun in the nineteenth century as an offshoot of Wesleyan perfectionism propagated primarily by John Wesley. The holiness tradition, in turn, influenced Phoebe Palmar and Asa Mahan of Methodist perfectionism and Oberlin perfectionism respectively. Thus, if Wesleyan perfectionism influenced the holiness movement which in turn influenced the early Keswick movement predominantly through the Higher Life movement, then the Methodist and Oberlin perfectionism must be the holiness movement's offspring. This could be graphically

---

94. Mbiti, *Introduction to African Religion*, 174.
95. Naselli, *Let Go and Let God*, 45.
96. This is a movement from 1875 to 1920 that was conservatively evangelical. It held the view that most Christians live in defeat and that the secret to living the higher life, the deeper life, or the victorious Christian life is consecration followed by Spirit-filling (Naselli, 45).

presented in the following, adapted illustration from *Let Go and Let God? A Survey and Analysis of Keswick Theology.*⁹⁷

Wesleyan Perfectionism

Wesleyan perfectionism, sometimes referred to as entire sanctification, was a view held by John Wesley, a renowned evangelical preacher of the nineteenth century. He held that Christians could to some degree attain perfection in this life. Indeed he separates justification and sanctification and restricts sin to voluntary sinful acts. He further argues that unintentional transgressions do not hinder the best of persons from being called perfect or sinless. Thus, Wesley seems not to object to the term sinless perfection.⁹⁸ He viewed sanctification as Christian perfection and "affirmed a second transforming work of grace that advocates the eradication of sin . . ."⁹⁹ Packer further asserts that Wesley's doctrine of perfection emphasized the power of perfect love to counteract a sinful countenance. He regarded personal knowledge of being sanctified (without known sin) as a due consequence of not breaking any known law.¹⁰⁰

It is thus critical to consider some resemblances between the Keswick and Wesleyan views of sanctification. McQuilkin argues that the expression of Wesleyan holiness appears in the Keswick growth pattern: a process-crisis-process that starts at regeneration.¹⁰¹ Thus the view that Keswick integrates the Wesleyan idea of the possibility of God entering the Christian life is suggestive of the holy life. Daily victory over sin is believed to be attained by

---

97. Naselli, *Let Go and Let God*, 77.
98. Naselli, *Keswick Theology*, 3.
99. Packer, *Keep in Step*, 132–135.
100. Packer, 137–139.
101. McQuilkin, "Keswick Perspective," 185–186.

entire consecration to God in a complete surrender that delivers the believer from the domination of inherited sin.

Thus Thompson, a Wesleyan author, recorded some critical connections between Wesleyan and Keswick theology. These theologies agree that a life of victory in Christ comes through a definite crisis experience or second work of grace. They believe that sanctification could be lost and agree on the second blessing.[102] However, while the Wesleyan holds that the second blessing is a normal occurrence in the economy of God, Keswick teachers state that the second blessing comes after justification because of man's ignorance of the need of being filled with the Holy Spirit.[103]

These intricate beliefs underline the strife for holiness. Indeed, as illustrated above, the Wesleyan movement inevitably gave birth to the holiness movement.

The Holiness Movement

Three offshoots from the holiness movement which began in 1835[104] will be discussed briefly to familiarize the reader with the emergence of Keswick theology. These are Methodist perfectionism, Oberlin perfectionism, and the Higher Life Movement. It was through the Higher Life Movement that Keswick theology grew and prospered in England and beyond.

Methodist Perfectionism

Despite Palmer's (1807–1874) claim to propagate Wesley's perfectionism, she modified it to emphasize her teaching, known as altar theology. As Smith observes, according to Palmer, there is a shorter way to holiness which she popularized through the holiness camp meetings.[105] Thus, Methodist perfectionism stressed Christian perfection and not a consequent process.[106] These camp meetings propagated Palmer's doctrine of sanctification. The early Keswick Convention to some extent became a British equivalent of the camp meeting movement.[107]

---

102. Thompson, *An Appraisal*, 14.
103. Dunlop, *Critique*.
104. Dayton, *American Holiness Movement*, 26.
105. Smith, *Called Unto Holiness*, 24.
106. Naselli, *Keswick Theology*, 4.
107. Smith, *Called Unto Holiness*, 24.

Oberlin Perfectionism

Warfield claims that the higher life teaching was an offshoot of the Oberlin theology. "If Oberlin Perfectionism is dead, it has found its grave, not in the abyss of nonexistence, but in the Higher Life Movement, the Keswick Movement, the Victorious Live Movement, and other kindred forms of Perfectionist teaching."[108] Warfield observes how Asa Mahan of Oberlin experienced a movement from sanctification by works alone to sanctification by faith alone. Henceforth he would not allow any place for work in sanctification, thus seeming to get it wrong because work and prayer must go together. This knowledge led Mahan to experience a "second conversion in which he seemed to himself to rise into a higher plane of Christian living . . . from twilight into the full light of Christian experience."[109]

Thus, Barabas recognizes Asa Mahan as a Keswick antecedent as well. Mahan and his associate Charles Finney, the primary propagators of Oberlin perfectionism, viewed holiness as the perfection of a human's autonomous free will.[110] They limited Christian perfection to a believer's intent to follow the moral law and regarded Spirit-baptism as the crisis following justification that initiates Christian perfection.[111] Mahan moved to England in the early 1870s, and no doubt influenced the Keswick movement by his leadership and teaching (the necessity of Christians receiving Spirit baptism) in the Oxford and Brighton Conferences that immediately preceded the first Keswick Convention.[112]

The Higher Life Movement

It wasn't until the publication of William E. Boardman's influential book "The Higher Christian Life"[113] in 1858 that interest in the subject of higher life grew in unprecedented magnitude.[114] The central argument of the book

---

108. Warfield, *Perfectionism*, ix.
109. Warfield, 52.
110. Barabas, *So Great Salvation*, 16.
111. Naselli, *Keswick Theology*, 21.
112. Barabas, *So Great Salvation*, 21–24.
113. This book guided the movement until Robert Pearsall Smith's removal from public ministry in 1875.
114. Naselli, *Keswick Theology*, 21; Barabas, *So Great Salvation*, 16.

according to Pearce[115] was that sanctification was experienced sometime after justification. This assertion must have caught the attention of the church as it sold over 100,000 copies both in America and Europe with a far-reaching influence. The book awakened a sense of spiritual poverty and powerlessness in the hearts and minds of believers and a quest for victory over besetting sins and power in Christian service. This led to a new scriptural study of holiness.[116] However, Abbot argued that the book lacked historical truth.[117] Furthermore, the book was found by some people to have been based more on experience than Scripture.[118]

Despite criticism, the book breathed new life into America and Britain. William Boardman began an itinerant convention ministry through which he met Robert Pearsall Smith and his wife, Hannah Whitall Smith. The couple became prominent higher life teachers popularizing Boardman's views throughout Britain in the early years of the fourth quarter of the nineteenth century.[119]

Smith's higher life meetings did much to set the pattern for the Keswick movement. Their emphasis was reinforced by their entry into the deeper spiritual experience.[120] They propagated post-conversion Spirit baptism[121] promulgated by the doctrine of "physical thrills."[122] This is what came to be regarded as the second blessing that brought one into the way of victory by faith. The Smiths had thus struck what they viewed to be the secret of the daily Christian life. They believed they had been delivered from the power of sin and its guilt.[123]

This understanding of sanctification was brought to England in 1872. The Smiths were the catalysts that brought lasting change in English religion[124] as they taught higher life theology in Broadlands (1874), Oxford (1874) and

---

115. Pearce, *Examination of the Higher Life*, 14.
116. Stevenson, *Keswick's Authentic Voice*, 14.
117. Abbott, "Boardmans' Higher Christian Life," 509.
118. Pearce, *Examination of the Higher Life*, 15.
119. Brown, "Higher Life Theology," 301.
120. Thompson, Appraisal of the Keswick, 12.
121. Pollock, *Keswick Story*, 35.
122. Physical thrills, a form of Quaker expression of the Holy Spirit, sometimes associated with sexual activity and immorality.
123. Barabas, *So Great Salvation*, 18.
124. Pollock, *Keswick Story*, 13.

Brighton (1875) that led to the first England Keswick Convention on 28 June 28 1875. They did not care about denominational labels, and speakers came from various denominational backgrounds. For example, "F.B. Meyer was a Baptist, A.T. Pierson, J. Elder Cumming, and George H.C. Macgregor were Presbyterians. Andrew Murray belonged to the Dutch Reformed Church. H.C.G. Webb-Peploe, H.W. Griffith Thomas, and J. Stuart Holden were Anglicans."[125] Thompson notes that Keswick soon became the recognized center of the movement.[126]

The Smiths suffered opposition from the evangelical leadership of the day like John Charles Ryle (later Bishop of Liverpool) who adversely contrasted Moody's teaching with that of Brighton.[127] Their doctrine of physical thrills ended their public ministry but did not stop the spiritual fervor. Successors like Henry Bowker steered the movement away from the excesses of American higher life to the deepening of spiritual life.[128]

Boardman asserts the higher life proponents used Romans 6:1–14 to argue that a believer could live as a defeated Christian. They taught that victory could be obtained through a crisis of surrender. Their theory of sanctification, that a believer could enter life on the highest plane, comprised the need for a second blessing, consecration and a victorious life of surrender – "let go and let God."[129] These components will be discussed in detail later.

Thus, both the Holiness and Higher Life Movements contributed immensely to Keswick theology which is profoundly grounded in the sin principle. The preceding views so far articulated by the movement's teachers bring to the fore the fundamental influence of sin in the believer. Knowing how to deal with it was of utter importance. Thus, sanctified life was not only encouraged but was seen as a hinge upon which victorious Christian life could find an outlet. It is therefore critical for this study to discuss early Keswick views of sanctification theology. This will help to conceptualize the driving force behind the Keswick theology.

---

125. Thompson, *Appraisal of the Keswick*, 13.
126. Thompson, 13.
127. Pollock, *Keswick Story*, 33.
128. Pollock, 40.
129. Boardman, *Higher Life Doctrine*, ii.

Keswick Views of Sanctification Theology

The historical view of early Keswick theology has been embedded in the teachings of prominent Keswick exponents. This section deals with major pillars that defined sanctification theology through the eyes of Keswick teachers. However, before engaging these historical tenets, the researcher shall briefly conceptualize the phrase "sanctification theology" in the contemporary understanding of the term.

Contemporary Conceptualization of Sanctification Theology

The Greek word that is used for sanctification in the New Testament is ἁγιασμός *(hagiasmos)*; this is defined in Louw and Nida's Lexicon as the process of making holy, dedicating, sanctifying or consecrating, as the operation of the Spirit making holy, causing to belong entirely to God and sanctifying work (cf. 1 Cor 1:2; 1 Thess 4:3; 1 Pet 1:2).[130] Louw and Nida further describe it as the careful moral behavior that expresses one's dedication to God's pure way of life, upright behavior and holy living (1 Thess 4:4, 7; Heb 12:14), and as the moral goal of the purifying process resulting in holiness and right behavior (Rom 6:22).[131] The opposite of sanctification, argue Louw and Nida, is ακαθαρσια *(akatharsia)* which translates as uncleanness, moral impurity, and filthiness (Rom 1:24).[132]

Thus Hoekema, writing in the last quarter of the twentieth century, comes closer to the dictionary definition above: "sanctification as that gracious operation of the Holy Spirit, involving our responsible participation, by which He delivers us as justified sinners from the pollution of sin, renews our entire nature according to the image of God, and enables us to live lives that are pleasing to Him" as sons and daughters of God.[133] Hoekema further distinguishes the pollution of sin from guilt. He observes, on the one hand, that guilt is a condition deserving condemnation because God's law has been violated. However, God's declarative (judicial) act in justification declares us not guilty of our sin on the basis of Christ's atoning work. On the other hand, pollution

---

130. Louw and Nida, *Greek-English Lexicon*, 538.
131. Louw, 538.
132. Louw, 770.
133. Hoekema, "Reformed Perspective," 61.

is the result of sin, the corruption of our nature that produces further sin. Thus the old and the new nature appear to coexist in the same person.[134]

Keswick Conceptualization of Sanctification Theology

The definition of Keswick theology of sanctification by Keswick teachers has been elusive. Indeed, there has been no single concise definition. However, Naselli asserts it is possible to come up with a view of sanctification theology shared by the prominent propagators of the early Keswick movement from 1875 to 1920.[135] This would be made possible, argues Naselli, if activities of the Keswick week were to be traced from the first day to the fifth day.[136] These activities shall be explored later in this section. But meanwhile, individual attempts at definition by the Keswick teachers should be considered.

Prof. Handley Moule[137]

Prof. Moule writing in the last quarter of the nineteenth century might give general guidance: "The aim of Christians who genuinely desire sanctity: To be [like Christ]; to displace self from the inner throne, and enthrone Him; to make not the slightest compromise with the smallest sin. We aim at nothing less than to walk with God all day long, to abide every hour in Christ and He and His words in us, to love God with all the heart and our neighbours as ourselves."[138] This view seems to reflect higher life teaching and though comprehensive, appears repetitive as many words used to describe the subject of sanctification are more or less synonyms.

McQuilkin

McQuilkin, an American Keswick exponent, believes that a commonly-held view is possible. His view on the Keswick teaching of sanctification is threefold: First, at justification and regeneration, the believer is declared to have the righteousness of Jesus Christ (positional sanctification or righteousness in Reformed circles). The second is an experiential sanctification or the practical

---

134. Hoekema, 61.
135. Naselli, *Keswick Theology*, 28.
136. Naselli, 29.
137. Bishop Moule, Bishop of Durham for nineteen years, confessed to have received blessing during the 1884 convention following Evan Hopkin's address on putting the Lord first (Pollock, *Keswick Story,* 70).
138. Pollock, *Keswick Story,* 74.

daily life in Christ; this is the primary focus of the Keswick emphasis. Then, the third aspect is complete sanctification which comes only at the end of this life, usually understood to be the glorification of the believer.[139]

Barabas[140]

Barabas, a renowned writer on Keswick theology, argues that in Keswick there is no holiness without the cross and the Holy Spirit is the agent of sanctification.[141] Barabas summarizes McQuilkin's general belief on sanctification as placing the dynamics of the overcoming life into their proper perspective, as far as Keswick theology is concerned.[142] Integrating McQuilkin's experiential sanctification with the Barabas argument about the cross could give a working definition of Keswick theology, as to the focus of this study. The experiential sanctification is significant in this context because it underpins the achieving of Keswick theology of sanctification that is believed to inform EARM's concepts and practices.

Indeed, Barabas argues that experiential sanctification in Keswick is best understood by use of the term *counteraction*. Undeniably, Keswick leaders claim that God's way of sanctification is counteraction, not suppression or eradication. They further argue that the law of sin (Romans 7), has hidden potential to express the old nature which is not utterly annihilated in this life. It is a regular threat to the life of a believer. This potential is only put to subjection by the counteracting power of the Holy Spirit.[143]

The attempted definitions of McQuilkin and Barabas, though moderate and descriptive, lack precision and clarity. Thus, it has been a challenge to conceptualize the Keswick theology of sanctification from the *Keswick* point of view. This was perhaps because the Keswick teachers came from various denominational backgrounds. At the same time, their teachings were not doctrinal, but mainly devotional. Pollock observes even Moody and Edward Moore could not give a precise definition of sanctification as they used scriptural phrases like "the rest of faith" or "the blessing", which

---

139. McQuilkin, *Keswick Perspective*, 158–160.

140. His book *So Great Salvation* is widely considered the standard interpretation of Keswick theology.

141. Barabas, *So Great Salvation*, 94.

142. Barabas, 94.

143. Barabas, 94.

could not satisfactorily define the doctrine of sanctification theology.[144] In light of this, it is critical to examine the theology of sanctification as taught by Keswick teachers.

Theology of Sanctification as Taught by Keswick Teachers

The hallmark of the Keswick movement revolves around the theology of sanctification as taught by Keswick teachers following a successful first convention held at Keswick on 28 June 1875. Its catchphrase (motto) as coined by Robert Wilson during the 1882 eighth Keswick Convention was *All one in Christ Jesus*.[145] Barabas observes that this motto was always placed strategically at the "entrance to the large tent in which the meetings are held at Keswick, and also over the platform . . ."[146] This watchword was said to be the foundation stone upon which Keswick's harmony held together.

The general message of the early Keswick Convention was the practice of holiness expressed by what Brooke referred to as surrender of the will or self-release to God.[147] Since the expectations from the Keswick Convention were "to develop the highest Christian character," practical deliverance from besetting sin was emphasized.

As indicated earlier, a brief survey on the view of sanctification shared by the prominent propagators of the early Keswick movement from 1875 to 1920 will be considered. This will be done in accordance with the five days of progressive teaching in a typical early Keswick Convention.[148] The views espoused in the Keswick Convention sequence below could help explain Keswick theology and perhaps provide a definition. First are its views on sin.

The sin principle (Day 1 and 2): the diagnosis and the cure

This is what Keswick proponents referred to as the diagnosis in which the law of sin was counteracted by the law of the Spirit of Christ (Rom 8:2) as a means of gaining dominion over sin. Although Keswick teachers agreed on

---

144. Pollock, *Keswick Story*, 67.
145. Pollock, 63.
146. Barabas, *So Great Salvation*, 35.
147. Brooke, "Message: Its Methods," 80.
148. Naselli, *Keswick Theology*, 29.

a likelihood of living without known sin, they rejected what they perceived as sinless perfection,[149] as was taught in Wesleyan theology.

Certainly, this view of sin was a key concept in Keswick theology as exemplified in *The Keswick's Authentic Voice* edited by Stevenson. This unique book contains outstanding addresses delivered from the Convention platform in the earlier years by speakers whose lives had been transformed by the very message they were convincingly proclaiming.[150] Nearly half of the book addressed two fundamental topics: sin in the believer[151] and God's remedy for sin,[152] the topics covered the first two days of a typical Convention. These themes are what Naselli recorded as the diagnosis (of sin) and the cure (victorious Christian living).[153]

Canon Harford-Battersby and Robert Wilson instituted the phrase *For the promotion of practical holiness* to chart the purpose and way forward of the Conventions. On the one hand, it was believed before true holiness can be experienced, sin in the believer had to be dealt with. On the other hand, God's remedy for sin "is summed up in one word – Jesus, whose vicarious passion of His cross, has borne the penalty and blotted out the guilt of every sin of every believer. When the believer renounces the sin principle, desire for cleansing follows and a sincere intention of walking in the light will be the due reward.[154] Pollock, a Keswick historian, writes: "Keswick acted on the belief that many listeners would yield and trust in an instant . . . This had its dangers . . . There were many testimonies of a practical deliverance from the power of besetting sin."[155]

Therefore, to avoid Keswick meetings becoming a breeding ground for counterfeit believers, focus on sin and its remedy received a wide treatment. The gravity of the sin principle not only led the conveners to allocate the first two days of the Keswick week to the subject but to hinge subsequent messages on it. The aim was to discourage a maimed walk with God, lack of a Christocentric life and lack of love among Christians. These three aspects

---

149. Naselli, *Keswick Theology*, 29.
150. Stevenson, *Keswick's Authentic Voice*, 9.
151. Stevenson, 123–144.
152. Stevenson, 135–244.
153. Naselli, *Keswick Theology*, 29.
154. Stevenson, *Keswick's Authentic Voice*, 25, 137.
155. Pollock, *Keswick Story*, 75, 76.

appeared to take a central place in defeating besetting sin, against which a consecrated Christian had to declare war. Brooke argued that Keswick became a place for casting off the weight of besetting sins[156] and of Christian service. It acted like a clinic where diagnosis and prescription of sin were made, declaring the believer ready for the Master's use.[157] At least three rudimentary facts upon which Keswick teachers based their messages on sin should be surveyed.

The carnal mind

The carnal mind was viewed as the enemy within, the human lacking the divine, and which Inwood terms deadliest to the spiritual life. Alluding to 1 Corinthians 6–10, he conveys Paul's realm of ethics that challenged attending the theater, dancing, nudity and erotic entertainment.[158] Pollock, furthering this argument, sees a need to overcome besetting sins; gossiping, impatience and an angry countenance.[159] Thus, in the Convention, the ministry of conscience encouraged believers not only to attain acceptable socio-ethical standards, but a full surrender as well. This is what Lees seemed to refer to as a pure, cleansed and healthy conscience.[160]

The deliverance

When the carnal has been unveiled, the natural consequence would be deliverance from besetting sins. Hopkins saw salvation from the penalty of sin that pollutes the inner self as the sole reason for Keswick meetings.[161] Thus, the need to put off the old man (as opposed to the flesh(and put on the new man (Romans 6; Ephesians 4; Colossians 3). The action of putting off the old man meant putting off the old man's clothes (habits or besetting sins). Head, alternatively, uses the phrase death of the natural man and newness of life of the spiritual man with reference to baptism into Christ (Rom 6:3–5; Eph 2:6).[162] Though this points to the mortification and vivification effects on a regenerate person, this was not a major concern for Keswick theology where the interest was enhancement of Christian character. However, sin was

---

156. Those sins that keeps recurring in our lives (Gitari, *Troubled but not Destroyed*, 294).
157. Brooke, "Message: Its Methods," 79–80.
158. Inwood, "Unveiling of the Carnal," 71, 75.
159. Pollock, *Keswick Story*, 16.
160. Lees, "Ministry of Conscience," 90.
161. Hopkins, "Deliverance from the Law," 162–166.
162. Head, "Watchword of the Convention," 115.

recognized as an ever-present snare. Therefore, there was a need to cling to Christ, our Deliverer from the law of sin and death.

Early gatherings in Oxford (1874) and Brighton (1875), viewed deliverance from sin in the light of receiving the blessing.[163] This view or experience was brought to England by Smith and his wife Hannah through higher life teachings. Pollock confirms similar teachings on consecration and purity for eight years at Keswick led many to the heresy of sinless perfection.[164]

The grace of God

The unveiling of the carnal and the deliverance from sin were not a means to an end in themselves except by the grace of God. It is by that grace that we can share in the forgiveness of sins, not because of our righteousness but by one righteous act of our Lord and Savior Jesus Christ. Therefore, Webb-Peploe argues that the grace of God can quench every desire of the heart through Jesus Christ.[165] Paul in Romans 6:14 asserts that we are not under the law but under grace. The law curses, but Christ delivers (Gal 3:10–14). Stockmayer concurs, and refers to Paul's thorn in the flesh to avoid self-praise (2 Cor 12:9).[166]

In addition, Figgs develops the theme of grace further, to what came to be referred, in Keswick circles, as "keeping." This was taken to mean, by the grace of God, the believers commit their helplessness to God to do for them more than they ask or think.[167] This understanding may have led to the teaching about the rest of faith or what came to be negatively referred to as passivity.

Accordingly Mackinnon, expounding on 2 Peter 3:18, pointed out that there are only two possibilities in relation to Christian growth, progress or retrogression. He encouraged the 1911 Keswick congregation to grow in grace to be of service to God.[168] From Paul's letter to the Romans, Mackinnon argued that baptism into Christ's death meant possessing his holiness and pure lifestyle, that is being dead to the persistence of sin. He declared that sin could not be eliminated from human nature. He implicitly challenged the

---

163. Head, 115.
164. Pollock, *Keswick Story*, 64.
165. Webb-Peploe, "Christian Walk," 254.
166. Stockmayer, "Sufficiency of Grace," 183.
167. Figgs, "Some Characteristics," 106.
168. Mackinnon, "Christian Growth in Grace," 121.

doctrine of counteraction, which he claimed was a departure from the previous Keswick teachings. He reiterated that Keswick taught the possibility of exercising by faith victory over besetting sins through the power of the Lord Jesus Christ.[169] Thus, Christians needed to undergo a process of what came to be referred as a "second blessing," a concept which was largely influenced by the Higher Life Movement. A crisis of consecration achieved this process.

Consecration and sanctification

The first two days, according to Naselli, laid the foundation for the third day, i.e., the crisis[170] of consecration.[171] The emphasis was no crisis before Wednesday. So, Hopkins states that consecration and sanctification were a dedication or committal of the whole being on the one hand, and on the other hand, conformity to Christ's character.[172] Boardman was of the view that the Christian who senses his need of sanctification could enter into the blessings of Romans 6:1–14 through surrender or consecration.[173] The truths of Romans 6 could be appropriated through surrender and faith, and the only surrender acceptable to God is the surrender of the entire life.[174] Boardman contends that crisis prepares a man for surrender and surrender is the entrance into a life of faith on a new and higher plane.[175] The believer must believe that he is dead to sin and alive to God to experience deliverance. Thus, victory depended upon daily reliance upon Christ to defeat sin and using Christ's power with a view to having dominion over temptation.[176]

The Keswick writer McQuilkin speaks of why this view of sanctification has been referred to as the "victorious life."[177] It is believed that a decision could initiate victory at a point in time. Thus, the new person in Christ can choose the right consistently. Such a person shouldn't willingly infringe the known will of God.

---

169. Mackinnon, 122–123.
170. Edmond ("Notions of Sanctification," 13) contends that sanctification by crisis is rooted in John Wesley's doctrine of Christian perfection.
171. Naselli, *Keswick Theology*, 32.
172. Hopkins, *Deliverance from the Law of Sin*, 332–333.
173. Boardman, *Higher Life Doctrine*, iii.
174. Pearce, *Examination of the Higher Life*, 58.
175. Boardman, *Higher Life Doctrine*, iii.
176. Boardman, iv.
177. McQuilkin, *Keswick Perspective*, 178.

The victorious life or the "victory in Christ" movement was promoted by Charles Gallaudet Trumbull.[178] It is said that he often began his discussions by prudently explaining that justification and sanctification are two separate gifts of God obtained independently through different acts of faith. He appeared to base his argument on Wesley's error of separating sanctification from justification.[179]

This view suggests that consistent victory depends upon the continual exercise of faith. This meant that the believer must avoid all self-reliance or energy of the flesh when seeking to obey God's commands. The Christian shouldn't employ effort, but give his battle to Christ for victory.[180] Trumbull concurs with Boardman in his argument that the secret of full victory is faith. Jesus has done it all and effort has no place in a victory over the power of sin because it (effort) thwarts victory.[181] To understand the significance of consecration in the life of Keswick gatherings, its two main strands, crisis and process, and the Christian walk require elaboration.

Crisis and process

Hopkins, a formative Keswick theologian, justified his argument by quoting from 2 Corinthians 7:1, where he singles out separation from defilement as a sole definitive and decisive action. The act of cleansing ourselves is decisive, and brings to the fore the aspect of the crisis in a believer. He also quotes Ephesians 4:31, asserting that putting off evil habits and laying aside every weight (Heb 12:1) point to a crisis.[182] Pollock, addressing the issue of crisis and the process, claims that a crisis experience (surrender and experience) was a prerequisite to entering the higher life.[183]

Additionally, Naselli outlines Hannah Smith's twofold description of surrender in the light of "let go and let God." That is, entire surrender or complete abandonment (letting go) and absolute faith (letting God). These two steps or twin doors of faith and surrender were necessary "in order to enter this blessed interior life of rest and triumph . . . Man's part is to trust, and God's

---

178. Warfield, *Perfectionism*, 351.
179. Warfield, 355.
180. Boardman, *Higher Life Doctrine*, iv.
181. Trumbull, *Victory in Christ*, 48, 84.
182. Hopkins, *Deliverance from the Law*, 333.
183. Pollock, *The Keswick Story*, 74.

part is to work... The believer can do nothing but trust; while the Lord, in whom he trusts, actually does the work..."[184]

Commenting on the twin door, Naselli associated step one with surrender – let go (Jesus becomes the Master of the believer's life) and step two with faith – let God (God was to keep the believer from the power of sin). Thus, the sum of steps one and two equals consecration. The secret to consecration was trusting (not trying), and resting (not struggling).[185] Figgs[186] understood the rest of faith as a state of calm in the Lord in the midst of strife and desolation, referred to by some as quietism.[187] It was believed that passivity allowed God to work through an individual by promptings and impressions and that annihilation of selfhood was fundamental.[188]

When it comes to a process, Hopkins cites Colossians 1:11, which points to an idea of spiritual strengthening, progressive purity (1 John 3:3) and transforming of character (Rom 12:1–2). He argues that consecration is repeatable in the sense of restoring back – "see that, every morning, and every day, and many times during the day, you can say Amen to the fact that you have handed yourself wholly to Him."[189] Holden in reference to Jonah 3:1 reckons that there is a second chance for those who had ceased to follow Christ.[190] This is made possible because of our confidence in God's marvelous love made manifest in Jonah's going to Nineveh which he had hitherto dreaded.

Naselli notes that Frederick Brotherton Meyer taught three steps of crisis experience: conversion, consecration and the anointing of the Spirit. Meyer, who was a Baptist minister, spoke at the largely Anglican Keswick Convention twenty-six times, and he successfully spread the Keswick message to America and beyond.[191] Naselli observes that Hopkins attained a crisis of surrender and faith in 1873 following higher life messages under Robert Smith and

---

184. Naselli, *Let Go and lLet God*, p.105.
185. Naselli, *Keswick Theology*, 33.
186. Figgs, "Some Characteristics," 99.
187. May be in reference to Hannah Smith's influential book, *The Christian's Secret of a Happy Life*, which encouraged believers to entire surrender - let go and absolute faith - let God separating the point of justification and sanctification.
188. Packer, *Keep in Step*, 155–157.
189. Hopkins, *Deliverance from the Law*, 335–337.
190. Holden, "Gospel of the Second Chance," 154.
191. Naselli, *Keswick Theology*, 24.

Boardman in England. Hopkins later led Harford-Battersby, one of the founders of Keswick, to enter the rest of faith.[192]

Edmond understandably and helpfully attempted to clarify what sanctification by crisis meant from the perspectives of the Holiness and the Pentecostal traditions, ascribing entire sanctification to the former and second blessing to the latter. While he recognized the sanctification by crisis terminology, he identifies its theological position of a second, definite and decisive experience, following regeneration, by which the Christian believer is sanctified. It is a crisis moment, sometimes preceded by much distress for the believer.[193]

Inwood, however, sounds a warning by asserting that one of the most efficient ways in which the devil hinders the work of Christ in the hearts of God's children is putting before them a counterfeit consecration, a counterfeit Christian.[194] Thus, the congregations at Keswick were solemnly charged to exercise discernment with regard to false and genuine consecration and were encouraged to crown Christ as King in their hearts.[195] Brown, commenting on 1 Samuel 15:14, encouraged the believers to shun defective consecration likened to Samuel's probing of Saul's plunder that ought to have been slain.[196] The unconscious sin must be made conscious and cleansed by the blood of Jesus Christ. Brown argued this happens when supplicants go back to Calvary – to the cross of Christ – confess their defective obedience and avoid being a religious deceiver.[197]

The Christian walk

Mantle tackles the theme of a Christian walk from the perspective of a great song based on Revelation 5:9–14.[198] The song[199] suggests that believers shall overcome by the word of their testimony in retrospect to the victory of the Lord Jesus at the cross over death and his resurrection. Webb-Peploe asserted that the command to be perfect is predominant in almost every epistle, but

---

192. Naselli, 23.
193. Edmond, "Notions of Sanctification," 13.
194. Inwood, "Unveiling of the Carnal," 117.
195. Inwood, 123.
196. Brown. "Defective Consecration," 124.
197. Brown, 126.
198. Mantle, "Victorious Life," 165.
199. This song echoes EARM's favourite hymn which has been translated into Kiswahili and to some extent confirms Keswick's DNA in the spiritual life of the Brethren.

people dread it. He noted that all apostles spoke well of it and seemed to encourage people to seek moment by moment the fullness of Christ (Eph 4:13) though he acknowledged none could reach perfection.[200] However, walking into a new experience, argues Shipley, is a matter of faith. Joshua 1:4–9 elucidates walking in God's presence as a requisite of full surrender.[201] Thornton further contends that this is not a do-nothing calling but doing all that the Lord commands (John 2:5) as a matter of trusting and obedience.[202]

While addressing the subject of "rest in Christ" as a condition of the soul to enable believers to walk closely with God in their daily life, Harford-Battersby warned against the heretical teachings of his day. On the one hand, that perfection is attainable; consequently no further attempt to walk closely with God is needed. On the other hand, the assumption that falling back is inevitable after conversion.[203] However, Pollock asserts that what mattered was God's power to keep the consecrated soul, and not human struggle.[204] Pollock further noted that Evan Hopkins, one of the great teachers at Keswick, contended that a nobleman's son was cured because his father arrived at a crisis, passing from seeking faith to a resting faith, and this kind of faith was lacking in Victorian Christianity.[205]

Spirit-filled life

The activity of Spirit-filling occupied the fourth day in which a prescription for spiritual growth was administered to avoid any setback. Naselli notes that Spirit-filling was at work at the beginning of the crisis of consecration and continued through the life (of consecrated believers only) of surrender and faith.[206]

Reading from Ephesians 5:18, Morgan reiterates that these words (Spirit-filling[207]) were addressed to the saints. He attributes the Ephesian phrase, "be

---

200. Webb-Peploe, "Christian Walk," 255.
201. Shipley, "Dependence of Faith," 258.
202. Thornton, "Trust and Obey," 261.
203. Hafford-Battersby, "How to Walk," 265, 267.
204. Pollock, *Keswick Story*, 34.
205. Pollock, *Keswick Story*, 28.
206. Naselli, *Keswick Theology*, 33.
207. The early Keswick proponents (including Hopkins) generally use Spirit-filling and Spirit-baptism terminology synonymously, but in the 1900s Keswick proponents gradually began to use Spirit-baptism terminology for what all believers experience at conversion and

filled with the Spirit," as referring to a heavenly calling with earthy responsibilities of Christian conduct. This is our inheritance, being sealed by the Spirit, as the possession of God, following regeneration.[208] Robert Pearsall Smith's main reason for coming to Keswick was to promote the full sanctification of believers.[209] Packer articulates that this blessing was an experiential event triggered by God subsequent to the new birth (first experience). It leads to an elevated full and genuine level of Christian living that regularly overcomes sin by the power of the Holy Spirit. Packer further asserts that this idea was founded on Wesley's doctrine of entire sanctification. This doctrine, sometimes referred to as Christian perfection or perfect love, states that sin is rooted out, rendering evil desires and motives obsolete; part of the blessing of heaven. However, higher life and Keswick teachers modified Wesley's idea of sin eradication into counteraction of sin, a term which also came to be contentious.[210]

Figgs argued that the blessed experience becomes a reality when one gets filled with the Spirit, as a sponge fills with the water.[211] Thus, Holden asserts that Christians were encouraged as they left Keswick for the environments that filled most of their daily routine. He argued that those were the environments to testify about the reality of God's will in all circumstances.[212] Thus, Hopkins called upon Christians to give a testimony of the definite blessing so as to have their conscience at rest.[213] Harford-Battersby, as we have seen, had rested his faith in Christ (acknowledged the blessing) at the end of one of the Keswick conferences.[214]

Hannah Smith appealed to believers to attain a complete salvation in this life from the power and dominion of sin. Spirit-baptism according to Hannah was a preserve of some people although she and her husband apparently never

---

to reserve Spirit-filling terminology for what only some believers experience after conversion. This helped distinguish Keswick from Wesleyanism and Pentecostalism (Naselli, 33).

208. G. C. Morgan, "Secrets of Power," 180–181.
209. Pollock, *Keswick Story*, 32.
210. Packer, *Passion for Holiness*, 110–111.
211. Figgs, "Some Characteristics," 106.
212. Holden, "Gospel of the Second Chance," 187.
213. Hopkins, *Deliverance from the Law*, 209.
214. Pollock, *Keswick Story*, 29.

lived happily.²¹⁵ The couple was accused of spreading American perfectionism – sinless perfection of the flesh. Moody referred to the fall of Pearsall Smith as a dreadful stumbling block.²¹⁶ This is because Smith's teaching continued even after exiting the Keswick's ministry.²¹⁷

Keswick missions
Christian service took center stage on the fifth day with a sharp focus on soul-winning and foreign missions. This was a fitting consequence for consecrated and Spirit-filled believers. Accordingly, Inwood during his closing address challenged the Keswick gathering to contemplate the commission of the Lord Jesus to his disciples (John 11:21–22).²¹⁸ It was evident to him that missionary passion ought to be the outcome of the fullness of the Spirit. Therefore many Keswick missionaries took Smith's theology to the mission fields.

However, initially Keswick's message was aimed at reaching out to Christians and not heathens, and that people were sent out to the mission field as Keswick missioners, to reach those already linked to Keswick and not as missionaries.²¹⁹ It was not until 1888 that Bowker (chairman of Keswick) accepted the missionary work, saying consecration and evangelization ought to go together. This led to the official sponsorship of missionary meetings.²²⁰ Keswick missionaries, as well as missioners, were mandated not to start their missions. Keswick missionaries in the field, irrespective of denomination, were funded through recognized mission societies.²²¹ Keswick declined to start its mission which could not only have proved expensive but worked against its interdenominational ideals.

Every year there was a special missionary gathering referred to as *A Morning with the Missionaries*²²² where remarkable speeches from the various mission field were delivered. For instance, Bishop Tucker of CMS, Uganda; Rev. H.S. Gamman of Congo Balolo Mission; Mrs. Gates of South Sea

---

215. Naselli, *Keswick Theology*, 22.
216. Pollock, *Keswick Story*, 66.
217. Pollock, 26.
218. Inwood, *Unveiling of the Carnal*, 233.
219. Stock. "Missionary Element," 137–38.
220. Pollock, *Keswick Story*, 83.
221. Stock, "Missionary Element," 89.
222. This was twenty-fourth great missionary meeting arranged by the committee and trustees of Keswick (*Keswick Week 1911*, 244–247).

Evangelical Mission, Australia and The Rev. Evan Mackenzie of the Scottish Mission in the Eastern Himalayas.[223] This interdenominational Keswick mission made a significant contribution to the world of missions, despite earlier fears. It was within this context that Joe Church arrived in East Africa as a representative of Keswick faith that had influenced Christian undergraduates of the Cambridge Christian Union in 1920s with victorious life teachings, second blessings, deeper holiness or simply the Highest.[224]

This section has explored the historical view of early Keswick theology. It established that its foundation was based on the five topics that constituted the five days of the Keswick week convention as was taught by prominent Keswick exponents. These seem to form the core pillars that defined sanctification theology from the perspective of the Keswick teachers. However, due to its interdenominational character, it has been difficult to arrive at a standard definition. Nevertheless, it can be said in principle that Keswick sanctification theology is a definite experience following regeneration and the subsequent ongoing crisis of consecration, which paves the way to a Spirit-filled life for powerful Christian service, epitomized in soul-winning and overseas mission.

Thus, the influence of the Keswick antecedents steered by Wesleyan perfection gave Keswick theology a unique expression that found acceptance among some evangelicals in America and Europe, before finding its way to East Africa in the early twentieth century. The question of what might have attracted Keswick theology to the East African soil deserves an answer.

Affinity Between Sociological Circumstances and Keswick Theology

The answer to the question why EARM was attracted to Keswick theology cannot be overstressed. This is because the bond between the sociological predisposition of much of East African social life and Keswick theology seems to be natural and fundamental. This bonding has enabled Keswick theology and the East Africa sociological worldview to have a significant exchange of concepts and meanings. Claims of the affinity of Keswick theology and EARM's sociological circumstances need little elaboration. The question will

---

223. Keswick Week, *Keswick Week 1911*, 244–247.
224. Church, *Quest for the Highest*, 14.

be answered from six-pronged influences on the East African's social life at the dawn of Keswick theology. These are as follows: racial segregation, faith in the supernatural, community ethics, rites of passage, blood symbolism and seclusion period.

Affinity on the Segregation of Human Beings

By the time of the advent of Keswick theology in East Africa in the first twenty years of the twentieth century, East Africa was just emerging from the effect of the First World War. One of the most significant outcomes was African soldiers realizing they were discriminated against by the colonial government.[225] The white soldiers were rewarded with land while Africans became squatters in their land. As if that was not enough the best of Kenyan land, the so-called white highlands, were exclusively reserved for European settlers. The schools and hospitals were also racially segregated. This led to a policy of separate development aimed at protecting European civilization in East Africa.[226] Such policies as taxation, labor and *kipande* (the identity card) system directed against Africans, made Kenyans tenants.

The teachings of Keswick theology tended to differentiate one Christian from the other (see footnote 20, on page 5). This description outlines two levels of Christians. Barabas observes that those invited as speakers at the Keswick Convention were neither eloquent preachers nor renowned theological professors but those "who can bear testimony to a definite experience of the fullness of blessing."[227] In other words, they must have experienced a crisis of consecration after Spirit-filling, without which they would be segregated simply because they have not surrendered themselves entirely to God.

The fact that this view was held by Canon Battersby and Evan H. Hopkins, key founders of the Keswick Convention, indicates the teaching that was carried out to the mission world. A survey of three graduates of Cambridge will suffice to illustrate the spread of Keswick teachings in East Africa.

---

225. Sagay and Wilson, *Africa: A Modern History*, 371.
226. Odhiambo, *History of East Africa*, 155.
227. Barabas, *So Great Salvation*, 33.

George Pilkington

Pilkington had a heritage of Keswick teaching as a student at Cambridge, 1885 – 1887. His fundamental significance to EARM was his testimony at the 1896 Keswick Convention in Uganda about the work of the Holy Spirit.[228] He and other CMS evangelical Anglicans diagnosed the shallowness of the conversion of their adherents and thought a revival was the remedy. In 1893 he inspired a revival in a limited way in Uganda.

Leonard Sharp and Algie Stanley Smith

Algie Smith,[229] who co-founded the Rwanda mission with Leonard Sharp, was the son of Stanley Smith,[230] one of the leaders of the Cambridge Seven.[231] They had deep evangelical convictions and missionary vision. They initially met at CICCU and like many other Cambridge students influenced by Keswick movement had concluded the only way to reciprocate Christ's love was to surrender their lives to His service in a foreign land.[232] They arrived at Mengo hospital in 1914 or 1915 and entered Gahini, Rwanda, an outpost of the Anglican Church of Uganda, in the early 1920s.[233]

Dr. Joe Church

Dr. Church according to Osborn[234] had a conversion experience in his student days at Cambridge in 1920. He was an active member of CICCU, which was quite influential in foreign missions. Makower[235] observes that CICCU thrived after Dwight Moody's revival at Cambridge and through the missionary zeal of the Cambridge Seven.[236] A favorite book among the Cambridge students,

---

228. Hafford-Battersby, "How to Walk," 23- 34, 261.
229. Langley, *Serving People*, 200.
230. Stanley Smith and C.T. Studd were members of the Cambridge Seven. They had experienced crises and endowment of power that started the Cambridge Inter-Collegiate Christian Union (CICCU) missionary zeal (Pollock, *Keswick Story*, 71).
231. Pollock, *Keswick Story*, 71.
232. Guillebaud, *Grain of Mustard Seed*, 11.
233. Nthamburi, *From Mission to Church*, 189.
234. Osborn, *Pioneers in the East African*, 55.
235. Makower, *Coming of the Rain*, 27.
236. A young band of birth and wealth and athletic prowess whose going out as missionaries to China early in 1885 caught the imagination of the nation and profoundly moved universities. C.T. Studd and Stanley Smith, the leaders, both had experienced crises

How to Lead a Victorious Life[237] had an immense influence on the young Dr. Church's spiritual and theological formation, particularly on daily victorious life. Thus, in June 1928, Dr. Church, a Cambridge-educated and Anglican physician with a background in the Higher Life or Keswick Movement, took charge of an unfinished hospital located in the first station established by the CMS in Gahini, Rwanda.[238]

Thus, the arrival of bearers of Keswick teachings to East Africa met with Africans who were already used to the idea of discrimination. Consequently, a teaching about a crisis of victorious life or receiving a blessing that would predispose an individual or a group of people to privileges over and above others who do not think or feel like them was not difficult to comprehend. This tendency might have contributed to the proliferation of the prosperity gospel in some African churches, especially the mushrooming Pentecostal churches.

Affinity with Faith in the Supernatural

Apart from racism and segregation, Keswick theology found in East Africa a fertile ground for helpless people in the face of diseases and famine. Keswick teaching on the higher life of surrender and victorious living made sense in an African context open to anything that could herald hope. The teaching of surrender and faith, or let go and let God, could have been understood as magical. Africans were already used to submitting themselves to a *mundu mugo* (medicine man) who on their behalf would expunge ailments, use witchcraft or engage malevolent spirits. Traditional Africans had full trust in *mundu mugo* who also provided them with protective gear like amulets and talismans that were endowed with the power to prevent accidents and diseases.[239] It would not have sounded strange for them to surrender their entire being to the supernatural to defeat the present malady.

Likewise, Keswick's emphasis on self-release to God for consecration to conquer the power of evil and sin would have been understood as cleansing from evil spirits through God's agency – the medicine man. Thus the

---

of consecration and endowment of power. The Seven brought their own alma mater and its CICCU to a peak of evangelistic zeal (Pollock, *Keswick Story*, 71).

237. This book emphasized the post conversion experience of a second blessing, or Spirit filling, and a strong desire for the higher Christian life.

238. Pahls, *Born of Revival*, 74.

239. Wambugu, *Agikuyu*, 194.

traditional way of dealing with evil would have provided a replica or model in Keswick theology's expression of a life victorious over sin.

Affinity with Community Ethics

Community fabric was highly regarded. This seemed to hedge around most of the African lifestyle from birth to death. Mbiti's dictum, "I am because we are, and since we are, therefore I am," defines the African concept of a community.[240] That is, I am because we are related. This signature symbolized shared communal existence. Anything or anybody found contravening the accepted social norms was swiftly reprimanded and a sacrifice made as a way of propitiating the spirits. Karanja observes that the victim was psychologically taken through a cleansing ritual as a way of recanting the wrongdoing.[241]

This view of the treatment of the victim could have had the closest affinity with Keswick theology regarding the Keswick "spiritual clinic" that addressed the sin principle with terms like diagnosis and prescription. Thus, an African, a Kenyan for that matter, would have quickly felt at home with Keswick theology.

Affinity with Rites of Passage

The rites of passage ceremonies were the preserve of the majority of African cultures even before the arrival of western Christianity. The Keswick theology concept of second blessing after regeneration that ushered a believer to a status of Christian victorious living or "spiritual maturity" would have found affinity with some Africans rites of passage. The early Keswick movement emphasized Christian experience that set some Christians apart from the rest; thus, the rise of a concept of two sets of Christians was inevitable. This doctrine could have had consequences on East African soil.

For a Kenyan Gikuyu youth to graduate to a privileged status of adulthood, he or she had to undergo a rite of passage called circumcision (cut). Following the cut, the initiates attained exempt status. He could marry, own a hut and be expected to defend the tribe against enemies. Since Keswick theology found an African context that respects rites of passage, a Gikuyu person could have easily seen that one group of individuals had a more recognized

---

240. Mbiti, *African Religion and Philosophy*, 109.
241. Karanja, "Confession and Cultural Dynamism," 147.

status than others. In fact, the young people who underwent the cut together were referred to as age-sets or *Rika* as explained earlier.

The *Rika* group protected and loved each other. They referred to one another as brothers and sisters and their parents as fathers and mothers.[242] Also, the senior age-sets were to be respected as elders by the junior age-sets as exemplified by the Nandi of Kenya age-sets system.[243] Similarly, the gathering at Keswick was organized and facilitated by prominent leaders of the movement who must have stood out amongst others with respect to the moment they had experienced a crisis of full surrender. Thus, the respect for senior age-sets could have found affinity in the Keswick hierarchical structure. Notwithstanding this, the Keswick and *Rika* structures cultivated a mutual love for their respective members. This must have inspired the emerging Brethren Christians to express themselves as brothers and sisters.

Affinity with Blood Symbolism

The practice of the pact of blood brotherhood, where young people would exchange and share their blood, symbolized and expressed life. This signifies giving one's life over to the other.[244] In other words, they became blood friends and would never betray the other. They often had stronger bonds than kinship ties. Keswick theology taught that for one to qualify for Spirit-filled life and thus be full partakers of victorious life, one had to surrender their lives by faith in God. One was expected to let go and to let God, that is, to live the life of the other (God). Blood brothers could have found resemblance in the concept of living the life of the other and thus could have easily embraced Keswick theology. Barabas notes that the most enduring feature of the Keswick Convention was the oneness of spirit among Christians.[245] No wonder, *All one in Christ Jesus* had been the prevailing theme at the Convention meetings. Perhaps that is why Brethren care so much for each other.

Blood symbolism was also used during various sacrificial rituals to counteract an evil spirit. Since the Gikuyu people believed that goats have a protective prodigy, their sacrificial blood was commonly used to quench evil

---

242. Kariuki, *Bishop Facing Mount Kenya*, 23; Magesa, *African Religion*, 103.
243. Magesa, 105.
244. Magesa, 106.
245. Barabas, *So Great Salvation*, 35.

spirits.[246] The victory of Jesus at the cross, illustrated in Revelation 5:9–14,[247] signifies the power of Christ's blood over the dominion of evil. Thus, Keswick theology could not have found better affinity than in the East African context. The shedding of Christ's blood at Calvary would have resounded clearly, for example to a Gikuyu of Kenya who used the blood of goats to appease evil spirits.

Affinity with a Seclusion Period

The initiates had a special time before and after circumcision to learn about the history of their people, their beliefs and practices, and importantly how to raise a family.[248] The seclusion period among the Gikuyu took up to eight days. The third day was the day of actual operation and was marked by the initiates discarding their children's clothing and putting on the youth's garment symbolizing the imminent transition from childhood to adulthood. This action resembled the Keswick week's exhortation that challenged those attending the convention to put off the old man's clothes, i.e., habits or besetting sins, and put on the new man's clothes. Head described this action as the death of natural man and newness of life of the spiritual man with reference to baptism into Christ.[249] This outstanding likeness would no doubt have provided a fitting environment in East Africa for the proliferation of Keswick theology.

The previous action is expounded by further events following the seclusion time when the youths were received in their respective homes with a ceremony.[250] Mbiti argues that returning home was like a new birth; as new, full and responsible people who acquire new names and new roles.[251] Wambugu state that the young initiates were now referred to as *anake* (young men) and *airitu* (young women).[252] The circumcised group took a particular name after the most significant event of the year. As seen earlier in this study the late Bishop Obadiah Kariuki's circumcision group of 1919 assumed the name *Rika ria*

---

246. Wambugu, *Agikuyu*, 190.
247. Mantle, *Victorious Life*, 165.
248. Mbiti, *Introduction to African Religion*, 94.
249. Head, *Watchword of the Convention*, 115.
250. Wambugu, *The Agikuyu*, 90–101.
251. Mbiti, *Introduction to African Religion*, 96.
252. Wambugu, *Agikuyu*, 101.

kimiri (Kimiri age-set), following the global epidemic that annihilated tens of thousands in Gikuyuland.[253]

The yearly five-day Keswick week convention in some ways was similar to the African practice of seclusion discussed above. Evidently, from the African perspective, those who persevered to the end would be regarded as having undergone the cut. That is, they have experienced "spirit-filled life," after the "crisis of consecration." They would be considered to have attained spiritual maturity and thus privileged to undertake responsibilities on behalf of the Keswick movement or community.

Thus, despite the difference in the number of days between the Gikuyu seclusion period and the Keswick week, the affinity was strong. The fact that groups of people pursuing similar interest would meet for some days would have found affinity with East African people at the dawn of the Keswick movement.

In this section, an attempt has been made to answer why EARM was attracted to Keswick theology. It has been found that East Africa sociological bonding had profound parallels with Keswick theology. Thus, the claim of the affinity of Keswick theology and EARM's sociological circumstances cannot be overstated. This combination no doubt led to the emergence and growth of EARM with remarkable higher life undertones propagated through Keswick teachings. These teachings permeated EARM's lifestyle impacting the church's participation in the *missio Dei*.

Evaluation of the EARM against *Missio Dei*

The preceding discourse hints at what led to Keswick theology getting attracted to East Africa and consequently pervading its daily life. As a result of this contact, certain features have been most dominant and shall be condensed into four manageable segments which will help evaluate EARM against *missio Dei*. They include, but not exclusively, the exposition of Scripture, the centrality of Christ, public testimony and legalism. These features define the movement's religious identity within a framework of walking in the light.

---

253. Kariuki, *Bishop Facing Mount Kenya*, 22.

Exposition of the Scripture

Brethren are ardent readers of the Bible. albeit through thematic devotions. They make little attempt at exegesis and thus lack a theological dimension. This seems to have been a historical problem whereby some founders of Keswick theology like Robert and Hannah Smith had little or no theological education and training. Thus, the Smith's mishandling of Romans 6:6,[254] consequently amplified higher life messages of second blessing leading to religious hypocrisy.[255] Though EARM did not embrace teachings of a second blessing, it nevertheless inherited their literal approach to scriptural interpretation oblivious of the context. Their reading of Ephesian 5:14 has been blamed for the split in EARM[256] resulting in some members aligning to the Arise and others to the Stand factions.

According to Bosch, the historical world is a constitutive element in the understanding of mission and not just a peripheral state for the church's mission.[257] Moreover, Wright argues against spiritualizing interpretations, particularly when the typological method of relating the Old Testament to the New Testament treats the Old as merely foreshadowing the New, thus losing its historical significance. The Bible shows that when it is read correctly, it challenges readers to recognize their participatory role in God's mission so as to avoid the Pharisaic hypocrisy of religious justification.[258]

Historical-critical scholarship could be a formidable mission tool to help members of EARM in making biblical applications to participate fully in God's mission. It is by so doing that we shall agree with Paul sentiments, "I, therefore, the prisoner of the Lord beseech you that you work worthy of the vocation where you have been called" (Rom 15:18–19). This realization is important because the success of the church's mission is the Lord's work, done the Lord's way. Indeed, a successful mission of the church must be found at the cross of Christ.

---

254. Naselli, *Let Go and Let God*, 102.
255. Pollock, *Keswick Story*, 36.
256. Nthamburi, *From Mission to Church*, 117.
257. Bosch, *Transforming Mission*, 426.
258. Wright, *Mission of God*, 279.

Centrality of the Cross

The Brethren's emphasis on the cross of Christ as the basis of their salvation no doubt puts evangelical Christian orthodoxy into its right perspective of proclaiming the Gospel and calling the world to repentance and faith. Wright argues that the cross was the inevitable cost of God's whole mission and the unavoidable center of our mission because all Christian mission flows from the cross.[259] Thus, the central nature of Christ in the salvation of the world provides a critical link for the *missio Dei* in the Old and New Testaments.

Osborn observes that the overriding theme of the revival meetings and Keswick Conventions were the messages of sin, repentance and forgiveness by the blood of Christ.[260] Osborn further states that Joe Church and his associates were said to preach only the crucified Christ.[261] Senyonyi, a Ugandan Brethren scholar, has been specific about Revivalists statements with regard to the centrality of Jesus in their preaching and teachings, based on the belief that Jesus paid the price for their sins. Thus, the name Jesus and the cross have been viewed synonymously. Brethren pray to the Holy Spirit to show them only Jesus because to them real revival is walking with Jesus, victoriously, moment by moment, day by day.[262] However, when this spirituality is viewed from the perspective of *missio Dei*, it seems to lack balance. Wright claims that the cross must permeate both social and evangelistic engagements.[263] Although the EARM appears to understand this to the fullest, their application of it tends to lean inwardly towards self rather than outwardly towards those outside their camp. Thus, it tends to fall short of holistic mission informed by a comprehensive mission of the cross.

Bosch also observes that following the Willingen Conference of 1952, the mission came to be understood as flowing from the very nature of God, and thus Trinitarian.[264] There is no doubt that God affirmed His supremacy in missions by confirming supremacy of his Son, Jesus Christ as the conscious center of the church.[265] Thus, EARM's Christocentric emphasis could be understood

---

259. Wright, *Mission of God*, 314.
260. Osborn, *Pioneers in the East African*, 87.
261. Osborn, 87.
262. Senyonyi, "GAFCON EA Revival Distinctives," 4.
263. Wright, *Mission of God*, 315.
264. Bosch, *Transforming Mission*, 390.
265. Piper, *Let the Nations*, 133.

in that perspective. But it becomes a problem when the Trinitarian thrust of mission appears blurred within the revival fellowships that mostly focus on one member of the Trinity. Bosch observes the doctrine of the *missio Dei* as God the Father sending the Son, and the Father and the Son sending the Spirit, and the Father, the Son and the Holy Spirit sending the church into the world.[266] Thus, a movement towards Trinitarian worship and holistic mission needs to be encouraged as a new model in EARM's theology of mission. This realization should pervade not only the Brethren's worship pattern but also be the basis of their public testimony.

Public Confession

We have seen public confession of sins has been rooted in both the Scripture and the African cultural practices. In both cases, it has earned its place in the light of setting norms and boundaries against which law is breached, and cleansing and confession required. It has been a common practice in the EARM to give a public testimony or confession. Brethren believe that by expunging their misdeed openly, they will clear their conscience not only before God but humanity as well. Winter observes that it is paramount for people to witness the glory of God in the lives of believers as a reason to turn away from evil to God.[267] Perhaps that could be one of the reasons Brethren seek to confess their sins openly – so that others can see and glorify God.

One of the primary Scripture passages that appear to approve public confession is James 5:16. Whereas it is right to seek assembly of the saints for confession, the amount of publicity we give depends upon how public the sin was (Matt 18:15–17). If the sin is publicly known, then to specify it during public confession is a matter of the responsible ethics of a good neighbor. However, as Price argues, wisdom should be used to declaring the sin – not so much because it might seem disgraceful to tell exactly what the sin was but to spare the sinner unnecessary hardship over a sin he has repudiated.[268] It is a good rule of Scripture to say that sin should be explicitly confessed to the extent that knowledge of sin exists. This could be a real mission emphasis because it handles the complexities that could arise in the church where a

---

266. Bosch, *Transforming Mission*, 390.
267. Winter, "Future of Evangelicals," 183.
268. Price, *Bible Answers*.

public sin goes unacknowledged. Indeed, since human mission has no life of its own, except in the hands of the sending God who is the initiator of missionary enterprises;[269] acknowledging public sin is a welcome mission factor. If Brethren could be discreet in handling various sins, informed legalism could help participation in the *missio Dei*.

Legalism

The members of EARM display passion for God in their conventions and fellowship meetings as they achieve experiential sanctification in their lives. This practical holiness, blended with Keswick theology, has not only been contextualized in EARM but has also acquired socio-ethical dimensions. There is nothing wrong with being ethical. However, the moral problem has been viewed from the perspective of creating two categories of Christians in the EARM, based on beliefs and practices of walking in the light, hedged with do's and don'ts. Langley and Kiggins observe that conformity to an accepted pattern of behavior becomes the gauge for one's religious commitment and this displaces the gospel of God's love and grace. Thus, the ensuing legalistic tendencies:[270] do not drink; do not smoke; do not wear short skirts; do not take bank loans; do not receive or give a dowry.[271] From this viewpoint, walking in the light is not within the precepts of the mission of God. Bosch claims that human mission has no life of its own, except in the hands of the sending God who is the initiator of missionary enterprises.[272]

Moral transformation by all definitions is not a problem in itself, but in the way it has been applied or misapplied within a framework of community rules of living vis-à-vis the biblical framework of an ethical community. Wright images ethical obedience from the perspective of walking in the ways of the Lord, as to reflect God in just human life relationships within an ethical community.[273] Therefore, the concept of walking with God is a practice

---

269. Bosch, *Transforming Mission*, 390.

270. This is comparable to Keswick teachings against indulgence or amusements like beer, theatre, dance, tobacco and questionable employment. Anything done to please self apart from Christ as Master and Lord and neighbor in all things lawful, was discouraged (Pierson, "Message: Its Practical Application," 91, 93, 94).

271. Langley, *Serving People*, 202.

272. Bosch, *Transforming Mission*, 390.

273. Wright, *Mission of God*, 364.

that all godly loving people ought not only to envy but also strive to achieve. Unfortunately, it seems that the ensuing ethical obedience has created a wedge in the EARM. This divisive attitude appears to put more emphasis on outward moral conformity expressed in walking in the light at the expense of the gospel and mission of Christ.

As earlier stated, Brethren's moral formation provides for evangelism and social responsibility, but falls short of replicating these outside their camp. Unlike the past, when evangelism and Christian social action went together,[274] it is mostly not the case currently as exemplified by *Mfuko ya Bwana*[275] ("the Lord's bag").[276] The Lord's bag has been exclusively for the Brethren's activities oblivious of general needs in the church. David Bosch argues for adding justice and social responsibility to evangelism in dispensing the promises and gifts of the Kingdom of God.[277] Thus, a need for a paradigm shift from the prevailing socio-ethical informed morality to a Gospel-focused mission because as Wright argues, the mission of the church includes both verbal proclamation and ethical living.[278] We must not be conformed to the world in any way (Rom 12:1–2). Just because the majority of EARM accept certain ethical behaviors within their camp does not mean it is right in the light of *missio Dei*.

Further, if a person is not a regular member of Brethren fellowships she or he would be labeled as not saved because salvation was understood and expressed through walking in the light. From this viewpoint, walking in the light is not within the precepts of the mission of God. Bosch claims that human mission has no life of its own, except in the hands of the sending God who is the initiator of missionary enterprises.[279]

In this section, the author explored certain features arising out of contact between Keswick theology and East Africa sociological circumstances leading to the proliferation of EARM. Consequently, an attempt has been

---

274. Langley, *Serving People*, 201.

275. A fund contributed by Brethren according to their ability to assist with organizing of conventions and other social needs among the Brethren.

276. Mambo, "Revival Fellowship", 115.

277. Bosch, *Transforming Mission*, 418.

278. Wright, *Mission of God*, 390.

279. Bosch, *Transforming Mission*, 390.

made to evaluate EARM against *missio Dei* and to define the movement's religious identity.

Conclusion

This chapter discussed the socio-historical circumstances that led to the influence of the Keswick theology of sanctification on EARM's walking in the light. It has endeavored to answer questions concerning socio-historical conditions that provided affinity for Keswick theology in East Africa. To elucidate the concept of walking in the light, it was placed in the context of *missio Dei* and subsequently described in the socio-historical context of East Africa. To explore the affinity between the sociological circumstances and the Keswick theology, a historical view of Keswick theology was critical. Finally, it has evaluated EARM against *missio Dei* and established the outstanding features that buttress EARM.

Further, the study noted that EARM has not only contextualized much of its inheritance from Keswick but also seems to have gone a step higher in its expression of practical holiness. The socio-historical concept and practice of walking in the light appear to have underpinned the boundaries within which the saved ones ought to trace their daily walk with God. Thus, while Keswick theology seemed to herald a new dawn of spirituality in East Africa in the wake of seemingly dry orthodoxy, it has nevertheless taken a contextual perspective, fashioning a theology with an African face. In order to comprehend the emerging theology, it is critical to examine the place of Anglican scholarship on Keswick theology of sanctification from the viewpoint of historical and empirical perspectives of walking in the light within EARM.

CHAPTER 3

Anglican Scholarship on Keswick Theology of Sanctification and Walking in the Light in the EARM

Introduction

This chapter focuses on the Anglican Church's scholarship perspective on Keswick theology as propagated by scholars of Anglican or non-Anglican Church origin. The scope incorporates an overview of Anglican scholarship from the viewpoint of historical literature and documents on the one hand, and the findings and analyses of the current situation on the other. It is divided into four parts.

The first part is the introduction, and it introduces the issues that provide a platform for engaging and investigating the existing historical nature of church scholarship. It also brings to the fore the current situation of the influence of Keswick theology on EARM's social-ethical beliefs and practices of walking in the light in the Anglican Church, Mount Kenya region.

Next is an historical overview of scholarship in the Anglican Church. The study of Anglican Church scholarship on Keswick theology's influence on EARM's walking in the light has yet to attract much interest from scholars. Even today, Anglican-Keswick theology's scholarship and influence on EARM's walking in the light has not been given the prominence it deserves in churches and theological institutions in East Africa. Indeed, the suggestion by the GAFCON 2013[1] meeting in Nairobi that the Anglican Church should return to the faith of EARM confirms this lack. Certainly, this failure has prevented Anglican-Keswick theology's scholarship and influence on EARM's walking in the light from occupying its proper place in shaping mission in the Anglican Church, Mount Kenya region.

This second section, therefore, will offer a fresh historical overview of the nature and influence of the Anglican Church scholarship on the emerging social and ethical beliefs, and practices of walking in the light and suggests a viable perception. The aim is to situate the Anglican Church scholarship in Keswick theology and walking in the light in the Anglican Church of Kenya. This section deals with Anglican Church scholarship concerning historical literature and documents. A highlight of key scholars will serve to assess credibility and authenticity of information. The work of these scholars forms the backbone of the summarized history of the genesis and spread of the revival to Kenya.

The following section of the study will look at the nature and current trends in scholarship within the Anglican church.

The final section of the chapter will analyze the data collected from oral and email interviews. It is graphically presented. Based on the findings, the study assesses the nature and current situation concerning the influence of Keswick theology on walking in the light. The study used qualitative approaches and conducted self-administered email interviews of EARM's leadership, ordinary membership, theological students, clergy, bishops and prominent stakeholders. This part comprises various sections which examine issues ranging from demographic distribution of respondents to understanding the Anglican Church scholarship on the influence of Keswick theology in EARM's concept of walking in the light in Mount Kenya region.

A Historical Overview of Anglican Church Scholarship on EARM

The East Africa Revival has touched millions of lives in East Africa and beyond, as the Holy Spirit has moved Christians to share the gospel with others. Indeed, it has been in the revival that the gospel has been powerfully

---

1. *Nairobi Communique*, GAFCON.

used to seek and save the lost and to transform the church, rather than seeing the church conformed to the world. Since the beginning of the last century, Africa has been crisscrossed by divergent missionary movements that heralded the gospel of Christ. As a result, the mission field was flooded with conflicting doctrines packaged with mission agencies and personnel sent to work overseas.

Anglicans were not the pioneer missionaries in East Africa; the Roman Catholic Church was the first to set foot in East Africa in 1498, courtesy of the Portuguese explorer, Vasco da Gama.[2] The CMS that heralded Protestant missionaries arrived in Mombasa much later in 1844 led by Ludwig Krapf and in 1877, Alexander Mackay arrived in Uganda.[3] Both were missionaries with CMS, though not from an Anglican background. It is from the Anglican mission of CMS that Keswick theology found its entry into East Africa. CMS played a significant part in the origin and spread of EARM that influenced social-ethical life particularly in the Anglican Church in the East African region. Scholars and popular writers mostly affiliated with the Anglican Church have recorded the genesis and spread of revival in East Africa. Although they appear to differ on some occurrences, they have attempted to depict the nature and characteristics of Anglican scholarship in the light of the influence of Keswick theology on EARM's walking in the light.

A Brief Overview of Anglican Scholarship on EARM

Early Anglican church scholarship reflects European dominance, with few having been active participants[4] in the origin and spread of the revival. The other group of participants could be considered inactive in the sense of not being involved in the actual events. Some of these are academicians or key revival members, both Africans and Europeans who have been engrossed in tracing the history and impacts of revival. The main active participants were Dr. John (Joe) Edward Church and Rev. Harold Guillebaud.[5] Dr. Algie

---

2. Langley, *Serving People*, 1.

3. Ward, *History of Global Anglicanism*, 166.

4. Active in the sense of being present (personally or through family representation) in the events and circumstances that led to the beginning of the revival.

5. Guillebaud and his family have been well represented by his daughter, Lindesay Guillebaud and his granddaughter, Margaret (Meg) Guillebaud, who have respectively authored *A Grain of Mustard Seed: The Growth of the Ruanda Mission of CMS* and *Rwanda: The Land God Forgot? Revival Genocide and Hope*.

Stanley Smith and Dr. Leonard Sharp may not have written a book or article, but Dr. Church and Rev. Guillebaud have commonly cited their contributions in the form of memoirs and in the Ruanda[6] notes. The study now considers a brief review of the active participants.

Active Participants

First, Dr. Joe Church (not to be confused with his son, John Church), was an Anglican missionary in Ruanda Mission at Gahini, where the Movement as it is known today started. He and his African colleagues felt the need for personal renewal through turning to the Lord, and a renewal of the church unfolding in the events that resulted in the revival. His book *The Quest for the Highest* is a classic, a diary of the East African Revival in which he records chronologically the sequence of events beginning on Tuesday, 19 December 1927 to 13 September 1961.[7] His further works, referred to as the "Dr. Joe Church Papers," are archived in the Martin-Henry Centre, Cambridge and provide a mine of information on the genesis of the revival in East Africa.[8]

The strength of this book is depicted in the way he wrote down his impression in a historical narration from 1927 to 1961. His memory of dates, places and names of people indicate he was deeply involved in the revival. Indeed, without his contribution future scholars would have lost a critical source of reference for the origin and growth of the East Africa revival.

However, his presentation falls in the class of popular writing and thus lacks an academic angle. Again, his bringing together all available records, written or oral, over about thirty-five years[9] from the beginning of the revival could lack accuracy regarding daily occurrences. Nevertheless, his habit of preserving records is a trait for current scholars to emulate.

Second, the Guillebauds have given two accounts of life experiences in Ruanda in their separately written books. The Lindesay Guillebaud book, *A Grain of Mustard Seed: The Growth of the Ruanda Mission of CMS*, was written earlier than Meg Guillebaud's book *Rwanda: the Land God Forgot? Revival, Genocide and Hope*. Lindesay's (1917–1971) writing begin with the early

---

6. The name Ruanda was the name of Rwanda in the early years. These names will be used interchangeably in this study.

7. Church, *Quest for the Highest*, 22, 252.

8. Ward and Wild-Wood, *East African Revival*, 228.

9. Church, *Quest for the Highest*, 11.

years of the partition of Africa by Europeans with Ruanda-Urundi falling into the hands of Belgium.[10] The book reveals the inner side of challenges that were facing Africans, like leprosy and the effects of war. It also depicts the beginning and spread of revival. The book brings to the fore interaction of African Brethren and European missionaries. The former received praise from Dr. Stanley Smith for playing a significant role in the revival while he accused the latter of hindering it.[11] Meg Guillebaud, born in 1943, gives a vivid and personal account of missionary witness in a land which had known not only the triumphs of faith but also the terrible events of the genocide in 1994. Meg faced up to the challenge of the questions that arose, when church leaders were implicated in the genocide.

The strength of the two authors is in their engagement in the story of succession in the Guillebaud family. They bring out the intrigues of the revival in their narration, showing the tremendous work of the Holy Spirit. Meg also carries the joys and pains of all the peoples of Rwanda.

However, their weakness is in the scanty explanation of the link of revival to Keswick theology except in mentioning the works of Stanley Smith and Leonard Sharp, who like Dr. Church had some Keswick background. Nonetheless, the books are a must-read for scholars who want to know the joy of revival and the pain it could prevent when taught faithfully by theologically informed servants of God.

Non-active Scholars

These are Anglicans in terms of denominational affiliation. They were selected based on their relevance to the study. Also included are scholars from other faiths, writing on the influence of Keswick theology on EARM's practice of walking in the light in the Anglican Church of Kenya.

First, Rev. Dr. Kevin Ward has taught in Uganda and has been a Senior Lecturer in Theology and African Religious Studies at the University of Leeds.[12] He co-edited *The East African Revival: History and Legacies* (2012) and has

---

10. Guillebaud, *Grain of Mustard Seed*, 14.
11. Guillebaud, 65.
12. Ward and Wild-Wood, *East African Revival*, viii.

written several articles on EARM. He is the author of *A History of Global Anglicanism* where he has also written on the origin and spread of the EARM.[13]

Second, Rev. Prof. John Karanja is a professor of Church History and African Studies at Trinity Lutheran Seminary in Columbus, Ohio. He was born in central Kenya and ordained in the Anglican Church of Kenya. He has a PhD in modern history from Cambridge University and has taught at St. Paul's and Nairobi University in Kenya. His publications include a collaborative work, *Rabai to Mumias: A Short History of the Church of the Province of Kenya, 1844–1994* (1994); *Founding an African Faith: Kikuyu Anglican Christianity 1900–1945* (1999); and "Confession and Cultural Dynamism in the Revival" In Ward and Wild-Wood's *The East African Revival: History and Legacies* (2012). Most of his writings engage African traditional culture and Christianity; for example, he compares the Gikuyu cultural way of vomiting (*gutahikio*) evil (*thahu*/taboo) with public confession in the EARM.

Third, Dr. Colin Reed was congratulated by The Most Reverend Donald L. Mtetemela, the then Primate of the Anglican Church of Tanzania. He termed Dr. Reed as a gifted missionary and Christian leader who made a significant contribution to the life of the church in East Africa. His celebrated book, *Walking in the Light: Reflections on the East African Revival and its Link to Australia'*(2007) provides many pointers for those who want to see revival today. The book explores the main factors behind the beginning of Christian revival in Rwanda.

Fourth, Prof. Bethwell A. Ogot has co-authored *A Place to Feel at Home: A Study of Two Independent Churches in Western Kenya* (1966). Bethwell has a doctorate from the University of London (1965) and was head of the History Department at the University of Nairobi. A renown Kenyan historian, Prof. Ogot brings to the fore the emergence of the CCA following the uncompromising stance by the Anglican Church. He gives a detailed investigation of revival in Nyanza that eventually led to *Kuhama* (separation) of CCA from the Anglican Church, creating *Joremo* and *Johera* factions. *Joremo* is a Luo word, for people of blood, i.e., signifying emphasis by the revivalists on the blood of Christ. *Johera* referred to the people of love, which seemed to be lacking in the *Joremo* and to an extent in the Anglican Church of the day.

---

13. Ward, *History of Global Anglicanism*, 175–179.

These scholars have widely researched the history of revival in East Africa. Dr. Ward and Prof. Karanja are perennial Anglican Church scholars on the influence of Keswick theology in the EARM. Specifically, Dr. Ward appears to have been a consistent EARM scholar writing freely on the *Balokole* (referred to as Brethren in Kenya) movement in Uganda. He has labored to see the relationship of revival and Keswick theology on the one hand, and revival, Keswick and Frank Buchman's Oxford Group,[14] on the other. Prof. Karanja brings the traditional cultural perspective as an influence on social-ethical life. He matches symbolic vomiting of evil to a public confession of sin. The subject of Keswick theology is only implied in his work.

Though Dr. Reed and Prof. Ogot seem to have written only once on this subject, their work is seminal in understanding the origin and growth of revival. Dr. Reed takes a historical-theology point of view while Prof. Ogot's perspective is historical. Whereas Reed's work starts from Gahini, Ruanda,[15] Ogot's begins from Nyanza, Kenya.[16] Another striking difference between Reed and Ogot is the content; the former engaged Keswick theology and revival, while Ogot appears to highlight the ensuing splits.

Thus, in spite of these scholars (active and inactive) somewhat distinctive approaches in content, depth, and presentation, they seem to complement each other. This assists the reader to get a clear perspective of the events from the beginning to the present generation. Their writings help the researcher knit together the loose ends in the history of revival and unveil the connection between Keswick theology and walking in the light.

Having reviewed the main Anglican Church scholars and scholarship, a summary of the origin and spread of the revival is necessary.

A Brief Overview of the Genesis of EARM

To comprehend the origins of EARM, it is crucial to examine the introduction of CMS into Buganda and Ruanda.

---

14. Ward, "Introduction," 3–5.
15. Reed, *Walking in the Light*, vii.
16. Ogot, "Church of Christ in Africa," 28.

Entry of CMS into Buganda and Ruanda

Langley and Kiggins reckon that the first missionaries of the Church Missionary Society arrived in Uganda in 1878 and were warmly welcomed by the Kabaka Mutesa I. The church expanded rapidly both geographically and numerically, but the spiritual foundations were compromised with traditional culture and a thirst for materialism.[17] While Anderson concurs, he adds that the missionaries had lost their spiritual fire as well. This fact was realized by the evangelical Anglicans of the CMS.[18] Ward and Anderson saw this scenario as a precursor to the outbreak of revival.[19]

The other cause for revival, though presumably related to the growing nominalism in the Anglican Church of Uganda, was the activities of the Ruanda Mission. This Mission stood for a "conservative evangelical theological position with regard to the Bible, promoting an urgent quest for renewal and personal holiness as understood by the Keswick Movement."[20] Indeed, the events of 1921 saw the emergence of the Bible Churchmen's Missionary Society, a CMS dissenter over the question of biblical authority. Henceforth Ruanda Mission, a semi-autonomous arm of CMS, received a mandate to guarantee that missionaries met conservative evangelical views on the Bible.[21] This decree cannot be overemphasized as the ground for the revival.

Date of Origin/Outbreak of Revival

While some scholars argue for the date of the origin of revival to be as early as 1927,[22] others suggest a date as late as 1935.[23] Indeed there had been some pockets of revival ranging from personal to group levels from the end of the 1920s. The following discourse attempts to set the background to the beginning of the revival.

---

17. Langley, *Serving People*, 60–61.
18. Anderson, *Church in East Africa*, 22, 123.
19. Ward, "Introduction," 3; Anderson, *Church in East Africa*, 123.
20. Ward, 3.
21. Reed, *Walking in the Light*, 16.
22. Mambo, "Revival Fellowship", 111.
23. Ward, *History of Global Anglicanism*, 176.

The arrival in the Ruanda Mission of the two young medical doctors, Leonard Sharp and Algie Stanley Smith,[24] pioneer missionaries in Ruanda-Urundi, appeared to set the pace. The two doctors, in their College days at Cambridge, had been eager for a missionary calling to some place unreached with the gospel. An invitation in 1914 from renowned missionary Albert Cook to work in Mengo Hospital, Uganda, seemed to confirm their calling.[25] Sharp and Smith were joined in 1922 by Dr. Joe Church and his wife Decie.[26] Reed argues that like most of the Ruanda missionaries of this period, Dr. Church was a creation of CICCU,[27] influenced by revivalist ideals and Keswick holiness spirituality.[28]

Perhaps this religious background worked in 1929 on Joe Church so that he became aware not only of his own spiritual bankruptcy but that of the Anglican Church in Uganda. He met Simeon Nsibambi who seemed to share his need for Bible study, prayer, and mutual encouragement. Nsibambi and Church surrendered themselves to Christ and sought the fullness of the Holy Spirit that led to personal transformation. This realization could have had historical significance because revival Brethren preferred 1929 as the date of the origin of the East Africa Revival when Joe Church and Nsibambi met at Gahini resulting in the latter supplying the mission at Gahini with committed hospital workers and teachers. It is reckoned that revival emerged first among these workers at Gahini in the 1930s and spread to other Ruanda Mission stations and Kigezi in Uganda.[29]

However, Reed gives the year 1933 as the earliest date following a conference after Christmas:

---

24. His father Stanley Smith was a leading member of the Cambridge Seven interested in oversees missions; no doubt he listened to some of Keswick teachers who frequented the University's CICCU.

25. Guillebaud, *Grain of Mustard Seed*, 12.

26. Ward, *History of Global Anglicanism*, 176.

27. The Union was a powerful force in the spiritual formation of many leaders of evangelical Anglicanism of this era (and of the English evangelical missionary movement for several generations). In the early years of the Rwanda Mission, most of the male missionaries shared this background – among others, doctors A. Stanley Smith and L. Sharp, and clergy such as J. Warren, L. Barham, H. Guillebaud and Arthur Pitt Pitts (Reed, *Walking in the Light*,18).

28. Reed, 19.

29. Ward, "Introduction," 3.

> After formal prayers, one of the Africans stood up and spoke earnestly of a personal conviction of his sinfulness, of God requiring changes in his life. He then began to confess openly what he saw as his sins. With tears, he publicly revealed the things that burdened his conscience. The atmosphere became electric, with person after person standing to follow suit. They confessed their perceived sins, with two or three speaking at the same time sometimes, as a wave of spiritual conviction swept through the group. A new dynamic had appeared in the church, with repentance as its central theme. This was perhaps the first obvious event of the Christian revival that swept through Rwanda, Burundi, Uganda, Kenya, Tanganyika, and parts of the Congo from the mid-1930s onwards.[30]

But Ward and Guillebaud give the year 1935 as the first outbreak of revival by hospital workers at Gahini.[31] Ward further observes that Blasio Kigozi, a brother to Nsibambi, brought the message of revival a year later to the Church Synod of Uganda with a plea to *zuzuka* (awake).[32]

Considering the different dating by scholars and the lack of a living source of information, Dr. Church's Ruanda notes, mostly written in the first person singular, are pivotal.

> Christmas, 1933: The beginnings of the Revival at Gahini. I will copy this account of the beginnings of the outpouring of God's Spirit as I wrote it in Ruanda notes in March 1934: There are signs that God is working. A few days ago I suggested an early Morning Prayer meeting to the hospital staff, and when I said 5 o'clock they smiled and said they were always up earlier than that praying. At 4 a.m. I found them all on my veranda waiting, and we had a wonderful two hours of prayer until it was light . . . The hospital staff is joining with the Evangelists' Training School for prayer this week. There is an air of expectancy that God will give us times of real blessing.[33]

---

30. Reed, *Walking in the Light*, 15.
31. Ward, *History of Global Anglicanism*, 176; Guillebaud, *Grain of Mustard Seed*, 7.
32. Ward, *History of Global Anglicanism*, 176.
33. Church, *Quest for the Highest*, 98.

Church goes on to add to his notes the beginning of a convention on Tuesday, 27 December 1933, a date alluded to by Reed when a wave of conviction swept through the conference, and African Christians started confessing their sins.[34] It would, therefore, suffice to assert 1933 as the date of the beginning of the revival as claimed by Reed and Dr. Church though as Ward observes the first outbreak could be traced to 1935.[35]

Reactions and Impact on the Ugandan Scene

The revival message was received inversely as it moved across Uganda. Some like Blasio Kigozi took the message of revival with its catch-word *zuzuka* (awake) to the 1936 synod of the Church of Uganda with a three-point message. He, however, died suddenly from a relapsing fever and his message was delivered posthumously.[36] The message which was in a question form was summarized[37] as the "coldness and deadness" of the church, open sinners at the Lord's Table and the way forward for revival in the church of Uganda.[38] These were weighty points and could have challenged the Anglican Church of Uganda. The reactions were diverse in their range from within the mainstream churches to the missionaries themselves.

Mainstream Churches

The *zuzuka* campaign was not well received by either the Anglican Church or the Catholic Church. Dr. Church avers that Algie Stanley Smith reported opposition and persecution from the Roman Catholic Church.[39] The *Balokole* attacks on clergy rubbed both the missionaries and the African clergy the wrong way.

For example, argues Ward, Bishop Cyril Stuart of Uganda wanted the young *Balokole* to train for the ministry of the church. However, their inflexible conduct led to expulsion of twenty-six of them from the theological

---

34. Church, 98–99.
35. Ward, *History of Global Anglicanism*, 176.
36. Langley, *Serving People*, 198.
37. The elaborated text is: "What is the cause of the coldness and deadness of the church of Uganda? Why are people allowed to come to the Lord's Table who are living in open sin? What must be done to bring revival to the church of Uganda?"
38. Church, *Quest for the Highest*, 122–123.
39. Church, 97.

college at Mukono.[40] The administration and faculty banned revivalists' early morning prayer meetings, but the *Balokole* stubbornly resisted, which led to a prolonged crisis in 1941. Consequently, their leader William Nagenda refused ordination and remained a lay evangelist wishing to preach the radical message of equality between Whites and Blacks.[41]

The teachers

The teachers' reactions were diverse. On one end of the continuum, there were those who blamed their poor performance on too much preaching about sin to the new lifestyle propagated by the *abaka* (those on fire) evangelists. They complained that they were baptized and confirmed Christians and wondered why they were required to be born again. On the other end, the accused including Blasio and Yosiya decided to pray, and later witnesses against Blasio recanted their evidence claiming they had since become saved.[42] Likewise, a headmistress of a girl's school had to expel some girls who had sneaked out in the night for a prayer meeting.[43] But as Dr. Church observes, some of these adamant teachers were eventually saved.[44] The ensuing lifestyle took a rigid stance resulting in a public confession of sin signaled by the revival hymn of absolution, *Tukutendereza Yesu*.

Balokole

In 1929 an afternoon United Bible study started with about two hundred assembling for doctrinal instructions following great scriptural themes, starting with sin, and traced out in the Scofield Bible. Eventually, these notes were enlarged and made into a study book first published in 1938 by Scripture Union of London under the title "Everyman a Bible student."[45] Church asserts that the subject of study was not only simplified but ran consecutively starting with God, man and sin.[46] As Church avers "Bibles were used until they fell into pieces."[47]

---

40. Ward, *History of Global Anglicanism*, 177.
41. MacMaster and Jacobs, *Gentle Wind of God*, 55.
42. Church, *Quest for the Highest*, 113.
43. Church, 118.
44. Church, 119.
45. Church, 62.
46. Church, *Every Man a Bible Student*, 15.
47. Church, *Quest for the Highest*, 114.

The Convention of 1935, regarded as the first to be organized by Africans at Kabale, followed the pattern of a Keswick Convention closely: Sunday and Monday were quiet days, Tuesday (sin), Wednesday (repentance), Thursday (new birth), Friday (Holy Spirit and victorious life), Saturday (gospel service), Sunday (eight testimonies) and Monday (a praise meeting). Every speaker followed the Bible reading for the day and hammered the message home from a living experience.[48]

As a result, some *Balokole* like Simeon Nsibambi went out boasting that they could tell after shaking hands with a new missionary whether he had the "real thing" in his heart or not.[49] Following this, some *Balokole* students of Bishop Tucker Theological College, Mukono, could even question their teachers on their understanding of the Bible. They engaged spirited campaigns against evils in the college like sin, theft and immorality.[50] Similarly, clerks at Entebbe were spending their weekends preaching against sin.[51]

Missionaries and clergy

Some missionaries like Lawrence Barham were in the heart of revival and noted ongoing activities like "confession of sin, restitution, sometimes receiving strong impressions to read certain verses of the Bible which led them to put away some habits like beer drinking." They preached in bands and stirred many people amidst opposition and a level of persecution.[52] But as Guillebaud observes through the words of Dr. Stanley Smith, the missionaries' contribution as a body to the revival was negligible until they had received a conviction of their sins.[53] No wonder Kosiya thought the convention of 1934 could not arouse conviction of sin because of what he termed as "people praying beautiful long prayers, many of them hypocrites he knew who needed to be broken down before God."[54] This resonates with MacMaster and Jacobs' observation of Erica Sabiti's confession that many clergy including himself were not saved as illustrated by his repentance following a confrontation by

---

48. Church, 116–117.
49. Church, 87.
50. MacMaster, *Gentle Wind of God*, 54.
51. MacMaster, *Gentle Wind of God*, 51.
52. Church, *Quest for the Highest*, 117.
53. Guillebaud, *Grain of Mustard Seed*, 65.
54. Church, *Quest for the Highest*, 99.

one of the members of the congregation who questioned whether he had experienced the cleansing blood of Jesus.[55]

Having seen the reactions in the Ugandan scene, following the start of the revival, the scholars' perspective on Kenyan soil is critical. This is outlined in three epochs.

Entry and Spread in the Kenyan Scene: 1937 to 1950

As with the date of the beginning of the revival, scholars seem to disagree on the year revival entered Kenya. While Dr. Church, Mambo and Macmaster and Jacobs identify the date as 1937,[56] Langley and Kiggins and Ogot claim 1938 as the date of entry.[57] If the two claims are authentic, then 1937 or 1938 would be regarded as the time of entry. However, it seems more credible to consider the prerogative of the Ruanda notes (on the strength of Dr. Church being a witness) in which Dr. Church cites the Convention at Kabete in Kenya, held on 30 March to 7 April 1937.[58] Thus, 1937 seems like the most likely date of entry. This date is further confirmed by Macmaster and Jacobs who affirm that revival arrived in Kenya in April 1937 when Nsibambi and a team from Ruanda visited Kabete, near Nairobi, where they met Obadiah Kariuki, a later bishop of Mount Kenya.[59]

Thus, the entry of revival into Kenya through Nyanza in 1938 as claimed by Welbourn and Ogot among others might be off the mark.[60] However, his survey of the spread of revival from the Maseno to Ramba pastorates is praiseworthy.

The year 1938 could perhaps be not the date of entry but of a second visit to Kenya. Mambo notes a second revival team from Ruanda at the Pumwani CMS station in Nairobi where some Christians were saved, including Anglican clergy.[61] However, between 1938 and 1945 nothing much was

---

55. MacMaster, *Gentle Wind of God*, 57.
56. Church, *Quest for the Highest*, 145; Mambo, "Revival Fellowship", 111; MacMaster, *Gentle Wind of God*, 58.
57. Langley, *Serving People*, 198; Ogot, *Church of Christ*, 28.
58. Church, *Quest for the Highest*, 145.
59. MacMaster, *Gentle Wind of God*, 58.
60. Ogot, *Church of Christ*, 28.
61. Mambo, "Revival Fellowship", 111.

heard about a revival in other parts of the country except Nyanza because of severe opposition from the established churches.[62]

In Nyanza, the revival continued to cause ripples in the Anglican Church. Besides the message of conversion and purity of heart receiving a lukewarm reception, it found a natural leader, Ishmael Noo in 1942, and by 1944 the revival membership was about two thousand, organized in what Welbourn and Ogot referred to as small armies led by faithful followers, moving from one place to another using crude megaphones and demanding their listeners to straighten their crooked paths.[63] They composed hymns to beckon people to get saved. Welbourn and Ogot quote an example:

> I heard the voice of Jesus say to me:
> Get up, and start to work;
> Start to work, because the night is near
> When a man does not work. So I say,
> The shepherd has sacrificed
> His live for the sake of the flock,
> For the sake of his flock, because he loves his sheep.
> Oh! Jesus, you were an only child!
> The shepherd has lost his life in order to save the sheep.[64]

As a result, many were radically resolving to serve Christ. Welbourn and Ogot assert that only the first wives kept their marriage vows as others decided to leave their unsaved husbands to follow Christ. Likewise, the saved women left their unsaved monogamous husbands. It is said that from 1945, most of Noo's congregation was made up of these women resulting in the revivalists being accused of promiscuity.[65]

The developing social ethics were disturbing. Both sexes were encouraged to sleep together simply because they were saved. The statement used was, "To the pure all things are pure,"[66] a quite deceiving statement because some got into immoral sexual relationships. The teaching of Noo preceded a sequence of other nefarious practices in the name of revival.

---

62. Mambo, 111.
63. Welbourn and Ogot, *Place to Feel*, 29.
64. Welbourn, *A Place to Feel at Home*, p.29.
65. Welbourn, 30.
66. Welbourn, 30.

Welbourn and Ogot observe that in 1946 Bildad Kaggia deserted the Anglican Church and formed a non-denominational church – The Voice of the World Wide Salvation and Healing Revival – which was registered in 1955. His followers in Central Nyanza, Jokaggia (Followers of Kaggia) began to preach Kaggiaism in 1948, emphasizing confession of sins, speaking in tongues and spiritual healing. They also rejected the Anglican Prayer Book and parts of the Bible that deal with Jewish customs and practices. Eventually, Kaggians broke with Noo when the former demanded the latter confess his sins, leading to three factions, namely Noo, the Stanway and the Kaggians, all claiming to be revivalists.[67]

On one pendulum swing, these disturbances destabilized the Anglican Church in Nyanza. Welbourn and Ogot note that the revivalists had to seek advice from their Ugandan counterparts to remain in the church and to place emphasis on conversion and confession of sins. This spelled doom for Noo and Kaggia, giving a lifeline to the Nyanza Revival.[68] Noo formed his own church in 1948 called The Christian Universal Evangelical Union which he headed until his death in 1960. With the departure of the Nooists faction from the Anglican Church, a group of Revivalist known as *Joremo*[69] was left in the church.[70]

On the other pendulum swing, the Revival Fellowship faced tribulation, particularly from the mainstream churches. Mambo avers that "church leaders predominantly reviled the Brethren's open confession of sin and their constant claim to have been born again." On top of that, some looking for a Luo word for fellowship, unfortunately, chose *lalruok*, a word translated as the conspiring together of thieves to commit a robbery. They were thus referred to as "that gang." The Gikuyu suffered a similar fate in their description of the Christian experience of rebirth in Christ. They were accused of reintroducing their traditional rite of *guciaruo ringi*[71] (second birth). At the same

---

67. Welbourn, 31.

68. Welbourn, 32.

69. A Luo word meaning "people of blood"; they sang and preached salvation through the blood of Christ.

70. Welbourn, *Place to Feel*, 32.

71. This phrase refers to the *Gikuyu* custom rite of passage involving an outsider who intends to join a group or a family. A sacrificial ceremony was performed to usher the individual into the community with full rights and privileges.

time, the fellowship was despised and termed *Dini ya Ruanda* or Ruanda heresy. They were denied access to church buildings, resulting in meeting in unusual places.[72]

After the Second World War, Mambo notes a steady growth in the Revival Fellowship in Kenya exemplified by the rise of big conventions.[73] This is echoed by Langley and Kiggins who record a major convention in Kikuyu land at Kahuhia in 1947 followed by others at Kigari in Embu in 1948, Kabete in 1949 and Thogoto in 1950 where attendance was close to 20,000.[74] Certainly, Gathogo observes that the ensuing conventions exposed their leaders' lack of theological training, developing a legalistic lifestyle and sometimes making ignorant decisions. Nevertheless, their influence was bountiful, as former criminals and renegades, particularly during the Mau-Mau rebellion, confessed and denounced their past sins.[75] Some of these confessions were disastrous and embarrassing. For instance, Bishop Peter Mwang'ombe of the Anglican Diocese of Mombasa lost his bishopric when a lady in 1970 publicly confessed that he had fathered her son when he was just a Reverend.[76]

Revival 1950 – 1980

Welbourn and Ogot open the second part of their brief survey with the important question, "Was the revival to be conducted within or without the church?"[77] Already *Nooism* had severed its relationship with the Anglican Church, and the remaining wing of the revival felt disillusioned by the Anglican Church hierarchy. Consequently, the laity felt a need for spiritual separation from the mainstream church, leading to the *Kuhama* movement whose members were called Separatists, *Wahamaji* (vacating) or Joremo. The separation took place in 1953 in what Welbourn and Ogot likened to Abraham living away from the land of his birth; they felt they had been called by God to leave the church and everything else behind, to devote themselves to a devotional life away from the powers of darkness exemplified

---

72. Mambo, "Revival Fellowship", 111–112.
73. Mambo, 112.
74. Mambo, 198.
75. Gathogo, "Retracing Diakonia," 7–8.
76. Gitari, *Troubled but not Destroyed*, 74.
77. Welbourn, *Place to Feel*, 33.

by admission into their fellowship, those who were not walking in the light.[78] They had been aggrieved by the *Wahamaji*,[79] who chose to defy the church on some key elements,[80] were the majority of the Revivalists, believed themselves to be God's elect and carried their cross daily.[81]

Baur credits the Revival Movement for giving life to the Anglican Church.[82] Nevertheless, Welbourn and Ogot observe that the majority of the church leaders decided to fight the *Kuhama*, who were accused of spiritual pride.[83] Maseno was chosen as the headquarters for the rival group that had the support of the Rural Dean, the Rev. Festo Olang', Archdeacon of Nyanza, E.K. Stovold and was believed to have received blessings of the Bishop of Mombasa, Leonard Beecher.[84]

Controversy between Joremo (Raba) and Johera (Maseno) Groups

By 1953, the Anglican Church in Nyanza had been split into two rival groups, a large one under lay leadership and the other under church leadership with a sizeable group of Christians expressing disaffection with the situation.[85]

The Maseno group, argue Welbourn and Ogot, believed that pure revivalism should remain in the church, and supported it fully because Christians can only separate from sin and not from Christ's body, the church.[86] Further, unlike the Wahamaji, the Maseno group encouraged lay leaders to support the leadership of ordained ministers and based their stand on love (Luo, Johera)

---

78. Welbourn, 33–34.

79. Musa Amoke, a layman who emerged as the leader of *Wahamaji* (Joremo) and who ordained ministers.

80. They emphasized extempore prayers and not a fixed church liturgy; preferred Christ as the only recognized leader and not episcopacy; church leaders perceived not to walk in the light were referred to as worldly; opposed to being church teachers because it involves teaching sinners, collecting church monies and working with teachers who had not seen the light; against serving on church councils, committees or boards and could not be god-parents or best-men to non-separatists – these are things of the world; opposed to wearing of cassocks or wedding rings; no free choice of spouse, this was the work of the movement; refused to recognize social obligations of a non-religious nature like registering as voters and were engrossed with personal salvation to the extent of neglecting family responsibilities.

81. Welbourn, *Place to Feel*, 34–35.

82. Baur, *2000 Years of Christianity*, 487.

83. Welbourn, *Place to Feel*, 36.

84. Welbourn, 36.

85. Welbourn, 36.

86. Welbourn, 37.

meaning those who love as espoused in John 23:34f, John 4:16 and Rev 2:2ff.[87] Doctrinally, Wahamaji (Joremo) believed people are saved through repentance and confession of sin and that one can be saved many times because we are still under the dominion of sin. Johera affirmed that salvation is through faith in Christ (Heb 11:1–12) and taught that salvation of the soul takes place once, though they acknowledge backsliding and restoration through repentance. Johera believed they are saved from the power and dominion of sin and thus are righteous and holy.[88]

Welbourn and Ogot further note that the main difference between the Ramba (Joremo) and the Maseno (Johera) groups was on the doctrine of salvation.[89] Whereas Joremo believed in the inner light and the invisible church, thus mistrusting the intellectuals but upholding charismatic leadership and contentment with living for Christ, Johera believed in the visible church (Christ's body) and respected church authority, tradition and reason as a way of bringing necessary changes in the church.[90]

The two rivals clashed in 1955 following the elevation of Olang' to the position of Assistant Bishop of Mombasa. Johera group believed he was tribal and would discriminate against the Luo. Olang' aligned himself to Wahamaji who had now agreed to return to the institutional church.[91] However, Olang's move to join Joremo annoyed the Johera clergy who could not accept laymen having authority over clergy.[92]

In 1956, Rev. Abednego Matthew Ajuoga, the leader of the Maseno group, defied orders from the mainstream church leadership and wrote a complaint letter to the Bishop of Mombasa over disciplinary action against a member of the clergy who was sympathetic to the Johera group.[93] Ajuoga's letter led to the reinstating of Rev. Nathan Sila Awour but made reconciliation between the Maseno group and the church leaders in Nyanza difficult.[94] He again challenged the church leadership in a letter titled "Light" addressed to the

---

87. Welbourn, 37.
88. Welbourn, 38.
89. Welbourn, 38.
90. Welbourn, 38.
91. Welbourn, 40, 41.
92. Welbourn, 42.
93. Welbourn, 43.
94. Welbourn, 44.

Bishop of Mombasa upon which he was demoted and transferred to Bondo, a stronghold of Joremo.[95]

In March 1957, Olang' invited the Bishop of Mombasa to a meeting at Maseno to try to unite the two factions. The Bishop urged the warring groups to reconcile against the wishes of Olang', who wanted the Maseno group to join the Ramba group. Another meeting was called in May 1957, and this time the bishop agreed with his assistant bishop's wish and reprimanded Johera leaders to stop "preaching their nonsense."[96] Eventually, Ajuoga and his lieutenants' licenses were withdrawn by the Bishop of Mombasa and the schism was inevitable.[97] The tragic outcome of the Anglican Church in Maseno, observes Baur, was the rivalry not only between the two factions but also of the two churchmen in the name of Bishop Festo Olang' and Rural Dean Matthew Ajuoga.[98] In 1958, Ajuoga was elected bishop of the Church of Christ through Presbyteral Ordination, because the Archbishop of Canterbury declined their ordination.[99]

Revival through the Years of Political Independence

In the midst of the ongoing intrigues in the spread of EARM, the excitement of freedom led to some members of the revival to join political parties. This brought new challenges as African Christians were motivated to demand independence from the mission churches. Thus, a dispute ensued between leaders of African churches and the mainstream churches. The revival's practice of walking in repentance and the fullness of the Spirit was put to the test.

The Revivalists hated tribal differences, denominationalism, class society and political alignment. As a result, many, particularly Gikuyus, were persecuted by the colonial settlers. Baur refers to the Revivalists as defenders of Christian non-violence who died a martyr's death for their Christian faith. They were accused of non-involvement in public issues and criticized for their concern for personal salvation.[100] Gatu argues that during the state of emergency in Kenya (1952–1960) revival Brethren refused to align with any

---

95. Welbourn, 52.
96. Welbourn, 53.
97. Welbourn, 54.
98. Baur, *2000 Years of Christianity*, 482.
99. Welbourn, *Place to Feel*, 57.
100. Baur, *2000 Years of Christianity*, 480.

side of the political divide and declined to take the oath of allegiance. They argued that since they had been washed with the blood of Christ, they had no business with the blood of goats.[101] They had to pay dearly with their blood. In fact, Gatu, Langley and Kiggins state that renewed oath-taking in 1969 saw many Brethren tortured or killed.[102] Langley and Kiggins further assert that the Anglican Diocese of Mt Kenya was the first to host an anti-oath rally attended by 50,000 people while still pledging loyalty to President Kenyatta and his government.[103]

During this time there was a robust and acrimonious suspicion between the loyalists and supporters of the freedom fighters. The Revivalists' call for peaceful co-existence was echoed by the first President of Kenya, Mzee Jomo Kenyatta in 1963, when he startled both his foes and friends. Instead of retaliation, his call to the young nation was "forgive and forget" and "love your neighbour as yourself."[104] He thus exemplified his strong revival heritage of preaching love. Perhaps being a friend of Bishop Obadiah Kariuki who was one of the leaders of the movement impacted Kenyatta at this time. Thus, the revivalists' influence was overwhelming; none could have resisted it within or outside the church. Their efforts helped in keeping bloody confrontation at bay after independence. Thus, many churches in Kenya united in revival following the suffering under the Mau Mau uprising and the painful struggle for independence.

On the flip-side, the revival fellowships did not need independence from any mission board or denomination because they were not attached to any formal organization. They handled their affairs including money generated from the fellowship separately as they planned missions or conventions. They just "walked in the light" about finances. Don Jacobs, recalling the years he had worked closely in the ministries of fellowship that he never heard any accusation of misuse of finance.[105]

Brethren in Kenya developed an internal mechanism of handling money in the name of *Mfuko ya Bwana* (The Lord's Bag) into which Brethren would

---

101. Gatu, "Jesus Christ, The 'Truthful Mirror,'" 39.
102. Gatu, 39; Langley, *Serving People,* 202.
103. Langley, 203.
104. Baur, *2000 Years of Christianity,* 481.
105. MacMaster, *Gentle Wind of God,* 181.

contribute to meet the needs of the fellowship, each according to his ability.[106] This money, however, brought serious repercussions because the Brethren did not approve of accounting and auditing procedures as they believed in walking in the light; accountability was not necessary for they trusted each other.[107]

Thus, beginning from 1964, Brethren were opposed to financial procedures and formed new movements within the revival referred to as *Ufufuo* or *Kufufuka* (Resurrection) or *Kuamka* (Awakening) in Kenya and Uganda, and *Okuzuzuka* (Awakening) based on Ephesians 5:14–15. Mambo further notes that Awakened Brethren saw the evils caused by money like extravagant lifestyle, ruinous loans and a thirst for prosperity.[108]

Indeed, Gathogo contends that re-awakened Brethren were discouraged from taking bank loans because Jesus could come at night and would find some in debt, yet he paid their debts through the cross. They were also not required to keep dogs for protection in their compounds, nor security officers among other security measures as God protects Balokole. As in the case of St. Paul, to "live is Christ and to die is gain" (Philippians 1:21).[109] Gathogo further claims that the *Arahuka* (Arise) revival of 1967, saw masses of people from the mainline churches converted to this faith. He asserts that Ephesians 5:14 powerfully taught liberation from hypocrisy and all sorts of darkness.[110] Gathogo observes that to some extent, it was surprising to hear confessions of cheating spouses (some church elders) despite hitherto appearing trustworthy. Thus, the 1970s came to be referred to as the generation of being born again.[111]

The interpretation and application of the Ephesian text led to sustained controversy in the ensuing years. *Kufufuka* and *Kusimama* held their meetings separately at St. Stephen's Church, Nairobi on the first Sunday and the second Sunday of each month, respectively. Likewise in the Mount Kenya region, *Kufufuka* and *Kusimama* held their monthly meetings at Maragua and Murang'a cathedral, respectively.[112]

---

106. Mambo, "Revival Fellowship", 115.
107. Mambo, 115.
108. Mambo, 115.
109. Gathogo, *Retracing Diakonia*, 7.
110. Gathogo, 8.
111. Gathogo, 8.
112. Gitari, "Paper on East African," 5.

Events of 1980 to 2015

The third epoch portrays a stabilized situation though *Kusimama* (Stand) and *Kufufuka* (Awakened) continue to meet separately particularly at national and regional levels. Local meetings have seen them mingle and one may not notice their differences. However, the Stand group which claims to be the original EARM has the majority of members across the four selected counties. Some of the traits of this period depict a continuity of the past as shown.

Convention resilience

In 1875, the first Convention was held at Keswick by the teachers of higher life and continued in the English Lake District until today. On African soil too, it has taken a journey of resilience since the 1935 East African Convention at Kabale, Uganda[113] and has gone on unabated for about eighty years. Mutembei further observes the unbroken sequence of the Conventions by dates, places, and themes all the way from 1935 to 2007, but notes that it was only 1997 and 2007 when there were no conventions.[114]

The Kabale convention met for a full week, Sunday to Sunday,[115] an updated version of early Keswick which met for five days.[116] The recent Kabale Convention in Uganda, which had the theme: "Brethren, consider your call" (1 Cor 1:26), shows a thinned timeline of three days (20 to 23 August 2015). But they still covered five topics as it was with Keswick. Keswick's first day dealt with sin and the final day with a mission. The Kabale Convention shows a paradigm shift from specific topics to generalized ones, whereby the first day was on revitalizing the spirit of revival and the final day was on evangelism and discipleship. They seem to have adopted the characteristics of the modern Keswick Convention, called Keswick Ministries.[117] The approach may have shifted, but the focus on mission and holiness has remained the same, albeit with a wider spectrum, and a definite move away from anything related to the "higher life" teachings of the past.

---

113. D. Mutembei, *Historia Fupi ya Ushirika [Short History of Brethren Fellowship]*, 7.
114. Mutembei, 38.
115. Church, *Every Man*, 116–117.
116. Naselli, *Let Go and Let God*, 171.
117. Naselli, 140.

Mfuko wa Bwana (The Lord's Bag)

The Lord's Bag was mentioned in the second phase of this survey and seems to have been practiced in Kenya ever since. Kamau highlights a controversy in the late 1990s within the Stand group associated with the *Mfuko wa Bwana*. The district team had prepared an exaggerated budget for the Kirinyaga Convention in the Mount Kenya Region. The matter went up to the Diocesan Bishop for mediation, resulting in a smaller budget which managed the convention activities, while raising questions what the Brethren wanted to do with the rest of the money.[118] However, the damage was already done leading to a split within the Stand; but the wound has healed. Perhaps the Kenyan team needs to learn from its Tanzanian counterpart, which opened a bank account to handle the revival's financial transactions.[119] Thus, they avoided trusting money to a few individuals under the guise that they will walk in the light.

Generation gap

Strict legalistic behavior associated with Brethren like "do not drink; do not smoke; do not part your hair; do not wear short skirts"[120] alienated many admirers. Young people in particular have not been attracted to EARM because of these stringent social ethics. However, there have been attempts to bring young people into the revival as attested by the recent big gathering of youth at the Lenana School Convention for young Brethren. The theme of the Convention had been taken from Ephesian 5:1, "Be imitators of God as dearly beloved children" (ESV).[121]

GAFCON communiqué

The GAFCON meeting at All Saints Cathedral, Nairobi in October 2013 found solace and inspiration from EARM's theology of salvation. They noted the revival had touched millions of lives as the Holy Spirit moved Christians from the beginning of the last century, to share the good news of Christ with others. They identified three features consonant with EARM:

- In the East African Revival, people learn about a change of heart.

---

118. Kamau, "Critical Analysis," 28.
119. Mambo, "Revival Fellowship", 115.
120. Langley, *Serving People*, 202.
121. Lenana School Document.

- Repentance of sin is followed by a confession of guilt and a desire to make amends.
- The gospel's power is twofold; to save the lost and transform the church as opposed to the church conforming to the world.

The meeting repented of indifference, prayerlessness, and inactivity in the face of false teaching. They affirmed that the sins from which they must repent are not necessarily those which the world also believes are wrong; they are those that God himself abhors and which are made clear in his Word.[122] The conviction of sin was noted by Dr. Senyonyi of Uganda Christian University to be central to revival.[123]

While GAFCON 2013 was centered on the conviction of sin, the GAFCON Nairobi communiqué 2016 concentrated on unity. Members expressed a desire to walk together in spite of the geographical distance between them. The phrase to walk together demonstrates familiarity with the perspective of beliefs and practices of EARM. It seems to resonate with the spirit of the revival's dictum of walking in the light; that is, the spirit of repentance and "walking in the light, as he is in the light" (1 John 1:7–9). The fact that six out of ten of the nations[124] in the communiqué 2016 were from Eastern Africa indicates the dynamics and influence of EARM on the GAFCON. The outgoing Chairman of the GAFCON, the Most Rev. Dr. Eliud Wabukala of the Anglican Church of Kenya has been a keen member of the EARM. Having said that, the meeting seems to regret the distance attributed to the Episcopal Church walking away from the Anglican Communion's doctrine on sexuality and the plain teaching of Scripture.[125]

EARM's Heritage of Keswick Theology

Having established some of the legacy of EARM coming from Keswick theology, it is prudent to identify some theological underpinnings of EARM, which was apparent in the historical survey of Anglican Church scholarship. These foundations may have prompted beliefs and practices of walking in the light.

---

122. Nairobi Communique.
123. Walton, *Legacy of East African*, 2.
124. These nations are Congo, Kenya, Myanmar, Nigeria, North America, Rwanda, South America, South Sudan and Sudan, Tanzania, Uganda.
125. http://www.ad-ne.org/global-communion/gafcon-nairobi-communique-2016/.

Naselli, an scholar and critic of early Keswick theology, believes this theology is erroneous and dangerous in spite of its being within the confines of evangelical orthodoxy.[126] Naselli concedes that his college days were permeated with the saved and surrender mantra in the sense of "I was saved at 13 and surrendered my life to the Lord at 18 years."[127] The second step (surrendered life) has been what Naselli came to call "Let go and let God."[128] Naselli acknowledges that he got disillusioned and wondered whether the teaching was biblical because it wasn't in line with what he was reading in the Bible.[129]

Naselli suggests that the "let go and let God" concept is not supported by the Scriptures. He argues that the "Let go" perception in the life of a believer was thought to occur when one surrenders everything to God, including himself. The role of the believer henceforth was to "praise God for victory" and "not to pray for victory." The "let God" notion leads to quietism or passivism, from believing that God's grace is sufficient to meet all needs. Romans 8:2, "God has set us wholly free from the law of sin," has been misinterpreted to mean "not will do this, but has already done it."[130] In other words, no need to struggle, just surrender all (let go) and rest in faith (let God).

About this scenario, Guillebaud observes a peculiar situation in Uganda, which could be translated as "let go and let God." While sleeping on a makeshift bed, Blasio Kigozi had this to say when two boys woke him up because they had spotted a leopard:

"Would you be frightened if there was a soldier here with a gun?" "No." "Well, we have better than a soldier. Jesus Christ is our protection. Go back to sleep."[131] While no religious person would deny that God protects his people, Kigozi demonstrates the kind of Christian faith prevailing among the revivalists. Years later in Kenya, the reawakened Brethren would not keep security dogs because Jesus protects them.

In respect to saved and surrender concepts in Kenya, the former refers to the converted in the sense of Spirit baptism. The latter refers to the filling of the Spirit that accompanies victorious life in the sense of a daily walk in

---

126. Naselli, *Let Go and Let God*, 74.
127. Naselli, 27.
128. Naselli, 28.
129. Naselli, 27.
130. Naselli, 200, 202.
131. Guillebaud, *Rwanda*, 57.

the light and attending fellowship meetings. The Brethren liken a truly saved person to an uprooted carrot, shaken free of all the soil clinging to it. This seems to parallel early Keswick theology of victorious life on one hand, and Brethren's victory at the cross of Christ on the other. It seems true that a significant element of the early Keswick theology could still be traced in EARM.

Indeed, Anglican scholars and associates[132] have written substantially on the socio-ethical beliefs and practices which could have contributed towards the concept of walking in light in the EARM. However, little has been said concerning its relationship with Keswick theology in spite of the fact that the pioneers of revival had Keswick theology undertones. For instance, Dr. Church was influenced by the Keswick theology flourishing in the CICCU that emphasized the post-conversion experience of a second blessing, or "Spirit-filling," and a strong desire for the higher Christian life.[133] Indeed, Dr. Church, during his early years in Ruanda, believed that Africans could also experience a second blessing.[134]

Additionally, in the early days there were Keswick Conventions in East Africa which had significant impact on the East African Conventions. The reason for this is twofold. First, the Keswick teachings found fertile ground in the East African soil as discussed in chapter 2. Africans easily appropriated the teachings into their traditional cultural milieu to the extent that Keswick theology lost its original edge.

The East African conventions emerged as an offshoot of the Keswick conventions, but they soon developed their own distinct African character. The Keswick Conventions emphasized personal holiness and heart examination, while the East African Revival Movement (EARM) prioritized evangelism, transparency, and open confession, resulting in a unique African character within East Africa's religious context

Second, the general wave of classical evangelical revivalism of the late nineteenth century that came to East Africa, thanks to CMS Ruanda Mission, could also have claimed parenthood for the revival. This is because Ruanda Mission emphasized conservative evangelical views on the Bible[135] and

---

132. This term will be used to refer to those called upon to write on the EARM's influence in the Anglican Church.

133. Church, *Needs Spiritual and Temporal*, 18.

134. Church, 18.

135. Ward, *History of Global Anglicanism*, 176.

"promoted urgent quest for renewal of personal holiness as understood by the Keswick movement."[136] In other words, as claimed by Ward the two views point to Keswick's seed and are thus authentic.[137]

Hastings summarizes the two views.[138] Whereas the East African revival exhibited characteristics of global classical Protestantism revival drawn from Keswick Conventions and the Buchman's Oxford Group, it nevertheless acquired a unique African face. Therefore, the question of the influence of Keswick theology on EARM's walking in the light deserves investigation. This section, therefore, strives to discuss six key elements that constitute experiential sanctification or practical holiness in EARM largely informed by Keswick teachings. Some elements, like baptism of the Spirit and being born again, are closely related but will be discussed separately to understand the perspectives of Keswick and EARM on both of them. Also, note that the second blessing concept runs through some of these elements, implying its significance in the history of the Keswick movement.

Baptism of the Spirit, a Second Blessing?

Barabas argues that Keswick's view of the baptism of the Spirit is not a spiritual experience after regeneration but a primary blessing of regeneration or what could be referred to as being born again.[139] This negates some early higher life teachings, that the baptism of the Spirit is a spiritual experience subsequent to regeneration, which they refer to as a second blessing, which was to be received as it was on the day of Pentecost. This resonates with Naselli's argument that Spirit-baptism like justification is Christ's judicial, positional, non-experiential gift and occurs at regeneration and never occurs again (1 Cor 12:13). At the moment of accepting Christ, a person receives the baptism of the Spirit.[140] That means all Christians are Spirit baptized at regeneration and since they cannot experience a second Spirit-baptism, argues Naselli, they should not try to find it.[141] This is because the Spirit-baptism is an endowment for those forming Christ's body the church, and believers have no part

---

136. Ward, "Introduction," 3.
137. Ward, *History of Global Anglicanism*, 175.
138. Hastings, *History of Christianity*, 52.
139. Barabas, *So Great Salvation*, 131.
140. Naselli, *Let Go and Let God*, 138, 234.
141. Naselli, 234.

to play in obtaining it. It is within the church that sanctification of believers is manifested.

In a bid to describe the believer's lifetime fight with sin in respect to the struggle between the believer's old and new nature, that is flesh and spirit, Naselli rightly cites Galatians 5:16–26.[142] Thus, there is no second blessing apart from God's work in the believer at conversion, which is judicial and ushers a Christian into the spirit-flesh struggle while in this world. Unfortunately experiential sanctification or what some believers call Spirit-filling experiences is supposed to have elevated the saved ones or *Balokole*[143] to a higher status of holiness than ordinary Christians. The saved or Brethren are believed to walk in the light, whereas those outside the Brethren circle, even though they have received Spirit-baptism, are regarded as not born again.

Then, it can be asked whether EARM advocated for second blessing theology. Dr. Church's assertion is in the affirmative.[144] He further claims that second blessing is a spirituality that portrays a deeper holiness and continuous surrender which came to be known by the Cambridge Christian Union in the 1920s as the victorious life or the Highest.[145] Macmaster and Jacobs concur and assert that Dr. Church witnessed to Nismbabi about the filling of the Spirit and the victorious life.[146] It is true then that some of the early revivalists propagated a second blessing theology.

But some scholars are skeptical. Ward states that whereas the Keswick movement taught a second blessing after initial conversion, EARM emphasized brokenness at the cross of Christ.[147] Ward indicated that "previous Christian experience apart from this event [initial conversion] was not recognized by the revivalists as *kulokoka* – the state of being saved."[148] But brokenness or *kulokoka* ought to be an experience subsequent to initial conversion, although ways of presentation may differ from that of the second blessing.

---

142. Naselli, 272.

143. Kenyan revivalists are referred to as Brethren or *Wandugu wa mizigo* (burden carriers in respect to bearing other Christians' burden andproblems, and particularly among the Brethren).

144. Church, *Needs Spiritual and Temporal*, 18.

145. Church, *Quest for the Highest*, 14.

146. MacMaster, *Gentle Wind of God*, 28.

147. Ward, "Introduction," 4.

148. Ward, "Introduction," 4.

Thus, the born-again element among the Brethren ought to occur consequent to initial conversion.

If this is the case, there might have been a change from second blessing emphasis. Indeed it seems like this experience had begun to lose its power (in Britain) even before the end of the nineteenth century and had gradually been replaced by an emphasis on activism and dedication to the cause of Christ and mission.[149] However, its possible resilience had a significant impact on the African soil. As stated by Dr. Church above, it seems to some extent to have defined East African spirituality.

However, the early Keswick's emphasis on a second blessing received severe criticism from the renowned English evangelical Bishop, J.C. Ryle, through his writings on holiness and practical religion.[150] The form of early Keswick theology that influenced EARM to a large extent would be called a partially-modified form of the higher life teachings which had come from America, courtesy of Robert Pearsall Smith and his wife, Hannah Whitehall Smith. Its partial modification in response to Ryle's work was a welcome gesture that shaped evangelical teaching up to the mid-twentieth century when again it met with criticism from other evangelicals.[151]

The second blessing would make sense when paralleled to the filling of the Spirit which will be discussed later. Baptism of the Spirit as argued by Naselli is not only judicial and theologically valid but also scriptural (Luke 3:16).[152] Indeed, one reason why Bishop Ryle condemned Keswick theology was its misappropriation of the baptism of the Spirit to the second blessing, which lacks sound biblical and theological support.[153] Additionally, Ryle's book *Holiness*, written in 1879, surveys the subject of holiness and raises questions on the teaching of Keswick theology. For example, on the one hand, great harm has been done by those claiming that there are different "levels" of the Christian life and that we are to strain to be like those who have reached a state of perfection (or even of near-perfection). On the other hand, many people believe that becoming more godly is not a battle, but simply a process

---

149. Reed, *Walking in the Light*, 56.
150. Reed, 56.
151. Reed, 56–57.
152. Naselli, *Keswick Theology*, 39.
153. Reed, *Walking in the Light*, 56. See for example Acts 1:8, 2:4; 8–12; 32–33; 10:44–46, Matt 3:11.

of leaning on Christ and expecting him to change us. But the testimony of Scripture is clear–we are to exert ourselves in pursuing holiness; we are to strive after it.[154]

Born Again

Undeniably, the outcome of Yosiya's rendezvous with Nismbabi would link the born-again and conversion experiences. Dr. Church recounts Yosiya's born-again crisis: "In the motor lorry on the road back to Gahini I kept pondering over these things, and before I got back, I was deeply convicted. My sins became a burden upon my back, and I yielded to Christ . . . this new life that began in me has never left me, and I am always longing to excel more in it."[155] In the words of Naselli, he became saved and then followed a new lifestyle.[156] This kind of conversion appears to be different from the initial conversion after justification and the baptism of the Spirit. The theological question here is whether he had been converted before his baptism. Dr. Church refused to have his child baptized in Uganda because he did not like Roman Catholic teaching that baptism *ex opera operato* (i.e., by the act performed) saved a child. He went on to claim that Uganda was full of baptized heathens. His son was thus baptized in England by his grandfather in "a private family baptism service, modifying the prayer book stress on the phrase, 'seeing now . . . this child is regenerate.'"[157] The confusion surrounding application of this sacrament requires a brief unpacking. In his online article, Tom Schenk argues that

> *Ex opere operato* . . . refers to the fact that the sacraments confer grace when the sign is validly affected – not as the result of activity on the part of the minister or recipient but by the power and promise of God.[158]

Schenk's assertions underscore the significance of the baptismal sacrament, in that it belongs to God and not to the officiating minister. Furthermore,

---

154. https://www.challies.com/reading-classics-together/reading-classics-together-holiness-introduction/accessed on 18th July 2024
155. Church, 79.
156. Naselli, *Let Go and Let God*, 27.
157. Church, *Quest for the Highest*, 80.
158. Schenk, "Ex Opere Operato" – Assumption Catholic Church, accessed online on 19th July 2024 downloaded from ttps://www.assumptiongranger.org/ex-opere-operato-2

the relegation of this sacrament to a supposedly holy church minister in a convenient context does not seem to add more value to its efficacy than when administered by an apparently unacceptable priest, in an unsuitable environment.

Nevertheless, baptism is a significant rite for a Christian's salvation journey. It therefore should not only be done scripturally but also the person entrusted with this ceremony ought to be beyond reproach (1 Tim 3:1–4). And the phrase "this child is regenerate"[159] could further the argument that the baptismal rite, is an outward sign of inward grace, ought to commence a Christian's born-again lifestyle.

Keswick theology invoked a second blessing experience as a phenomenon following the initial conversion of Christian undergraduates of the 1920s. Dr. Church argues that these undergraduates were seeking for deeper holiness, a second blessing or what was referred to by CICCU as victorious life.[160] This was the spirituality that Dr. Church strived to see realized not only in himself but in Uganda and Ruanda. At this juncture, Dr. Church was still under the immense influence of early Keswick theology. Thus, one could understand why he had to struggle to get a holy person to baptize his child.

The concept of being born again or twice-born and of second blessing is significant in the sense that they seem to be a second stage in the salvation process in the EARM and Keswick theology, respectively. However, the meaning of the terms seems to change with the circumstances, as discussed earlier. It seems correct to assume that the controversy brought about by the second blessing was replaced by stress on devotion to serving Christ which has been expressed through various term like "saved ones."[161] Thus, the phrases twice-born and saved ones[162] seemed to have gradually evolved from previous second blessing theology to become the trademarks of *Balokole*.[163] The other profound characteristic of the *Balokole* is the centrality of the cross.

---

159. Church, *Quest for the Highest*, 80.

160. Church, 14.

161. Reed, *Walking in the Light*, 56.

162. Bruner cited this reference, "Activities of the "Abalokole", "Twice Born" or "Saved Ones", 30 April 1944, TNA CO 536/215/4, f. 9, p. 9]. This reference was extracted from a letter, probably intercepted by the Protectorate Government, seemingly from a female British teacher.

163. Bruner, "Public Confession," 267.

Brokenness at the cross ought to be a due and instantaneous response following the initial conversion.

The Cross of Christ – Daily Victory

Senyonyi observes that revivalists like Nagenda saw Jesus as the focus of the revival meetings. Indeed, the name Jesus and the cross were used interchangeably.[164] Mambo further notes that Brethren strongly "emphasize daily spiritual deliverance, cleansing, and power for Christian living, through the blood of Jesus which was shed on the cross."[165] Certainly, the central symbols that stand out in the mind of the Brethren are the crucifixion of Jesus on the cross and the shed blood.

Surely, revival meetings would not have realized its goal without invoking the blood of Jesus for the forgiveness of sin. Dr. Church and his fellow evangelists were said to preach the message of brokenness, the message of the cross – Christ crucified. In one incident, the overwhelming sense of guilt led government and even respected church leaders to seek "the cleansing blood of Jesus Christ."[166] At Gahini school, Guillebaud records a striking incident as girls met with Jesus: "One girl was kneeling apparently in a trance with tears running down her face, crying out, 'can't you see him – look, there – Jesus is on the cross, dying for me."[167] Indeed, the convicting presence of Christ saw many remorseful souls seeking his cleansing. This is consistent with Osborn who observed that the Brethren contend that the Holy Spirit leads believers back to the cross, to Christ's cleansing blood.[168]

Unlike the early Keswick movement, which stressed a second blessing experience beyond initial conversion, Ward and Wild-Wood assert that the East African Revival Movement focused more on the initial conversion as "an overwhelming experience of brokenness at the cross."[169] This assertion leads to difficulties because while there were some who experienced brokenness immediately after initial conversion (Spirit-baptism), others had this experience later in life.

---

164. Senyonyi, "GAFCON EA Revival Distinctives", 4.
165. Mambo, "Revival Fellowship", 116.
166. MacMaster, *Gentle Wind of God*, 40, 41.
167. Guillebaud, *Rwanda: The Land God*, 66.
168. Osborn, *Pioneers in the East African*, 87.
169. Ward and Wild-Wood, *East African Revival*, 14.

Indeed, Meg Guillebaud alludes to a revival at Mukono Anglican Training College led by Joe Church in which many people responded to Christ. However, some staff members were unhappy that the "message was unsettling their baptized and confirmed students."[170] Thus, it looks like there are two classes of conversion. First, at baptism after initial conversion, i.e., becoming a Christian and second, when one is converted to a new way of expressing brokenness at the cross as per the overwhelming power of the Holy Spirit. Indeed the two types of conversion are prevalent among Christians in the present day Protestant mainstream churches in Kenya. Many converted believers of the first category would not be considered Brethren unless by their daily lives they exhibit brokenness.

This being the case, there is some resemblance between Keswick and EARM teaching concerning the two types of Christians; that is the born again, by virtue of experiencing brokenness. The one group is said not to have been born again and yet have been baptized, simply because they could not express brokenness by constant confession of their sin.

Public Confession of Sin

Anne Coomes details the events of 1935 that led to the conversion of Festo Kivengere following a convention at Kabale, Uganda in which Dr. Joe Church was the main speaker. The convention had run from Sunday 22 September to Monday 30 September 1935 and kept to one theme per day[171] with sin occupying the first slot on Tuesday.[172] As a result, Coomes observes a wave of conviction across Kabale as people wept for their sins and sought repentance and forgiveness.[173] This led to restitution (translated in Gikuyu as *guthondeka mehia*).

So, when Festo Kivengere gave his life to Jesus Christ, the natural consequence was to confess publicly his sins of smoking, drinking and stealing. This also meant leaving behind cultural taboos like eating chicken, eggs, and fish,

---

170. Guillebaud, *Rwanda: The Land God*, 66.

171. Other themes were: repentance, Wednesday; the new birth, Thursday; coming out of Egypt (separation from the world), Friday; the Holy Spirit and the victorious life, Saturday; praise meeting, Sunday.

172. Coomes, *Authorized Biography of Festo Kivengere*, 68–69.

173. Coomes, 69.

which a Muhima (Festo's tribe) should not touch. Such denials constituted his new life as he openly shared his faith in Christ.[174]

The nagging question here is how he came to acquire knowledge of confession. Was it from Dr. Church, a beneficiary of Keswick theology? Or was it a natural order following the dictums of the African traditional culture that compels a wrongdoer to confess his wrongs publicly?

Keswick theology shows that the sin principle has been a key subject at Keswick meetings since 1875. Indeed, the entire Keswick week appeared to focus its attention on sin; other topics were hinged on it.

Although Ward argues that Dr. Church had been influenced by Frank Buchman's Oxford Group Movement that emphasized public confession of sin, it seems likely that Buchman had a Keswick heritage.[175] An AA Pamphlet for Agnostics posted on 3 November 2013, notes Buchman's confession of his prideful behavior at the 1908 Keswick Convention in England. The full text of his confession after the preaching of Jessie Penn-Lewis is below.

> I thought of those six men back in Philadelphia who I felt had wronged me. They probably had, but I got so mixed in the wrong that I was the seventh wrong man ... I can only tell you I sat there and realized how my sin, my pride, my selfishness and my ill-will had eclipsed me from God in Christ. I was the centre of my own life. That big "I" had to be crossed out. I saw my resentments against those men standing out like tombstones in my heart. I asked God to change me, and He told me to put things right with them. It produced in me a vibrant feeling, as though a strong current of life had suddenly been poured into me, and afterward a dazed sense of a great spiritual shaking up.[176]

Certainly, this is brokenness at best, in a Keswick Convention context in which Buchman was convicted of his sins. Since it was a Keswick teaching that brought him to his knees it gives credit to Keswick theology and Dr. Church's religious heritage. Indeed, even Hooper concurs that from its foundation, the East African revival had been impacted by the teachings of the Keswick

---

174. Coomes, 72–73.

175. Ward, "Introduction," 4.

176. Lean, *A Life*, 30–31, cited from http://aaagnostica.org/2013/11/03/frank-buchman-and-the-oxford-group/.

movement.¹⁷⁷ As the teachings entered the mission churches, the Brethren attested to the cleansing power of the blood of the Lamb and confessed sin publicly (1 John 1:7).

Therefore, it seems fair to suggest that in spite of some of Keswick's questionable teachings, at least public confession was a Keswick distinctive. Indeed Pollock contends that Handley Moule, a Principal of Ridley Hall at Cambridge beginning in 1881 and later Bishop of Durham, publicly confessed.¹⁷⁸ Thus, it looks like public confessions at Keswick meetings were accepted phenomena. No doubt this practice could have gained leverage in the African context of vomiting and confessing evil or taboo.

Thus, perhaps Festo could have borrowed the art of public confession from his culture. Stanley acknowledges this feature among the Bahima (Festo's tribe) of North-Eastern Ankole, a traditional religious practice in which "the tutelary spirits were worshiped by local cult groups, entry into which was effected by an initiation ceremony where the initiate had to confess alleged infringements of sexual prohibitions. The initiate went through a ritual of being killed and being brought back to life before being accepted into the cult group."¹⁷⁹ This resonates with Gikuyu traditional religion and culture where the ceremony of *gutahikio* (symbolic vomiting) was administered to remove *thahu* (ritual defilement). In this ritual, the offender was called upon to confess his or her wrongs, known or unknown.¹⁸⁰ It thus looks like the art of confession has been rooted in various religious practices and has always been appropriated to serve the spiritual and psychological contexts of the client. However, this conclusion neither negates the influence of Keswick theology nor ignores the impact of African religious culture. One of the significant emphases here has been the habit of public confession of wrongs such as promiscuity. Although such public confessions have now been discouraged, they were regarded to be one of the key indicators that one had been born of the Spirit of God.

---

177. Hooper, "Theology of Trans-Atlantic Evangelicalism," 82.
178. Pollock, *Keswick Story*, 68, 70.
179. Stanley, "East Africa Revival", 14.
180. Karanja, "Confession and Cultural Dynamism", 147–148.

Filling of the Spirit

The Spirit-filled life was the climax of the teachings in the first three days (sin, cure, and consecration) of the yearly Keswick Convention.[181] Spirit-filling was believed to be the key theme of the Keswick week. Indeed, it was considered "a great sin not to be filled with the Spirit."[182] Spirit-filled Christians are believed to have the power of the Holy Spirit, enabling them to live a consistent Christian life. The choosing of seven men "known to be full of the Holy Spirit and wisdom" (Acts 6:3) suggests a biblical thrust on this subject and more so for Christians who hold church offices. A further lesson from this text is that some people fell short of the fullness of the Spirit. This raises the question of equitability of the fullness of the Spirit among Christians. This is a two-case scenario between those who have fullness versus those who have little or are lacking, and what that means for the church mission and ministry.

Referring to Ephesians 5:18 Barabas contends that Keswick teaches "While every Christian has the Spirit and has been baptized by the Spirit, not every Christian is filled with the Spirit or has the fullness of the Spirit."[183] This resonates with Naselli but adds that "to have the Spirit is one thing, but to be filled with the Spirit is quite another." He further refers to the question asked in Acts 19:2, "Did you receive the Holy Spirit when you believed?"[184] This question suggests that one can be born of the Spirit and not be filled with the Spirit, i.e., not sanctified wholly. Naselli reiterates that Spirit-baptism occurs once at a believer's crisis, while Spirit-filling frequents a believer's lifetime.[185]

Also, filling of the Spirit serves to equip a child of God for holiness and service without which living a consistent Christian life would be difficult.[186] Naselli notes the influence of Wesleyanism and Pentecostalism brought into early Keswick theology by the higher life teachings. Advocates of early Keswick theology such as Hopkins used Spirit-filling and Spirit-baptism terminology interchangeably.[187] It was not until the 1900s when Spirit-baptism terminology slowly came to be used for "what all believers experience at

---

181. Naselli, *Let Go and Let God*, 172.
182. Barabas, *So Great Salvation*, 131.
183. Barabas, 132.
184. Naselli, *Let Go and Let God*, 206.
185. Naselli, 207.
186. Murray, *Full Blessings of Pentecost*, 110.
187. Naselli, *Let Go and Let God*, 205.

conversion and to reserve Spirit-filling terminology for what only some believers experience subsequent to conversion,"[188]

Dr. Church and Nsimbabi, reeling from the impact of Protestant evangelicalism, particularly the Keswick influence, found themselves reading extensively about the Holy Spirit from the Scofield Bible. Guillebaud[189] avers that "the Spirit Himself lit up the Book and they saw in a new way not only their sin and failure but the marvel and sufficiency of God's remedy in Christ."[190] Meg Guillebaud adds that they knelt in prayer, "deciding before God to quit all sin in faith, and claiming the victorious life and the filling of the Holy Spirit."[191] It is likely that at this point, Spirit filling and being born again were viewed as two sides of the same coin. Yosiya's countenance after yielding to Christ[192] parallels Dr. Church and Nsimbabi's experiences of quitting all sin and becoming Spirit-filled.

The element of filling of the Spirit, as opposed to Spirit baptism, could have started among the *Balokole* Brethren around this time, in what has come to be referred to as being born again. If this is the case, then the practice of Brethren repeating continuously their born again experiences seems to demonstrate the fact that it was not an event but a process. Brethren were encouraged to walk daily with God in prayer and Bible study. While this was important for continuous spiritual discernment, some Brethren got puffed up with their spiritual experiences so as to regard those outside their Christian worldview as not saved or Spirit-filled. Nsimbabi claimed to discern whether visiting missionaries had the real thing in their hearts (filling of the Spirit) through a shake of hands.[193] Thus, a "holier than thou" attitude started to manifest itself within the revivalists.

Nonetheless, Dr. Church and Nsimbabi championed the spirit of brokenness at the cross of Christ, which became a signature for the fullness of the Spirit among the Brethren. While these findings were a significant breakthrough for the East African revival, they became somewhat divisive as had already been manifested with Nsimbabi's obvious spiritual pride. In spite of

---

188. Naselli, 205.
189. Lindesay Guillebaud is Meg Guillebaud's aunt (Guillebaud, 2002:8)
190. Guillebaud, *Grain of Mustard Seed*, 50.
191. Guillebaud, *Rwanda: The Land God*, 56.
192. Church, *Quest for the Highest*, 79.
193. Church, 87.

this shortcoming, the *Balokole* had an unquestioning belief in the authority of the Scripture.

Authority of the Scripture

Rodgers argues that "Anglicans have sought to build their theology on the supreme authority of the Holy Scriptures, with Jesus as the fulfillment, central climax and right perspective on the meaning of the whole of the Scripture."[194] The revivalists could not agree more with Rodgers. The pillar of the Brethren's strength has been the Scripture. Dr. Church's observation puts this assertion into perspective. The Scofield Bible had been the main text with a series of Bible studies leading to the publication of *Every Man a Bible Student*.[195] Thus "Bibles were used untill they fell to pieces."[196] Dr. Church and Nismbabi diligently used the Scriptures leading to the duo claiming "the victorious life and filling of the Holy Spirit."[197] Certainly, revival teams used the Bible to teach related subjects each day, reminiscent of Keswick Conventions. The topics of "sin, repentance, new birth, separation from the things of the world, the victorious life and the Holy Spirit"[198] were scriptural themes. At Gahini, Bible teaching, with "a sword of the Holy Spirit" (Ephesians 6:17) was a daily business for hospital workers.[199] As the leading teachers had little or no theological education, devotional reading of the Bible was bound to become the norm.

Dr. Church, a British medical doctor in Ruanda, had a meticulous leadership role in the early East Africa revival. But there is no evidence he attended a theological college except of course being a member of CICCU through which he came into contact with Keswick theology. A book popular in the CICCU at that time, *How to Live the Victorious Life*, had a profound influence on his religious convictions.[200] This book, argues Makower, represented the Keswick theology of the post-conversion experience – a second blessing, or

---

194. Rodgers, *Essential Truths for Christians*, 1.
195. Church, *Quest for the Highest*, 61, 62.
196. Church, 114.
197. Guillebaud, *Rwanda: The Land God*, 56.
198. Guillebaud, 67.
199. Church, *Quest for the Highest*, 78, 87.
200. Makower, *Coming of the Rain*, 27.

"Spirit-filling,"[201] and a strong desire for the higher Christian life.[202] According to MacMaster and Jacobs, Nismbabi had only a medical background, in Uganda's civil service.[203]

With this shallow theological context, proper biblical interpretation was a challenge. This could have been one of the causes of misunderstandings and splits over the years. The most profound division within the revival has been that of the Reawakened (Abazukufu) as a result of reading Ephesians 5:14, "Awake, O sleeper, and rise from the dead, and Christ will shine upon you." Those who continuously confess their sins after conversion were said to be dead, because they had not experienced the power of the Spirit to overcome sin. The ordinary *Balokole* were considered dead (*abafu*). For Nsimbabi this was a key text, but in 1972 he turned against the *Bazukufu*, and this formalized the split between the Reawakened and the ordinary *Balokole*. Nowadays in Uganda, these antagonisms are not so hotly debated, and both groups flourish to some extent.[204] In Kenya, the *Abazukufu* are known as *Kufufuka* (Awakened/Arise) and the *Abafu* (Kusimama/Stand). However, their differences are felt more during large meetings or conventions which each faction holds on its own. For example, the convention for the *Abafu*, "the 8th Kabale Revival Convention" took place at Kabale, Uganda from 20 to 23 August 2015. The *Abazukufu* held "the East African Reawakened Revival" in Uganda Sebei College, Tegers from 10 to 13 December 2015.

Reed notes the defect of Keswick teaching as lacking a clear theological viewpoint. This has been blamed for the weak theological standing of evangelicalism in the British Anglican Church in the early 20th century.[205] However, it would be unfair to develop a view that devotional reading of the Bible is wrong in itself. In fact, it would be an added advantage for a biblical scholar to also uses Scripture devotionally and prayerfully. Indeed, the church today

---

201. Makower, 27.
202. Church, *John Edward (1899–1989)*.
203. MacMaster, *Gentle Wind of God*, 28, 29.
204. Interview with Rev. Dr. Kevin Ward via email on 6 June 2016.
205. Reed, *Walking in the Light*, 58.

has been forthright in encouraging informed Bible preaching and teaching as exemplified in the GAFCON Nairobi communiqué[206] mission statement.[207]

The previous six themes construed from the historical survey or overview of scholarly literature and documents bring to the fore the intricate genesis and spread of EARM to Kenya since 1935. These themes could be claimed to have been substantively impacted by the Keswick theology of sanctification, albeit with an African face. The inferred achieving of experiential sanctification has been argued to have led to the socio-ethical practice of walking in the light. The following section concludes the perceived relationship between these themes and the practice of walking in the light.

Consolidation of Themes from the Viewpoint of Walking in the Light (1 John 1:7)

Walking in the light is a central theme in this study. Giving it a section here is not meant for discussion because that has already been done in chapter 2. The aim is to glean and consolidate themes drawn from the influence of Keswick theology on EARM, which have contributed to the prevailing situation in the Anglican Church of Kenya. These themes are namely the baptism of the Spirit, being born again, the cross of Christ, public confession of sins, the filling of the Spirit, and authority of the Scripture seem to define the socio-ethical concept of walking in the light. However, themes like the baptism and filling of the Spirit are no longer emphasized except in the Pentecostal churches and charismatic groups within the mainstream churches. This to some extent has weakened the Brethren's identity in Kenya. These themes will certainly form the basis for discussion in the subsequent chapters, but first the findings from the field research will be considered.

---

206. https://www.gafcon.org/news/nairobi-communique-and-commitment

207. The mission of GAFCON is to guard and proclaim the unchanging, transforming gospel through biblically faithful preaching, teaching, and program which free our churches to make disciples by clear and certain witness to Jesus Christ in the entire world.

Nature and Current Trends Regarding Anglican Church Scholarship on Keswick Theology's Influence on EARM's Walking in the Light: Findings and Analyses of the Prevailing Situation

Data Construction

This section provides summaries of the responses to research questions as they were put to the respondents. Some answers were recorded verbatim while others due to length were diligently summarized to reflect the actual text, mostly in the third person. This was done across the categories of respondents for each of the interview questions. The answer to each research question was collated in terms of comment or a note at the end of each category. This was done in all the subsequent categories. These fuller responses can be found in Appendix @@. Finally, these notations were put together to glean the most recurrent elements, which became the themes or findings of this research.

Merriam calls this process of making appropriate notations of bits of data that looks potentially useful in answering the research questions as coding.[208] This process is different from coding as a way of de-identifying sources of data, which also accompanied this analysis. Thus the interview centers and identifying personal information have been de-identified.

Describe the Way You Give a Testimony

This question was answered by only the ordinary members and the leaders of the EARM because of their unique way of giving testimony which is not common among theologians.

The majority of ordinary members across the four dioceses give their testimony in a threefold way. First, they disclose their full identity, where and when they met with the Lord, what led to their conviction; second, they repent and confess their past sins, then restitution and forgiveness of sins. Third their journey of salvation with Jesus, walk in light or with God. A few mentioned a fourth aspect, which is future hope.

The majority of the leaders of EARM begin their testimony by declaring their full identity. Then the context of an encounter with the Lord (what led to a conviction [lesson from the Bible], what one was saved from), confession and restitution. This was followed by stating your sojourn or walk with the

---

208. Merriam, *Qualitative Research*, 178.

Lord. The ordinary members and leaders of EARM started their testimony by saying *Tukutenderezza*.

Have You Ever Heard of Keswick Teachings? If Yes, in What Way Have They Influenced the Prevailing Socio-ethical life in EARM? If No, What Influenced Beliefs and Practices Apparent in the EARM?

As far as ordinary members are concerned members in three centers across the four dioceses have heard but none in Kirinyaga. Leaders of EARM in four centers across the four dioceses have heard, but none in the Mount Kenya West. Theological students in the areas have not heard of them, while clergy in at least once centre in every diocese has heard, and one bishop has heard, while prominent stakeholders have all heard.

The second part of the question concerned affirmative responses and was answered across the categories as follows: Out of the four dioceses, the Kirinyaga ordinary leaders had no knowledge of Keswick's influence on EARM. Others reported some awareness of its impact. Its influence on Christian identity, Bible decrees and salvation procedure was noteworthy. Amongst leaders there was some knowledge of Keswick teachings in Mount Kenya Central, Kirinyaga and Embu, but not in Mount Kenya West. A mention of the Higher Life Movement, biblical beliefs, renewal and convention show some significant elements of Keswick influence. Theological students did not show awareness of Keswick theology. Clergy showed indications of influence exemplified by the use of such terms as sanctification, piety, setting apart, renewal, and deeper experiences of salvation, legalism and the way of saying testimonies. Bishops were not aware of influence.

The stakeholders were aware of the influence exemplified by activities of the pioneer missionaries and first converts who entrenched legalistic evangelical theology and hypocritical spirituality. They noted an emphasis on daily devotion and accountability and a moral life with strict sexual morality and personal holiness. They stressed the importance of Bible study, Spirit revival, conversion theology of being saved and infilling of the Holy Spirit and daily sanctification, close to salvation by works.

The final responses to Question 2 dealt with alternative sources of influence of the socio-ethical practices of walking in the light apart from Keswick theology. This question was put to the participants in their categories and was mostly answered by those who had not heard about Keswick movement.

Amongst ordinary members influences came through Rwanda and other spiritualities. Stress on Bible reading, mentorship, hearing confession about Christ and forgiveness and humility. Also, the emphasis on love for one another, terms like legalism and setting apart, fellowships and conventions.

Amongst leaders of EARM Embu and Kirinyaga seem to have received indirect influences of Keswick theology and possibly from other spiritualities. The main components of responses from the perspectives of other purported forces apart from Keswick theology were as follows: the teachings of Rwanda and from the previous revival leaders, fellowships (convention) and Bible reading and instruction. The cross of Christ, confession of sin, love for one another, strict norms of dressing and conduct.

Theological students said that the socio-ethical life was influenced by the literal interpretation of Scripture. Amongst clergy those in Mount Kenya Central seem unaware of any other alternative influences to the current socio-ethical life except Keswick theology. Other dioceses were aware of alternative influences like Scripture reading and teaching (conservative), sharing testimonies, separate life from society, strong faith, walking in the light and love for and fellowship with each other. Bishops commented that interpretation of Scripture and challenges of modernity could inform church growth influenced by the revival.

For prominent stakeholders other alternatives influenced people with little or no theological knowledge. They noted the impact of Victorian ideals, born-again culture, other forms of evangelical Christianity and the strict moral discipline (legalistic theology) of walking in the light, repentance, and forgiveness.

Describe Walking in the Light, Showing How It Could Have Brought Division in the Revival?

Ordinary members noted openness – that is no hypocrisy and a daily walk with the Lord. But the open confession of sin and hypocrisy brought division. The majority of leaders in the EARM saw "walk in the light" as a daily walk with the Lord, a daily testimony, public confession and openness to God and humanity or sharing your personal life. The division came when one failed to share a testimony with other people. Thus, hypocritical holiness and exposure of one's secrets brought splits. That is, those who were perceived as not walking in the light were forsaken.

Theological students noted public confession of sin, Bible teaching, and stress on sanctification. Strict dress code and damaging testimonies were obvious influences. Clergy noted that the EARM teaches confession of sins, restitution, daily Bible study, sanctification and renewal, Christian discipleship, deeper salvation experience, walking righteously with God, Jesus as Lord and Savior, purity, brotherly love, prayer life and about fellowship with one another. It influences legalism; dress code, corrupted theology and is judgmental, leading to a church within the church or categorizing Christians, hypocrisy, and shedding of deep lights.

Bishops commented that walking in the light teaches the centrality of Scripture, repentance, forgiveness and restitution, open-hearted ethical life, being right with God and other people. It influences renewal and the new man, family life, moral code and openness in Christian life and leadership. Prominent stakeholders noted the significance of confession of sinful life, born again, holiness, moral rectitude, genuine conversion, walking in the light, the blood of Jesus, restitution, Bible study, prayer and firm testimony. Many were influenced including clergy, though some are hypocritical. Walking in the light teaches a strong disincentive to sin and repentance within the economy of grace.

What's the Dominant Text(s) Used by Members That Could Have Led to the Split

Ordinary members did not identify any dominant biblical text. Amongst the leaders of EARM there were some texts recurring: Daniel 1: 8ff; Genesis 12:1ff; Ephesians 5:14; 1 Corinthians 11:15–16; Romans 10:9; and 2 Corinthians 6:14–18 were also mentioned by the ordinary members. Theological students identified Genesis 12:1–3; Ephesians 5:14; and Daniel 1:12. Clergy identified 1 Corinthians 11:14; 2 Corinthians 6:14–18; Ephesians 5:14; Daniel 1:8ff. Bishops did not identify particular texts except for one suggesting Ephesians 5:14 and Daniel 1:12. Amongst prominent stakeholders the most recurring texts were Daniel 1:8ff, 2 Corinthians 6:17; 2 Corinthians 6:14; Ephesians 5:14.

Briefly Describe the History of the Split in EARM, Showing How It Has Affected the Mission of the Church

Ordinary members of EARM noted that division began in 1956; later *Nthama* in Nairobi became *Kuhama,* then became *Kusimama* (Eph 6:14–20) and 1967

Re-awakening (Eph 5:14) which was led by William Nagenda. Another faction was *Kupaa*. There were other internal splits of "lights" in 1969. Others claimed the 1970s and 1980s. But most of them noted the 1967 date. Leadership and legalistic codes of conduct, and devastating testimonies were also blamed for the split. This caused disharmony in the mission field which affected church growth.

Leaders of EARM noted the Uganda Convention, and Psalm 127:1ff encouraged people to rely on God's protection, not on dogs. Also, interpretation of Ephesians 5:14 led to reawakening. Some note that the fellowship was one before 1967. Some think in Kenya split began in Nairobi; there is mention of *Nthama* 1956 and another meeting in Nairobi that confirmed the split. Ephesians 6:14–20 was applied by *Kusimama* group to stand against Kufufuka group. 1969 oath-taking also led to divisions. Some left for Pentecostal churches due to the interpretation of 1 Corinthians 11:14–16 that oppressed the youth. In 1990s lots of youth left Anglican for Pentecostal churches. Genesis 12:1ff led to some parents abandoning their unwedded pregnant daughters. This has affected the mission of the church due to mistrust within the church, separation, inequality, excommunication and a poorly-biblically founded mission.

Theological students were generally not aware, while most clergy respondents avoided the history part of the question but were comfortable with effects. For example, they noted liberalism as women became clergy, declining morals as the youth left the fellowship, church hierarchy conflicts with fellowship, poor biblical teaching and theological differences, open confession of sins and hypocritical holiness. Some observe a declining evangelism and apathy.

Bishops were not quite aware of the earlier splits but impacts were construction of a new church, effects on conventions and a drop in spirituality.

Prominent stakeholders spoke of how splits in the revival began in 1937; *Joremo* vs. *Johera*. Some mention 1967; the *Abafu* (dead) and *Bazukufu* (reawakened). Brethren attacked clergy saying they were not saved. The youth were joining Pentecostal churches. This compromised witness though the majority of Anglican bishops claimed to be part of the revival, some accepting to criminalize LGBTI.

What Change Would You Recommend for the Current Socio-ethical Life?

Ordinary members' recommended: embrace a changed social life (modesty), return to old Brethren lifestyle, and good mentors for youth and clergy, church to use Brethren, proper use of the Bible and practice constructive testimonies. Leaders of EARM emphasized moderate dress code, encouraged fellowship to join social groups, good mentorship for youth, clergy to include Brethren in the Sunday Church program, proper use of the Bible and embracing healthy cultural norms and activities.

Theological students said that the Bible should be used correctly and wanted fellowship to be inclusive. Clergy recommended that to balance between nominalism and holier-than-thou hypocrisy, there should be dynamism in worship, a recognition of Brethren in church, proper exegesis of the Bible, embrace change, a workshop on spirituality, allow interaction of young people of both sexes and unity as per Ephesians 4, oneness of God. Bishops encouraged the church to address sin; allow change, repentance, and transparency. Others felt the church should embrace EARM (heritage) moral conduct.

Prominent stakeholders emphasized revival heritage, new forms of spirituality, encouraged flexibility and tolerance, value sexual minorities, holistic discipleship, re-reading the Bible from the perspectives of scientific discoveries, visionary leaders, socio-ethics led by life and ministry of Jesus. They noted there is no pure Anglican Church in Kenya. Indeed the Anglican Church mode of confession and testimony is EARM and Pentecostalism with some elements of African culture.

Is There Anything You Would Wish to Share Which Has Not Been Covered Above?

Ordinary members' noted that Brethren encouraged clergy and students to join the fellowship and that the Brethren should be recognized in the church (allow a revival week). However, Brethren were challenged to join social-economic groups while proper ministerial formation of clergy was encouraged. Brethren never recognize church leaders but Christ. They have stereotypical fellowship liturgy. They need to emphasize constructive testimony. Indeed some Brethren have relaxed moral codes. But fellowship has no denominational boundary and is not a movement and accepts marriage renewal. They have no membership list. They encourage preaching themes to trickle down from convention level.

Leaders of EARM noted that they emphasize a gender-separated sitting arrangement, a monthly guiding text, harmony between EARM and the Anglican Church. EARM is the backbone of the Anglican Church, and the Brethren contributes *Gicunji kia Mwathani* (portion of God's money [convention money]). EARM is not a faction and should welcome clergy and youth. The concept of sin should be taught at St. Andrew's College Kabare.

Theological students thought that the Brethren should accept change, acceptance of others and accountability. Clergy thought that Brethren should allow integrated fellowship and dynamic worship, and emphasis on proper communication (Isaiah 1:18). EARM is a fellowship (not a movement) across denominations. Clergy should incorporate Brethren in the preaching program. Brethren should include youth in EARM's leadership. Church leadership should end these divisions. Brethren assists eligible members in getting a marriage partner. They emphasize cleanliness and sound theology. Bishops thought that Brethren should be tolerant with other people (oneness in Christ). Clergy should appreciate Brethren and avoid having a beard. The church should refine Brethren's ways of conducting marriages, understand youth, address ethical issues and improve interpretation of Scripture.

Prominent stakeholders noted that revival reshaped post-colonial Kenya; compare thought and practice of the old *Balokole* and modern charismatic movements and Pentecostalism. This knowledge should strengthen the church and its witness. The church leadership and scholars should influence and be influenced by the revival.

The notations that accrued from the recurrent responses across the categories were compared to get the most consistent bits or units of data from which the following themes were sorted. On the construction and analysis of these themes hinge the remaining section of this chapter, which begins with demographical information about the respondents.

Demographic Data: Distribution of Respondents According to Their Categories

Table 2 below summarizes the demographical representation of the respondents involved in the field study in the four selected Anglican dioceses of Mount Kenya Region. The representation includes some of the current theological students at St. Andrew's College of Theology and the prominent stakeholders within and outside the region. The information was gathered on various dates from April through July 2016.

Table 2: Demographic

Respondents by categories	Frequency	Percentage
Ordinary members	228	75
Leaders of revival	29	10
Theological students	15	5
Clergy	21	7
Bishops	3	1
Prominent stakeholders	6	2
Total respondents	302	100

Table 2 shows that the biggest number of the participants was drawn from the ordinary members (75 percent) of EARM followed by the leaders (10 percent). Although categorized, the leaders are strongly intertwined and bonded with the ordinary members. The fact that these two categories comprise 85 percent of the total respondents elucidates the level at which this movement optimally operates.

Table 3 below shows the variant number of respondents in the four dioceses. On the higher side of the continuum, Kirinyaga Diocese scored 29 percent, followed by Embu and Mount Kenya Central at 27 percent and on the lower side, Mount Kenya West with 16 percent. This table suggests that while EARM in Kirinyaga, Embu and Mount Kenya Central dioceses is relatively thriving, in the Mount Kenya West, it appears to be nearer the end of its natural life.

Table 3: Data by Categories

Categories	Kirinyaga	Embu	Mt Kenya Central	Mt Kenya West	Total
Ordinary members	67	59	65	37	228
Leaders	9	10	7	3	29
Clergy	6	6	4	5	21
Bishops		1	1	1	3
Total	82	76	77	46	281
Percentages	29	27	27	16	100 approx.

The four categories in the above table plus theological students and prominent stakeholders make a total of six categories which will be used to construct themes which will guide this study.

Constructing Themes

As suggested by the word "construct," the qualitative research method of collecting data amassed detailed information that called for a particular analysis procedure. The process started with reading interview transcripts and field notes, as per the interview questions across the categories. The respondents' views and perspectives were recorded with precise detailed accounts. These accounts were shifted and reduced into their most significant key elements referred by Merriam as analytical coding,[209] which groups segments of accounts or comments and notes which appear to go together.

Merriam argues this coding technique extends beyond a description of data to interpretation and reflection on meaning.[210] This was done in a twofold way: First, the researcher rigorously sifted the details within the categories to establish the most consistent patterns or themes, which could have influenced Keswick theology on the EARM's beliefs and practice of walking in the light. Second, the emerging key patterns or themes were systematically analyzed to reduce them into six themes and sub-themes that the researcher used to write the findings. These are Brethren's born again testimony, acquaintance with EARM's precursor, the daily sanctification of the new man, Scripture

---

209. Merriam, *Qualitative Research*, 179.
210. Merriam, 180.

and moral codes, splits and mission of the Anglican Church of Kenya and synergized-diversified Anglican Church of Kenya.

Brethren's Born-again Testimony

The aspect of being born again among the Brethren could not be authenticated by the members unless accompanied by a sequential testimony. Indeed, the question "describe the way you give a testimony" generated a lot of enthusiasm in all four dioceses. Mainly the ordinary members and the leaders of the movement were asked this question. The reasons were twofold. First, just like the pioneer revivalists Dr. Joe Church and Simeon Nsimambi, they were not theologians. Certainly, the majority were uneducated. Thus they faithfully carried on the teachings of how to say a testimony as it had been passed to them by the former revivalists' leaders. Second, they shared an overwhelming and unique characteristic of asking for or giving testimony, which most often has not been familiar to the theologians.

The majority of the ordinary members gave their testimony in a threefold way, with a near uniformity across the four dioceses.

Full disclosure of identity

Brethren start their testimony by disclosing their full identity, saying where they came from, when they met the Lord and what led to their conviction. For instance, a leader of EARM in Embu said "Christ saved me on April 29, 1967, at 3.00 A.M when drunk with alcohol ... the specific sins that the Lord convicted me of I confessed and asked for his forgiveness ..." An ordinary member of Mount Kenya West said, "I was born again on July 26, 1981. I don't forget that day. *Uria utakanyumbura guku ndikamumbura iguru,*" which literally means "But whoever disowns me before men, I will disown him before my Father in heaven" (Matt 10:33). In this way, they seemed to identify with both God and humanity from the viewpoint of their heavenly and earthly relationships. They, therefore, appeared to claim the heritage of both realms; their identity is known and cannot be confused with any other. But a minority did not give a clear identity. A leader in Embu talked of overcoming with the word of testimony, defeating the devil and salvation from sin. This inconsistency could have been caused by the advanced age since the respondent was eighty-three years old but still a recognized leader of the movement. It is no wonder the generation gap has continued to challenge the growth of the EARM.

Confession, restitution and forgiveness of sins

As indicated above, Brethren repent and confess their past sins one by one followed by restitution and forgiveness. A group of ordinary members in Mount Kenya West said they repent and confess in details all the sins they had previously committed. Where it was necessary to repay back what was stolen, they did so. Those who had avoided paying taxes went to the revenue authority to report themselves. If one had committed adultery he would go back to repent and *guthondeka* (make amends). In other words, to receive forgiveness, they brought to the light their past dark practices. Thus, restitution became a precursor for forgiveness.

Although done with good intention, some public testimonies had led to fallout within the Brethren, particularly when incriminating confessions leaked out to non-Brethren. That is notwithstanding an admission of adultery could break marriages whether or not the culprits were in the fellowship. A woman lay leader in one of the dioceses suffered a lifelong blow when it emerged from a Brethren confession that she had had an extra marital relationship.

In spite of its negative side, a leader of EARM from Mount Kenya Central said public disclosure helps the believers to open up to each other, as they testify how the Lord has enabled them to overcome challenges in life.

Journey with the Lord Jesus

An ordinary member of EARM in Kirinyaga said that Brethren end their testimony by stating their sojourn with the Lord, affirming their growth in Christ every hour. Similarly, a leader from Mount Kenya West said, "You tell how the Lord is good, how he has sustained you, what he has done for you and how you have a daily walk with God." Another leader from Kirinyaga said, "I briefly narrate what my Lord Jesus Christ has done for me so far. However, the way [of saying testimony] may vary with situations." These responses seem to give a hint that informs the phrase "walking in the light." Phrases like "every hour," "how he has sustained you" and "what my Lord Jesus Christ has done for me so far," suggest an ongoing process.

Acquaintances with EARM's Precursor

In order to put this theme in its proper perspective, it is vital to study the following statistics concerning respondents' grip of Keswick theology. This will enable the reader to apprehend most of the respondents' level of understanding of Keswick theology of sanctification and appreciate its influence in their daily life.

As the following figures indicate, the majority of the respondents had not heard about Keswick theology. Ordinary leaders: approx. 81.6 percent; Leaders: approx. 86 percent; Theological students: 100 percent; Clergy: approx. 66.6 percent; Bishops: Approx. 66.6 percent and the Stakeholders: 0 percent.

This shows that 80 percent (242) of the 302 respondents have never heard of Keswick theology. Table 4 below explicates this phenomenon per category.

Table 4: Respondents Never Heard of Keswick Theology

Respondents	Kirinyaga	Embu	Mt. Kenya Central	Mt. Kenya West	Total frequency	Percentage
Ordinary members	67/67	47/59	50/65	22/37	186/228	81.6%
Leaders	8/9	9/10	5/7	3/3	25/29	86%
Theological students					15/15	100%
Clergy	4/6	4/6	2/4	4/5	14/21	66.6%
Bishops	-	1/1	1/1	0/1	2/3	66.6%
Prominent stakeholders					0/6	0%
Total	79/82	61/76	58/77	29/46	242/302	80%
Percentages per diocese	96%	80%	75%	63%		
Percentages for the four select dioceses	227/281 = 80.7%					

Table 4 shows theological students were the most ignorant of the existence of Keswick theology. This might be due to two reasons. First, most of them were young (in their twenties) and could be classified as non-active members of the EARM. Though this study was not looking at the age of its members, it was quite clear from the responses that Brethren were mostly older adults. Second, it suggests that studies of the antecedents of "Keswick theology" have not been emphasized in the church history syllabus at St. Andrew's College where these students undertake their studies. This trend of ignorance has been replicated by the clergy and the bishops most of whom received their theological education at St. Andrew's College.

The ordinary members and the leader's score over 80 percent in terms of ignorance despite the fact that there has been a consensus that they are "the Brethren." This is by being the majority adherents of the movement. The ignorance could be attributed on the one hand to the historical distance between the Keswick movement and the current crop of Brethren. Indeed, although the Brethren show keenness in mentioning the years they got saved, only one leader from Embu could recall a 1969 Keswick meeting. On the other hand, African church historians might not have done serious studies that could have connected Keswick theology with EARM. Perhaps if that had been done, a document could have been made available in a readable form for use by the ordinary members who are mostly uneducated.

By virtue of their academic pursuit and their revival backgrounds, all the prominent stakeholders have heard about Keswick theology and its influence on the EARM's beliefs and practices of walking in the light. Thus, concerning the 20 percent of those who have heard, the prominent stakeholders have a clean sheet of 100 percent knowledge of Keswick theology. Indeed out of the four dioceses, no one among the Kirinyaga ordinary members had any knowledge of Keswick influence on EARM. Likewise, no one among the Mount Kenya West leaders had any knowledge. As earlier mentioned, it is only one leader in Embu that had specific knowledge. Indeed his mention of the Higher Life Movement was the clearest expression of the knowledge of Keswick theology among the categories except for the prominent stakeholders. Clergy too had some grip on this teaching. In Mount Kenya Central one respondent among the clergy said that sanctification is a great doctrine that holds EARM together while another one said it has molded EARM's piety and set it apart from other Christians. But two clergy in Mount Kenya West confused it with the name of a Keswick Bookshop in Nairobi. This fact suggests the degree of ignorance by the clergy, let alone the ordinary Brethren. As seen in the second part of the following theme, the majority of the respondents except the prominent stakeholders attributed other factors besides Keswick to have influenced EARM.

Daily Sanctification of the New Man

The idea of experiential sanctification has been the bedrock of Keswick theology and somewhat flickers in the EARM's everyday life. This has been addressed under two subthemes: Keswick and non-Keswick antecedents.

Daily sanctification as a Keswick antecedent

This theme brings to the fore respondents who have at least some knowledge of Keswick theology. Affirming the influence of Keswick teachings in the EARM, some Embu clergy described Keswick theology as a wave of revival and renewal over East Africa, explicated by profound salvation experiences similar to the prevailing situation in Kenya. Likewise, some stakeholders not only positioned it within the wider holiness movement but also emphasized conversion and personal faith exemplified by the infilling of the Holy Spirit, and the purity of heart and body. Other stakeholders responded that Keswick teachings entrenched spirituality that became legalistic and prompted daily devotions and a profound sense of accountability. They also associated it with the strict pietistic theology of being saved and daily sanctification. Another stakeholder said it promoted a belief close to salvation by works other than by grace and faith in the resurrected Christ. All Bishops were unaware except one who could not recall its influence on EARM. This implies that unless some structures are put in place to salvage EARM, it could be approaching the end of its natural life in the Anglican Church of Kenya.

Daily sanctification as a non-Keswick antecedent

While the majority of the respondents cited other factors as the source of influence, there were some who supported both views of influence, i.e., the Keswick and the non-Keswick antecedents. This fact had been cited in the historical survey earlier in this chapter by scholars like Ward who described "its roots in classical Evangelical revivalism and the Keswick movement of the late nineteenth century."[211]

This phenomenon characterizes the data findings of the prevailing situation in the Anglican Church of Kenya. In Kirinyaga an ordinary member of EARM said this spiritual influence came through church conventions, the study of the word of God and the confession of Christ. Indeed, conventions provide a platform for the spiritual nurture of born-again Christians. A clergy member from Mount Kenya West added that conventions were based on one major theme of walking in the light within the districts of its jurisdiction.

This nurture conforms them to a daily lifestyle. A leader in Kirinyaga adds that Brethren hate sin, love God and look for help at the cross. These

---

211. Ward, *History of Global Anglicanism*, 175.

teachings have become basic to the Brethren and undoubtedly influence their daily walk with the Lord. An ordinary member from Mount Kenya West said most of them lack knowledge of the meaning of the EARM and that led to set themselves apart from others to strictly follow Jesus' teachings. This respondent appears to point out that their experiential holiness influences their distinct daily life.

A clergy member in Mount Kenya West said the influence comes from a personal encounter with the Lord Jesus and a firm faith that resist sin. Others in Kirinyaga locate the influence to conservative teaching. For instance, one of them said, "elders of my church including my grandfather could camp at home for *Kesha* (an overnight meeting) and fellowships, preaching, sharing testimonies and encouraging one another. I was much attracted to this." This acknowledgment seems to put the alternative source of influence in its right perspective. However, clergy from Mount Kenya Central has no knowledge of any alternative apart from Keswick. This might indicate that they were quite conversant with the history of EARM on the one hand and the other, they appeared insincere of the effects of the other spiritualities.

Some stakeholders said it was influenced by Pentecostalism and the born-again culture with the strict religious position. Other stakeholders attribute the influence to Victorian ideals that advocate for sexual restraint, low tolerance of crime and a strict moral code. Still others saw a lack of theological knowledge as a prelude to the belief and practice of walking in the light. This view was also expressed by a bishop and theological students who saw it as a consequence of literal interpretation of Scripture.

Scripture and Moral Codes

To elucidate scripture and moral codes it is vital to look at scriptural verses that inform splits and also interpenetration of scripture and ensuing moral life.

Scriptural verses that inform splits

The majority of respondents used various biblical texts to describe the history of the divisions. The most mentioned texts were Ephesians 5:14 and Daniel 1:8ff at sixteen and fourteen times respectively. Others were 2 Corinthians 6:14–18 at six, 1 Corinthians 11:14–16 at six, Genesis 12:1 at five, Ephesians 6:14–20 at five, Romans 13:8 at four and Psalm 127:1 twice. These texts seemed to contribute most significantly to the development of a unique

Brethren lifestyle. Texts that scored a frequency of less than two were not tabulated in Table 5 below.

Interpretation of Scripture and ensuing moral life

Table 5 below shows the frequency and percentages of the key passages of Scripture and their purported meaning that could have inspired splits in the EARM. Out of the eight most popular texts, Ephesians 5:14, was at the top end of the continuum while Psalms 127:1 was at the lower end. The disparity in frequency could be interpreted to mean their impact on EARM's socio-ethical life was various. That is, interpretation of these texts could have informed subsequent divergent beliefs and practices of walking in the light. However, none of the texts garnered 50 percent of popularity which implied their influence could have been local and sporadic. It could also have meant that other factors apart from the interpretation of biblical texts could have influenced the splits. Table 5 shows how some biblical texts were interpreted and applied to impact various distinct socio-ethical lives.

Table 5: Interpretation of Biblical Texts by Brethren

Bible text	Verse	Teaching	Freq.	%
Ephesians 5:14	Wake up, O sleeper, rise from the dead	Leave the dead (the EARM)	16	28%
Daniel 1:8–16	Do not defile yourself	Avoid affluent life style	14	24%
1 Corinthians 11:13–15	Issues of hair (v.15)	Sensual life	6	10%
2 Corinthians 6:14–18	Come out from them	Don't fellowship with sinners	6	10%
Ephesians 6:13–20	Stand firm (v. 13)	Remain steadfast in EARM	5	9%
Genesis 12:1	Leave your country	Leave your unsaved family	5	9%
Romans 13:8	No debts	Don't take loans	4	7%
Psalms 127:1ff	God's protection	Don't keep dogs	2	3%

1. Ephesians 5:14 "Wake up, O sleeper, and arise from the dead" (ESV)
As seen in the above table, most respondents who believe splits were brought by interpretation of Scripture mentioned the Ephesian text. Some ordinary members in Kirinyaga said the Ephesian passage led to Kufufuka (Arise) in 1967. The text was interpreted to mean they should leave the EARM. A leader in Mount Kenya Central said this text meant they had been raised from sins. They went on to say that Kufufuka members shared two testimonies. Firstly, they said when they were born again (saved) and secondly when they were raised or revived. This created two categories of Christians, the saved and the revived.

Some ordinary members from Embu said this split originated with William Nagenda, a leading lay evangelist from Baganda. In his sermons, Nagenda emphasized that resurrected Christians should avoid worldly involvement, particularly should refrain from taking bank loans. It required those who were saved to be saved again leading to the Awake (*Kwarahuka* or *kuriuka*) group. Similarly, a prominent stakeholder said this text is primary to the *Abazukufu* (Reawakened) which taught that those who continually confess sins after conversion were dead because they have no power of the Spirit to overcome sin. Therefore, the ordinary *Balokole* were considered *abafu* (dead). This led to a formal split in 1972.

2. Daniel 1:8, 12 "But Daniel resolved that he would not defile himself with the king's food, or with the wine . . . let us be given vegetables to eat and water to drink."
Some Kirinyaga leaders said the Daniel text was understood in 1969 to mean leaving EARM to form another group. Indeed, in 1987 some clergy from Mount Kenya West stated that this text was interpreted Mtama na Maji (sorghum and water) and led to a split from EARM in Kiambu. Another member of the clergy in Mount Kenya Central said this text laid foundation for Kupaa (rising up). The text was used by the Kupaa group to refuse good food from the king's table and instead be served only with vegetables and water. Some Mount Kenya Central leaders said the interpretation of the text made some Brethren shun social gatherings where sweets were served.

Another clergy member in Mount Kenya Central said the Kupaa became the people of the light in Murang'a and based their belief on 1 John 2:9–11, saying *ithui nituonete utheri* (ourselves, we have seen the light). It thus came to be called *Ngwataniro ya utheri* (fellowship of the light) based on Matthew 5:14. They accept greetings such as, "praise the Lord." They do not allow weddings of expectant girls or renewal of marriages. The third offshoot from Kupaa came to be called the Revival Fellowship which believes in walking in the light.

One of the leaders in Kirinyaga said this Kupaa group settled for a simple life. For example, their weddings have no wedding cake, and the bride wears a simple wedding dress. This is complemented by a leader from Embu who said the Kupaa group was against earthy influence (extravagance lifestyle).

3. 1 Corinthians 11:14–16 "If a man has long hair, it is a disgrace for him, but if a woman has long hair, it is her glory . . . her hair is given to her for a covering."

This text was interpreted by Kirinyaga leaders to mean that men should not keep beards and women should cover their heads. As a result members of EARM do not have beards and women either cover or shave their heads. This has become the norm whether inside the church or outside. A clergy member from Mount Kenya Central used 1 Corinthians 11: 5 to indicate that women should cover their heads while praying. Thus, a clergy member from Mount Kenya West termed issues of long hair and short hair as a dress code.

4. 2 Corinthians 6:14–17 "Do not be yoked together with unbelievers . . . Therefore come out from them and be separate, says the Lord." (NIV)

The second part of this text was quoted more frequently than the first part. This is perhaps due to its seemingly clear intent to separate the righteous from sinners. Thus some ordinary members in Kirinyaga and Mount Kenya Central responded favorably to this text. A prominent stakeholder also mentioned this text. Some Brethren have used it to hedge themselves from the rest of the Christian community, which is perceived to be living in sin. This has entrenched a holier-than-thou attitude. However the first part of the text, "Do not be yoked together with unbelievers" didn't attract as many respondents. Indeed, only a clergy member in Kirinyaga mentioned it. This shows the crux of the verse to have been the second part, maybe due to its forthright declaration of setting apart believers from unbelievers.

5. Ephesians 6:14–20, particularly verse 14 "stand firm."

The respondents were emphatic about verse 14, "stand firm." Mount Kenya Central and Embu leaders said that this text was used by the *Kusimama* "standing up" group to encourage Christians to withstand challenges. Indeed, *Kusimama* group has been noted for the utilization of the phrase *Yesu atosha* (Jesus satisfies). Some ordinary members in Embu said that *Kusimama* group was formed when some Brethren disagreed with *Kufufuka* campaign and saw nothing wrong with having bank loans to improve their welfare. This disagreement led to separate meetings that saw the *Nthama* (Embu word for Exodus) faction spring up in Nairobi in 1956. They regarded traditional nicknames to be sin and identified themselves with *the Kuhama* (Exodus or Lleave) group. Thus, the *Kufufuka* backlash led to *Kusimama* (Stand) and *Kuhama*. The connotation of *Kuhama* leans towards leaving, as to depart, in this case leaving *Kusimama* and *Kufufuka*. This brought to the fore a series of splits within the EARM.

6. Genesis 12:1 "Go from your country, your people and your father's household..."

The Kirinyaga leaders said some Brethren after reading this text sold everything they had and "physically" left their families to serve God in distant places. Theological students referred to this group as *Thama*, a Gikuyu word for leave or exodus. Although the origin of the term *Thama* is distinct from *Kuhama* mentioned above, the two complement each other in emphasis. Mount Kenya Central leaders said the interpretation of this text led some parents to desert their unwedded pregnant daughters and would not even attend their weddings. The same parent would attend the wedding of a daughter that married while not pregnant. This discrimination led to family feuds.

7. Psalms 127:1 "Unless the Lord watches over the city, the guards stand watch in vain."

Indeed Blasio Kigozi could have read this text when he slept soundly in a makeshift shelter well aware a leopard was lurking in the dark.[212] Thus some of the Kirinyaga leaders said this text was used in a Uganda convention, where it was emphasized that God was the protector and so there was no need of seeking any other form of security, for example keeping dogs. Likewise,

---

212. Guillebaud, *Rwanda, the Land God*, 57.

leaders in Embu said Brethren in Uganda refused to visit their colleague called *Matofu* because he kept dogs. The dogs came to be regarded as a sin, and some were killed.

8. Romans 13:8 "Let no debt remain outstanding..."
The Kirinyaga leaders said this text was viewed through the same lens that expressed intolerance of unwedded pregnant daughters and keeping dogs. Honestly one of the stakeholders commented in Kiswahili, *Tusiwe na deni* (we should not have debt). The text could have led to a split as some Brethren saw no problem with taking bank loans. This could be one of the reasons why the majority of Brethren have been economically poor. Indeed, in Embu, one of the leaders said that in the 1970s there were social and economic problems that challenged taking loans because of the inability to pay back. Another leader from Embu said members were asked to refrain from a bank loan.

Other causes of splits
As mentioned earlier, the majority of the respondents associated splits with other factors while the remaining ones had no idea. The other factors included leadership and open confession of sin.

1. Leadership
The majority of the respondents who said other factors contributed to the splits believed strong personality and leadership disaffection were the primary causes. One of the prominent stakeholders said some Brethren who were retired teachers imposed themselves too firmly leading to isolating other members.

Thus, most of the bishops said splits were occasioned by personal differences and social lifestyles. Indeed, one of them pointed at the dress code and shaving of hair as the essential elements that led to the emergence of *Utheri* (walking in the light) group.

One of the prominent stakeholders said Brethren's habit of attacking clergy as not saved weakened the Brethren's bargaining power in the church. For example, they dismissed one of the early church founders in Kirinyaga as not saved because he used tobacco. it is no wonder another prominent stakeholder observed the *Balokole* movement has always been at loggerheads with what they referred to as the "nominal" church.

Some clergy in Embu said EARM had been opposed to the Anglican Church hierarchy and had conflicted with bishops. Indeed one of the prominent stakeholders stated that Revivalists acknowledged their leader to be the Holy Spirit. Thus a lack of theological training had led to misunderstanding and the eventual split. Some Embu ordinary members expressed similar sentiments and added that a leadership dispute resulted in the beginning of some of the new denominations.

A prominent member of revival said one of the social, ethical issues that brought a split between Joremo (people of blood) and Johera (people of love) was the question of polygamy. Johera argued that polygamists were honest men and should be loved and accepted, but the true Anglicans who were strict or hypocritical did not want them near.

Apart from the church's hierarchy conflict, Embu leaders said there were divisions in the fellowship too. Some held their fellowship meetings in their homes while others were held in the church. Also, leaders in Embu said fighting for leadership positions had led to some members starting their own churches. Undoubtedly, splits could give rise to a new congregation as expressed by some Mount Kenya West leaders who said that some fellowship leaders were also members of the church leadership. This meant they had their followers in the church. So their divisions caused wrangles attributed to what some Mount Kenya Central leaders termed as unequal recognition of members.

2. *Open confession of sin*

Some Embu leaders said repenting and confession of sin could have led to dissension especially when someone was forced to repent sins the person doesn't even know. Again, before somebody was admitted as a member of EARM, one was required to promise before God and the assembled congregation (publicly) that one has left sin. This led to some leaving the movement due to the stigma that often accompanied confessions. Also, some leaders of Mount Kenya Central argued that Brethren sidelined anybody perceived not to walk in the light (not confessing sin). Some ordinary members of Mount Kenya Central attributed the division to not only the lack of openness but Brethren's doubt of other people's salvation. This brought enmity and mistrust within the Brethren and with other Christians. Thus, some Kirinyaga clergy said shedding of too much light, with open confession, brought division. This could be what some ordinary members in Kirinyaga termed as damaging testimony that led some Brethren to disagree with their vicar.

Some Embu ordinary members said division within the revival began in 1969 when two lights arose; one acknowledged open confession of sins and the other did not. After 1970 deep lights were discouraged because they brought mistrust among the members. Some of these lights or testimonies acted as codes of ethics that were used to address the dress code and hairstyle.

The administration of the 1969 oath also brought some division as was expressed by some of the Mount Kenya Central leaders. Those found culpable left the movement and some joined Pentecostal churches. The practice of open confession was termed hypocritical by some Kirinyaga clergy and some ordinary members of Mount Kenya central. Thus, some leaders in Mount Kenya Central added that Brethren did not appreciate a public address system (loud music) claiming praying loudly and speaking in tongues were sinful. This affected the youth, and some left the church.

Effects of Splits on the Mission of the Anglican Church in Kenya

As seen above, splits within the EARM led to some factions. Each group had its slogan, mostly drawn from a scriptural text. Most of these slogans resulted in the formulation of ethical rules of conduct befitting the catchphrases. For instance, Thama was applied literally by a Brethren in Kirinyaga who left his unsaved family to witness for Christ in Nairobi (a faraway country). So the question of the effect of the split on the mission of the church evoked varied reactions from the respondents which could be classified into several sub-themes.

Evangelism and witness

A prominent stakeholder said that evangelical revivalists have often been at the heart of church-sponsored mission activities and on a personal level evangelism. However, another stakeholder said EARM remained like an opposition party within a church assassinating one another while hiding under walking in the light. Still another one stated that splits compromised the real witness of the Brethren all over East Africa. Thus, some ordinary members in Mount Kenya Central said the fact that Brethren view themselves as holier-than-thou impedes the church mission. Others in the same diocese blamed the way Brethren say their testimony or share lights (walking in light), that exposed somebody's private life. This affects church witness and growth of the mission because many Christians see testimonies as an intrusion into their lives and an attempt to portray unequal standing with other Christians.

Some leaders in Embu said split did not only weaken EARM's unity and slowed its witness spirit but failed to witness to the church with each defending its theological stand. Others stated that in the 1960s there was a lapse in holiness and witnessing to the Spirit. This was due to strict moral codes like refraining from a bank loan and getting saved anew, which led to separate fellowship meetings. But ordinary members in Kirinyaga, said in the 1970s, splits impacted the mission of the church positively with smart dress codes and preaching from the Bible. Thus, some clergy in Mount Kenya West said competing interests of different groups affected the mission. Young people were most affected, and many left the fellowship leading to declining morals in the church.

A Pentecostal haven
Pentecostal influence in the Anglican Church in Kenya has resulted in outsiders confusing Brethren identity of being born again with that of the mushrooming Pentecostal churches. Some disgruntled Christians found their haven here. One of the prominent stakeholders stated that youth joined Pentecostal churches where they could fully exercise their gifts. Some of the Mount Kenya Central leaders said some people went to Pentecostal churches because of the strict moral code. They further said that in the 1990s youth left the church not just because of their hair, makeup, dress code, and use of public address system but because the Brethren did not tolerate Pentecostal worship in the Anglican Church. Thus Kirinyaga leaders said the split has led to new fellowships and new denominations, a fact shared by one of the bishops.

Again abandonment of unwedded pregnant daughters by their Brethren parents led to a further exodus of young people from the church. Kirinyaga ordinary leaders said young people declined to join the fellowships, citing lack of motivation. Some clergy from Mount Kenya Central said this brought a cloud of confusion and lack of synergy for the church's growth.

Disenfranchised church mission

Undoubtedly, splits led to a disenfranchised church mission due to lack of openness and doubt of others' salvation. Leaders in Mount Kenya West said EARM separates themselves from others (sinners), but Jesus came for such, not the righteous and this affected church mission. Thus some ordinary members from Mount Kenya Central said this brought enmity and mistrust among Brethren and with other Christians, particularly clergy, who were irked for being asked to get saved. One of the prominent stakeholders recently said that EARM saw itself as the legislators of the church with the majority of Anglican bishops claiming to be part of the revival. This could have been a big boost for the church mission if the declaration was not halfhearted, as to appear schizophrenic in faith as claimed by a prominent stakeholder.

Some of the Kirinyaga ordinary members saw no reciprocity between Brethren support for church activities and church support for Brethren activities. This deadlock has led to a lack of brokenness at the cross of Christ and affected the church mission. Some members of Mount Kenya Central said Brethren had been members of the church though governed by distinct rules of conduct. One of the bishops said this strained relationships and affected conventions, while another one noted the split led to church growth as a splinter group bought a plot and built a church.

Synergized-diversified Anglican Church in Kenya

Most respondents expressed the need for an all-inclusive and diversified church that allows reciprocating dynamics of different facets of church ministry and mission.

Leadership

About inclusion of Brethren in leadership, one of the prominent stakeholders said EARM was critical in reshaping post-colonial Kenya. Jomo Kenyatta, a friend of Bishop Obadiah Kariuki, used to say "forgive, they don't know what they do," a phrase which has been well propounded in the EARM. Indeed, in 1969 Bishop Kariuki, a member of EARM, confronted Kenyatta to stop humiliating church elders who were being stripped naked and forced to take the oath. Thus the bishop and the Brethren seemed to read from the same script. This shows mutual coexistence between the church leadership and the Brethren which enabled them to fight injustices.

Indeed, another bishop said the church should address ethical issues surrounding unmarried daughters who were not allowed to give birth at home. He also said Brethren should work towards the informed interpretation of the Scripture, appreciate and nurture youth to Christian maturity. Another bishop stated that Brethren should not behave like politicians by attacking other Christians. He said Bishop Mahiani had almost been chased away for associating with the *utheri* (light) splinter group. Thus it seems like bishops have been instrumental in the running of the Revival. On the one hand, some clergy in Kirinyaga said the retired Archbishop of the Anglican Church of Kenya, Dr. Eliud Wabukala, was a product of the revival movement. So, as expressed by the Embu clergy and Kirinyaga ordinary members, the Anglican Church should support EARM and include them in the church preaching programs. Kirinyaga ordinary members and Leaders respectively said that priests should provide mentorship for Brethren and youth and that Brethren should be members of church councils. On the other hand, Embu ordinary members felt that Brethren should also be good mentors for young people and clergy.

Thus, some Embu clergy said that bishops and clergy should end divisions in the church. This could be done, says some Mount Kenya Central clergy, by preaching and teaching the unity of purpose based on Ephesians 4 (one God, one Spirit, and one hope). Thus, some of the Mount Kenya Central clergy voiced a need for EARM and the Anglican Church to work together to fight the devil, not each other.

At the one end of the range, some Embu leaders said clergy and Brethren should have one fellowship Sunday every month. At the other end, the clergy was encouraged to walk in the light and to teach salvation. This aspect of inclusive fellowship was also advocated by the ordinary members in Kirinyaga, who said Brethren wished to have a revival week that would incorporate clergy, theological students, and youth. Thus, Mount Kenya West clergy and leaders said youth should not only be accommodated in the leadership of EARM but also given opportunities to preach in the fellowships.

A group of ordinary members in Mount Kenya Central was of the view that there should be changes in the revival leadership. This is in spite of the fact that Brethren claimed they have no leaders in fellowship because all are equal and Christ is the chief priest. In this diocese, the leaders of the movement said EARM does not have elective positions and no age limit. EARM leaders are referred to as burden bearers. During team meetings, they sit in a circle, united in Christ, maybe signifying they were among equals. But paradoxically they accept titled leaders of fellowship. However, a leader in Embu said a circular sitting arrangement in fellowship meetings is necessary because it appreciates positive values of African heritage. Although this could be an adaptation of the Gikuyu council of elders, the only difference was that Gikuyu had senior elders called chiefs.

A group of the Kirinyaga ordinary members said local church fellowships, regional fellowships and conventions should be encouraged. A member of Mount Kenya Central leaders said monetary contributions fondly called *Gicunji kia Mwathani* (the Lord's portion) in the local churches cater for team fellowships up to the East Africa level.

But they advised Brethren should not sacrifice their families to attend conventions referred to by a section of Embu ordinary members as stereotypical. That is, during these forums they follow a certain legalistic liturgy. A leader in Mount Kenya Central said they have conventions every April for senior Brethren and also for youth, and a mission every August. Another leader in this diocese said the fellowship has a guiding biblical text every month from District to local church level. Thus a group of ordinary members in Mount Kenya Central stated that EARM should be handled carefully. This is because it is the backbone of the Anglican Church in Kenya, it could become a church within a church.

Moral code dynamism
Issues of moral code had more to do with the dress code. A group of ordinary members from Embu said Brethren should accommodate fashion norms. They should not insist that women should dress according to St. Paul's instructions in 1 Timothy 2:9–15. The group argued that Paul's instructions were valuable for the principles they specify, rather than as specific instructions. They said the principle, in this case, is that one should not overdress in public. They argued that this law should apply to men as well.

So, the church and the fellowship should not make rules which appear burdensome for any sector of the congregation. They should avoid what looks like micromanaging some segments of the congregation like youth. One of the groups of ordinary members in Mount Kenya Central expressed a need for EARM to embrace change. Brethren should avoid legalistic rules that hinder young people from joining the fellowship. Thus, a leader in Embu and a group of Kirinyaga ordinary members said Brethren should relax the dress style, and the Embu leader adds that women should preach with or without a headscarf. Certainly, Mount Kenya West clergy was emphatic on ignoring some radical stands like prohibiting the plaiting of hair.

Group of ordinary members in Embu said those in authority consider it their right to shape the opinions of young people. The EARM should know the church needs the youth for its survival. The young people accused the fellowship of being too restrictive and exclusive. Some have left because they found the norms of conduct too tied to the interest of the older members. Indeed, some unmarried Brethren have complained of interference in their choice of marriage partners. They quoted Galatians 5:1 "it is for freedom that Christ has set us free. Stand firm then and do not let yourself be burdened again by a yoke of slavery." So no individual should burden another because of issues of faith. For example, Brethren should not challenge clergy to publicly confess sin if they were to be relevant as God's watchman.

Indeed, Kirinyaga ordinary members said a testimony should not be a measure of personal salvation; rather it should glorify God. They observed that Brethren should avoid rigid fellowship rules and instead rely on God's word. Thus, one of the Kirinyaga leaders said that the word of God should guide the converts, not socio-ethical rules.

A clergy member in Embu said people should dress decently and believers should walk as per their confession, while another from Mount Kenya West said everybody should be saved but confess sins to God alone. A group of ordinary members in Kirinyaga said there should be proper handling of the neophytes to avoid their leaving the fellowship. Thus, a cleric from Embu argued that Brethren should revisit public relations to deal with issues of dress code and morality. Indeed, a prominent stakeholder said the Anglican Church should encourage great flexibility and tolerance of different views. This respondent insisted that church leaders should learn from Anglicans in other parts of the world to value sexual minorities and to encourage the decriminalization of the old colonial sodomy laws.

However, some Kirinyaga ordinary members seemed retrogressive in their argument that people should observe gender rules of dressing and hairstyle. They said men behave like animals; girls should not go near them. They also said men should not wear earrings and necklaces. Women should either wear short hair or headscarf and should loathe decoration. Thus one of the Bishops said the church should emulate EARM's strict ethics like the shaving of the beard and at the same time bring people to church. Another bishop said the church should uphold EARM's heritage of addressing sin but allowing change. Thus, some Brethren wants the status quo. So, as a Kirinyaga clergyman argues there is a need to strike a balance between nominalism and a holier than thou attitude.

Worship (in the Spirit) dynamics
In order to accommodate everyone and especially youth, theological students expressed a need for dynamism in the fellowship. Thus theological students together with some Mount Kenya West clergy said there should be full participation of all ages in church departmental activities. Indeed, Embu ordinary members felt that hugging of the opposite sex particularly by the young people should be allowed.

Thus some Embu clergy and a leader in Mount Kenya West said to worship God in truth and the Spirit, there is a need to recognize the ministry of the Holy Spirit in the church. A section of Mount Kenya Central clergy added that Brethren should allow jumping, singing and dancing for the Lord because it is biblical, not evil. Furthermore, a clergy member from Embu said to bring harmony and growth of the church in the Spirit; Brethren should carefully handle the Scripture.

One of the prominent stakeholders argued that bishops should be transferrable to share their gifts with the whole Anglican Church of Kenya. The issue of transferring bishops has existed for decades but has never been implemented, perhaps due to fears of the unknown, but a significant agenda for the Anglican Church of Kenya. Another stakeholder argued that in spite of the fact that the mode of confession and testimony remains EARM; there is no pure Anglican Church in Kenya. This is because the church appears to have combined elements of African culture, Pentecostalism and EARM. Thus in the Kenyan ecclesiology, remains a rainbow spirituality, meaning that the church is losing its tradition.

However, another stakeholder said that Anglican tradition has always expressed concern for the whole life, in part because of its unique history as a church for the nation. He believes discipleship is holistic, committed to living as a Christ follower in ways that define the whole life. Another stakeholder expressed a need to look at the relationship between the older *Balokole* movement and modern charismatic Pentecostalism in the light of their thought and practice. This is because the earlier EARM was founded within the context of the overwhelming power of the Holy Spirit, which appears to anchor the proliferation of Pentecostal churches today. Thus a group of Embu ordinary members encouraged the fellowship members to revert to the former Brethren lifestyle. A leader in Embu inspired spiritual renaissance to address negative socio-ethical issues such as corruption in Kenya.

A prominent stakeholder adds that Anglican Church should value its revival heritage and encourage new forms of spirituality among young people, while teaching the importance of worship and practices of the Anglican Church. Thus a cleric in Mount Kenya Central requested EARM to be less conservative and accept the leadership of the Spirit of God.

Twenty-first century church academics

In order to improve the current socio-ethical life, the respondents' raised two pertinent issues.

1. Ministerial formation of clergy

A prominent stakeholder appeared ecstatic that African Anglican clergy were getting interested in their history. He said that this knowledge should strengthen the church and its witness to the nations of Africa and the wider world. Another encouraged clergy, bishops and ACK Academics like the researcher, to devote time for fellowship with East Africa Revival groups in their areas, to influence and be influenced by real spiritual and theological growth in the church and East Africa Revival Movement.

However, a group of ordinary members in Kirinyaga pointed out that ministerial formation for clergy has not been good. The other group urged lecturers to follow-up students during mission outreaches to correct and rebuke any unruly behavior. The students training for ministry should know it is a calling, not a job. Thus some leaders in Embu said theological colleges like St. Andrew's Kabare in Kenya should address sin in its ministerial formation of theological students. This should enable clergy to be good role models of salvation.

2. Reading the Bible in the twenty-first century

Some leaders in Mount Kenya Central expressed a need for Brethren to embrace the twenty-first-century cultural changes. A prominent stakeholder said there should be more re-reading of the Bible in the light of the scientific discoveries of today. The stakeholder said the life and ministry of Jesus should inspire a church leader's visionary and imaginative socio-ethical life. But some leaders in Embu cautioned that the Brethren should not use the New Testament as an instruction manual for norms and overly burdensome instructions. The Church should refocus on strengthening biblical knowledge and Christian witness to attract the younger generation.

Some Kirinyaga clergy voiced a need for special workshops for believers on spirituality. A leader in Embu said Brethren do not only need preaching lessons but also how to use lectionary readings in their sermon preparation. Furthermore, theological students argued that Brethren should learn proper exegesis and interpretation of the Bible. Certainly, as observed by a Kirinyaga cleric, this could be one way to entrench sound theology to revive the dying movement. Likewise, a clergy member in Mount Kenya Central said the church should exploit the principle of Isaiah 1:18. This would help to develop effective communication for an understanding of one another's sentimental values for Christian living and service.

Social-economic activities

Groups of ordinary members in Mount Kenya Central said Brethren should model biblical teachings on economic activities and embrace a changed social life. They were also asked to be sensitive to what they say at social gatherings to avoid fallout. Thus another group of ordinary members in Mount Kenya Central argued that formation of socio-economic groups to assist other people is not sinful. Helping the needy is biblical (1 John 3:17–18). Indeed some Brethren are wealthy and for them to discredit socio-economic actions confuse people. A leader in Kirinyaga asked Brethren to avoid self-centeredness and help the less fortunate to harness unity.

A leader in Mount Kenya Central said Brethren should avoid conservativeness and should not compare the 1930s or 1950s salvation standards with today's. The respondent urged Brethren to consider joining a self-help social group. Another leader said while Brethren address the dress code and morality they should engage in economic activities. A Kirinyaga leader added that there is need to encourage welfare groups, where people contribute money to help each other. This respondent also urged opening a saving account in the bank to get loans. But a Kirinyaga clergy member observes that Brethren abhor socio-economic projects such as bank loans.

Conclusion

This chapter focused on the Anglican Church scholarship perspective on Keswick theology as propagated by scholars of Anglican or non-Anglican church origin. The task incorporated an overview of Anglican scholarship from the viewpoint of historical literature and documents on the one hand, and the findings and the analysis of the current situation on the other. It is divided into four parts. Part 1 introduced issues that provided a platform for engaging and investigating the existing historical nature of church scholarship. It also brought to the fore the current situation of the influence of Keswick theology on EARM socio-ethical beliefs and practices of walking in the light in the light of the Anglican Church Mount Kenya region.

Part 2 discussed a historical overview of Anglican Church scholarship on Keswick theology's influence on EARM's walking in the light. This section offered a new historical summary of the nature and influence of the Anglican Church scholarship on the emerging socio-ethical beliefs and practices of walking in the light and suggested a viable perspective.

It also dealt with Anglican Church scholarship concerning historical literature and documents. A highlight of the main scholars served to assess credibility and authenticity of the summarized history of the genesis and spread of the revival to Kenya.

Part 3 discussed nature and current trends regarding Anglican Church scholarship on Keswick theology influence on EARM's walking in the light with findings and analyses of the prevailing situation.

This part (Part 4) analyzed the data collected from oral and email interviews. Based on the findings, the study assessed the nature and current status with respect to the influence of Keswick theology on walking in the light. The study used qualitative approaches and conducted self-administered email interviews on EARM's leadership, ordinary membership, theological students, clergy, bishops and prominent stakeholders. This part comprised various sections, which examined issues ranging from demographic distribution of respondents to understanding of Anglican Church scholarship on the influence of Keswick theology on EARM's concept of walking in the light in the Mount Kenya region. Following this it is vital to investigate the rudimentary missiological principles with the view to giving perspective on the prevailing trends.

CHAPTER 4

Prevailing Basic Missiological Tenets and Practices of Walking in Light

Introduction

This chapter focuses on the basic missiological tenets and practices of "walking in the light." The scope incorporates, on the one hand, interpretation of the central biblical texts which appear to have contributed to the prevailing situation. On the other hand, it debunks evangelical Anglican tradition by placing missiological viewpoints in the right perspective in this study. It is divided into seven parts. First, it introduces the chapter as a whole; second, it brings to the fore the basic missiological tenets that provide a platform to analyze the prevailing practices of walking in the light. Third, it interprets some of the key biblical texts to give historical-missiological perspective on the current situation. Fourth, the chapter attempts to explicate evangelical Anglican tradition which will hinge the missiological foundations needed to critique specific tenets of the prevailing model of walking in light in EARM. Fifth and sixth, the chapter inform the researcher's theoretical framework to analyze scriptural teachings related to sanctification, and culminate in a new EARM model of the theology of sanctification. Finally, the chapter offers a conclusion.

Basic Missiological Tenets That Provide A Platform to Analyze the Prevailing Practices of Walking in the Light

Although missiological studies have numerous tenets or principles; the researcher's focus is on the ones that appear pivotal to this work. These are the following: incarnational, cross-centered, centripetal-centrifugal, *missiologoi*, and *missio Dei*, which seem to inform and complement each other. These principles will help analyze the current beliefs and practices of "walking in the light" in the EARM.

As per the research findings conducted in early 2016, the following beliefs and practices, which are clustered into three categories, were found to be prevalent. First, the born-again testimony that incorporates confession of sin, and daily victory or sanctification. Second, worship in spirit dynamics, and Pentecostal haven. Third, Scripture and moral codes. These will be analyzed through the eyes of each of the ensuing five missiological principles.

Incarnational Principle

Certainly, the incarnation is a fundamental model of mission as it compels God to descend to the level of his creatures in becoming one with humanity. Athanasius explains the reason for this mysterious habituation: "it was our sorry case that caused the Word to come down, our transgression that called out His love for us so that He made haste to help us and to appear among us. It is we who were the cause of His taking human form, and for our salvation that in His great love He was both born and manifested in a human body."[1] While Athanasius seems to expound John 1:14, "The Word became flesh and dwelt among us", he further appears to echo the words of Paul in Philippians 2:6–8: "Christ Jesus, though in the form of God, did not count equality with God a thing to be grasped, but emptied himself, taking the form of a servant . . . and being found in human form, he humbled himself and became obedient unto death, even death on the cross."[2] This, observes Galgalo, demonstrates Christ relinquishing his "divine attributes in order to identify himself with humanity."[3] It is with this regard that Jesus could accomplish the intended

---

1. Athanasius, *On the Incarnation*, 29.
2. Galgalo, *African Christianity*, 34.
3. Galgalo, 34.

mission which culminated in his crucifixion. This action of God is not only incarnational, but kenotic, and is rooted in the mission of God.

According to this understanding, it suffices to say that incarnation is at the pinnacle of God's prototypical love and grace, which goes to the heart of God's mission to the world.[4] In a practical sense, by becoming human God entered into a special relationship with humanity. This integration of humanity with the divine nature of Christ looks like what Tizon calls missionary engagement with the local community,[5] and so places contextual faith in its proper perspective.

This is echoed by Hiebert and Meneses, who contend that incarnation serves as a model for human relationships, arguing that missionaries should not only identify with the people they serve but also adopt their lifestyle as a way of building trust and acceptance.[6] Hiebert and Meneses further raise a profound point that "just as Christ remained fully God when he took human form, so the Scripture remains divine revelation even when it is written in different languages . . . No other act of the missionary empowers people and dignifies their culture more than Bible translation. It takes people seriously and says to them that God speaks their language."[7] Thus, since language gives words and meaning to people's worldview, the translation must be precisely and meticulously applied to the context.

Following this, it is critical for the incarnate missionary to work towards a God-driven missionary task noting that God is already incarnate among people before the arrival of the missionary. This suggests the mission of God does not follow the missionary, but the missionary follows or participates in the *missio-Dei*. God is already ahead preparing the hearts of the local people to receive the transforming word of God through the power of preaching Christ crucified.[8] In addition, missionaries must admit they are still sociocultural outsiders sent by Christ to announce the good news of salvation. Indigenous people would expect missionaries to respect the local population's worldview. Missionaries' entry into the local indigenous context should,

---

4. Galgalo, 33.
5. Tizon, *Transformation after Lausanne*, 155.
6. Hiebert and Meneses, *Incarnational Ministry*, 371.
7. Hiebert and Meneses, 371.
8. Hiebert and Meneses, 373.

therefore, portray peaceful and cross-centered missionary intentions. Indeed, this understanding of incarnational mission serves as a measuring rod, to analyze beliefs and practices of walking in the light.

Born-again Testimony

A born-again testimony, which describes Brethren journey with the Lord Jesus, starts when a person accepts Jesus as Lord and Savior. He or she declares to leave behind worldly amusements, to cling to Jesus, in what Brethren call in Kikuyu, kuhikira mwathani (married to the Lord). By this action, they are expected to shun all evil activities. Thus, Langley and Kiggins elaborated a born-again experience by a carpenter during a Uganda convention in 1945:

> At their feet was a fire in which burned two native harps. Jeremiah, a senior carpenter, had been saved and had called his friends to witness the burning of things which he had used in his drinking bouts. "I used to work well," he said, "during the daytime, but as soon as the sun goes down I turned into another man. I became a demon. I drank, shouted, sang and abused people, playing heathen tunes on my native harps, often drunk . . . So I have burned the harps and my past. The devil has gone out. The Lord Jesus has come in!"[9]

The phrase "the devil has gone out, and the Lord Jesus has come" in describe a situation akin to a spectacular transformation from an ordinary Christian to a saved Jeremiah. He now has Jesus in his life. Note the senior carpenter referred to here had a baptismal name, but that to the Brethren didn't matter. A public confession has to be done heralding a moral transformation. In other words, Jeremiah gave up everything, so that, as they believe, Christ incarnate, at that very moment enters into his life. This is a typical born-again story by Brethren across Kenya today.

As far as EARM was concerned, Jeremiah had not been saved until he had burned his past evil practices. Indeed, in one of the interviews carried out by the researcher in April 2016, it came to the fore that to be born again, one had to mention evil things or sins committed in the earlier life, and make the necessary restitution as a precursor for forgiveness. Although public

---

9. Langley and Kiggins, *Serving People*, 192.

confession of immoral practices has been discouraged, one would still be expected to follow a threefold way of saying a testimony: declaration of one's status in the past (before being born again), present walk with the Lord, and future expectations from God, in that order. That is a prototype testimony from a brother.

Thus, born-again experiences naturally point to a particular routine, declaring victory over sin through daily sanctification, or a daily walk with Jesus, who they believe lives in their souls. This kind of testimony is a common feature during Brethren fellowship meetings. In such meetings, a neophyte is welcomed to an exclusive caring group of believers, who show distinct love for one other.

Spirit Dynamism

The Brethren Christian seems to believe in the gifts of the Holy Spirit, but with a noteworthy reservation in regard to Spirit dynamism in worship. Indeed, any serious Brethren would neither dance in worship nor entertain powerful musical instruments. This can be a challenge for the incarnate ministries conducted by Brethren in a multi-dynamic and open society. Thus, most young people and even relatively older ones seem to prefer charismatic worship sessions in the Anglican service. This scenario has led to a proliferation of Pentecostal churches, which are perceived to allow Spirit dynamism, and indeed, have encroached on most mainstream Protestant churches in Kenya.

Moral Codes

Since Brethren read and uphold literal teachings of Scripture, challenges of Scripture related to legalism have been inevitable. Thus, the Brethren in this context, appear to find resistance from believers who want the freedom of not only choosing a dress code but, also of association. Indeed, the born-again testimony informs not only the moral codes but also the subsequent spirit dynamism in worship.

Cross-centered Principle

Athanasius' explanation of why Christ had to suffer death on the cross for sinners' sake, gives a profound missiological focus.[10] Surely, Christ had to

---

10. Athanasius, *On the Incarnation*, 29.

become a curse as it had been written, "Cursed is every one that hangeth on a tree"[11] so that by His death, He became a ransom for all. Athanasius further evokes thought-provoking sentiments about the cross that puts the mission of God in its proper perspective.

> How could He have called us if He had not been crucified, for it is only on the cross that a man dies with arms outstretched? Here, again, we see the fitness of His death and of those outstretched arms: it was that He might draw His ancient people with the one and the Gentiles with the other, and join both together in Himself. Even so, He foretold the manner of His redeeming death, "I, if I be lifted up, will draw all men unto myself."[12]

It seems Athanasius views the cross of Christ as a focus point for salvation for *His ancient people;* no doubt the Israelites and the *Gentiles* were being called to share in the kingdom of God. Indeed, with regard to the missionary call to the Gentiles, Paul, an apostle to the Gentiles was forthright. Paul appears to convey his conviction of the significance of the message of the cross, in his letter to the Corinthians: "For I resolved to know nothing while I was with you except Jesus Christ and him crucified." (1 Cor 2:2) He further said, "Woe to me if I do not preach the gospel" (1 Cor 9:16). However, Hastings argues that while the cross must be preached in every culture, its message ought to be contextualized.[13] For example, Paul in Acts 17 used an Athenian narrative to convey the gospel message. Further, Hastings brings to the fore the implications of the wounded Jesus, which implies a servant Christ, who gave his life for the salvation of the world.[14] So, the disciples should not expect less, they should expect to suffer as they proclaim the redemptive mission to the world.

Unfortunately, Christianity has sometimes been used to oppress and displace people. For example, the Rwanda genocide has been said to have been influenced by Christians (the number of Christians in Rwanda is commonly

---

11. Athanasius, 55.
12. Athanasius, 55.
13. Hastings, *Missional God,* 223.
14. Hastings, 231.

agreed to be over 90 percent of the total population) through tribal lines.[15] This was in spite of the fact that Rwanda had been reckoned to have been the epicenter of East African Revival in the 1920s.

Surely, the image of Christ with nail-scarred hands and feet should be a clear enough message that the cross of Christ was and is to initiate forgiveness, reconciliation, and liberation of God's people. This should be the language of mission. Indeed, it is widely known that reconciliation and forgiveness have taken root in Rwanda today. This can be replicated in countries faced with ethnic tension.

Born-again Testimony; Daily Sanctification at the Cross of Christ

The cross-centered principle could be said to be a central concern that weaves through the Brethren born-again testimony. Indeed, the theme song of the revival sets the pace for the appropriation of the daily sanctification for the Brethren, at the cross of Christ. The following chorus in Luganda and English shows a precise description of the power of the cleansing blood of Jesus:

> "*Tukutendereza Yesu* (We praise You, Jesus)
> *Yesu Mwana Gw'endiga* (Jesus the Lamb)
> *Omusaayi Gwo Gunaziza* (Your blood has cleansed me)
> *Nkwebaza Omulokozi* (I thank You, Savior)"[16]

The third verse emphasizes the impact of the death of Christ on the cross, and his sanctifying blood. Indeed, most born-again testimonies include a spectacular aspect of Jesus passion at Calvary. While talking about EARM during the Nairobi 2013 GAFCON meeting, Senyonyi argued that EARM presented Christ crucified, saying that when a man meets the Christ of Calvary, self-effort dies away.[17] This again looks like Keswick ecclesiology of "let go and let God," which can lead to passivism. Their emphasis on Jesus' cleansing blood finds affinity in the cross-centered mission principle. Thus, Senyonyi points out that for Brethren, "real mission is just walking with Jesus, victoriously, moment by moment and day by day."[18]

---

15. Paul, *Integrated Research Institute*.
16. Reed, *Walking in the Light*, vi.
17. Senyonyi, "GAFCON EA Revival Distinctives", 4.
18. Senyonyi, 4.

Spirit Dynamism and the Cross of Christ

Spirit dynamism is less emphasized by Brethren in comparison with the preaching of the Christ crucified. For instance, Senyonyi observes that during the 1945 Kabale Convention it was reported that people were summoned to pray for the Holy Spirit to show them only Jesus.[19] Certainly, Brethren talk about guidance by the Holy Spirit, but themes on the Holy Spirit are rare within their fellowships and conventions.[20] Thus, the majority of them prefer rigid liturgy and are not convinced by Pentecostal-Spirit dynamic ministries.

Moral Code and the Cross of Christ

As mentioned earlier, most of the moral codes evolved out of certain biblical texts, which appear to have contributed to the development of a unique Brethren lifestyle. Certain dress codes that lack common decency, from the perspective of Brethren, could raise doubts whether the individual has ever accepted the crucified Christ as Lord and Savior. Certainly, Brethren believe in the authority of the Bible as the salvific word of God. Indeed, in the language of the Lausanne Covenant of 1974, the Bible is "the only written word of God, without error in all that it affirms, and the only infallible rule of faith and practice . . ."[21] The Brethren may have challenged the interpretation and appropriation of scriptural messages, but their firm belief in the authority of the Bible should be emulated. Thus, "Every man a Bible student"[22] was the fundamental philosophy of the founders of EARM. This has not changed in the present time and should be at the center of cross-centered mission.

Centripetal-centrifugal Principle

The centripetal-centrifugal mission principle can be viewed as two sides of the same coin, whereby centripetal invites in, while centrifugal sends out. While centripetal has traditionally been ascribed to the Old Testament understanding of mission, where nations were drawn to Israel, the centrifugal mission in the New Testament depicts Jesus sending out the disciples (Matt 28:19–20). Thus, Ott, et al. avers:

---

19. Senyonyi, 4.
20. Mambo, "Revival Fellowship", 113.
21. T. Yamamori, *Penetrating Missions'*, 178.
22. Church, *Quest for the Highest*, 62.

> The centripetal movement is that of nations being attracted as by a magnet to the glory of the Lord manifested in Israel, the nation's coming to Zion and the centralized worship of the Lord in the temple . . . The centrifugal movement of mission in the New Testament marks a reversal, with God's new people being sent out to the nations, to be a witness among the nations. The nations are not to come to God's people in Jerusalem, but God's people are to go to the nations.[23]

Consequently, the centripetal-centrifugal concept appears to have attracted debates on its suitability as a mission principle. Indeed, as noted by Blauw, "There is no thought of mission in the Old Testament in the centrifugal sense in which it comes to the fore in the New Testament."[24]

Indeed Bosch observes, "Astrologers came from the East to Jerusalem to look for the Saviour of the world (Matt 2) . . . The Roman army officer coming to Jesus (Matt 8:5) and the Greeks traveling to Jerusalem to see Jesus (John 12:20) give expression to the same idea: Salvation is to be found in Israel, and the nations who wish to partake of it should go there."[25]

However, it would seem the centripetal concept in the two testaments beckon nations for salvation, albeit differently as observed by Blauw above. Indeed, the centripetal mission in the light of the New Testament passages cited above could be viewed as mission par excellence. This is because the encounters with Jesus led to the proclamation of the gospel and thus a centrifugal mission. "As the Father has sent me, I am sending you." (John 20:21) The Father sends Jesus to win salvation; so Jesus sends his disciples to announce salvation.

As Bosch observes, there could be a tendency to understand mission in the Old Testament as entirely the work of God, and centrifugal mission in the New Testament as man's work.[26] This is because man and God appear to be competitors, whereby, man's activity tends to exclude God's and vice versa. But this shouldn't be the case because Christians expect God's presence in the believers' mission activities. Furthermore, argues Bosch, by recognizing

---

23. Ott, Strauss and Tennent, *Encountering Theology of Mission*, 23.
24. Blauw, *Missionary Nature*, 35.
25. Bosch, *Witness to the World*, 78.
26. Bosch, 78–79.

that the church's mission is God's activity, we may speak of it as our activity as we participate in it.[27]

Born-again Testimony and Centripetal-centrifugal Mission

Deep in the EARM's testimony is the concept of a daily walk with God, which informs their walking in the light. Therefore, the idea of going or sending, in the light of centrifugal mission, has been a rallying cry among Brethren missions. A Brethren faction like *thama* (Exodus), appears to have emulated the call of Abraham and left physically to a far country.

Spiritual Dynamism and centripetal-centrifugal Mission

The neophytes are put in a seclusion segment known as *gatia-uki*, "a pool of honey," where the local Brethren meet with them once a week, instilling rules and regulations of born-again Christians. As they mature spiritually, they may be allowed to attend and participate in other segments, such as district, national and East Africa conventions. Thus, a semblance of centripetal-centrifugal characteristics is seen as the neophytes come into *gatia-uki* for instructions. They are then sent out to participate in the mission field, from the district to the East Africa level.

Likewise, to counter the effect of legalization of homosexuality and other vices, the GAFCON 2013 meeting in Nairobi recommended that the Anglican Church go back to the faith of EARM-based scriptural authority.[28] This looks like a centripetal mission, in which EARM would become a school for the Anglican Church leadership, who would then be sent back (centrifugal) to preach a transformational mission in their churches.

Moral Code and Centripetal-centrifugal Mission

One thing that has fundamentally impacted EARM is its propensity to care for its members. Its beliefs and practices informed by a strict moral code seem to have enforced their typical inward looking mission. Nevertheless, in the 1970s, their smart dressing attracted admirers as observed by research participants (ordinary members in Kirinyaga). This could have contributed to

---

27. Bosch, 79.

28. https://www.gafcon.org/communique-updates/nairobi-communique-and-commitment/

increased membership because many people reviled the general fashion of the day. This inward-looking attitude, mostly influenced by the dress code, might have contributed to the centripetal mission and subsequently turnaround centrifugal mission. However, sending out of Brethren missions today, bogged down with these codes, have been faced with resistance, particularly from the younger generation. Furthermore, the majority of Brethren are elderly. Thus, the generation gap has been a challenge to the mission. Indeed, a clergy member in Embu, who participated in this research, argued for a respectable dress code. Thus, the tension between Brethren and the younger generation hinders mission.

Missio Logoi Principle

The principle of *missio logoi* is critical if a proper articulation of the gospel is to be realistic. Hiebert and Meneses seem right in saying that "divine revelation must take flesh in human languages and cultures. Just as Christ chose to live in a particular time and setting, so we must incarnate our ministry in the contexts of the people we serve."[29] Muck adds that *missio logoi* has to do with mission languages, such as languages of analysis, of media and languages of participation.[30] Furthermore, Muck contends that "the many languages of mission in each of these three categories can be used inwardly as ways for Christians to talk about their missions to one another, and outwardly as means of expressing the gospel to non-Christians."[31] Certainly, this might not be possible without the development of faith in the lives of communities served by the missionaries.

Additionally, Dunaetz observes that the Bible views faith as a double-edged concept, which is both relational and cognitive. On the one hand, the relational view emphasizes God's imitativeness (John 3:16) to reconcile humanity to Himself. On the other hand, the cognitive view describes a human rational process as depicted by the author of Hebrews 11:1.[32] Therefore, Dunaetz further notes that the relational and cognitive dimensions of faith are critical in

---

29. Hiebert and Meneses, *Incarnational Ministry*, 370.
30. Muck, "Missio-logoi," 5–6.
31. Muck, 6.
32. Dunaetz, *Missio-Logoi and Faith*, 67.

actualizing the biblical concept of πιστις.[33] This cognitive dimension, contends Dunaetz, is similar to what social psychologists call "attitude certainty", the degree to which an individual is certain that a particular opinion or belief is correct.[34] Besides, Dunatetz emphasizes that "findings from psychological science concerning attitude certainty may provide insights to missionaries as they seek to effectively minister to others through their *missio-logoi*."[35] The greater the attitude certainty that people have, the more confidence they will have to act on their beliefs, and the more likely they are to oppose distractors of what they believe to be true.

Unquestionably, colonizing Europeans came with a cynical mind about Africa. Indeed, Baur observes that in the eyes of colonizing Europe, the Africans were "savages" to be civilized, "cursed sons of Ham" to be saved, "big children" to be educated.[36] This derogatory and demeaning attitude towards Africans followed in hot pursuit of the pioneering missionaries, some of whom collaborated with colonialists, to the detriment of African mission.

Moreover, Walls narrates David Livingstone's description of a typical nineteenth-century missionary as dumpy sort of a man with a Bible under his arm, whose formal education was not high enough to have him receive Anglican ordination in the home ministry.[37] Thus, an attitude certainly might have given a low image of the missionaries going into overseas mission. Worse still, some missionaries were unworthy to be on the field on account of their bad conduct. Baur observes King Afonso of Kongo complained to King Manuel of Portugal,

> in this kingdom, the faith is still as fragile as glass on account of the bad example of those who came to teach it . . . Today our Lord is crucified anew by the very ministers of his body and blood. We would have preferred not to be born than to see how our innocent children . . . run into perdition on account of these bad examples.[38]

---

33. Dunaetz, 67.
34. Dunaetz, 67.
35. Dunaetz, 67.
36. Baur, *2000 Years of Christianity*, 281.
37. Walls, *Missionary Movement*, 199.
38. Baur, 2000 Years of Christianity, 59.

Indeed, such unscrupulous behavior spoke volumes and contributed to the cold reception of the gospel, particularly in sixteenth century Christianity. Missionaries must not only practice acceptable behavior but must also be willing to learn from the community to avoid any aspect of negative attitude certainty.[39] Behavioral-cultural norms remain critical and determine the success of missions.

Following this argument, when attitude certainty is conceived it will inform people's beliefs and subsequent practices, either positively or negatively. Thus, when attitude certainty of some Christians drives them to perceive things differently, it will be difficult to persuade them to abandon that belief. Indeed, as Njoku observes,

> Beyond the problem of communication posed by language and cultural barrier, preaching by European missionaries, with the intention to persuade the people rationally to abandon the faith of their ancestors and embrace the Christian faith, was at best a stalemate, but in general failed to convince the adult population . . . Some Christian doctrines were, in the eyes of the adult representatives of the traditional religion, simply illogical and even nonsensical.[40]

So, *missio logoi* should take cognizance of the mission languages to do justice in the communication of the gospel to people of other faiths.

Born-again Testimony and Missio Logoi

Undoubtedly, the language of the mission is a fundamental principle of mission that Brethren ought to propagate in the words of their testimony and in action. Indeed, the majority are illiterate but fluent in their mother tongue. Certainly, they are useful in the local mission, facilitating in their vernacular language. However, the majority requires services of an interpreter during national and international conventions.

They seem to delight in scriptural texts that teach about confession, forgiveness, and restitution. For example, they applaud Zacchaeus' decision

---

39. "The greater the attitude certainty that people have . . . the fewer doubts they have, the more likely they will be to act on their beliefs, and the more likely they are to resist persuasive augments to abandon their beliefs", Donaetz, Missio-logoi and faith, 67

40. Njoku, "Missionary Factor," 204.

(Luke 19:8) to put right what seemed to have contradicted Christian living. Many Brethren follow Zacchaeus' repentance model when they get born again, and this positively impacts the mission field. 2 Corinthians 3:1–3 has been taken as a mission text by Brethren, as they undertake the mission, as letters of Christ to the nation.

Spiritual Dynamics and Missio Logoi

Certainly, the language of the mission can be regarded as one of the most profound ways of expressing various forms of worship. In this way, Christians with different gifts find their bearing in contextual mission areas. In this regard, one of the prominent stakeholders of EARM argued that bishops should be transferrable to share their gifts with the whole Anglican Church of Kenya. Indeed, most of the Anglican bishops in Kenya have been influenced by the EARM, and are frequently given a speaker's slot during convention meetings. Others, like the late Archbishop David Gitari of the Anglican Church of Kenya and a renowned Rural Dean in the Diocese of Kirinyaga, Robert Kariuki, claim devotional Bible reading by Brethren without proper exegesis hinders mission.[41] Furthermore, a holistic discipleship of the neophyte, free to exercise gifts of the Holy Spirit has been tailored to suit a stereotyping lifestyle.

Moral Code and Missio Logoi

Indeed, the concept of *missio-logoi* from various biblical texts can be seen to have influenced the Brethren's Christian life, leading to their devotional reading of the Bible. The resultant socio-ethical beliefs and practices have created tensions between Brethren and other Christians, and sometimes among themselves. Certainly, the subsequent Brethren's language and behavior have at times led to dissensions and damaging self-righteous attitudes towards other believers.

The ensuing *missio logoi* moral code sometimes influences the direction that a dialogue would take between a Brethren and a non-Brethren. This certainly falls within the confines of dos and don'ts, whereby Brethren would claim to have social decorum, while non-Brethren, indecorum. So, one of

---

41. Gitari, "Paper on East African Revival," 5; Kamau, "Critical Analysis," 12.

the major challenges of this ethical reading is that it denies justice to the meaning of the text.

Missio Dei Principle

Most of the believers' prayers for mission work appear to lift humanity, and God is only invited to go with them. Indeed, one of the common prayers for the mission is, "Lord, we call upon you to go with us on this mission." Thus, humanity seems to have dethroned *missio Dei* for *missio homo*, forgetting that, it is not us inviting God to mission work, but that it is God who is inviting humanity to his mission to the world.[42] Believers are only invited to participate, and not sent to carry out God's mission.

Wright argues that if mission should be biblically cognizant and authenticated, then its meaning should include the believers' "committed participation as God's people, at God's invitation and command in God's mission within the history of God's world for the redemption of God's creation."[43] Wright further contends that God is the owner of mission while the Church is a participant upon the invitation and command of God.[44] Moreover, the fact that Wright mentions the purpose of God's mission as the redemption of God's creation[45] fits well with Bosch's version that the church is an instrument of God's love in the world.[46] So, it has nothing of its own. Thus, the mission mandate ought to be founded on being in a bonding relationship with God because "as invited participants believers are tasked to provide the medium through which God's redemptive activity can touch the world . . . believers are called to be God-bearers (*Theotokos*) in clarifying, fulfilling and furthering God's mission in the world."[47]

Born-again Testimony and Missio Dei

It is a challenge to participate in the mission of God while Brethren's spiritual self-awareness is predisposed to be better than other Christians. This seems true in Brethren's practice of walking in the light, in which giving testimony,

---

42. Galgalo, *African Christianity*, 37.
43. Wright, *Mission of God*, pp.22–23.
44. Wright, 23.
45. Wright, *Mission of God*, 23.
46. Bosch, *Transforming Mission*, 390.
47. Galgalo, *African Christianity*, 37–38.

signifies one is a born again (saved) Christian, therefore, a better Christian. Those who do not share their testimony are labeled not saved, and thus excluded from Brethren fellowship. Brethren appear keen on serving God, and seemingly, willing participants in the *missio Dei*. However, the challenge is that they display ego over and above other believers' ways of expressing their faith. This betrays the Brethren's perceived love of God, demonstrated in action and words of testimony. Indeed, they seem to front salvation by works, and that could set a wrong precedent for those entering the kingdom.

Spirit Dynamics and Missio Dei

Since the Holy Spirit has the unique attribute of regenerating unbelievers (John 3:5–8) and bringing them to faith in Christ, he is at the center of the mission. In this way, churches are brought into spiritual maturity, as to initiate missional impacts in community transformation. However, if believers do not subject themselves to the indwelling power of the Holy Spirit, the result is not only a lifeless teaching and preaching, but also a shoddy mission and failure in church growth. No wonder Ott contends that the Holy Spirit's ministry should be unrestricted, because "the Spirit's power is necessary for every aspect of missionary work."[48]

Therefore, when the Brethren tend to obstruct spiritual dynamics in their fellowships and missions, they appear to limit the ministry of the Holy Spirit. But *missio Dei* entails the priority of God in his mission, because He is a missional God. Again, since the mission is Trinitarian, God the Father and the Son sending the Holy Spirit, it means spiritual manifestations of the Holy Spirit are activities of God. Thus, an attempt to suppress the ministry of the Holy Spirit is tantamount to non-participation in the *missio Dei*. The result is the elevation of *missio homo*, rendering the Brethren's work human-driven and powerless, regardless of their tireless effort in the organization of missions, ranging from the weekly *Gatia-uki* to the yearly East African convention.

Moral Code and Missio Dei

Certainly, by constructing legalistic codes of conduct, based on beliefs and practices of walking in the light, the Brethren appear to have turned *missio*

---

48. Ott, Strauss and Tennent, *Encountering Theology of Mission*, 242.

Dei into *missio homo*, affecting the freedom of worship. Surely, the Brethren's task should be that of clarifying salvation, but not of blocking those who are entering into God's kingdom.

Indeed, moral codes are not wrong in themselves, and when applied correctly can become useful instruments to harness the demands of the kingdom. Undoubtedly, the Israelites were subjected to the Decalogue, to guide them in their walk with God. Indeed, the objective of the moral law was to give guidelines on Israel's participation in the *missio Dei*. That means moral codes ought to direct believers to participate in the mission of God, and not subject them to *missio homo* activities.

Interpretation of the Main Biblical Texts to Give Missiological Perspectives on the Prevailing Situation

A grammatical-historical method will be used to carry out an exegetical and theological study of the selected scriptural texts that form the bedrock of Keswick's influence on EARM beliefs and practice.[49] This is because the study seeks to ascertain the historical relevance of these texts to the EARM. So, the historical development of the interpretation of the texts will be necessary to appraise and critique beliefs and practices that have led to the prevailing situation. However, since this study has a missiological perspective, the researcher will not delve into an in-depth study of the selected texts.

In chapter three the researcher named the eight most dominant biblical texts that could have contributed to the practice of "walking in the light." These are: Ephesians 5:14; Daniel 1:8–16; 1 Corinthians 11:13–15; 2 Corinthians 6:14–18; Ephesians 6:13; Genesis 12:1; Romans 13:8 and Psalms 127:1ff. This sequence is in the order of dominance and significance of the text to Brethren's beliefs and practices of walking in the light. But since this exegetical study is only a section of this chapter, attempting to interpret all these texts will not be possible. So, four texts will suffice based on their dominance and possible influence on the prevailing practice of walking in the light by members of EARM in the selected ACK Dioceses of the Mount Kenya region. These are: Ephesians 5:14; Ephesians 6:13; 1 Corinthians 11:13–15

---

49. Marshall, "Evangelicalism and Biblical Interpretation," 100–123.

and Daniel 1:8–16. Since the main theme of Daniel 1:8–16 and 2 Corinthians 6:14–18 is separation, the Daniel text has been preferred, not only by virtue of representing the Old Testament context but also for its popularity among the research participants.

Since this is a historical study, at least three epochs of interpretation have been outlined. These are early Christianity, Reformation, and modern. Due to the apparent growth in the interest of interpretation in the modern era, the texts have been broken into parts. This would make it possible for the researcher to analyze the scholars' perception of words and phrases effectively. Further, to put the texts into their proper historical perspective, an attempt at the examination of the wider and the immediate contexts is pivotal.

Historical Development of the Interpretation of Ephesians

This section examines the historical setting and interpretation of Ephesians 6:13

Historical Setting of Ephesians

Although the researcher acknowledges various viewpoints on the authorship of this letter, this thesis specifically engages interpretation of the text from the historical point of view. This is to ascertain the influence of such texts in the prevailing beliefs and practices of walking in light in EARM.

Hoehner argues the date of this letter is severely affected by various theories associated with the venue of Paul's imprisonment.[50] The traditional view of Roman imprisonment is profoundly supported by the Bible (Acts 25:6—28:31), a view championed by most scholars. Hoehner appears to suggest that Ephesians was written towards the end of his Roman incarceration in early 62 CE.[51] Certainly, Hoehner and Arnold observe that Paul could have sent Tychicus with both the Ephesians and the Colossians letters (Eph 6:21; Col 4:7).[52] Indeed, Arnold implies that Paul saw it as an excellent opportunity to send Tychicus with a more general letter to address Ephesian Christians and other nearby churches.[53] But Perkins contends that most scholars think the

---

50. Hoehner, *Ephesians: An Exegetical Commentary*, 96.
51. Hoehner, 96.
52. Hoehner, 96; Arnold, *Ephesians: Exegetical Commentary*, 43.
53. Arnold, 43.

letter is pseudonymous.[54] This is because it appears to lack Paul's presence. However, the researcher is convinced that this letter is most likely written by Paul because the circulation of a letter via proxy is quite normal.

Having placed the dating into its perspective, it is critical to understand the background of Ephesian believers. The city of Ephesus has been branded the mother city of Asia in respect to her influence as "the headquarters of the Roman Proconsul and the seat of the Confederacy *(the Koinon)* of the Greeks in Asia."[55] By virtue of Ephesus' position as a cosmopolitan and multiethnic city, it became a home for various religions. The goddess Artemis (Diana), observes Arnold, had a strong bonding relationship with the city, so that she was referred to as "Artemis of the Ephesians," aside from other deities (up to fifty gods and goddesses).[56] Thus, Perkins observes that the Artemis cult shows the preeminence of the goddess above all other powers.[57]

In addition to religious deities, there were magic and folk belief phenomena. One of the best examples was the failed exorcism attempt by Sceva's sons (Acts 19:13–20) when they were overpowered by the demonized man for allegedly failing to account for Jesus and Paul's name. This led to what Arnold termed as dreadful fear and conviction among the believing community. It also suggests many of those who were becoming Christians had not only been involved in magical activities but also pointed out their attachment to the spiritual realms.[58] Moreover, Perkins claims that Paul's "emphasis on Christ's exaltation above the powers of the cosmos and the identification of believers with their exalted head forms the centre of the book of Ephesians."[59]

"There were indications of a Jewish presence in the city since the third century BC."[60] Thus, Arnold asserts that many Jews had become Roman citizens and were granted permission, *religio lecita*, to practice their religious traditions, like food laws.[61] No wonder Aune observes that the traditional Roman forms of public and private worship were mostly practiced by those

---

54. Perkins, "Letter to the Ephesians," 351.
55. Arnold, *Ephesians: Exegetical Commentary*, 30.
56. Arnold, 31, 33.
57. Perkins, "Letter to the Ephesians," 361.
58. Arnold, *Ephesians: Exegetical Commentary*, 33.
59. Perkins, "Letter to the Ephesians," 361.
60. Arnold, *Ephesians: Exegetical Commentary*, 36
61. Arnold, *Ephesians: Exegetical Commentary*, 36–37.

who were ethnically Roman.⁶² This means non-Romans as well as those who acquired Roman citizenship were allowed to practice their religion.

Concerning the Imperial cult, Arnold suggests it was based more on political than religious inclinations and served to influence the status of imperial power.⁶³ Also, Aune (2000:923) attests to the fact that towards the end of the third century BC, many cults were instituted by the Greek cities. Thus, Julius Caesar and Augustus were deified by an official act of the Roman Senate to assume the status of the official pantheon of the Romans.⁶⁴ This may serve to support Paul's insinuation that "our struggle is not against blood and flesh but the authorities . . ." (Eph 6:12). This warlike claim by Paul depicts a picture of contention between believers and evil powers. Thus, a call to awake in 5:14 and to stand in 6:13 to contend with powerful forces that might have taken captive the Ephesian believers.

Immediate Context of Ephesians 5:14

"Therefore it says, Awake, O sleeper, and arise from the dead, and Christ will shine on you" (διὸ λέγει Ἔγειρε, ὁ καθεύδων, καὶ ἀνάστα ἐκ τῶν νεκρῶν, καὶ ἐπιφαύσει).

The phrase "therefore it says" (διο λεγει), seems to give authority to the text regarding its origin. But, its source, argue scholars like Eadie and Thielman, is shrouded in uncertainty.⁶⁵ However, the majority including Aquinas refer to Isaiah 60:1,⁶⁶ though Arnold disagrees and suggests it was part of the oral tradition within early church worship.⁶⁷ Indeed, interpreters like Perkins place it in the baptismal rites in the early church.⁶⁸ This is supported by Klein, who adds that whatever the source of the hymn it has a moral appeal.⁶⁹

Nevertheless, Perkins observes that it depicts images of Jerusalem, as the Lord calls the city to awake, rise and shine, a description consistent with the

---

62. Aune, "Religion, Graeco-Roman,", 921.
63. Arnold, *Ephesians: Exegetical Commentary*, 40.
64. Aune, "Religion, Graeco-Roman," 923.
65. Eadie, *Commentary on the Greek Text*, 348.
66. Aquinas, *Commentary on Saint Paul's Epistle*, 208.
67. Arnold, "Ephesians," 331.
68. Perkins, "Letter to the Ephesians," 438.
69. Klein, "Ephesians," 140.

coming Messiah.[70] Thus, Thielman claims that waking from sleep, resurrection from the dead, and enlightenment was part of the Middle East antiquity which has metaphorical significance; in Jewish contexts it shows a change in a person who has joined God's covenant community.[71]

Therefore Paul likely used this setting to contrast darkness vs. light, death vs. life images to describe conversion (Gal 2:19–20; 2 Cor 4:4–6; Rom 6:3–11). Paul introduces this text as if it carries the authority of Scripture, Διο λεγει (therefore it says),[72] meaning that like Scripture this text speaks to the present.

Ancient Interpretation

Some of the early church interpreters, for example Ambrosiaster,[73] seems to have understood sleep as lethargy of mind, associated with a sort of death or darkness from which the Ephesians were called to rise to light and life in Christ.[74] But Chrysostom appears to suggest Paul was addressing both unbelievers and believers who were deep in sin, and he was therefore prudent to call them to awake.[75] While Ambrosiaster seems to interpret the text metaphorically, Chrysostom seems more forthright that sin is sleep.

Medieval Interpretation

Aquinas, one of the most influential medieval thinkers of Scholasticism, claims that this text is inconsistent with Paul. He perceives it as an image borrowed from Isaiah 60:1. He understands that the ones asleep are called to arise from the dead (evil works) to receive Christ's enlightenment and perform good works of light. He contends that justification of a sinner comes after a free decision to cooperate in the act of rising from sin.[76]

---

70. Perkins, "Letter to the Ephesians," 438.
71. Thielman, *Ephesians*, 349.
72. Thielman, 349.
73. "Despite the elusive identity of Ambrosiaster, several facts about him can be established. Internal evidence suggests he was active in Rome during the reign of Pope Damasus (366–384), and almost certainly a member of the Roman clergy" (https://en.wikipedia.org/wiki/Ambrosiaster).
74. Ambrosiaster, "Metaphors of Sleeping," 179.
75. Chrysostom, "Addressed Also to Believers," 179.
76. T. Aquinas, *Commentary on Saint Paul's Epistle*, 208.

Reformation Interpretation

Calvin observes that the light[77] of Christ enlightens and delivers unbelievers from death to life. Thus, Calvin encourages believers to work hard to awaken the sleeping and the dead and bring them to the light of Christ.[78] Therefore Sarcerius, a Lutheran reformer, maintains that when every work of darkness is exposed, confessed and repented it becomes light and does works of light.[79] Also, Bucer[80] contends that evil should be called by its name because light makes plain what was hitherto hidden.[81] Otherwise one would not be worthy to be called a child of light. Further, Diodati alludes to conversion as an antidote to awake from the sleep or death of sin, which would lead to enlightenment by the light of the gospel.[82] Hence, one walks according to the gospel statutes.

Similarly, Dickson brings to the fore the preaching of the gospel as a way of raising those who are asleep and dead to repentance, by faith in Christ.[83] In other words, awaking from the dead to life implies re-awakening to faith in Christ. So, to deal with sinners, he is of the opinion that this understanding of the text should be commended to others.

Modern Interpretation
Awake O sleeper, Ἔγειρε, ὁ καθεύδων,

The phrase, awake O sleeper, ἐγείρε, ὁ καθεύδων, appears to indicate in Paul's mind the condition of those addressed, that they were sound asleep, καθεύδω (fall asleep). Eadie, argues that the Apostle was calling them awake from this slumber, described as the stupor of death.[84] On the one hand, Eadie appears to view sleep as a euphemism for death, and falling asleep as a metaphorical description of dying. On the other hand, he depicts rise from the dead as an

---

77. Calvin (*Commentaries*, 313) cautions that light does not begin to shine after rising from death to life because human works do not precede God's grace.
78. Calvin, 312–313.
79. Sarcerius, "Repentance Brings Light," 372.
80. Influenced English reformation through revising the 1549 Prayer Book.
81. Bucer, "Call Evil by its Name," 372–373.
82. Diodati, "Everyone is Called," 373.
83. Dickson, "Children Must Preach," 373.
84. Eadie, *Commentary on the Greek Text*, 399.

imperative, standing up in the face of satanic assaults (6:11, 13–14).[85] By doing this, argues Barth, the Messiah will shine upon you.[86]

The imperative ἐγείρε is used to rouse people from their sleep (Matt 8:25). But although the verb καθεύδων can be used for natural sleep, Paul seems to use it here for spiritual lethargy (1 Thes 5:6), where some believers had become collaborators with works of darkness and needed awakening towards deeds that please God. Believers are therefore encouraged to wake up from spiritual laziness, because as sleepers they may not realize their spiritual ignorance.

Certainly Eadie appears to view it as a prophecy addressed to Zion, which had been sleeping and dead.[87] Indeed, Findlay connects the quotation with the Old Testament, especially Isaiah 60:1–3.[88] Lincoln concurs and moreover links the heritage of the text to early Judaism, which illustrates the imagery of death for sin and sleep for physical death. Furthermore, sleep is viewed as the condition of forgetfulness and drunkenness, part of belonging to the sinful darkness (1 Thess 5:5–8; Rom 13:11–14). Baptism is arising from the death of sin (Rom 6:13; 6:4). In the same way, the church in the armor of light and joy of salvation, ought to confront the darkness for the time has come for the dead to hear the voice of Christ and live.[89]

Indeed Stott on the one hand likens darkness with ignorance and evil, while on the other hand compares light with righteousness and truth.[90] So, the change from darkness to light gives the impression of union with the Lord, the light of the world. This means that for a Christian, when anything is exposed by the light, it becomes visible.[91] Thus, Stott sees "conversion as awaking out of sleep, rising from death and being brought out of darkness into the light of Christ."[92] So, argues Lincoln, "these words [Eph 5:14] heard at their baptism function now to remind the readers of the power of the light, of the transformation of their new status that has taken place and of

---

85. Eadie, 399.
86. Barth, *Ephesians: Introduction*, 576.
87. Eadie, *Commentary on the Greek Text*, 399.
88. Findlay, *Epistle to the Ephesians*, 335.
89. Lincoln, *Ephesians*, 331.
90. Stott, *Message of Ephesians*, 199.
91. Stott, 200.
92. Stott, 201.

its ethical implications. Their baptism, then, signified a movement from the sleep of spiritual death into the light of life in response to the divine call.[93] Thus, Lincoln maintains that both divine initiative and human effort are represented in conversion.[94]

Arise from the dead (ἀνάστα ἐκ τῶν νεκρῶν)

Concerning the phrase "rise from the dead" (ἀνάστα ἐκ τῶν νεκρῶν), Hoehner observes the imperative ἀνάστα denotes an urgency to rise from death. It is used to signify rising from the dead (physically), but in the present context, it seems to refer to rising from a spiritual deadening illustrated by the unfruitful works of darkness. Paul urges unbelievers to awake and with urgency arise from the path that leads to death.[95] In addition, the command to arise (ἀνίστημι), argues Eadie, is similar to that given by the Lord to the man with the withered hand, "Stretch out your hand" (Mark 3:5).[96] Moreover, Arnold likens the phrase to a person dead in transgressions and sins. So, Paul calls the believers to consider themselves as dead to the power of sin, but alive to God in Christ Jesus (Rom 6:11).[97]

Therefore, believers should not only shun darkness but exemplify their new identity in Christ who will then shine on them. Beet asserts that Paul used Ephesians 5:14 to bring hidden things to light because a sleeper is a sinner who needs to arise from the dead, or from the sleep of sin. He reckons Christians are the medium through which the light shines.[98] Therefore, Westcott states that the light has transforming power, ἔγειρε . . . ἀνάστα, awake from sleep, arise to action.[99] Gore suggests this power should separate believers from the morally dead works of darkness and reprove the dark world of sin.[100] Therefore, the charge is to arise and be light for your light has come.[101]

---

93. Lincoln, *Ephesians*, 332.
94. Lincoln, 335.
95. Hoehner, *Ephesians: An Exegetical Commentary*, 687–688.
96. Eadie, *Commentary on the Greek Text*, 400.
97. Arnold, *Ephesians: Exegetical Commentary*, 335.
98. Beet, *Commentary on St. Paul's Epistles*, 354.
99. Westcott, *St. Paul's Epistle*, 79.
100. Gore, *St. Paul's Epistle*, 195.
101. Eadie, *Commentary on the Greek Text*, 399.

No wonder Thielman claims that the phrase appears to envision a preacher of the gospel calling the unbeliever, who is imagined as asleep and dead, to a resurrected life in which the light of Christ will shine (ἐπιφαύσει ὁ Χριστός) on him or her. Thus, "Get up, O sleeper, and rise from the dead" appears to recall the language of 2:1 and 5–6. Here Paul describes his readers as formerly dead in their trespasses and sins and now not only are they made alive and raised, but are seated with Christ. Thus, ἔγειρε has been interpreted like waking someone from sleep (Mark 4:27) and has the same idea of rousing a believer to vigilance and sobriety (1 Thes 5:6).[102]

Christ will shine on you (ἐπιφαύσει σοι ὁ Χριστός)

The verb to enlighten, ἐπιφαύω is likened to a flash of light of Christ upon the dead, to bring them (ἀνάστα) into life. Hoehner contends that ἐπιφαύω is directed to the believer who is a partaker of the deeds of darkness. The believer is commanded to awake from his spiritual sleep and rise from spiritual deadness so that Christ will shine on him.[103] Thus, Moule seems to call upon the light of God to shine on the awfulness of human darkness. In this way, the enlightened (believers) would carry God's transforming radiance to those in darkness.[104] But this, says Barth, happens not on the ground of man's power but because of the radiant Messiah himself.[105] In other words, the shining Messiah communicates something of his essence to those illuminated, so that in his light they become light. The enlightenment described here is equivalent to the justification of the sinner.[106]

With regard to the phrase "Christ shall shine on you" (ἐπιφαύσει σοι ὁ Χριστός), Thielman, argues that unbelievers should awake to embrace the gospel and rise from their previous ways of darkness.[107] By so doing, contend Thielman and Snodgrass, Christ will not only enlighten (expose) unbelievers but also transform them into the life-giving light.[108] This means that believers should not avoid rebuking sin, even if they need to be aware of the damage

---

102. Thielman, *Ephesians: Baker Exegetical Commentary*, 350–351.
103. Hoehner, *Ephesians: An Exegetical Commentary*, 688.
104. Moule, *Ephesian Studies*, 261.
105. Barth, *Ephesians*, 576.
106. Barth, *Ephesians*, 577.
107. Thielman, Ephesians: *Baker Exegetical Commentary*, 351.
108. Thielman, 351; Snodgrass, *Ephesians*, 274.

that doing this wrongly can do. Nevertheless, with discernment, believers cannot afford to not call darkness dark.

Certainly, Dale sees the Ephesian Christians as carriers of this light into the darkness of heathenism. Indeed, verses 8 and 9 shows that Christians were charged with walking as children of light, having acceptable moral habits and alertness of mind.[109] Since, this light was not to be concealed but to illuminate the dark places, Eadie and Gore observe that "true enlightenment is not the privilege of a few, but is open to all who will come to Christ."[110] Indeed, Paul's model of Christianity "has everything to gain and nothing to lose by disclosure of life in the light."[111]

Thielman depicts this phrase as a recalling of 5:8, which describes Paul's readers' movement from their former existence, defined by darkness, to a life defined by light.[112] Thus, the church should live by values that oppose darkness. But this, argues Lincoln, is not meant to isolate the church from the world because believers should shine, illuminating how life should be lived. This would give the church a distinct identity of transforming the darkness around it and play its crucial missionary role as the domain of light.[113] As a result, Arnold claims that this phrase urgently admonishes believers living in sinful lifestyle (sleepers) and calls them to have exemplary conduct.[114] That is, they should be alert and sober.

Appraisal of Interpretation of Ephesians 5:14 by the Brethren
Awake O sleeper

As implied earlier, Ambrosiaster and Stott understand this phrase as a metaphor and symbolism respectively.[115] While not literally applicable, the figures of speech signify the interpreters did not understand the expression ἔγειρε, ὁ καθεύδων in the literal sense. Thus, Ambrosiaster's term "sleep," as a stupor of

---

109. Dale, *Epistle to the Ephesians*, 334.
110. Eadie, *Commentary on the Greek Text*, 198.
111. Gore, *St. Paul's Epistle*, 201.
112. Thielman, *Ephesians: Baker Exegetical Commentary*, 351.
113. Lincoln, *Ephesians*, 335.
114. Arnold, *Ephesians: Exegetical Commentary*, 334.
115. Ambrosiaster, "Metaphors of Sleeping," 179; Stott, *Message of Ephesians*, 199.

mind, estranged from the truth,[116] while Stott contrasts darkness and light.[117] Whereas the Brethren[118] would be happy to compare works of darkness and works of light, they will not likely associate sleep with the status of mind, but a spiritual condition inclined to worldliness. So, the dictums of the dos and the do nots characterize their fellowship. The dos represent things they consider of light, such as righteousness and truth, while do nots represent worldly[119] things of darkness, ignorance and evil. Anyone who does not conform to this concept of being awake is excluded from their fellowship.

Since Stott and Diodati view conversion as awaking out of sleep or rising from death,[120] then there is a disconnect with the Brethren who seems to see conversion as a prelude to becoming a Brethren, being born again. It seems these two scholars were referring to justification, God's gift of salvation, which is believed to be a one-time occurrence. However, it seems Brethren do not think justification alone qualifies a believer to join fellowship. Some outward signs like saying a testimony or public confession of sin and consequent moral transformation would serve as sufficient parameters to qualify to join the Brethren.

Chrysostom observes that it is necessary to "wake up" believers who "sleep in sin," and the metaphor inspires the Brethren's desire to have dominion over sin.[121] Recurrent sins are what Keswick teaching called "besetting sin,"[122] a phrase that to some extent was adopted by EARM to depict recurring sins.[123] That could be the reason for daily cleansing or walking in light among Brethren. However, "awake" as interpreted by Chrysostom could mean arising

---

116. Ambrosiaster, 179.

117. Stott, *Message of Ephesians*, 201.

118. As mentioned earlier, the term Brethren (saved ones) refers to EARM in Kenya as opposed to *Balokole* in Uganda. Indeed, research participants, particularly in the Diocese of Mount Kenya West were categorical that they are not a movement, but a revival fellowship. Thus, the term Brethren (Fellowship) seems preferable in this study.

119. Keswick movements abhorred worldly amusement like alcoholism, smoking and immorality. Indeed, Pearsall Smith, one of the founders of Keswick Movement lost his ministry for being suspected of sexual impropriety.

120. Stott, *Message of Ephesians*, 201; Diodati, "Everyone is Called", 373.

121. Chrysostom, *Addressed Also to Believers*, 179.

122. Brooke, "Message: Its Methods," 80.

123. Gitari, *Troubled but not Destroyed*, 294.

from sin or leaving sin,[124] a fact Brethren would endorse. A respondent from Mount Kenya Central said they had been raised from sins.

Again, the fact that Eadie sees the church as the one that "sleepeth" and should awake[125] would be welcomed by Brethren. This is because it has always been the Brethren's contention that the church (non-Brethren members) has been profoundly asleep and should awake. The Brethren, unlike Calvin, do not usually associate the term sleep with unbelievers[126] but with believers who are worldly. A similar observation is made by Hoehner, that Paul was admonishing believers indulging in the unprofitable work of darkness.[127] So, it seems Hoehner's views complement the Brethren's concept of being awake, though if the text was a baptismal formula, it could likewise apply to unbelievers' conversion. But since the addressee of this text is vague the Brethren's view of the addressee appears valid.

Thus, Brethren would be happy with Stott's contrast of light and darkness, and Ambrosiaster's concept of sleep as a lethargy of mind might not be accepted. Nevertheless, Ambrosiaster's description could be accurate because of the rational human character that might prove inept in matters of God. It seems therefore, different views whether the sleeper is a believer or not has been held to by different commentators throughout the ages.

Arise from the dead

Ambrosiaster assoicates the dead with non-Christians who need to leave the pagan life and be born again.[128] However, Brethren go beyond this, requiring born-again Christians to exclude from their fellowship anyone who does not live according to their rules of conduct. This creates a syndrome of two kinds of Christians: on one end of the continuum is the born-again Christian who does not comply with the Brethren moral code, while on the other end is the born-again Christian who subscribes to Brethren beliefs and practices. This divide has unfortunately led to apathy and suspicion in the Anglican Church, Mount Kenya region, and no doubt has hindered the church's participation in the mission of God.

---

124. Chrysostom, *Addressed Also to Believers*, 179.
125. Eadie, *Commentary on the Greek Text*, 400.
126. Calvin, *Commentaries on the Epistles*, 312–313.
127. Hoehner, *Ephesians: An Exegetical Commentary*, 687.
128. Ambrosiaster, "Metaphors of Sleeping," 179.

The command *arise* (ανασta) appears to have put a wedge within the revival movement with the implication that some members are *dead* (νεκρους). This command, though viewed as a figure of speech, convinced many among the Brethren that some of their members are "dead." Therefore, some respondents in Kirinyaga claim this text led to the *Kufufuka* (Arise) faction in EARM in 1967, which came to be called in Gikuyu *Arahuka*, sometimes referred to as *Uriukio* (Resurrection). At the point of this split, the general welfare of the church was not necessarily *Arahuka's* concern, though they were still members. Indeed, some of the church members had already been labeled unsaved (dead). So, the split was an EARM's matter and has persisted to date.

In an attempt to interpret the phrase "from the dead," Beet understands it as a potent metaphor of darkness translated to mean the sleep of sin. The Ephesians ought to arise and censure sin around them to bring hidden things to light.[129] The phrase "sin around them" appears exclusive and could have been applied by Brethren to signify that other Christians are dead and need to arise and walk with them as children of light. Subsequently, Brethren appear to regard themselves as righteous. Others around them need to arise and join them. This strong appeal seems to fit Brethren's resolve to preach salvation, as they understand it, aggressively.

Thus, Arnold observes that "rise from the dead" appears to mean arise from those who are dead in transgressions and sins.[130] This could have easily been associated with Paul's summons to believers (5:7) to differentiate themselves from unbelievers in their conduct. This does not mean Christians are called to isolate themselves from the world but are called to live differently from their non-Christian acquaintances. Indeed, Aquinas understood to arise from sleep or death to denote leaving behind bad works of sin.[131] He did not seem to mean geographical separation from unbelievers as applied by Brethren. Surely, Christians should nurture fellow believers wallowing in sin to maturity without loading them with unnecessary burdens of dos and do nots.

---

129. Beet, *A Commentary on St. Paul's Epistles*, 354.
130. Arnold, *Ephesians: Exegetical Commentary*, 334.
131. Aquinas, *Commentary on Saint Paul's Epistle*, 208.

And Christ will shine on you

The verb επιφαυσκω, "to shine," notes Hoehner, is directed to the believer who is a partaker of the deeds of darkness. The believer is commanded to awake from his spiritual sleep and rise from spiritual deadness so that Christ will shine on him.[132] Brethren would love this as it justifies their clamor for believers to walk in the light. This light is not to be hidden; it is to illuminate the dark places.[133] Perhaps Barth's understanding of enlightenment and justification[134] could further aid understanding of Brethren's position with regard to this verb. He appears to apportion divine initiative to Christ and human effort to believer's lifestyle (5:15). This could be explained by the works of God at justification and sanctification, where the latter could involve experiential sanctification, with strict moral obligations on the part of the believers. This is where Brethren's spirituality revolves as they work out daily sanctification of their lives.

Thus, Aquinas' interpretation that justification of sinners is a requisite to rising from sin[135] might differ from Brethren's view. Brethren do not seem to regard justification as a departure from sin, but a beginning of the spiritual journey to conversion. Indeed, Diodati alludes to conversion as a prerequisite to being enlightened by the light of the gospel and walking according to its statutes.[136] Ordinarily, justification is meritorious, but to Brethren good works must prevail. This is what Keswick theology appears to call the victorious life or higher Christian life.[137] Thus, Barabas notes that Keswick was like a spiritual clinic for spiritual casualties in the church who needed spiritual remedies or cures.[138] No doubt this resembles Brethren's exclusive fellowship, whereby those outside the fellowship are termed spiritually sick and needing a cure. The remedy (victorious living), according to Brethren, is found in the daily walk with Christ.

---

132. Hoehner, *Ephesians: An Exegetical Commentary*, 688.
133. Dale, *Epistle to the Ephesians*, 399.
134. Barth, *Ephesians*, 577.
135. Aquinas, *Commentary on Saint Paul's Epistle*, 208.
136. Diodati, "Everyone is Called," 373.
137. Naselli, *Let Go and Let God*, 45.
138. Barabas, *So Great Salvation*, 30–31.

Also, Calvin seems to understand Paul to mean that when Christ enlightens unbelievers, they rise from death to life.[139] So, Calvin appears to see Christ's light as life-giving to the dead (sleepers) at justification. But Brethren appear to view it as Christ's sanctification, which is experiential to those who are already justified, but living in sin and should arise.

Gore's practical aspects of darkness and light could be crucial in apprehending the phrase "and Christ will shine upon you."[140] This is because the phrase seems to speak into the Brethren aspect of seeing they are the best, forgetting this light is open to all, even those who may interpret differently. Actually, application of this phrase could bend towards moral intelligence or scientific views. But these could still be dark alleys and far away from the light of Christ. There is nothing to lose by disclosing the light, though some Brethren's public testimony might need censorship by the church. Thus, Lincoln contends that the church should have a distinct identity in the midst of society to transform darkness into light, by showing a right attitude in worship and fellowship.[141] Indeed, Brethren lifestyle should shine a light on darkness through interaction and not separate coexistence. Surely, architects of spiritual indifference cannot claim to have been exposed to light when they are not in the light.

Bucer, a Swiss reformer, comes very close to Brethren beliefs and practices of calling evil by its name.[142] This is because light makes plain what is hidden and children of light ought to do likewise. This borders on public confession of sin which has long been discouraged because of what may be referred to as washing one's dirty linen in public. But Sarcerius argues that when every work of darkness is exposed and confessed it becomes a light to those who repent, because repentance brings light and does works of light.[143] Thus, Dickson claims the phrase implies that the children of light must preach the gospel.[144] This could only succeed when Brethren interact with other believers and even

---

139. Calvin, *Commentaries on the Epistles*, 312.

140. Gore, *St. Paul's Epistle*, 200. "it is possible to be awake and enlightened in the speculative and practical intelligence, i.e. in the region of the senses . . . yet to be asleep and in the dark in the region of the will and conscience towards God . . . It is possible to be enlightened about evil and in the dark as regards goodness"

141. Lincoln, *Ephesians*, 335.

142. Bucer, "Call Evil by its Name," 372.

143. Sarcerius, "Repentance Brings Light," 372.

144. Dickson, *Children Must Preach*, 373.

with unbelievers. Indeed, earlier years of the Keswick movement saw Keswick missionaries directed to preach only to Christians and not to pagans.[145] Thus it seems Dickson had a hand in influencing Keswick theology which in turn seems to have influenced EARM beliefs and practices of walking in the light.

In addition Moule, one of the proponents of the Keswick movement, argued that Christ shines from believers to carry his transforming radiance to those in darkness.[146] Westcott adds that the transformative power of the light of Christ leads to rising to action.[147] No wonder Brethren are very aggressive in preaching what they understand to be light. But their seeming overemphasis on experiential sanctification may have led them to plummet down the other side of the precipice.

Missiological Perspectives on Brethren's Interpretation of the Ephesians 5:14

The research participants found this text to be one of the most popular with respect to causing dissension in the EARM. The thrust of the passage, "awake, rise and shine," was used by some members of the EARM (Brethren) to insinuate some believers were asleep. Thus, the sleepers (the "dead") were subsequently excluded from the fellowship because, on the one hand, from the Brethren's viewpoint, the sleepers were still lurking in the darkness of sin. On the other hand, the awake, the risen and resurrected ones (ἀναστα) were depicted as the righteous group, thus named the Arise/Awakened faction. They claim that they were not only born again but also resurrected, thus referred to as the *Uriukio* in the Gikuyu language.

The Uriukio faction acclaimed itself self-righteous and is still distinct, but not as clearly as in the beginning. This sanctimonious exclusiveness appears to have blurred missiological dynamics in the church. This is in spite of the fact that *Uriukio* like any other members of Brethren, claim salvation through Christ. But the fact that *Uriukio* at this point appeared to have played down justification as the basis of salvation, and instead elevated experiential sanctification and practical holiness, rendered the noncompliant ineligible for Brethren membership.

---

145. Stock, "Missionary Element," 137.
146. Moule, Ephesian Studies, 261.
147. Westcott, *St. Paul's Epistle*, 79.

However, Wright observes that exclusivity was used in the Bible to depict a godly model of God's people to the nations.[148] Certainly, even though God used exclusion or setting apart of certain people, places and items, it was never done to lock out the covenant people, albeit some were stiff-necked towards evil. It was to identify the people of God amongst the nations.

Thus, Bosch avers the following concerning the all-inclusive mission of Jesus: "both poor and the rich, both the oppressed and the oppressor, both the sinners and the devout . . . dissolving alienation and breaking down walls of hostility, of closing boundaries between individuals and groups."[149] Indeed, Jesus's mission model would appear impossible for *Uriukio*, who seemed to exclude not only other Christians but other Brethren as well. In contrast, Jesus's model brings to Jesus's fold all and sundry. This model of Jesus would likely be termed anathema, not only by *Uriukio* but by the entire Brethren family.

But Wright argues that unity among Christian believers (1 Pet 2:9) is pivotal because they are all in Christ and God.[150] It follows that mission set up in the context of exclusiveness is not in the spirit of God, nor does it serve the interest of the entire community of believers. In addition, Bosch claims the inclusiveness of Jesus' mission is exemplified mostly in the *logia* (sayings), which can best be described by the preaching of love, even to the adversary.[151] Indeed, Hastings states that believers should be *shalom* (peace), experiencing and expressing a community influenced by the risen Christ.[152] Surely, a community of radiant and born-again missional believers, reconciled to Christ and with one another, cultivates informed peace.

With regard to mission as an invitation to this community, Henriksen avers, "to be a church called to serve the world and to proclaim the gospel is thus to be a church called to be in and for the world of God – a world often gone astray, but God's world."[153] This means that a Christian community like the *Uriukio* should embrace what it might term worldly, for example, keeping dogs or getting bank loans. The most obvious problem with members of

---

148. Wright, *Mission of God*, 380.
149. Bosch, Transforming Mission, 28.
150. Wright, *Mission of God*, 387.
151. Bosch, Transforming Mission, 28.
152. Hastings, *Missional God, Missional Church*, 127.
153. Henriksen, "Mission: Invitation to the Community," 72.

Uriukio is the uninformed elevation of practical holiness. *Uriukio*, certainly, needs to come down, not necessarily to be worldly but to raise the perceived earthly to the level of the ideal Christian community. Such a community would not only attract members of the Brethren but non-Brethren, as well. Therefore, as Hastings observes, "the church's mission is fulfilled in participation with Christ and that its function as such is to point to Christ and what he has already done by way of reconciliation and revelation."[154]

Historical Development of the Interpretation of Ephesians 6:13

"Therefore, take the whole armor of God that you may be able to withstand in the evil day, and having done all, to stand" (διὰ τοῦτο ἀναλάβετε τὴν πανοπλίαν τοῦ θεοῦ, ἵνα δυνηθῆτε ἀντιστῆναι ἐν τῇ ἡμέρᾳ τῇ πονηρᾷ καὶ ἅπαντα κατεργασάμενοι στῆναι).

Immediate Context of Ephesians 6:13

While Ephesians 5:14 appeared to have been used by some members of Brethren (the Arise faction) to justify their righteousness over and above others, Ephesians 6:13 seemed to have been used to describe spiritual warfare within the Brethren camp on the one hand, and with the mainstream Anglican Church on the other. This scenario appears to have called on Brethren to stand firm in their faith – thus the *Stand* faction. The contention with the Anglican Church in Kenya could be likened to what Wild-Wood described of *Balokole*, who used to throw a salvation challenge to all and sundry, except to themselves.[155]

Thus, to do justice to the interpretation of this text, it is critical to place it in its immediate context. In verse 12 Paul emphasizes the inherent danger and suggests that the Ephesians' struggle is not against flesh and blood but evil forces. Indeed, as Calvin intimates, the enemies are so powerful that no human power could withstand them.[156] Thus, verse 13 appears to summarize the armor of God explained throughout Ephesians 6:10–17. No wonder the majority of Brethren made this verse their motto: it appears to describe

---

154. Hastings, *Missional God, Missional Church*, 129.
155. Wild-Wood, "East African Revival," 201.
156. Calvin, "Paul's Exhortation," 400.

their weapons of warfare against some of their accusers from the mainstream Anglican Church, and to some extent from the Arise faction, among others. Therefore the central verse for this discussion will be Ephesians 6:13. Indeed, Hoehner, notes this verse begins with διὰ τοῦτο ("because of this"), suggesting a causal conclusion from the previous verses, presupposing formidable superhuman evil powers pitted against the believers.[157] Thus, a call to put on the whole armor of God to resist the adversary. Arnold notes the phrase (διὰ τοῦτο) points to verses 11–12 and the hosts of spiritual evil forces led by the devil that threaten the church.[158] Thus, the appeal (verse 11) to believers to dress for war; to put on the armor and to stand and resist attack from enemies. Paul envisions a demonic assault happening on the evil day.

Paul is seen repeating the command, therefore, take the whole armor and again gives the purpose for doing this. This phrase begins with ἵνα followed by δυνηθῆτε. The verb δύναμαι, which means to be able, or withstand, denotes a defensive and not an attacking posture.[159] Hoehner states the purpose of armor is to assist believers to stand against evil cosmic powers (vv. 11–12).[160]

Ancient Interpretation

Jerome[161] provided interpretation of most of the Bible for the early church, and his work on the Ephesian text cannot be ignored. In the present study, his interpretation of the phrase, "to stand in the evil day," is twofold. First, it may refer to the final consummation and judgment when the enemy will have to fight to keep believers in his control. Second, it also may serve as an encouragement to the Ephesians to stand in the faith of the gospel, and not lapse under temptations and persecutions.[162] Thus, he appears to hold to both views, suggesting the phrase stands for both the final day of judgment, and also for the present age. Ambrosiaster, on the other hand, complements Jerome's interpretation by going further to interpret the phrase, "the whole armor of God." He argues that believers are at war with vicious foes who

---

157. Hoehner, *Ephesians: An Exegetical Commentary*, 831.
158. Arnold, *Ephesians: Exegetical Commentary*, 449.
159. Hoehner, *Ephesians: An Exegetical Commentary*, 833.
160. Hoehner, 832.
161. Jerome was an early church priest, confessor, theologian and historian, best known for his Bible translation that came to be known as the Vulgate).
162. Jerome, "Being Able to Stand," 198–199.

are skillful in every deception. So, they must be alert for spiritual combat, using weapons of soberness and self-denial to subjugate combatant spirits.[163] However, it appears that Ambrosiaster understands that warfare will thrive in the present age, while Jerome holds the two views.

Medieval Interpretation

Aquinas interprets the text from the immediate context, citing Paul's explanation of the devil's snares (6:12) and in verse 13 advises the Ephesians to arm themselves. In verse 14 he elucidates the categories of weapons.[164] Indeed, Paul talks about the powers of "this dark world" and "spiritual forces of evil in the heavenly realms," so he cautions the Ephesians, take up the whole armor of God, that is, take up spiritual weapons ready for combat. Why? "For the weapons of our warfare are not of the flesh but have divine power to destroy strongholds." (2 Cor 10:4)

It is therefore critical for Paul to admonish the believers to take up the whole armor so that they may be able to withstand, that is, to resist the devil (Jas 4:7). He interprets in the evil day from the perspective of what takes place in it. In other words, the believers were encouraged to prepare beforehand for the battle because the days are evil. So follows the phrase, "and to stand in all things perfect," in hardship and progress, trusting perfectly in the grace of Jesus Christ. Indeed, by the phrase, "everything perfect," Aquinas appears to mean sufficiency in salvation.[165] That is, the total will with the Father, striving to withdraw from passing realities and progressing towards the imperishable.

Aquinas seems to anticipate an imminent battle with the devil and his retinue as a present reality in the lives of believers.[166] The reliance on God for spiritual blessings is critical during this difficult time. However, Aquinas appears not quite clear on the eschatological battle but is emphatic on the present life.[167]

---

163. Ambrosiaster, "Whole Armour of God," 199.
164. Aquinas, *Commentary on Saint Paul's Epistle*, 239.
165. Aquinas, 240–241.
166. Aquinas, 241.
167. Aquinas, 242.

Reformation Interpretation

About the evil day, Brenz suggests that "the day is not evil in itself but because of the evil temptation that every temple [of the human body] is full of," such as carnal minds and issues of faith and practice.[168] Calvin concurs with Brenz that Paul was exhorting the Ephesians to arm themselves against evil temptations.[169] Thus Calvin claims that the phrase, "you may be able" suggests a promise of victory, implying resolve to withstand the devil by putting on the whole armor of God to fight to the end.[170] Calvin is emphatic that Paul was likely insinuating that anyone properly armed against Satan will never be defeated in his spiritual journey.[171] Thus, Calvin and Brenz look like they understood the evil day to signify the present life of believers full of dangerous carnal adversaries.

Modern Interpretation

"On account of this, take up the full armor of God"
(Διὰ τοῦτο ἀναλάβετε τὴν πανοπλίαν τοῦ θεοῦ)

Eadie asserts that the charge, take up the whole armor (panoply) of God, is loaded with military aphorisms first mentioned in verse 11. He further stresses that the Christian armor is worn to encounter the enemy on the evil day.[172] Moule alludes to this fact, and further states that putting on the panoply of God is a necessity to enable believers to withstand formidable opponents in the evil day, such as the crisis of temptation or terror.[173] Gore seems to bring to the fore another perspective of the armor of God as something like the righteousness of God, which is Christ, the believers' armor.[174] So, by putting on Christ's as armor, the believers are guaranteed victory in the hour of evil. Thus, Gore unlike other commentators so far has not only likened armor to Christ's righteousness but has gone on to appropriate it as clothing for believers.

---

168. Brenz, "We Must Resist Temptations," 401.
169. Calvin, "Paul's Exhortation," 401.
170. Calvin, 401.
171. Calvin, 402.
172. Eadie, *Commentary on the Greek Text*, 474–475.
173. Moule, *Ephesian Studies*, 327–328.
174. Gore, *St. Paul's Epistle*, 242.

In addition, Barth, contends that this armor "is equated with the new man who in Romans 13:12, 14 and Galatians 3:27 is identified with Christ."[175] Barth further adds the adjective "splendid" to describe this armor, so that he interprets the phrase as, "put on the *splendid* armor in order to be able,"[176] to signify that believers are able as long as they take up the unique armor given to them.

Stott goes on to describe the armor, and further claims that the phrase "the whole armor of God" translates the Greek word *panoplia* (the full armor of a heavy-armed soldier), referred to as divine armor.[177] This may compare with Barth's description of splendid armor equated with the new man analogy of putting on Christ (Rom 13:12).[178] The emphasis on the divineness rather than just *panoplia* appears to indicate that *panoplia* is God's. That is, God shares it with believers by putting it on as they march to war against evil powers. An quotation of the Puritan minister William Gurnall in Suffolk in 1655 by Stott might help understand divine *panoplia*:

> In heaven, we shall appear not in armour but in robes of glory, but here they (the pieces of armour specified) are to be worn night and day; we must walk, work and sleep in them, or else we are not true soldiers of Christ. In this armour, we are to stand and watch, and never relax our vigilance, for the saint's sleeping time is Satan's tempting time; every fly dares venture to creep on sleeping lion.[179]

Gurnall's claim that we must walk and sleep in them appears to summarize Stott's perspectives of the divine armor as putting on the whole armor of God.[180]

Thus, Lincoln likens the armor analogy with putting on the new humanity by putting off the old self (Eph 4:25), a fact observed above as putting on Christ.[181] Therefore, believers are solemnly encouraged to take up the full armor of God and appropriate the divine resources (pieces of armor) ensuing

---

175. Barth, *Ephesians 4–6*, 762.
176. Barth, 764.
177. Stott, *Message of Ephesians*, 275.
178. Barth, *Ephesians 4–6*, 762.
179. Stott, *Message of Ephesians*, 276.
180. Stott, 276.
181. Lincoln, *Ephesians*, 442.

from it.[182] So, to Lincoln, like Stott, the full armor is divine and sums up divine resources.[183] Thus, the full armor is critical to withstand ἀντιστῆναι or "resist the devil" in the evil day. Thus, Hoehner, argues that putting on the full armor connotes putting on weapons to contend against the assaults of the devil.[184] Indeed, Hoehner asserts that the use of the imperative "take up" (ἀναλάβετε), may suggest urgency on the part of the believers who were described in the preceding verses as being in the battle with heavenly evil forces.[185]

"So that you may be able to resist in the evil day"
(ἵνα δυνηθῆτε ἀντιστῆναι ἐν τῇ ἡμέρᾳ τῇ πονηρᾷ)
Eadie interprets ἐν τῇ ἡμέρᾳ τῇ πονηρᾷ as a day of the definite satanic attack in terms of damaged reputation, bitter repentance, and recollections of the past.[186] It is a preview of the ultimate evil amongst humanity, marked by persecution and apostasy, indeed a time of desperate terror for weak believers.[187] Thus, Findlay undoubtedly appears to bend more towards pronouncing the evil day as a foretaste of the last things,[188] putting him on a collision course with Eadie who seems to claim the evil day is not futuristic.[189]

Barth observes, "As much as Ephesians expresses a realized eschatology of salvation, it also speaks of the experience of eschatological tribulations at present. The struggle against the spiritual hosts of evil is necessary now, just because it anticipates and participates in, the final opposition of God to all evil and God's victory over it."[190] Lincoln, intimates Paul is warning his readers against complacency in the face of threats of evil principalities of this world.[191]

But the meaning of the phrase "in the evil day" has been disputed. Indeed, the dispute has been long-standing. Three case scenarios will suffice. In one instance, Lincoln proposes four competing interpretations. First, shortly before *parousia* (events immediately preceding the *eschaton*); second, any

---

182. Lincoln, 445.
183. Stott, *Message of Ephesians*, 275.
184. Hoehner, *Ephesians: An Exegetical Commentary*, 832.
185. Hoehner, 831.
186. Eadie, *Commentary on the Greek Text*, 475.
187. Findlay, *Epistle to the Ephesians*, 412.
188. Findlay, 412.
189. Eadie, *Commentary on the Greek Text*, 475.
190. Barth, *Ephesians 4–6*, 804–805.
191. Lincoln, *Ephesians*, 445.

time of crisis or an extraordinary temptation; third, a reference to the entire present age and fourth which is favored, a synthesis of the first and third interpretations.¹⁹² The readers are to awaken to the fact that they are in the evil days, which will culminate "a final time of evil at the end of history."¹⁹³ Thus, Lincoln like Findlay and Barth appear to combine present and indefinite future.¹⁹⁴ Lincoln argues that this evil day is a current phenomenon in the lives of humanity and there will also be the last day of evil.¹⁹⁵ The armor will be necessary to enable believers' battle with evil now and in the future. Believers ought therefore to stand firm, having accomplished their preparations for battle.

In the second case, Hoehner claims that ἐν τῇ, ἡμέρα τῇ πονηρᾷ ("in the evil day") has five possible interpretations. First, satanic outbreak immediately before *parousia*; secondly, the entire period of a believer's life or the whole of the present age (5:16); third, critical times in a believer's life; fourth, combining views one and two, the present time (evil day) that will culminate in the final spate of evil in a future day, and fifth, combining views two and three, referring to the present age compounded with perilous times of satanic events against believers.¹⁹⁶ Hoehner suggests the fifth view to be most representative as it alerts believers to be prepared for both everyday evils as well as times of heightened spiritual battles.¹⁹⁷ Hoehner thus appears to stand in solidarity with Eadie at this point, where the majority of the preceding commentators suggest evil days are now *and* in the unpredictable future in the present day believer's lifetime.

A third case has been cited by Arnold, in which he views, first, events immediately preceding the *parousia* as one of many evil days (5:16) or second, extraordinary trials in the lives of believers. Arnold appears content with the last view which he claims to have support from the majority of commentators. He seems to be of the opinion that verses 11–12 and verses 14–18 portray a context of how to achieve victory and that believers have not already won.¹⁹⁸

---

192. Lincoln, 445–446.
193. Lincoln, 446.
194. Findlay, *Epistle to the Ephesians*, 412; Barth, *Ephesians 4–6*, 804–805.
195. Lincoln, Word Biblical Commentary: *Ephesians*, 446.
196. Hoehner, *Ephesians: An Exegetical Commentary*, 833.
197. Hoehner, 834.
198. Arnold, *Ephesians: Exegetical Commentary*, 449–450.

However, it is certain that believers will face demonic attacks in the present age. Thus they are called upon to prepare, to stand from falling into temptations and to advance the good news of deliverance on enemy territory.

It would appear that Arnold, Eadie and Hoehner's stance depicts this evil day as the present age of the Ephesian believers. Findlay, Barth, and Lincoln, although staunch supporters of the evils of the present time, appear to have an indefinite future in mind. This is also the mind of the researcher because it is difficult to delineate and confine the evil day to present-day believers only, without anticipating an ultimate battle with the devil and his entourage in the indefinite future.

"And having done everything, to stand" (χὰι κατεργασάμενοι ἄπαντα, στῆναι)

Eadie argues that some classical writers used κατεργασάμενοι to mean "having subdued" and others as "having done all or accomplished all."[199] However, Eadie challenges the former assertion and indicates that verses 11 and 14 signify to stand, not when the combat is over, but to stand before the foe, in the very attitude of resistance and self-defense, or in expectation of an immediate assault.[200] Certainly he gets support from the subsequent verses: "stand, therefore" (vv. 14–17), with the belt of truth, breastplate, shoes, shield, helmet, and sword and praying at all times. This interpretation makes sense in light of the description of the elements of warfare suggesting the emphatic need for complete military attire, which would be illogical if the battle is over.

Findlay captures the term "stand" as the watchword for this warfare where Gentile believers were encouraged to hold their ground. This strategic defense is required to withstand in the evil day, which is more than daily temptations that co-exist within humanity.[201] By using the words "more than daily temptations," Findlay, interprets the clause to mean that Paul was foreseeing imminent danger over the infant church of Christ. Perhaps he had in mind the AD 64–70 crisis that extended from the fire of Rome to the fall of Jerusalem, a time that might look like the day of judgment for Israel and the ancient world.[202] Indeed, persecution of the young church by the Roman emperors

---

199. Eadie, *Commentary on the Greek Text*, 475.
200. Eadie, 476.
201. Findlay, *Epistle to the Ephesians*, 410–411.
202. Findlay, 411.

beginning with Nero and ending under Constantine could be a further reference point, that battle is an ongoing concern.

Moule further suggests that when believers have completed preparation for the battle, they are to stand firm, unmoved, unshaken, and ready to engage and tread down their enemies.[203] With regard to "stand" in verses 13 and 14, Barth claims it carries the sense of verse 11, that is, to resist in the present-day warfare against the devil on earth.[204]

Regarding the phrase "having done everything," Barth argues it has duplicate meanings such as to carry to victory, to defeat, to finish a job.[205] Thus, Barth claims that nowhere in the New Testament has "everything" (*katergazomai*) been used to mean to conquer or to subdue, but rather to prepare (2 Cor 5:5) or to accomplish (Rom 7:15–20), that is to work out, to bring about, to effect (2 Cor 9:11; Phil 2:12). He further contends that it is unlikely for Paul to speak of the result of the battle in verse 13 and then in verse 14 to go on to discuss the fundamental standpoint during the combat unless the words κατεργασάμενοι ἅπαντα ("having done everything") somewhat summarizes the preparations for warfare.[206]

In interpreting this phrase, Hoehner suggests that the reason for putting on the full armor of God is to help believers resist in the evil time and having accomplished all, to stand.[207] Hoehner suggests two versions of this phrase. The first conveys the idea that victory has been achieved so that believers can stand. The second suggests that since all preliminaries are complete, believers are to stand against the devil's attack.[208] This is the better version because believers are urged to stand as they are prepared to engage the enemy.[209] So the preferred interpretation of this phrase is to prepare for the battle, as opposed to subdue or conquer. This preference is consistent with most scholars.

---

203. Moule, *Ephesian Studies*, 328.
204. Barth, *Ephesians 4–6*, 764.
205. Barth, 765.
206. Barth, 766.
207. Hoehner, *Ephesians: An Exegetical Commentary*, 834.
208. Hoehner, 835.
209. Hoehner, 836.

Appraisal of Interpretation of Ephesians 6:13 by Brethren
"On account of this, take up the full armor of God."

Most scholars like Stott, Barth, and Lincoln have identified "panoply" (armor) with Jesus Christ.[210] Thus, putting on the full panoply of God has been likened to putting on Christ, in what is further compared to putting on new clothes and putting off old ones. Similar words are said by Brethren after getting born again, and frequently accompany their public testimonies in their Christian journey. Most of their testimonies attest to the concept of overcoming a spiritual enemy and sometimes the real adversaries of Brethren fellowship. They tend to describe their weapons, in the words of Paul: "For the weapons of our warfare are not carnal, but mighty to God unto the pulling down of fortifications, destroying counsels" (2 Cor 10:4). This verse seemed to be key to Aquinas' theology of spiritual warfare.[211]

Thus, Brethren embrace various pieces of armor almost literally. Certainly research respondents and participants in Mount Kenya Central and Embu claim this text was used by the Kusimama (Stand) group to encourage Christians to withstand challenges. They often use the phrase *Yesu atosha* (Jesus satisfies) signifying their need of Jesus in their lives. Thus, thirst for righteousness and the word of God have continued to challenge their passion for fellowship, evangelism, and mission. No wonder Joe Church, one of the pioneers of EARM, wrote a book called "Every Man a Bible Student."[212] Certainly, Brethren love to read the Bible, albeit devotionally, a fact they could have borrowed from Keswick teaching which emphasized "on personal devotion and service, rather than on theological understanding."[213] This led to the exegetical challenge of the Scripture, a fact observed by Guillebaud that evangelical scholarship was largely missing.[214] Indeed most of the Keswick exponents were not theologically equipped, except a few like Handley Carr Glyn Moule who was a Professor of Divinity and Principal of Ridley Theological College at Cambridge, and later Bishop of Durham.[215]

---

210. Stott, *Message of Ephesians*, 275; Barth, *Ephesians 4–6*, 762; Lincoln, *Ephesians*, 442.
211. Aquinas, *Commentary on Saint Paul's Epistle*, 239.
212. Church, *Quest for the Highest*, 62.
213. Reed, *Walking in the Light*, 58.
214. Guillebaud, *Rwanda: The Land God Forgot*, 73–74.
215. Pollock, *Keswick Story*, 68.

Brethren understand the whole armor as a full regalia for spiritual warfare. Thus commentators like Gore, writing in the early twentieth century, not only likened armor with Christ's righteousness but as clothing for believers as well.[216] Also, Stott's viewpoint of walking and sleeping in the panoply no doubt summarizes the Brethren's perspective.[217] Thus, Brethren urge their members not to leave behind any weapon of war until all the enemies are vanquished, now and in the future. Indeed, this is attested to by their testimonies that have past, present and future components.

"So that you may be able to resist in the evil day, and having done everything, to stand."

Brethren do not regard the phrase "in the evil day" as having eschatological perspectives, as some scholars like Jerome and Aquinas appear to conceive it, but a present reality as understood by scholars like Eadie, Arnold and Hoehner. This reality seems to have been internally and externally perpetuated.

Internally, in the 1960s and 1970s the re-awakening wave of *Balokole* inspired by the interpretation of Ephesian 5:14's "Awake, O sleeper . . ." infiltrated the Kenyan soil splitting the Kenyan EARM, fondly referred to as Brethren,[218] into two main factions. One came to be referred to as the Arise or Awakened, and the other came to be called the Stand, derived from Ephesian 6:13 – to stand [firm] (in the original faith of the EARM). The Stand faction faced severe tribulations from the Arise faction accusing them of being dead, and therefore that they should arise. Thus, Embu respondents contend that the *Kusimama* (Stand) group was formed after some Brethren disagreed with Kufufuka, especially on issues of obtaining bank loans, which Kusimama endorses. Indeed, Kamau states that Kusimama is the largest group of Brethren in the Mount Kenya region,[219] and for that matter, the term Brethren, by and large represents their views. As observed by one major stakeholder (participant), most of the Anglican leaders including bishops,

---

216. Gore, *St. Paul's Epistle*, 242.

217. Stott, *Message of Ephesians*, 276.

218. It is critical to indicate that Arise and Stand factions appear to coexist mutually today in their local Brethren fellowships, though they tend to hold separate conventions nationally, and in the Eastern African region. The use of the term Brethren in this study, unless specifically stated, will incorporate the two factions.

219. Kamau, "Critical Analysis," 22.

identify themselves with *Stand*, probably because Stand appears to work relatively harmoniously with the church hierarchy.

Externally, there were at least three factors. The first wave of tribulation came mainly from a section of the Anglican Church, which was not happy with Brethren beliefs and practices. Although Stand did not break away like Johera in western Kenya in the 1950s, following unfair treatment by the church hierarchy,[220] this conflict has continued to date, mainly due to a consistent claim by the Brethren that clergy are not saved. As a result, some clergy have refused to recognize Brethren's ministry in the church. Thus, a passive stand phenomenon threatens the wellbeing of the Brethren's lifestyle. The "day of evil" appears to persist to date and might go on into the foreseeable future. If not checked, this day might annihilate them, as the population of Brethren has continued to dwindle.

The second wave of the perceived day of evil analogy for Brethren came with the struggle for independence in Kenya. Indeed, some adherents were martyred for refusing to join forces against the colonial regime. Others were persecuted for refusing to take the oath of allegiance, saying since they had drunk the blood of Jesus, they would not drink the blood of goats.[221] In this regard, it would seem their day of evil was at that present time. But the point is they stood firm in their faith in the face of persecution.

It is as if the Brethren had read Aquinas' interpretation of this phrase.[222] If it is matter of salvation, they practice daily sanctification as if it is the presence of God in their lives. They daily "walk in the light" as if it is withdrawal from the world (the passing reality) in pursuit of the infinite, they are on the glory train towards heaven, and other Christians are locked out.

The third wave concerns isolation and stigma by the general society. Brethren appear to face the wrath from society for refusing to participate in some social gatherings. A group of participants in this research in Kirinyaga, said they refuse to attend some meetings because they perceive traditional rituals performed during such get-togethers invoke ancestral spirits (which they regard to be evil). By refusing to attend such meetings, Brethren lose

---

220. Ogot, *Church of Christ*, 43, 57.
221. Gitari, *Troubled but not Destroyed*, 185.
222. Aquinas, *Commentary on Saint Paul's Epistle*, 239–240.

opportunities for evangelism and mission. This attitude has also led to their weak impact in the socio-economic activities, and many of them remain poor.

However, it is important to note that Brethren's testimony seems to answer the question of spiritual warfare that they encountered then and now. A standard text frequently used by Brethren has been "and they have conquered him by the blood of the Lamb and by the word of their testimony, for they loved not their lives even unto death" (Rev 12:11). Certainly, one of the favorite Brethren songs has been *kaza mwendo, utasinda* (Be steadfast in your walk [with the Lord], you will be victorious), which seems to allude to the fact that nothing shall prevail against the power of God. So, Calvin and Brenz writing during the Reformation era, argued that Paul was exhorting the Ephesians to arm themselves against evil temptations.[223] This could have encouraged Brethren to stay away from situations that could compromise their faith. It could also reinforce Brethren's bold testimonies of daily trials and temptations. Indeed, they see putting on armor as a prelude to the prevalent battle, not only amidst internal wrangles but also from the Anglican Church, which they accuse of being lukewarm.

Missiological Perspectives on Brethren's Interpretation of the Ephesians 6:13

The putting on a panoply as a righteousness of God's motive to stand against the evil day has been the keynote subject for the Stand faction in particular, and later for the entire Brethren Fellowship in general. The appropriation of panoply as a cloak of righteousness, to stand against evil, is a common subject or testimony during Brethren's weekly revival fellowships. This subject has been used against the perceived perpetrators of evil. Thus, Brethren explicates the subject in the two-word phrase "stand firm" clothed in the splendid armor of righteousness so as to contend with the evil powers.

The concern of the Stand (Brethren, unless stated otherwise) is to stand firm against the present evil whether imagined or real. Thus, Bosch claims that "we need an eschatology for a mission which is both future-directed and oriented to the here and now . . . an eschatology that holds in creative and redemptive tension the already and the not yet . . . moves in all three times: past, present, and future. The reign of God has already come, is coming, and

---

223. Calvin, "Paul's Exhortation," 401; and Brenz, "We Must Resist Temptations," 401.

will come in fullness."²²⁴ This observation seems consonant with the Brethren method of sharing a testimony, which is based on the past (status before salvation), present (sojourn with Christ), and future (the fullness of time, when the Son of Man will return). This indicates their struggle is not only current, but futuristic (indefinite), or as they call it, before the Son of Man returns. To Brethren, the uncertain future signifies the end of their earthly life (when Jesus comes to take them home), which should not be confused with the last events before the end of the world. Indeed, Livingston's differentiation is worth noting:

> Traditionally understood, eschatology means the doctrine of last things, pointing to the end of time . . . Understood in terms of the Second Coming of Christ, the resurrection of the dead, the final judgment, the coming of the kingdom, and the future states of heaven and hell. Within much of modern theology, however, eschatology is used to refer to the power of God in Christ through the Spirit working out his purposes within world history as well as beyond it.²²⁵

The Brethren's commonly sung hymn during their fellowship is *kaza mwendo, ndugu yangu, Yesu yuaja kutusukua* (be steadfast, my friend, Jesus is coming back to take us home). This compares with "and they have conquered him by the blood of the Lamb and by the word of their testimony, for they loved not their lives even unto death" (Rev 12:11). This appraisal is consistent with the Brethren adherents who were martyred for refusing to join *Mau Mau* forces against the colonial regime.²²⁶ This assertion is also supported by Stand's constant firm stand against distractors like *Uriukio* on one hand, and some Anglican Church members, on the other. Thus, Brethren's eschatological perspective in the light of Livingston's definition, appears to tilt towards the modern view.

One of Livingston's models see the kingdom of God "as invisibly present in the hearts of true believers – with a corresponding lack of interest in the institutional church."²²⁷ Undoubtedly, this model, which Livingston call pietist

---

224. Bosch, *Transforming Mission*, 508.
225. Livingston, *Missiology of the Road*, 256.
226. Gitari, *Troubled but not Destroyed*, 185.
227. Livingston, *Missiology of the Road*, 273.

(a renewal movement within Protestantism), believed that "the true church was ... the small, authentic church within the larger institutional church" that sought to convert persons into their little communities of true believers – fundamentally a spiritual mission was their concern, and not social action issues.²²⁸ So, Livingston argues further, with regard to this model, "the eschatological kingdom of the future was a glorious reality, but the present dimension of the kingdom was privatized: the kingdom became an individual, inward and invisible experience of the believer with his or her Lord."²²⁹ Thus, this mission theory and practice somewhat reflect the prevailing situation of Brethren, who sometimes excuse themselves from the missional church function to attend their own missions.

Historical Development of Interpretation of 1 Corinthians 11:13–15

"Judge for yourselves: is it proper for a woman to pray to God with her head uncovered? Does not the very nature of things teach you that if a man has long hair, it is a disgrace to him, but that if a woman has long hair, it is her glory? For long hair is given to her for a covering." (13 ἐν ὑμῖν αὐτοῖς κρίνατε· πρέπον ἐστὶν γυναῖκα ἀκατακάλυπτον τῷ θεῷ προσεύχεσθαι; 14 οὐδὲ ἡ φύσις αὐτὴ διδάσκει ὑμᾶς ὅτι ἀνὴρ μὲν ἐὰν κομᾷ, ἀτιμία αὐτῷ ἐστιν, 15 γυνὴ δὲ ἐὰν κομᾷ, δόξα αὐτῇ ἐστιν; ὅτι ἡ κόμη ἀντὶ περιβολαίου δέδοται)

Historical Setting of 1 Corinthians

Corinth's rise from ruin is traced to Julius Caesar in 44 BC.²³⁰ This fact is collaborated by Winter who further claims that following its destruction by the Romans in 146 BC, it was redesigned and reconstructed 102 years later in the manner of the Romans' cultural architectural taste, becoming a new Roman city.²³¹ Sampley claims that it enjoyed colonial status signifying its unique connection with the Roman Empire operatives.²³² Winter and Sampley observe

---

228. Livingston, 274.
229. Livingston, 274.
230. Sampley, "First Letter to the Corinthians," 775; and Gill, "1 Corinthians," 105.
231. Winter, *After Paul Left Corinth*, 8–9.
232. Sampley, "First Letter to the Corinthians," 774.

that the official government language was Latin.²³³ Indeed, Winter notes that magistrates were indulged against replying to Greeks apart from in Latin.²³⁴

In Paul's era, Corinth was not only a center of commerce and religious diversities, but also the principal city in the province.²³⁵ Indeed, Sampley argues that during the reign of Emperor Claudius (AD 41–54) Corinth had a higher status than Athens as a key administrative hub of the Roman province of Achaia.²³⁶ This suggests that Corinth thrived within the context of Roman laws and dictums of the imperial cult.²³⁷ Gill concurs, and asserts that the Roman colony of Corinth "housed the cult to the Roman emperors."²³⁸ Indeed, argues Gill, Julius Caesar was deified in 44BC, and subsequent emperors, beginning with his adopted son Augustus, enjoyed divinity status.²³⁹

Moreover, Corinth was reputed for having a somewhat superficial cultural life, which Sampley claims was an aftermath of Julius Caesar's restoration of Corinth in 44 BC, which allowed entry of migrants into the city, besides a sailors' lifestyle, which led to Corinth's reputation as a sinful city.²⁴⁰ No wonder Mare claims that Aristophanes used the term *korinthiazomai* to express a notion of losing a life, i.e., "to live like a Corinthian in the practice of sexual immorality."²⁴¹

Thus, Mare and Sampley argue that Paul²⁴² arrived in this immoral city in AD 50 (Acts 11) and suggest that 1 Corinthians²⁴³ is written from Ephesus

---

233. Winter, *After Paul Left Corinth*, 12; and Sampley, "First Letter to the Corinthians," 774.
234. Winter, 13.
235. Mare, "1 Corinthians," 176.
236. Sampley, "First Letter to the Corinthians," 774.
237. Sampley, 773–774.
238. Gill, "1 Corinthians," 105.
239. Gill, 105.
240. Sampley, "First Letter to the Corinthians," 775.
241. Mare, "1 Corinthians," 176.
242. It is important to add that authorship of 1 Corinthians is credited to Paul. Indeed, Mare ("1 Corinthians," 179) claims early Christian writers like Clements of Rome and Polycarp appear to acknowledge Paul's authorship. Verbrugge ("1 Corinthians," 248) claims Paul's authorship of 1 Corinthians has been uncontested, probably because of its strong textual evidence (1:1; 16:21; 1:14; 3:6). However, Gill ("1 Corinthians," 108) indicates Paul and Sosthenes, a Corinthian synagogue ruler (Acts 18:17) as joint authors, though Paul appeals to his apostleship role. This appeal could suggest Paul's principal authorship in retrospect of Sosthenes' designation as "our brother."
243. Sampley ("First Letter to the Corinthians," 776) contends that what the Bible refers to as 1 Corinthians is Paul's second letter. The first letter, the so-called previous letter (1 Cor 5:9–

(1 Cor 16:8, cf. Acts 18:18–19) following the establishment of the mission there.[244] Sampley adds that Junius Gallio arrived in Corinth in AD 51 as Roman governor of the province of Achaia (Acts 18:12–17), and mentions Jews bringing him a case against Paul.[245] Furthermore, Mare contends that Gallio was in office in the first half of AD 52, meaning he must have started his proconsulship by 1 July AD 51, "being the time each year when Roman proconsuls took office."[246] Furthermore, Gill argues that the presence of Gallio can fix the date because "An inscription from the sanctuary of Apollo at Delphi shows that he was the governor in Greece when Claudius had obtained Tribunician power twelve times and had been acclaimed emperor twenty-six times. From other inscriptions, these events place the Delphi inscription between the end of 51 and August AD 52 (when he was acclaimed emperor for the twenty-seventh time)."[247] This is further collaborated by Verbrugge's claim that "an inscription found at Delphi mentions Gallio as proconsul of Achaia during the period of Claudius's twenty-sixth acclamation as emperor. Thus, most scholars' hold that Gallio was proconsul from 1 July AD 51, to 30 June AD 52."[248] Therefore, the preceding discussion seems to place Paul's arrival between AD 51 and 52 and is consistent with the historical Junius Gallio proconsulship and Claudius's specific crowning as emperor.

This, argues Sampley, could have happened a few years "after Paul had left Corinth in late summer of 51 . . . The likely date for writing 1 Corinthians would be late fall or winter of 53–54 CE."[249] This range appears likely in light of Gill's and Verbrugge's claim of a date in AD 55, from Ephesus (1 Cor 16:5–9).[250] So, it seems safe to suggest that Paul wrote 1 Corinthians sometimes in AD 55, about three years following his arrival in Corinth.

---

12) cannot be traced. This is what is referred to by Mare ("1 Corinthians," 178) as the sorrowful letter (2 Cor 2:4; 7:8, 9).

    244. Mare, "1 Corinthians," 176; Sampley, "First Letter to the Corinthians," 776.
    245. Sampley, 775.
    246. Mare, "1 Corinthians," 176.
    247. Gill, "1 Corinthians," 106.
    248. Verbrugge, "1 Corinthians," 247–248.
    249. Sampley, "First Letter to the Corinthians," 777.
    250. Gill, "1 Corinthians," 101; Verbrugge, "1 Corinthians," 248.

That aside, it is said that the Corinthian congregation was made up of Jews and Gentiles.[251] Sampley and Verbrugge further claimed that the congregation of believers were poor – lower socioeconomic class (1 Cor 1:26), and that the rich among them sometimes treated the lower class believers shamefully (1 Cor 11:17–34).[252] Furthermore, Sampley argues that Paul depicts Gentile believers as not only the majority in the Corinthian congregation but describes them as former idolaters (1 Cor 12:2).[253] Besides, Verbrugge indicates Gentile believers loathed eating food implicated or associated with the worship of idols, which to them was tantamount to honoring pagan gods.[254] Thus, to effectively incorporate these Gentiles into people of God, Sampley describes their re-socialization so that they would perceive themselves as a segment of "the Israel of God" (Gal 6:16).[255]

That being the case, 1 Corinthians has to be located in the cultural milieu of Paul's day. This puts 1 Corinthians 11:2–16 into its proper perspective concerning the interpretation that cultural norms constitute elements of honor or shame. Sampley observes that the most significant cultural norm in Paul's era was to pursue what promotes honor and to minimize what brings shame, where society was hierarchically structured. The lower strata or the subordinate persons were expected to praise and honor the ones at the helm of leadership.[256] Accordingly, Sampley argues that arrangements of seats at social gathering were carefully allocated according to the grade of status and shame was accorded anyone who went against the decorum.[257]

Immediate Context

It is apparent from the above that some Christians in Corinth were offended by their fellow believers eating meat that had been sacrificed to idols. This sets into perspective the Roman background into which the church is founded and nurtured. No doubt Paul appears to reinforce issues of common decency to avoid backlash from the apparently disgruntled believers who had just left

---

251. Mare, "1 Corinthians," 177.
252. Sampley, "First Letter to the Corinthians," 777; Verbrugge, "1 Corinthians," 244.
253. Sampley, 778.
254. Verbrugge, "1 Corinthians," 244.
255. Sampley, "First Letter to the Corinthians," 778.
256. Sampley, 782.
257. Sampley, 782.

pagan worship. Certainly, issues of decorum in worship, just like eating meat offered to idols were contentious. Indeed, observes Verbrugge, the matter of head covering in worship has been a contentious issue which triggers various interpretations.[258] It is thus audacious to suggest with finality, in this short section, the crux of the text (1 Cor 11:2–16). Indeed, 11:13–15 is considered by the researcher as the thrust of this text, which is viewed as a precis of the entire text.

Winter in reference to 11:4 (veiling of men) appears to dispute the view that this passage is about the veiling of women.[259] Citing D.W.J. Gill, Winter depicts "the Roman convention of men covering their heads while praying and offering up libations. . . ."[260] Winter and Gill observe that evidence of men wearing a toga over their heads "while praying or offering a libation to a god or gods" is found in Corinth. It was the prerogative of the social elite including emperors to wear a veil while offering up a sacrifice.[261] This meant that only the persons taking a leadership role in a pagan ritual veiled their heads. But, Winter (2001:123) states that, though it isn't only the elite that prophesied, this culture spread to the Christian community so that "they covered their heads after the manner of the pagan priests," a concept that appears to have attracted the lower strata of the society.[262] Certainly, claims Mare, women believers attending church with an unveiled head would mostly create confusion as to whether one is mourning or had committed adultery.[263] Indeed, Winter asserts that an unveiled wife is regarded as a woman who has been shorn (11:5), conventionally equated to an adulterous woman,[264] who should have her hair shaved in the manner of a prostitute.[265]

Thus, at the founding of the Roman city of Corinth, the royal values accorded to Roman wives found themselves challenged through what Winter

---

258. Verbrugge, "1 Corinthians," 350–351.
259. Winter, After Paul Left Corinth, 121.
260. Winter, 121–122.
261. Winter, 22 & Gill, "1 Corinthians," 157.
262. Winter, After Paul Left Corinth, 123.
263. Mare, "1 Corinthians," 256.
264. "An adulterous wife should be shorn or have her head shaved as a punishment intended to humiliate her publicly" (Winter, *After Paul Left Corinth*, 128).
265. Winter, 128.

calls new wives²⁶⁶ who could now compete with those they were hitherto customarily differentiated from. This led to an inevitable revolt by the Roman wives of social status against customary and prejudiced values.²⁶⁷

Winter argues that the term wife or woman (γυνή) begins with ages fourteen to sixteen years, which were considered ideal ages for the Roman girls to marry in the first century. Since single girls aged sixteen and below were not allowed to speak in an open gathering, they were unlikely to have prayed or prophesied publicly.²⁶⁸ So the term γυνή, as used by Paul (11:2ff) "would not include the pre-teen or the unmarried woman in her early teens."²⁶⁹ This is collaborated by Verbrugge, although he cautiously suggests that it could also refer to unmarried females.²⁷⁰

However, Winter suggests that the word veil in this context indicates the subjects under discussion were married women. This is because "the marriage ceremony involved what was called in Greek veiling the bride . . . and taking off the veil of a bride was one of the essential components of marriage.²⁷¹ It was the social indicator by which the marital status of a woman was made clear to everyone."²⁷² Thus, unveiled woman in public, argues Verbrugge, may attract men's attention, which could even be more distractive and indecorous in a worship context.²⁷³

So, adds Winter, Paul used the terms veil and woman together to indicate she is married, meaning a widow would not be required to wear her bridal veil.²⁷⁴ Thus, any mention of a woman and a veil to a first-century person signifies a married woman. It appears then, argues Winter, "the issue here was

---

266. This is best described by a conventional speech, the bedroom speech, at the marriage bed of a wedded couple. "Plutarch, writing in the first century A.D, provides an example of such a speech delivered to two young friends. It demanded of the woman religious faithfulness to her husband's gods and the acceptance of his casual sexual encounters with a maidservant or with high-class prostitutes at dinners . . . these sexual liaisons were a means of gratifying lust, for he loved his wife and it would be inappropriate for him to find this sexual release with her . . ." (Winter, 124).

267. Winter, 123.
268. Winter, 126.
269. Winter, 126–127.
270. Verbrugge, "1 Corinthians," 351.
271. Winter, After Paul Left Corinth, 127.
272. Winter, 127.
273. Verbrugge, "1 Corinthians," 354.
274. Winter, After Paul Left Corinth, 127.

married women praying and prophesying without their veil in the Christian meeting."[275] Winter claims the core issue is that the text suggests neither that every married woman attending the meeting uncovers her head nor that every man covers his head, but addresses those who were praying and prophesying with their heads uncovered or covered.[276]

Having placed the text into its historical perspective, the crux of the study will now proceed to the analysis of commentaries by various scholars.

Ancient Interpretation

In expounding this text, several ancient church writers demonstrate aversion for practices that go against natural law. Chrysostom speaks about Paul's appeal to the social convention which is palpable to barbarians and wonders what is wrong with the Corinthians who cannot acknowledge the obvious.[277] Thus, on one end of the continuum, Augustine questions why men wear long hair contrary to Pauline teachings,[278] while on the other end, Clement of Alexandria terms profane and misleading the attitudes of women wearing wigs [hairpieces]. Indeed, Clement of Alexandria's further lament deserves restating: "If a man is the head of the woman, is it not impious for her to deceive him with all that extra hair and at the same time offend the Lord by dressing like a harlot, when her natural hair is so beautiful?"[279]

Reformation Interpretation

Calvin, one of the sixteenth-century Reformers, appears to clarify the relationship between the sexes and affirms its authorship is God. So, male and female "ought with humility to accept and maintain the condition which the Lord has assigned to them . . . [Otherwise they] are rebels against the authority of God," which is tantamount to hurting each other.[280] Furthermore, reckons Calvin, nature dictates short hair as a universal decorum, even amongst the Greeks, a fact endorsed by ancient interpreters.[281] Indeed, Calvin argues that

---

275. Winter, 127.
276. Winter, 128.
277. Chrysostom, "Judge for Yourself," 106.
278. Augustine, "Why Such Long Hair?," 107.
279. Clement of Alexandria, "Long Hair a Woman's Pride," 107.
280. Calvin, *Commentary on the Epistles*, 361.
281. Calvin, 361.

Paul's use of the phrase αὐτὴ ἡ φύσις meant nature itself, and thus upholds the fact that it is disgraceful for a man to display effeminate marks.[282] But Calvin claims ancient chronicles indicate men used to grow long hair.[283] It appears then, argues Calvin, by the time Paul was writing the practice of short hair for men had not come into use in Germany and Gaul. Nevertheless, in Greece men who wore long hair were reckoned indecorous for displaying signs of effeminacy.[284]

Modern Interpretation

"Does not nature itself teach you?"

The phrase "judge for yourself" is viewed by Fitzmyer as Paul's concluding argument as he appears to revert to verses 4–6, to ask rhetorical questions in verses 13–14. In answering the first question, Paul tends to depict the proper decorum in which a woman addresses God in prayer, *vis-à-vis* merely praying in a holy gathering (v. 5).[285] Paul's concern here seems to arise from woman's search for parity with man displayed by her uncovered head.

The second question, contends Fitzmyer, appeals to nature, φύσις which Paul personifies as an instructor of humanity.[286] But, Fitzmyer notes, unfortunately the general order of nature (instructor) has been somewhat overshadowed by social convention.[287] So, in unpacking the phrase "does not the very nature of things teach you?" (Οὐδὲ ἡ φύσις) Ellicott appears to state that the term φύσις denotes the outward more than an inward feeling, but adds that Οὐδὲ seems to appeal "to the support given to the inward feeling by the light supplied by the general order of nature."[288] Also, Garland points out that nature, ἡ φύσις to Paul, refers to male and female hairdos that conform to the expectations of society.[289] Of interest, in this case, is the apparent notion that Roman men kept short hair.

---

282. Calvin, 361.
283. Calvin, 361–362.
284. Calvin, 362.
285. Fitzmyer, *First Corinthians*, 420.
286. Fitzmyer, 420.
287. Fitzmyer, 420.
288. Ellicott, *St. Paul's Epistle*, 207.
289. Garland, *1 Corinthians*, 530.

Indeed, Ellicott recognizes that men in antique times used to wear various lengths of hair depending on their background. For instance, Hebrew men wore hair short, though they were well aware long hair was fashionable (2 Sam 14:26). Also, Greek men initially had long hair, but subsequently it was primarily short.[290] Likewise, Romans after 300 BC had short hair, a fact affirmed by Beet.[291] In addition, Edwards notes men keeping long hair had been reckoned as a mark of honor among the upper classes in Athens though it was later tainted with pride.[292] Thus Ellicott avers, "in early Christian days short hair was the mark of the Christian teacher, as contrasted with the usual long hair of the heathen philosopher."[293] In other words, short hair for men was the acceptable and honorable social convention. Indeed, argues Garland, the general social connotation in Roman Corinth is that men with long hair were effeminate, unnatural and showed signs of moral perversion.[294] Garland further observes that long hair in a Roman context depicted the relationship of the wife to her husband.[295] Thus, Fitzmyer claims that the phrase "wears the hair long" κομάω with regard to men, means more than wearing a beard, a distinguishing mark for the two sexes.[296]

Perhaps Paul's call for attention to what nature teaches might have been precipitated by Romans' obedience to natural law, where short hair for men was standard practice. Since men do not use hair as cover (dishonor for them), as a sign from nature it is only women who need this cover. Thus, Corinthian women should follow the hints of nature and cover[297] their heads since nature has endowed them with an excellent natural cover.

Surely, the ensuing discussion seems to borrow a cue from the previous interpretations in which divine differentiation of men and women is shown by natural affinities to maleness or femaleness, respectively. Barrett contends that nature has made a clear distinction between man and woman in the light

---

290. Ellicott, St. Paul's Epistle, 208.
291. Beet, *Commentary on St. Paul's Epistles*, 187.
292. Edwards, *Commentary on the First Epistle*, 281.
293. Ellicott, *St. Paul's Epistle*, 208.
294. Garland, "1 Corinthians," 531.
295. Garland, 531.
296. Fitzmyer, "First Corinthians," 420.
297. This covering περιβόλαιον is depicted as an article of apparel that covers much of the body, such as a cloak or a mantle (Garland, "1 Corinthians," 531).

of the quantity of hair assigned to each.²⁹⁸ A reverse of this difference renders the outcome artificial. Barret goes a step further and observes that a man has hair on the chin and a woman generally has a gentler voice.²⁹⁹ These signs naturally distinguish the gender.

This being the case, the issue of homosexuality as implied by Barrett that is behind Paul's arguments shouldn't arise on the basis of this clear distinction.³⁰⁰ By following their sexes as intended by God, human beings, argues Barrett, attain the highest glory.³⁰¹ Also, Barrett further observes that Paul did not believe only women should be covered because both sexes ought to cover their nakedness.³⁰² This is expounded by Edwards later in this study.³⁰³ Barrett however lays weight on women on the basis of more hair and thus should follow the clue suggested by her naturally long hair.³⁰⁴

Heading further depicts Paul's explication of natural sensitivities of Christians, based on their previous experiences of synagogue services before their conversion. He seems to suggest that this issue was not a spiritual matter, but gives a hint of sensibility that it was shameful for a man to wear long hair.³⁰⁵ However, as observed by Ellicott, it was not an issue as some O.T. texts like 2 Samuel 14:25–26 and Numbers 6:5 would show. But Ezekiel 44:20 describes the command for the priest, neither to shave nor keep long hair.³⁰⁶

Long hair, a covering, a woman's glory

In this section, Paul draws attention to natural modesty which commonly understands woman's hair as a covering (περιβολαίον) which Edwards relates to πέπλος meaning it is in excess of a veil (κάλυμμα). He further asserts that this veil is worn during prayer to God in addition to the long hair.³⁰⁷ The inten-

---

298. Barrett, *Commentary on the First Epistle*, 256.
299. Barrett, 256–257.
300. Barrett, 257.
301. Barrett, 257.
302. Barrett, 257.
303. Edwards, *Commentary on the First Epistle*, 281.
304. Barrett, *Commentary on the First Epistle*, 257.
305. Heading, *First and Second Corinthians*, p.163.
306. Ellicott, *St. Paul's Epistle*, 208.
307. Edwards, Commentary on the First Epistle, 281.

tion, argues Edwards, is to mark voluntary adoration towards God in worship, on the one hand, and to distinguish worship from social life, on the other.[308]

As a counterpart to the previous verse, Ellicott elucidates the phrase "for long hair is given to her as a covering" (ὅτι ἡ κόμη ἀντὶ περιβολαίου δέδοται), to denote acceptance for women, viewed as a beautiful natural veil.[309] This distinction of sexes (verse 15b) argues Beet, necessitates women having more hair and suggests that long hair deprives men the dignity accorded to the stronger sex. Efforts by men to appear like women misinform feminine nature and disgrace men. In addition, he argues that long hair for women draws admiration and is nature's endowment to them.[310] Beet thus avers:

> Nature has made a visible distinction of the sexes by covering woman's head with more abundant hair. This teaches that the God of Nature designs the sexes to be distinguished, in the most conspicuous part of their body. This natural distinction is recognized in the general judgment of mankind that it is a dishonour for men or women to assume, in this respect, the appearance of the other sex. Now when men stand uncovered before God and women covered, they accept formally and visibly by their own action this distinction of sex and the position in reference to the other sex which God has given. Whereas, if women appear in public unveiled, they do something to obliterate a distinction visibly and conspicuously by nature in the very growth of their hair.[311]

Thus, there is no excuse for women to ignore the natural rhythm of things that uphold physical distinction of sexes, just as there is no reason for men to go against this difference.

Therefore, like his predecessors, Heading acknowledges long hair is for woman's glory and covering. He argues that in Greek, περιβολαίον is a different word from the previous verses 4, 5, 6 and 13.[312] This word, contends Heading, means something cast around (Heb 1:12), connoting the hair is a

---

308. Edwards, 281.
309. Ellicott, *St. Paul's Epistle*, 208.
310. Beet, Commentary on St. Paul's Epistles, 186.
311. Beet, 186.
312. Heading, *First and Second Corinthians*, 163.

veil of glory and beauty.³¹³ Since this natural beauty has no spiritual value in the service it requires a second artificial covering; an observation Edwards alluded to earlier.³¹⁴

In advancing the question why a woman should not pray to God uncovered, Garland brings to the fore the adjective "uncovered," ἀκατακάλυπτος. He suggests that uncovered "does not refer to the woman's hairstyle but a cover over the head."³¹⁵ The matter raised by Garland regards what is fitting, πρέπειν (cover), as contrasted to what is shameful and disgraceful (11:4–5, 14), and what is unnatural (11:14). This concept appears to link to Paul's appeals to nature to reveal what is fitting or suitable.³¹⁶ Therefore, Paul calls for social propriety, which he appears to link to what is dishonorable or shameful³¹⁷ (ἀτιμία) and distinguishes from glory (δόξα), in human social life.³¹⁸ Besides, Paul depicts in verse 15 the ideal conventional display of a woman's long hair, her glory, as opposed to being shaven or uncovered, her disgrace (vv. 5b-6). Further, Fitzmyer advances this argument on the fact that long hair for women is given for covering (περιβόλαιου),³¹⁹ for her glory. Paul wants her to cover herself when praying in public with a wraparound cloak.³²⁰ Maybe as previously observed some hair styles were presumed not fitting before God. So, an extra covering was preferred.

Edwards further mentions a significant point which, so far, may help balance this discussion. He observes, "In previous verses, the Apostle has spoken of the man's shorn head and the woman's long hair as symbols of subjection, in one case to the man, in the other to Christ." That is, man's long hair is a disgrace, and the woman's long hair is her beauty. In this case, the subjection of man to Christ is his glory and "the woman's glory consists in being the glory

---

313. Heading, 163.

314. Edwards, Commentary on the First Epistle, 281.

315. Garland, "1 Corinthians," 530.

316. Garland, 530.

317. Fitzmyer, ("First Corinthians," 421) discredits the argument that Paul thought long hair was a sign of homosexuality.

318. Fitzmyer, 421.

319. Fitzmyer (421) captures an argument by some modern interpreters, like T. W. Martin (*Paul's Argument*, 84) who confuses a testicle, περιβόλαιον with a head covering, an argument completely untenable. This is somewhat linked to the idea that the hair of a woman in this passage is part of female genitalia.

320. Fitzmyer, "First Corinthians," 421.

of the man by subjection to him."³²¹ That being the case, everyone must abide by the acceptable propriety in sacred assembly and prayers addressed to God.

Appraisal of Interpretation of 1 Cor 11:13–15 by Brethren
"Does not nature itself teach you"

This phrase resonates with Brethren worldview of dictums from nature that expects a clear gendered social setup. By expounding the phrase "does not the very nature of things teach you?" (Οὐδὲ ἡ φύσις), Ellicott presents the hairstyle as it should be³²² in the eyes of Brethren. Indeed, argues Beet, maxims of nature necessitate women to have more hair. He suggests that long hair deprives men of the dignity accorded to the stronger sex.³²³ As Fitzmyer implies, men who wore long hair could easily be branded homosexual,³²⁴ a thorny issue in the church today especially in the Anglican Church. The GAFCON 2013 meeting in Nairobi expressed the need to return to the theology of Brethren Fellowship centered on the repentance of sin, confession of guilt and a desire to make amends. This indicates Brethren are not alone in this homosexuality dilemma, which appears to sever the partnerships between Western churches and African churches. In this, Brethren's dictum of walking in light or being willing to suffer isolation might appear like a good thought for the Anglican Communion.

Issues of sexuality are critical to Brethren and inform the separate sitting arrangement of men and women, even in fellowship meetings. Even at the end of fellowship when each of the Brethren is expected to greet one another, embracing of the opposite sex is not expected. In other words, anything that could arouse sexual feelings should be avoided. But some misinformed leaders of revival like Noo contravened this teaching and suffered repercussions. Noo had taught that both sexes could sleep together just because they were believed to be holy ("to the pure all things are pure"), but unfortunately some engaged in sexual relations.³²⁵ Beside this, seriousness on separation of

---

321. Edwards, Commentary on the First Epistle, 281.
322. Ellicott, *St. Paul's Epistle*, 207.
323. Beet, Commentary on St. Paul's Epistles, 186.
324. Fitzmyer, *First Corinthians*, 421.
325. Ogot, Church of Christ, 30.

men and women could have been a lesson from Keswick teachings.[326] This is in spite of the fact that, early church tradition discouraged women (not necessarily wives) from sitting next to married men at public functions as it was construed they would be sexual companions in the evening.[327]

Moreover, Barrett claims that nature has made a clear distinction between man and woman by the nature of hair apportioned to each.[328] This differentiation applies to the teachings of Brethren because they expect men to have hair as men and women to have hair as women. It is important to indicate here that the Brethren's desire is for the two sexes to glorify God. So, as far as this concept is observed within perspectives of well thought out theology, Brethren deserve a commendation.

Again, since women's abundance of hair is universally accepted, the answer to the rhetorical question, "does not the very nature of things teach you?" is affirmative. This confirms Brethren's years of teachings on this issue. Surely, Brethren might feel vindicated by this study, following the onslaught on the dress code, particularly by the younger generation.

Long hair, a covering, a woman's glory

The issue of hair has remained contentious, more so within the Brethren circle where wearing a hairpiece is tantamount to a good dress code. Indeed, Clement of Alexandria seems to take Paul's views literally and castigate extra covering. He claims God had already endowed them with their own beautiful natural hair. Why then offend the Lord by wearing a head covering like a prostitute (Gen 38:12–15)?[329] In other words, extra cover to Clement was a contradiction to the social convention of his day. This to some extent contravenes Brethren who drum up support for a cover, understood as a headscarf as opposed to a wig or artificial hair. Indeed, some Brethren advise their women adherents to either cover their long hair or keep it short (11:6), though Paul regards this as shameful. However, with respect to the anti-wig

---

326. Pearsall Smith's leadership in Keswick meetings ended dramatically in 1875 following accusation of adultery (Pollock, *Keswick Story*, 34–37). Thus, the fact that Smith could suffer such a ruthless end to his ministry, for a mere conjecture of sexual impropriety, reflects the hard-line stance on moral code by Keswick precursors of East Africa Revival.

327. Winter, After Paul Left Corinth, 128.

328. Barrett, Commentary on the First Epistle, 256.

329. Clement of Alexandria, "Long Hair a Woman's Pride," 107.

campaign, there could be influence from the teachings of early church fathers like Clement of Alexandria[330].

But pro-wig interpreters might challenge Clement of Alexandria with regard to what Paul meant by a covering. Indeed, Edwards, Heading and Garland associate a covering (περιβολαίον) to something more than a veil, a second cover which is cast around (Heb 1:12).[331] If this is what Paul means, then artificial hair or cloak as a covering for women's natural hair is not only within the preferred decorum but also theologically informed. This understanding violates the Brethren view and somewhat shakes their socio-ethical belief and practice of walking in the light. But the covering as a second cover cast around is meant to cover possible impropriety posed by sometimes excessive hair styles and has been embraced by most ladies in church leadership today.

Thus, to avoid hairdos becoming a stumbling block to believers, this extra cover apart from artificial hair might placate the Brethren's point of view. This covering in the context of the Brethren is a headscarf, which is fashionable and socio-ethically tenable to them. However, moderate hairstyles and properly tended hair are gaining acceptance. This sounds alarm bells to the Keswick ethos that emphasizes simple lifestyle.[332]

When it comes to men, the expectation for Brethren is short hair, shaved beards and clean shaven faces. A modest and smart dress code is a distinguished mark of the Brethren. One of the bishops who participated in this survey discourages bearded clergy in his diocese. This is perhaps a borrowing from Augustine who shows disgust to men who wear long hair contrary to the teaching of Paul.[333] Edwards and Barrett point out that men too are expected to dress decently and that like ladies they are also symbols of subjection to Christ. As a woman's short hair is disgraceful to Christ, so is man's long hair.[334] Indeed, Ellicott explains the acceptable social convention of men's short hair

---

330. Clement of Alexandria in about AD 190 succeeded Pantaenus "as the most prominent teacher and leader in the Christian schools of Alexandria" (MacCulloch, *Christianity*, 147).

331. Edwards, Commentary on the First Epistle, 281; Heading, First and Second Corinthians, 163; Garland, "1 Corinthians," 350.

332. Pollock, Keswick Story, 143.

333. Augustine, "Why Such Long Hair?," 107.

334. Edwards, Commentary on the First Epistle, 281; Barrett, Commentary on the First Epistle, 257.

exemplified by the fact that Christian teachers wore short hair.[335] Admittedly, Brethren have tried to depict brokenness at the cross of Christ by the way they relate to one another, in the Lord. Indeed, they call their colleagues *muru wa Ithe witu* (my brother in God), *mwari wa Ithe witu* (my sister in God), perhaps as a way of displaying their subjection before the Lord Jesus. In this regard, Brethren display a strikingly similar understanding with the majority of scholars.

Missiological Perspectives on Brethren's Interpretation of 1 Corinthians 11:13–15

Indecorum as an exclusion motif for women and men in true Christian worship is a genuine concern across Brethren circles. No wonder Wright observes that Genesis 1:27 implies "that there is something about the wholeness of human gender complementarity and the mutual relationship it enables that reflects something true about the very nature of God. Not that God himself is sexually differentiated, but that relationship is part of the being of God and therefore also part of the very being of humanity, created in his image."[336] Indeed, this concept speaks to the gender complementarity model, and appears to challenge the Brethren interpretation of 1 Corinthians 11:13–15, which seems to emphasize women's hair style more than men.

Though the text has been interpreted to mean the issue of the covering of hair is for married women, Brethren have generalized it to apply to all women. This is irrespective of the fact that the text challenges both men and women to observe social decorum without which one might be termed a prostitute. Thus, Egnell arguing for the community of equals, concludes that there is a need for "an equal, receiver-oriented" relationship in church worship.[337] Putting this in context, men and women should be expected to dress in a way that differentiates their gender. If this decorum is to be followed, then a model of a new woman and a new man is necessary.

Egnell, contending for a community of difference, recalls the differentiation of the Christian community in Corinth.[338] While admitting the health

---

335. Ellicott, *St. Paul's Epistle*, 208.
336. Wright, *Mission of God*, 427.
337. Egnell, "Minority Community of Equality," 186.
338. Egnell, 188.

side of this distinction, Egnell asserts that hybrid identities – the informing identifying lifestyles – may help Christians to appreciate interreligious multiplicities.[339] Moreover, Wright sees this theme of identity (Jesus shares the identity of Yahweh), expressed in Κυριος Ιησους, (Jesus is Lord), which became a Christological formula for Christian identity, requires no explanation, because it is a universal truth.[340] Moreover, argues Wright, this two-word phrase was familiar with Greek-speaking Jews in the first century CE.[341]

Thus, this differentiation concept in a worshipping community, where individual identities are recognized on the basis of confession of the lordship of Christ, puts gender complementarity in its right perspective.

Historical Development of Interpretation of Daniel 1:8–16

Having looked at the interpretation of Paul's teaching about hair in 1 Cor 11:13–15, the author turns attention to the interpretation of Daniel 1:8–16.

Historical Setting

The claim by early Christian interpreters that the book of Daniel is the work of a single author born during the era of Jeremiah and living in exile in Babylon has been challenged by Porphyry, a third-century pagan philosopher.[342] This challenge has been noted by McCollough as a call for Christian commentators to make clear that the book of Daniel was written during the Babylonian exile.[343] Indeed, many Christian writers have defended Daniel's authorship asserting that Daniel was endowed with wisdom (Dan 1:3–5; 2:48–49) and was loved by God (Dan 9:23).

Thus, McCollough argues that the Babylonian Talmud and Theodoret of Cyr's Commentary on Daniel criticize the Jewish placement of the book of Daniel in the writings rather than the prophets.[344] However, as Collins claims the challenge of authenticity came to the fore again through Uriel da Costa in the seventeenth century, Antony Collins (the English Deist) in the eighteenth century and Bertholdt and Von Lenerke's commentary in the nineteenth

---

339. Egnell, 188.
340. Wright, *Mission of God*, 107.
341. Wright, 108.
342. McCollough, "Introduction to Daniel," 151.
343. McCollough, 151.
344. McCollough, 152.

century.³⁴⁵ Collins further argues that, though there was a consensus in favor of Maccabean dating by the turn of the nineteenth century, the conservative defense of Daniel's authorship persists to date.³⁴⁶ This conservative view seems most plausible to the researcher because matters of faith and unbelief will always pull in different directions. It is, therefore, reasonable to conclude that Daniel is not only the author of the Book of Daniel but also a prophet of God.

Having established the authorship, it is noteworthy to say that the book of Daniel is divided into two sections, chapters 1–6 and 7–12. While the former depicts Daniel's narratives of faith in Yahweh, the latter conveys Daniel's visions.³⁴⁷ Smith refers to these as the historical and prophetical portions.³⁴⁸

The historical setting of chapter 1 places Daniel's ministry in the "third year of the reign of Jehoiakim" (v.1) and marks its end in "the first year of King Darius" (v. 21), which is precisely, 605–539 BCE.³⁴⁹ Indeed, the chronology of this epoch is well documented. For instance, Miller states that Daniel was most likely born in 620 BCE during the reign of Josiah (640–609 BCE) whose first son, Jehoiakim reigned (609–597 BCE) after Jehoahaz, his younger brother's three-month rule (2 Kings 23:30–34).³⁵⁰ But it was during the three months reign of Jehoiakim's son, Jehoiachin in 597 BCE (2 Kings 24:6–16), that Jerusalem was again invaded by Nebuchadnezzar. During this raid, observe Miller and Farrar, Jehoiachin and ten thousand people of Judah were taken captive to Babylon (2 Kings 24:12–16).³⁵¹ Smith notes that they either carried or damaged the holy vessels.³⁵²

Miller indicates that Zedekiah, another son of Josiah (2 Kings 24:17–25:21), was the last king of Judah (597–586 BCE). Like his predecessor, Zedekiah defied the king of Babylon and Jerusalem was eventually seized in 586 BCE.³⁵³ Furthermore, Farrar claims that Zedekiah was killed and

---

345. Collins, *Daniel*, 25.
346. Collins, 26.
347. Longman, *Daniel . . .* , 19.
348. Smith, *Daniel and the Revelation*, 23.
349. Longman, *Daniel*, 19, 42.
350. Miller, *New American Commentary*, 43–44.
351. Miller, 43; Farrar, *Expositor's Bible*, 124.
352. Smith, *Daniel and the Revelation*, 24.
353. Miller, *New American Commentary*, 43.

832 people were taken to Babylon (Jer 29:2; Kings 25:11).[354] Miller argues that Daniel's life cut across the reigns of the five kings of Judah that saw the collapse of Judah and the ruin of Jerusalem.[355]

Immediate Context

This historical background puts Daniel chapter 1 into its proper perspective. It introduces the narration of the four young men aged twelve to fourteen years who were among the captives.[356] They were selected because they were full of splendor and acumen to be trained as pages in the service of King Nebuchadnezzar for three years. This argument is supported by Lucas and further notes that their names Daniel, Hananiah, Mishael, and Azariah were changed to Belteshazzar, Shadrach, Meshach, and Abednego, respectively.[357] The names that exalt Yahweh,[358] contends Lucas, were substituted with designations that most likely invoke Babylonian's god.[359] Farrar observes that the four youths were put under the care of Ashpenaz, master of the eunuchs,[360] and were provided with food and wine from the king's table.[361]

Ancient Interpreters

Theodoret of Cyr notes that Daniel and his friends were well aware of the omnipresence of God, so they continued to worship him even in difficult circumstances (in exile).[362] Thus, Theodoret of Cyr observes that they vowed not to eat the king's food because they saw "Babylonians offer defiled meat to the idols and the polluted libations at the temple."[363] Also, Jerome states that Daniel gained favor in the eyes of the Lord. Subsequently, the prince of the eunuchs somewhat aided him to execute a plan to desist from eating

---

354. Farrar, *Expositor's Bible*, 124.
355. Miller, *New American Commentary*, 44.
356. Farrar, *Expositor's Bible*, 126.
357. Lucas, *Apollos Old Testament Commentary*, 45.
358. Daniel (God is my judge), Hananiah (Yahweh has been gracious), Mishael (who is what God is?) and Azariah (Yahweh has helped) (Lucas, 53). See also Montgomery (*Critical and Exegetical Commentary*, 128–130).
359. Lucas, *Apollos Old Testament Commentary*, 53.
360. It is likely the boys were made eunuchs (Isaiah 39:6, 7).
361. Farrar, *Expositor's Bible*, 126.
362. Theodoret of Cyr, "Youths Reject the Kings Food," 158–159.
363. Theodoret of Cyr, 159.

defiled food from the king's table.³⁶⁴ To this regard, Tertullian conceptualized partial fasting informed by Daniel and his friends' preference for vegetables and water instead of royal delicacies.³⁶⁵ It appears the test was successful because they ended up not only more handsome but more spiritually refined. Furthermore, Daniel was endowed with much wisdom. Truly, God gifted the four young men with much knowledge and understanding.

Reformation Interpreters

The saying that "to the pure all things are pure" (Titus 1:15) looks like an affront by Calvin to Daniel and his companions, whom he accused of moroseness.³⁶⁶ Indeed, Calvin wonders why Daniel should temporarily reject the king's luxuries only to resume later (Dan 10:3).³⁶⁷ Calvin argues that the first reason that led Daniel to reject a luxurious lifestyle was to mourn his motherland. Second, to escape the possible danger of allurements and temptations associated with the royal diet (snares of the devil), that could not only compromise his piety and worship of God but also endanger his health.³⁶⁸ Thus, argues Calvin, it is the consequences of partaking the king's delicacy that makes it abominable to Daniel; the diet is not polluted in itself.³⁶⁹

Calvin argues that the chief eunuch's favor (v. 9) is shown in not reporting Daniel to the king when Daniel had described the royal food polluted. Daniel attributes this favor from a pagan official (prefect) to God's mercy by comparison to previous contemptuous treatment of Jews by their conquerors.³⁷⁰ Thus, Calvin observes that God can make the "most cruel, become humane when the Lord wishes to spare us."³⁷¹ Calvin sees the warm and courteous denial (v. 10) of Daniel's request as another favor of not jeopardizing their

---

364. Jerome, "God Gave Daniel Favor," 159.
365. Tertullian, "Value of Partial Fasts," 159.
366. Calvin, *Commentary on Daniel*, 97.
367. Calvin, 97.
368. Calvin, 98–99.
369. Calvin, 99.
370. Calvin, 100–101.
371. Calvin, 102.

lives.³⁷² Calvin again reckons God's providence (v. 11) to enable Daniel to bend the mind of the servant in charge of Daniel towards his request.³⁷³

Calvin (vv. 12–13) recollects that it was not pollution that made Daniel and his friends reject the royal food, since the Hebrew Scripture (Num 6:2) allows drinking of wine, except for Nazirites.³⁷⁴ By this, Calvin means they could eat any food at the king's table. Thus, the only reason for Daniel to reject the royal food is to avoid adapting "himself to the delicacies of the palace, which would cause him to become degenerate."³⁷⁵ Hence, Calvin thought that would help Daniel lament his country, as opposed to giving into the king's diet.

Following ten days of testing, Daniel and his friends came out shining. Regarding this phenomenon, Calvin (vv. 14–15) claims their simple lifestyle was nourished by God's gracious providence, for they were not lured by the taste, but remained steadfast in their duty to obey and fear God.³⁷⁶

But Calvin claims "it would be very frivolous to subsist entirely on pulse and water; as greater intemperance [self-indulgence], sometimes displays itself in pulse than in the best and most dainty dishes."³⁷⁷ Furthermore, Calvin observes, "For if anyone asks the medical profession, whether pulse and other leguminous plants are wholesome, they will tell you they are very injurious [harmful], since they know them to be so."³⁷⁸ The point Calvin is making is that God is behind the positive outcome of the test and not the choice of the diet.

Modern Interpreters
The youths reject the king's diet (v. 8)
Farrah describes the food at the king's table as meat, game, fish, joints and wheaten bread, which the four young men reject, as they perceive it is polluted.³⁷⁹ Hence, they chose to live on pulses, vegetables and water. The verb, to defile (גָּאַל), argues Collins, has to do mostly with issues of blood (Isaiah

---

372. Calvin, 103.
373. Calvin, 105.
374. Calvin, 106.
375. Calvin, 106.
376. Calvin, 107.
377. Calvin, 108.
378. Calvin, 109.
379. Farrar, *Expositor's Bible*, 126, 133.

59:3), contaminated offerings (Mal 1:7, 12) and matters of exclusion from the priesthood (Ezra 2:62).[380] The royal diet as described here is not forbidden by the Levitical laws. Collins argues that "interpreters since Josephus have thought that the request for a vegetarian diet implied that the rejected foods included meat. Even if the food in question was not specifically defined as unclean in the Torah, the vegetarian diet requested can be understood as an attempt to safeguard the observance of the Levitical laws."[381]

So, these Hebrew youths, observes Miller, were confronted with the dilemma of remaining true to the teachings of Mosaic Law (1 Macc 1:62–63) without suffering from moral and ceremonial defilement.[382] Indeed, argues Collins, Israelites would rather die than eat polluted food. Truly, Hosea 9:3–4 implies the food in exile is defiled. Thus, Jubilees 22:16 elucidates this phenomenon, "keep yourself separate from the nations, and do not eat with them; do not imitate their works nor associate with them, for their works are unclean and all their ways polluted."[383]

Certainly, Daniel's decision to stand firm borders on holiness, a fact supported by many interpreters. Collins, Miller and Goldingay argue that many of the dietary provisions at the king's court were presumed unclean since the laws of clean and unclean were not observed (Lev 11; Deut 14). Again, a portion of the provision (meat and wine) would typically be offered to Babylonian gods before finding their way to the king's table, while in Israel it would have been offered to Yahweh (Exo 34:15; 1 Cor 8–10).[384] Smith concurs and adds that the Babylonians used wine as a libation.[385]

Furthermore, Goldingay claims that abstaining from meat and wine, while in exile, is consonant with mourning and penitence in memory of Judah,[386] a statement affirmed by Calvin.[387] Also, Goldingay asserts that entertaining the

---

380. Collins, *Daniel*, 142.
381. Collins, 142.
382. Miller, *New American Commentary*, 66.
383. Collins, *Daniel*, 143.
384. Collins, 142; Miller, *New American Commentary*, 66; Goldingay, *Word Biblical Commentary*, 18–19.
385. Smith, *Daniel and the Revelation*, 29.
386. Goldingay, *Word Biblical Commentary*, 19.
387. Calvin, *Commentary on Daniel*, 98.

king's delicacies is tantamount to reliance on him.[388] A similar observation is made by Collins who agrees with Calvin that Daniel was avoiding being interfered with and an affluent lifestyle.[389]

Indeed, Lucas argues the manner of an offering to gods could also have applied to a vegetarian diet. Daniel's rejection of the king's diet comes against a framework whereby only the king or high-placed officials had the privilege of their food and drinks, specially offered to the deity for a blessing.[390] But Lucas observes that since Mosaic laws do not exclude wine (except in a vow, Num 6:2–4), Daniel had another reason for his abstinence.[391] Indeed, it is assumed the partakers of the king's food are likely to have an unwavering allegiance to him (11:25b–26a). Furthermore, the importance of meals in the Ancient Near East with regard to covenant-making, for example Exodus 24:1–11, could have influenced Daniel's decision. So what Daniel is rejecting is total control by the king: but then, argues Lucas, the term "defile" isn't explicable.[392]

Daniel and his friends subsequently stood before the king as courtiers and the nature of this role itself seems to the researcher to constitute defilement. Moreover, Collins alludes to the fact that Daniel later ate meat and drank wine, though not from the king's table (10:3).[393] But as Lucas observes, the term "defile," גָּאַל (ga.al) in other contexts refers to cultic defilement, for instance, as used in Ezra 2:62 and Nehemiah 7:64, which in the case of Daniel goes further to give his allegiance to Yahweh.[394] Furthermore, Nebuchadnezzar's plunder of the Jerusalem temple constitutes defilement and a reasonable factor to reject anything that could jeopardize his loyalty to God.

No doubt then, Gaebelein portrays Daniel as a faithful servant of the God of Israel in Babylon. Even though only fourteen years old, he seems to have understood the law of God that he should not defile himself with what he considers to be unclean.[395] Furthermore, Montgomery argues that refraining from meat sacrificed with blood (Acts 15:20) and wine graced with religious

---

388. Goldingay, Word Biblical Commentary, 19.
389. Collins, *Daniel*, 142; Calvin, *Commentary on Daniel*, 97–98.
390. Lucas, *Apollos Old Testament Commentary*, 54.
391. Lucas, 54.
392. Lucas, 54.
393. Collins, *Daniel*, 143.
394. Lucas, Apollos Old Testament Commentary, 54–55.
395. Gaebelein, *Prophet Daniel*, 13.

libations (1 Cor 10:21) was the pious Jews' religious practice to escape defilement. For instance, Judas and his company (2 Macc 5:27) isolated themselves from pollution to eat grass in the mountains.³⁹⁶ Nevertheless, Miller reckons that defilement with wine is not in Jewish law and its profane nature here would be associated with religious libations.³⁹⁷ Thus, Daniel's dilemma was based on his religious convictions that he should remain faithful to Yahweh.

However, contends Collins, not all Jews in the diaspora had a problem with food. For instance, Jehoiachin (2 Kings 25:29–30) and Nehemiah (as a cup bearer) must have eaten from the king's table.³⁹⁸ So the issue of Daniel and his friends must have been occasioned by a need to limit assimilation into the Gentile culture. Thus, they resolved not to pollute or defile (גָּאַל) themselves with the royal delicacies. Miller and Calvin observe that Daniel did not refuse the kingly diet because it had covenant significance,³⁹⁹ but also agrees with Goldingay that Daniel saw the king's delicacies as a snare towards abiding by the king's policies.⁴⁰⁰ Besides, Smith claims that his abstinence was occasioned by his infirmity, a fact earlier observed by Calvin.⁴⁰¹ Nevertheless, this food was unclean by Jewish standards and Daniel decided not to defile himself.

God's favor endangers the eunuch's life (vv. 9–10)

It looks obvious from the way the king appointed the diet for Daniel and his friends that he was interested in their welfare. No doubt, argues Smith, the eunuch was reluctant to grant the young men's request as it could lead to his execution. Moreover, he had specific instructions from the king, failure to do such endangered his head (רֹאשׁ אֶת־חוּב) with the king.⁴⁰² Thus, Miller portrays Ashpenaz the eunuch's response (1:9–10) as God's favor (לְחֶסֶד) and sympathy (וּלְרַחֲמִים) as he worked through the pagan official to grant Daniel's request.⁴⁰³

Montgomery does not think רֹאשׁ אֶת־חוּב indicates the death penalty but understands it to mean the chief official is solely answerable or responsible

---

396. Montgomery, *Critical and Exegetical Commentary*, 130.
397. Miller, New American Commentary, 67.
398. Collins, *Daniel*, 143.
399. Miller, New American Commentary, 67; Calvin, Commentary on Daniel, 99.
400. Goldingay, Word Biblical Commentary, 19.
401. Smith, Daniel and the Revelation, 29; Calvin, Commentary on Daniel, 98.
402. Smith, 30.
403. Miller, New American Commentary, 68.

for the welfare of the youths.[404] But Goldingay views the phrase "endanger my head" as indicating the death penalty. It seems his fear is not imaginary but well-founded (2:12; 3:19–20) if the boys were to end up unhealthy. Therefore, he would not wish to provoke the king to anger and is understandably sad.[405] However, as Smith observes, the fact that Nebuchadnezzar wanted the very best mental and physical growth for these young men shows a praiseworthy kingly picture.[406]

Daniel and his friends appear to be aware of the pressure they were exerting on the chief official (Ashpenaz), and on themselves as well. Certainly, as Goldingay notes, they could have been accused not only of insubordination to Nebuchadnezzar's orders but also of causing disharmony among the other captives who had no problem with the diet.[407]

So, Montgomery observes that the eunuch's compassionate answer was divinely inspired so that after ten days of water and vegetables, they came out stronger and more beautiful.[408] Collins agrees with Montgomery and reckons this favorable attitude to the Jews by Gentile leaders is consistent in chapters 1–6.[409] Montgomery observes similar favors to other Jews such as Zerubbabel, Ezra and Nehemiah.[410]

Lucas notes that the chief official's reply is not an outright refusal[411] but raises a problem that leaves Daniel's request supressed with the possibility of evading the problem.[412] But, argues Lucas, a proposal by Daniel for a test period on a vegetarian diet to a junior officer was successful.[413]

---

404. Montgomery, Critical and Exegetical Commentary, 131.
405. Goldingay, Word Biblical Commentary, 19–20.
406. Smith, Daniel and the Revelation, 30.
407. Goldingay, Word Biblical Commentary, 19.
408. Montgomery, Critical and Exegetical Commentary, 131.
409. Collins, *Daniel*, 143.
410. Montgomery, Critical and Exegetical Commentary, 131.
411. Lucas, *Apollos Old Testament Commentary*, 55.
412. Montgomery, *Critical and Exegetical Commentary*, 131.
413. Lucas, *Apollos Old Testament Commentary*, 55.

Testing for ten days (vv. 11–16)

Farrar observes that they were allowed to experiment for ten days on water and pulse[414] or vegetables (הַזֵּרֹעִים).[415] Smith agrees with Farrar but acknowledges an overwhelming presence of God's favor in their request.[416] However, this request does not imply that eating meat is wrong because as Miller points out, the Passover meal constitutes a meat diet.[417] Indeed, Lucas observes that Daniel later returned to his regular diet of meat and wine (10:3).[418] This shows the issue was not a vegetarian diet, but as mentioned earlier, the implication of partaking the royal food at this point. As Gaebelin notes, this reason would justify Daniel's petition to the chief eunuch to be excused from defiling himself with the heathen food.[419]

Indeed, after the test, Farrar, Smith and Miller assert that the young men appeared healthier and better nourished than the other youths who dined from the king's table. Therefore, they were permitted to continue with a diet of vegetables and water for their entire time of training.[420] Thus, Smith states that pulses, vegetables and water, for only ten days, cannot account for this improvement, except by God's extraordinary intervention.[421]

Conversely, Collins notes Josephus' argument that the young men's fresh look is not a result of a simple lifestyle, but because "they did not oppress and weigh down their souls with a variety of food."[422] Nevertheless, going by the description in the above footnote, the writer believes pulse is a health food. This claim is supported by Miller's contention that nutritional experts advise

---

414. Pulse is a vegetable food of the leguminous kind like peas, beans, etc., plants that are either pulled or plucked, but not reaped (Smith, *Daniel and the Revelation*, 30). In addition, Miller (*New American Commentary*, 69) points out that the term refers to "that which grows from sown seed" and "include not only vegetables but fruits, grains, and bread that is made from grains."

415. Farrar, *Expositor's Bible*, 134.

416. Smith, *Daniel and the Revelation*, 30

417. Miller, *New American Commentary*, 69.

418. Lucas, *Apollos Old Testament Commentary*, 55.

419. Gaebelein, *Prophet Daniel*, p.14.

420. Farrar, *Expositor's Bible*, 134; Smith, *Daniel and the Revelation*, 30; Miller, *New American Commentary*, 69.

421. Smith, *Daniel and the Revelation*, 30.

422. Collins, *Daniel*, 142.

fruits and vegetables for best health.⁴²³ But, Calvin, writing in the sixteenth century, says medically they are injurious.⁴²⁴

Furthermore observes Farrar and Gaebelein, they were endowed with knowledge and wisdom. Indeed, Daniel's respect among the Chaldeans grew due to his understanding of dreams and visions.⁴²⁵ After three years of training, Farrar notes that the four were found superior and worthy to become personal assistants to the king.⁴²⁶

Notwithstanding, Collins doubts the claim that their refusal of the king's food is attributed to asceticism or fasting.⁴²⁷ However, going by Calvin's assertion that Daniel's rejection of the king's diet was to perpetually remember his country,⁴²⁸ and Goldingay's observation that abstaining from a festival diet constitutes mourning or penitence,⁴²⁹ then fasting cannot be overruled.

Appraisal of Daniel 1:8–16 by Brethren
Refusal of "tea" at Gatundu (defiled diet)

As observed earlier, most of the Brethren have interpreted biblical texts almost literally and Daniel 1:8–16 is not an exception. In 1969 the phrases "Daniel resolved not to defile himself" (v.8) and "let us be given vegetables to eat and water to drink" (v. 12), were the rallying call for the disgruntled members of EARM (Brethren) in Kenya. This date is confirmed by some respondents from Kirinyaga who understood the text meant leaving EARM to form another group. The idea of leaving was orchestrated by a demand directed at members of the Kikuyu community to take the tribal oath, called "tea," meant to pay allegiance to Jomo Kenyatta's presidency following the assassination of Tom Mboya in Nairobi. The ordeal is described by Gitari⁴³⁰ as the most humiliating experience:

> They were made to squat and ordered around by unruly youths and given the most unpalatable concoction to drink. Those who

---

423. Miller, *New American Commentary*, 70.
424. Calvin, Commentary on Daniel, 109.
425. Farrar, *Expositor's Bible*, 134; Gaebelein, *Prophet Daniel*, 14.
426. Farrar, 135.
427. Collins, *Daniel*, 143.
428. Calvin, Commentary on Daniel, 98.
429. Goldingay, Word Biblical Commentary, 19.
430. Gitari, *Troubled but not Destroyed*, 185.

resisted were beaten up and some were killed. This brought President Kenyatta into his first major conflict with the church. Many members of East African Revival Movement had refused to take the Mau Mau oath because they could not mix the blood of Jesus that had washed their sins away with that of goats. Many revivalists had been killed for refusing to take the Mau Mau oath and were willing to die rather than drink the "tea" at Gatundu with the president.

Certainly, this is a pagan ceremony, in all its trappings, that could not have been accepted by many members of EARM. Indeed, as hinted by Gitari above, serious oathing preceded the one of 1969. Baur observes that during the *Mau Mau* rebellion against the white regime in Kenya, some Christians succumbed to pressure and participated in the pagan oathing rituals.[431] However, many members of EARM died as martyrs. This boldness in the face of persecution provided the necessary impetus to reject the diet of a goat at Jomo Kenyatta's home in Gatundu.

Like Daniel and his friends, the demand by EARM was to be excused from defiling themselves. Indeed, the situation that EARM found itself in is similar to what the early church interpreter, Theodoret of Cyr,[432] and indeed, most modern commentators, like Collins, Miller and Goldingay perceived of Daniel.[433] That is, like Daniel and his friends, EARM refused Kenyatta's food because it was perceived as polluted.

Taking "tea" at Gatundu with the president would have signaled subjection of their faith to Kenyatta. This could have compromised their faith in God. Similarly, commentators like Calvin and Collins show Daniel's piety and worship of God as enough reason to refuse the king's diet.[434] Thus, the fact that Brethren sought to abstain from what appears profane signifies a missiological model towards the sanctity of the Christian faith in Christ.

---

431. J. Baur, *2000 Years of Christianity*, 480.
432. Theodoret of Cyr, "Youths Reject the Kings Food," 159.
433. Collins, *Daniel*, 142; Miller, *Daniel*, 66; Goldingay, *Daniel*, 18–19.
434. Calvin, *Commentary on Daniel*, 98; Collins, *Daniel*, 143.

Mtama na maji (pulse and water)

The oathing context most likely made some members of EARM choose to separate themselves from those of their members perceived to have participated. This led to the birth of *Mtama na Maji* (sorghum and water) which also came to be referred to as *Kupaa*, which means to rise up, to separate, or to leave EARM. This split was actualized in 1969, a date confirmed by some leaders of EARM who participated in this research.

Thus, like Daniel, the *Kupaa* group was opposed to the eating of contaminated food at the king's or president's table and took the symbolical slogan "only sorghum[435] (pulse) and water." Though the *Kupaa* group did not necessarily drink water and eat sorghum, they were sending a strong message of their call to the salvation of God. Like Daniel they had no problem with meat, *per se*, but with the pagan oath.[436]

The *Kupaa* faction has had a long-standing impact on social lifestyle. Undeniably, some respondents from Mount Kenya Central claimed that *Kupaa* stopped its adherents from attending social gatherings where delicacies were served. This is complemented by a respondent from Embu who contends that the *Kupaa* group was against worldly influence.[437] Indeed, Figgs observes that the attitude of Christians living in affluence and yet giving little gifts to the mission field were frequent reports in Keswick meetings.[438] This inconsistency in giving to the work of God, particularly by Brethren fellowships, has remained a hindrance to the church mission. Most members of *Kupaa* and indeed, most members of EARM/Brethren are inherently poor. Furthermore, many appear not be interested in church missions except in their self-initiated conventions. Additionally, Mambo suggests that they seem to give money to their project through what is called *Mfuko wa Bwana* (The Lord's Bag).[439] This has led many of them to avoid socio-economic programs.

Indeed, a focus group discussion in Kirinyaga attributed this problem of social gatherings to some traditional rituals that precede slaughter of a designated animal on some occasions. The argument has been that some

---

435. Sorghum is a common plant in Kenya and so is easy to apply directly to the text.
436. Calvin, *Commentary on Daniel*, 99.
437. Lucas, *Daniel*, 54.
438. Figgs, "Some Characteristics", 101.
439. Mambo, "Revival Fellowship", 115.

traditional spirits are invoked, rendering the meat unclean to the Brethren. However, this wholesale condemnation of social events today may not be justified, because not all ceremonies may invoke traditional rituals. Not all traditional rites amount to pollution.

Yet they have developed strict morality. On the one hand, they oppose weddings of pregnant girls and renewal of marriages. On the other hand, they emphasize simple weddings devoid of luxuries, where even cutting of the cake is not done. The lifestyle still borders on water and vegetables. This self-denial could be linked to fasting and mourning, most likely for other Christians, who to them are languishing in extravagant lifestyles and pride.[440] However, Pollock states that Keswick taught against reverting to old temptations of pride,[441] so it might serve right for Kupaa to descend to the level of other Christians to inform and be informed.

Evidently, this group of Brethren might have misunderstood the Scripture, taking it out of context and applying it to themselves. As said before, Keswick devotional reading of the Bible could be attributed to almost a century-long style, propagated through leaders of revival. Indeed, the days at Keswick Conventions were spent entirely on the exposition of some key biblical topics dealing with holiness and sanctification.[442] However, the Keswick teachers, as noted before, were mostly theologically unschooled. Little has changed today among the Brethren fellowship leaders. Indeed, the fact that most theologians and clergy seem unwelcome in the Revival Fellowship means the status quo remains.

This creates a distance, not only between Kupaa and EARM but also with other Christians and the surrounding community. Nonetheless, some respondents in Mount Kenya Central argue that later the Kupaa faction developed into the people of light or fellowship of the light (Matt 5:14). Thus, the offshoot of the Brethren Revival Fellowship, which believes in walking in the light, is Kupaa. They exchange greetings, praise the Lord, a hallmark of not only Brethren but of most evangelical Anglicans today.

---

440. Calvin, *Commentary on Daniel*, 98; Goldingay, *Daniel*, 19.
441. Pollock, *Keswick Story*, 67.
442. Reed, *Walking in the Light*, 21.

Missiological Perspectives on Brethren's Interpretation of Daniel 1:8–16

Interpretation of this text by the Kupaa (Rising Up) faction appears to have strengthened their resolve to protect their faith in God against defilement. However, if Kupaa's simplicity is Christ-centered, then their participation in the mission of Christ would have seen the growth of the faction and the Brethren as a whole. But as Iversen observes, Christ in us (Col 1:27) is an essential concept to missional ecclesiology.[443] This makes sense for beliefs and the practice of walking in light because if Christ is in us, then our body is Christ's. That means Christ's body (the church) is not exclusive but welcomes all, even the tax collectors and the immoral people.

Indeed, Livingston depicts the church as God's alternative community in which it "exists simultaneously as a theological entity and a sociological entity,"[444] a concept supported by Iversen.[445] Livingston argues the church should be a genuine missionary community, which recognizes its dual nature in the matters of God and the matters of the world,[446] i.e., being in the world, but not of the world. However, Henriksen claims that the church exists because the world is God's, but it is in a state that somewhat contravenes the dicta of its creator.[447] This dual nature has been problematic: on the one hand, more aspects of the world have entered the church and, on the other hand, the church appears to have less impact in the world. In order to make maximum use of this tension, a preferred future model is necessary.

Following this, Kupaa, like any other member of EARM bases its faith in Christ, and should depict a Christocentric community of forgiveness and reconciliation.[448] Moreover, Hastings states that since the nature of the church is one with the missional Christ, it ought to be attractive and incarnational to the poor and the rich.[449] The Brethren fellowship is prone to exclusiveness and poses a missional challenge. An exclusion motif against affluence forced Kupaa to confine itself to a simple lifestyle. This simple way of life raises a

---

443. Iversen, "Pro me," 193.
444. J. K. Livingston, *Missiology of the Road*, 292.
445. Iversen, "Pro me," 193.
446. Livingston, *Missiology of the Road*, 292.
447. Henriksen, "Mission: Invitation," 70.
448. Hastings, *Missional God, Missional Church*, 128.
449. Hastings, 129.

mission concern because the affluent and other outsiders should have the gospel preached to them. Furthermore, Livingston claims evangelism is the center of the mission, calling all people to join Christ's earthly community.[450] So, while simplicity is a virtue, Kupaa ought to welcome others into the community.

But Wright observes that the exclusiveness of Israel's worship (Deut 4:9–31) is a model for the nation's exclusive faithfulness to Yahweh, without which they would lose their distinctiveness.[451] Unlike Israelites, Kupaa's "Christocentric" distinctiveness is a superficial reflection of self-righteousness – a holier-than-thou attitude.

Anglican Evangelical Tradition Framework for Walking in the Light

In order to ground the missiological foundations needed to critique particular tenets of the current trend in EARM (in chapter 5), this section will explicate the Anglican Evangelical tradition. First, in order to culminate in a new EARM's model of the theology of sanctification, the Anglican Evangelical tradition will inform the researcher's theoretical framework to analyze scriptural teachings related to sanctification and holiness. Since these scriptural teachings have already been captured earlier in this chapter, contextually elucidated, interpreted and applied to the prevailing beliefs and practices of walking in the light, a critique of each will now be placed within the context of the Anglican Evangelical tradition. They will be classified into three themes; exclusion (Eph 5:14 and Dan 1:8–15), standing firm (Eph 6:13) and social convention (1 Cor 11:13–15).

Although standing firm and social convention are to a large extent both exclusive, for the sake of a comprehensive approach to demystifying Brethren scriptural teachings from the perspective of the Anglican Evangelical tradition, they will be analyzed as distinct themes. However, in the formulation of the current theological model of walking in the light, they will be subsumed in the exclusion concept.

---

450. Livingston, *Missiology of the Road*, 227.
451. Wright, *Mission of God*, 380–381.

Second, this section will describe the beliefs and practices of walking in the light in the Anglican Evangelical tradition, a faithful participant in the *missio Dei*.

It is not within the scope of this study to discuss where Anglican Evangelicals are going or who they are taking along.[452] It suffices to say that those in Anglican and Evangelical traditions do not view themselves as one distinct monolithic structure but as having a variety of theological and spiritual influences.[453] Also, Anglican evangelicals faithfully honor their mother traditions though not without theological and practical tensions.[454]

Having said that, it is critical to point out that the concern of this study is to use the Anglican Evangelical tradition framework as a benchmark to analyze Brethren's lifestyle. Three key Anglican Evangelical fundamentals anchor this analysis, namely: supremacy of Scripture, The Doctrine of Reformed ecclesiology and engaging the Prayer Book. Each of these fundamentals supports the themes of exclusion, standing firm and social convention.

Supremacy of Scripture

Packer holds the view that the Holy Scripture is θεόπνευστος (*theopneustos*), that is, God-breathed or inspired by God, and thus a sufficient guide for instruction in all matters of faith and practice (2 Tim 3:16).[455] Indeed, it is useful for correction and renewal of spiritual life for both individual believers and the churches.[456] Therefore, Scripture ought to hold together the seeming cracks that pervade Anglican and evangelical relationships. Turnbull claims Anglicans and evangelicals share basics beliefs concerning the Bible as the highest authority in matters of faith and practice.[457] Moreover, Gills notes that formularies of the Anglican Church were both biblical and evangelical and this appears to vindicate evangelicals' loyalty to Anglicanism.[458] This claim of scriptural supremacy is justified in Anglican and evangelical traditions of origin, canonical and liturgical expressions and in religious observance, which

---

452. Packer, *Evangelical Anglican Identity Problem*, 13.
453. Turnbull, *Anglican and Evangelical*, 49.
454. Turnbull, 93.
455. Packer, *Evangelical Anglican Identity Problem*, 20.
456. Packer, 20.
457. Turnbull, *Anglican and Evangelical*, 104.
458. Gills, "Forty Years on", 238.

upholds the Thirty-Nine Articles, the Lambeth Quadrilateral,[459] the Canons and the Declaration of Assent.[460] Furthermore, the issuing of the Bible in the ordination rites demonstrates its authority in the ministry and mission of the church, which is steadfast with evangelical belief.[461] Packer suggests that evangelical Christianity inside and outside Anglicanism has a high view of the ordained ministry as a personal calling, though the church is regarded as a shared priesthood where accessibility to God and service is open to all.[462]

Nonetheless, tension abounds within the traditions, particularly when some Anglicans quote authorities (reason and tradition) other than Scripture.[463] This is consistent with Wright's description of evangelicals' insistence on the primacy of the Bible and not the church, a perspective that has been pushed forward to depict the Scripture and the church as exclusive alternatives.[464] Wright points out that the interpretation of Scripture can be divisive particularly with respect to doctrinal and ethical debates like homosexuality and women's ordination.[465] Atherstone suggests that an apparent Anglican evangelical identity crisis brings to the fore significant ecclesial and theological questions about what it means to be authentically evangelical in the wider Church of England.[466] This polarization tends to keep the parties looking over their shoulders concerning the alternatives. Following this, a treatment of scriptural themes of sanctification and holiness ought to be considered from the perspective of the Anglican evangelical tradition.

Exclusion

The authority of Scripture is fully observed by Brethren, though they have been accused of literal interpretation and devotional reading.[467] This differs

---

459. 1. The Holy Scriptures, as containing all things necessary to salvation. 2. The Apostles' Creed as the baptismal symbol; and the Nicene Creed as the sufficient statement of the Christian faith. 3. The two Sacraments ordained by Christ himself – baptism and the supper of the Lord. 4. The historic episcopate, locally adapted (Schaff, *Lambeth Quadrilateral*).
460. Turnbull, *Anglican and Evangelical*, 104.
461. Turnbull, 105.
462. Packer, *Evangelical Anglican Identity Problem*, 22–23.
463. Turnbull, *Anglican and Evangelical*, 106.
464. Wright, *Evangelical Anglican Identity*, 25.
465. Wright, 11.
466. Atherstone, *Anglican Evangelical Identity Crisis*, 68.
467. Reed, *Walking in the Light*, 58.

from the Anglican evangelical view, which has been championed by towering theological figures like J.I. Packer and John Stott. Perhaps Brethren need to borrow a leaf from their book and entertain more clergy in their fellowship without losing their spiritual fervor. Certainly, the Bible is central in their life, a tradition that reaches as far back as early Keswick Conventions where themes on various holiness passages were expounded.[468] This is reflected in the writings of the pioneer members of EARM like Dr. Joe Church and Simeon Nsibambi, who fervently devoured the Bible resulting in the famous clarion call, "Every Man a Bible Student."[469] With guidance, this is the way to go. Indeed as Gills observes the International Fellowship of Evangelical Students (IFES) required proper guidelines on the handling of Scripture, but unfortunately, overemphasis on evangelicalism had led them into a "logical dilemma," expressed by Gills in this way: "If the Church is indeed the communion of true believers and its local manifestation was 'the gathering in fellowship of all who are in Christ', what then of those whose denominations were led by men who were clearly not evangelicals and therefore were not in Christ?"[470]

A more "godly worldliness" should be considered, which calls for living in a creative tension, where good from either side is shared. Anglican evangelicals have endured tension, more so after the 1966 disagreement between John Stott and Martyn Lloyd-Jones about whether evangelicals should remain in the Church of England (Stott) or withdraw (Lloyd-Jones), but as Gills observes the tension has not been without consequences. Only time will tell the exact impact of the conflict.[471] Meanwhile, the Anglican evangelical identity has to some extent been elusive, one cannot fail to perceive the pressure of a church on edge despite its distinguished biblical and theological scholarship. The extent to which the church opens its doors to challenge its traditional basis in the Scripture will shape the course of the Church of England in the future. So when a prominent stakeholder participant in this research states that African bishops led by the American and English counterparts have

---

468. Ward, "Introduction," 3.
469. Church, *Quest for the Highest*, 62.
470. Grills, "Forty Years on", 233.
471. Gills, 233.

made claims against LGBT behavior[472] basing their reasons on the Bible and culture, one may not fail to notice obvious tensions that accompany the scriptural authority.

However, serious consideration of the primacy of Scripture without informed exegesis is not laudable either. The majority of the Kenyan wing of EARM, often referred to as Brethren, are illiterate yet faithful believers, who unquestionably apply their literal understanding of the Bible to daily life. Thus, biblically-reinforced dissensions had been the natural consequence over the years, which influenced beliefs and practices of "walking in the light," with the power to set norms of inclusion and exclusion from the fellowship. There is no easy way for such a community other than living on the edge looking over the shoulder at the ones excluded while marking the boundaries for the included. Surely a theology of inclusion of EARM factions and Anglican evangelicals ought to be the model for the future.

Standing Firm

Brethren's view of the primacy of the Holy Scripture cannot be overemphasized. It is so central that the majority of the splits were occasioned by their flawed interpretation of the Bible. Brethren appear to firmly accept the words of Paul to Timothy (2 Tim 3:16) unquestioningly, i.e. the Bible is inspired by God and thus suitable for instruction in righteousness. In this regard, some of them even preach to passengers inside public vehicles. Brethren, like Anglicans and evangelicals, shares fundamental beliefs concerning the Bible as the highest authority[473] despite exegetical challenges. Nonetheless, the Bible should be a focal point of Brethren unity and not a source of division. Brethren theology, like Keswick teaching, has been anchored firmly on the Scripture as the word of God. For instance, Keswick meetings were referred to as conventions for the promotion of scriptural holiness propagated through various Keswick Bible conferences and conventions.[474] It appears that in some ways, evangelicals too were influenced by Keswick, or at least shares antecedents of the Holiness Movement, which as intimated earlier was Keswick's precursor; as Turnbull observes, these emphasized exclusion from

---

472. Stands for lesbian, gay, bisexual, and transgender.
473. Turnbull, *Anglican and Evangelical*, 104.
474. Barabas, *So Great Salvation*, 30.

corrupting influences.[475] This appears consistent with Brethren's advocacy for strict ethical theology informed by what looks like the holiness tradition.

Thus Wright's view of evangelicals' resolve to elevate the Bible and not the church[476] seems plausible. Brethren do not look to the church as a guide to their faith and practice. What appears to matter is scriptural exposition, whether devotionally or not. Brethren view the Anglican Church of Kenya's spirituality as lukewarm for what they perceive as insensitivity to scriptural authority. Thus, some ordinary members of the Brethren who participated in this research questioned theological education at St. Andrew's College, Kabare for graduating students who appear fraudulent. This compares with Packer and Wright's observation of the contempt of Church of England clergy and laity of the 1930s and 1940s for biblical and theological studies. This has changed for the Church of England where theological scholarship has grown but not without divisive Anglican-evangelical viewpoints as seen in the 1967 Keele conference.[477] The standoff between Stott and Lloyd-Jones[478] is reminiscent of the "stand firm" theme, where Stand Brethren stood firm against contending and somewhat marauding forces ranging from the Arise demand for the awakening of those who "sleepeth" to the firm refusal of oathing at Gatundu.[479]

Social Convention

One of the strengths of Anglican evangelical Identity is the mutual sharing of the primacy of the Bible as the core fundamental concerning faith and practice.[480] On the one hand, McGrath associates this mutuality with the evangelical propensity to enjoin itself to any ecclesiology grounded in the Scripture.[481] On the other hand, Anglicans offer to evangelicals a vision of the church, which is not only consistent with the New Testament but also grounded in the Christian tradition that upholds pastoral and evangelistic

---

475. Turnbull, *Anglican and Evangelical*, 79.
476. Wright, *Evangelical Anglican Identity*, 25.
477. Packer and Wright, *Anglican Evangelical Identity*, 53.
478. Gills, "Forty Years on", 231–242.
479. Gitari, *Troubled but not Destroyed*, 185.
480. Turnbull, *Anglican and Evangelical*, 104.
481. McGrath, *Evanglical Anglicanism*, 19

functions.[482] This unique element of association sets the pace for a healthy biblical and theological engagement towards a harnessed and cohesive church. But as Wright observes, the extent to which biblical authority is endorsed will most likely inform doctrinal and ethical issues.[483] Thus, Wabukala claims that the Scripture has been rendered vague by church tradition. He cites a case in the United States where one of the Episcopal Church bishops, in support of same-sex relationships, sensationally attacked the authority of the Bible so as to say "we wrote the Bible and we can rewrite it. We have rewritten the Bible many times." Such provocative sentiments by a revisionist bishop go against social convention and most Anglican evangelicals would reject it.[484]

Certainly, early Keswick theology upheld a social decorum that abhorred sensual self-indulgence and focused on pleasing God and neighbor.[485] This social-ethical expectation informed beliefs and practices of the Keswick Movement, which influenced the East African Revival. No wonder born-again Brethren conversion demands leaving behind a carnal lifestyle and embraces a new life girded with moral codes.[486] Indeed, an accepted code of hair styles is one of the highlights of numerous dos and don'ts that pervade Brethren social life. Although the literal interpretation of the Bible informs Brethren social convention, it has, nonetheless, maintained a distinct spiritual identity that appears to confront Christian nominalism when some section of the church is silent. Indeed, one of the prominent stakeholders who participated in this research maintains that the place and role of LGBT individuals in the Anglican Communion has remained divisive. This is not only a challenge to the Anglican evangelical identity, but one of the main causes of concern in the Anglican Communion gravitated by the GAFCON agenda.[487] Admittedly, the majority of East African Anglican bishops, including the retired Primate of ACK Dr. Eliud Wabukala (GAFCON 2013, online) stand against homosexuality as is informed by the EARM.

---

482. McGrath, *Evangelical Anglicanism*, 19.
483. Wright, *Evangelical Anglican Identity*, 11.
484. Wabukala, "Thirty-Nine Articles", 59.
485. Pierson, "Message: Its Practical Application," 93–94.
486. Langley and Kiggins, *Serving People*, 202.
487. Wabukala, "Thirty-Nine Articles", 52.

Reformed Doctrine Ecclesiology

The theological roots of evangelical Anglican draw inspiration from the Reformed doctrine in what Turnbull calls moderate Calvinism because of its appeal to the Thirty-Nine Articles and The Eclectic Society.[488] In addition, Turnbull contends that moderate Calvinism brings together the Reformed and Puritan traditions alongside the perceptions of the revival with a renewed spiritual impetus, which resonates with the historic foundations of the Anglican tradition.[489] However, observes Gills, working in an eclectic ecclesiastical setting appears to hinder evangelical bishops' evangelical focus.[490] Gills notes remarks by a lecturer at Wycliffe Hall: "We are supposed to have more evangelical bishops in the House of Bishops than ever before, and yet the Episcopal attack on evangelicalism continues unabated."[491]

Turnbull clarifies this scenario by citing John Venn, the Vicar of Clapham who summarizes Anglican evangelicalism's moderate Calvinism at The Eclectic Society: "if to believe the truth of the gospel is enough, then all may be saved. If it be to believe savingly, then the range is more limited."[492] In other words, as Turnbull puts it, the elements of exclusivity still abide in the belief of a general redemption, on the one hand, and specific redemption via the covenant of grace for the elect, on the other.[493]

This puts the Anglican evangelical understanding of predestination into the right perspective whereby the Calvinist stress on sin and depravity is upheld, and signifies the sufficiency of the work of Christ on the cross for everyone.[494] Turnbull observes a Reformed doctrinal evangelism within Anglican evangelicalism in general and affirms a penal substitutionary view of the atonement in which sinners can be reconciled to God in particular.[495]

---

488. Turnbull, *Anglican and Evangelical*, 93. The Eclectic Society was instituted in 1783 by London Clergy who met weekly "for mutual religious intercourse and improvement and for the investigation of religious truth" (Anonymous). Eclecticism is "any system of theology or philosophy which, rather than adhere to one school of tradition, selects such elements as seem the best in several systems, and combine them" (Cross and Livingstone, *Dictionary of the Christian Church*, 527).

489. Turnbull, 93–94.

490. Gills, "Forty Years on", 241.

491. Gills, 241.

492. Turnbull, *Anglican and Evangelical*, 94.

493. Turnbull, 94.

494. Turnbull, 94.

495. Turnbull, 95.

Thus, a practical Calvinism achieved in doctrine, evangelism, ecclesiology and pastoral ministry illustrates crucial features of Anglican evangelicalism[496] albeit theological and practical tensions.

Pastor-scholars like Stott and Lloyd-Jones, at least before the 1966 disagreement, held a traditional evangelical ecclesiology that depicted the Church as an invisible community yet demonstrating a real spiritual partnership transcending all traditions across denominational limits.[497] It is noteworthy, argues McGrath, that evangelicalism has no central or defining ecclesiology and can co-exist within any form of church order, as well as the Roman Catholic Church.[498]

Packer and Wright claim that evangelicals are occasionally misunderstood to have a weak opinion of the church, although the truth is they regard the church as a community organism where fellowship is primary, and the structures are secondary.[499] Nevertheless, they are free to adopt any ecclesiology that is founded in Scripture and Christian tradition and is pastorally based.[500] This suggests Anglicans and evangelicals are interdependent and thus enabled to work together through the catholic structures of the Church of England.[501] But while admitting this interdependency, Gills cautions against damaging the very basis of the evangelical gospel.[502]

Exclusion

The moderate Calvinism as expressed in British Anglican evangelicalism in particular on the doctrine of election appears to stand against the Brethren's exclusive self-righteousness or "holier-than-thou" attitude that pervades their daily sanctification. They are fond of pointing at sin, mostly of other Christians apart from themselves, as if saying they are awake while others "sleepeth," or that they are holy while others are wallowing in defiling lifestyles. Indeed, during the early Keswick Conventions, the subject of the sin principle took the first two days where topics on diagnosis and the cure for

---

496. Turnbull, 95.
497. Gills, "Forty Years on", 237.
498. McGrath, *Evangelical Anglicanism*, 13.
499. Packer and Wright, *Anglican Evangelical Identity*, 51.
500. McGrath, *Evangelical Anglicanism*, 19.
501. McGrath, 19–20.
502. Gills, "Forty Years on", 240.

sin were taught.[503] This shows the remedy for sin is critical to a believer's spiritual life. This view of sin might resonate with Brethren's confession to one another of experiences of failed walking in the light during their weekly fellowships. This appears to negate their hitherto pious disposition and suggests that, like other Christians, they are prone to sin. In other words, they too are depraved sinners in need of Christ's forgiveness.

Indeed, their sanctimoniousness has not only regularly tended to put some of them on a collision course with clergy but have also denied themselves chances of being frontrunners in the evangelism activities of the Anglican Church of Kenya. The costs of this nature of tension appear to resonate with English evangelicals who in spite of producing an Archbishop of Canterbury (George Carey) remain undermined by the Church of England polity.[504] Indeed, the acclaimed conception that the majority Kenyan Anglican bishops are Brethren might be only superficial, if their attendance to the Brethren fellowship is considered.

This view is consistent with one of the prominent stakeholders in this research who contended that the theology of revival today is remote and it is more what some leaders say, but does not impact life. One of the stakeholders admits that most Anglican Church leaders have been influenced by it as far as the doctrine of salvation is concerned but it is not reflected in social-ethical life.

Certainly the lifestyle of Anglicans ought to influence and be influenced by the society around. This is true of the evangelical ecclesiology, which is not limited to any church order.[505] Indeed, a routine that Packer and Wright portray is that the structures of the Church of England ought to encourage interdependence as a community church entity of mutual fellowship.[506] Brethren stereotyping lifestyle is not limited to the ACK and pervades majority mainstream Protestant churches like the Methodist Church of Kenya and the Presbyterian Church of East Africa. This non-denominational community integration if well nurtured and theologically guided might hold the key for a rejuvenated, renewed and all-inclusive Brethren fellowship.

---

503. Naselli, *Let Go and Let God*, 171.
504. Gills, "Forty Years on", 241.
505. McGrath, *Evangelical Anglicanism*, 13.
506. Packer and Wright, *Anglican Evangelical Identity*, 51.

Standing Firm

The eclectic challenge to the Reformed tradition could have contributed to some Anglican evangelicals (like Stott), to believing "it is the will of God to remain in a Church that is sometimes called a 'mixed denomination,'" in this case, pitting evangelicals and non-evangelicals in the Church of England against each other.[507] The ensuing tension could have precipitated episcopal attacks on evangelicalism leading to fewer evangelical bishops in the Church of England.[508] This context puts the "stand firm" concept in its proper perspective as perpetuated by the two leading Anglican evangelical journals, the Churchman (now called the Global Anglican, from a more reformed and conservative evangelical perspective) and the Anvil (usually from a more "open" evangelical perspective that is more positive about being part of the wider denomination), which rival each other.[509] This resonates with the Keswick view of the church as comprised of wounded soldiers[510] where believers were expected to attend a spiritual clinic where diagnoses and cures are administered courtesy of the Keswick Week conveners.[511] But this standoff between the perceived sick and the purported nurse scenario culminated in the "let go and let God" procedure, which is not only unbiblical but misleading as a means of sanctification,[512] and therefore, a flawed means of the Christian doctrine of sanctification.

This sort of divisiveness arising from misappropriation of the doctrine of sanctification appears to have impacted the Brethren lifestyle of daily sanctification through definite beliefs and practices, which hedge them against the present evil now and in the unpredictable future. This creates a paradox. While Brethren appear to put their trust in a panoply of God's righteousness informed by daily sanctification as a defense against their adversaries, they nonetheless segregate themselves from other Christians. Certainly, Brethren appear to rally their defense behind rules of conduct more than reliance on God. Even though this is a significant departure from the early Keswick, "let go and let God" nevertheless, is like falling over the precipice. This trend

---

507. Grills, "Forty Years on", 238.
508. Grills, 241.
509. Atherstone, *Anglican Evangelical Identity Crisis*, 3.
510. Barabas, *So Great Salvation*, 30.
511. Naselli, *Let Go and Let God*, 171.
512. Naselli, 4.

appears to resonate with the worrying doctrinal drift in Anglican evangelicalism following the birth of the Anvil Journal (1984), which as Atherstone suggests continues to conflict with the Churchman.[513]

Social Convention

Roberts, while quoting Ryle's sentiments on the danger of a church that is unclear doctrinally, maintained that a church creed should not be excessively narrow but comprehensive.[514] This is consistent with Turnbull's suggestion that moderate Calvinism incorporates the Reformed- Puritan traditional spirit in the Anglican tradition, which stresses the sufficiency of the cross for all rather than on atonement only for the elect.[515] However, unchecked comprehensiveness on doctrinal purity, argues McGrath, can have counterproductive consequences in the relation between evangelicals and non-evangelicals in the Church of England.[516] It thus seems complicated to observe a conventional tradition that suits all; instead, coexisting in creative tension might be an option.

The early Keswick slogan watchword of "All one in Christ Jesus" sought to harmonize their comprehensive lifestyle informed by sanctification and practical holiness.[517] This slogan, adds Pollock, came into use at the 1882 mega-convention which brought together over twelve hundred delegates.[518] As seen earlier, the teachings of Keswick instilled into its gatherings a theological understanding that somewhat hedged them off from other Christians. This sort of arrangement was also observed with members of EARM. Indeed, Nsibambi, a key pioneer figure of EARM claimed to discern whether new missionaries were born again by shaking of hands.[519] This is consistent with Barrington-Ward's challenge by a Revivalist at Selly Oak, Birmingham to declare his walk in the light.[520] There is no doubt this explicates Brethren's practical social convention, a rigid mindset that has continued to inform

---

513. Atherstone, *Anglican Evangelical Identity Crisis*, 4.
514. Roberts, "J.C. Ryle," 35.
515. Turnbull, *Anglican and Evangelical*, 93–94.
516. McGrath, *Evangelical Anglicanism*, 16.
517. Head, "Watchword of the Convention," 114.
518. Pollock, *Keswick Story*, 62.
519. Church, *Quest for the Highest*, 87.
520. Barrington-Ward, *Revival Through CMS Eyes*, 53.

a two-Christian scenario. One is Brethren and the other is non-Brethren (Christians considered by Brethren to have not been born again), the reason being indecorum according to the Brethren code of conduct. This narrow disposition has affected Brethren's exponential growth, as they seem old-fashioned and out of touch with the Anglican Church of Kenya worship dynamism. In accordance with Packer's observations on Anglican evangelicals, Brethren should pursue clear goals of spreading pure Christianity that adapt and speaks to the life of both the church and the surrounding community.[521]

Engaging the Prayer Book

Turnbull assert that, the second Book of Common Prayer (BCP) of 1552 formulated under Edward VI, not only depicts the Reformed Anglican liturgy but is foundational to both the Elizabethan Settlement and the 1662 edition. This fact sheds light on the apparent relationship between the 1552 Prayer Book and the Elizabethan Settlement of 1559 that set religious uniformity across England.[522] Thus, by instituting the BCP and polity and thirty-nine articles of religion in 1571, Elizabeth appears to have set limits for the Church of England.[523] As McGrath further observes, Anglicanism in its initial phases was not steadfast "to any set of doctrines which can be designated as distinctively and exclusively Anglican," but notes throughout history Anglicanism has embraced some theological inclusiveness.[524]

This is supported by Chadwick who notes that the BCP and the English Ordinal provide the best expression of the Anglican theology of inclusion rather than of exclusion.[525] However, Turnbull observes excessive ritualism and exclusiveness of the Episcopal Church not only inspired formation of the Reformed Episcopal Church in 1873 but also provided opportunity for the Reformed church to organize its ecclesiology based on the supreme authority of Scripture, assent to the plain teaching of the thirty-nine articles and worship centered on the BCP.[526] However, Packer and Wright note devotion to the articles and the 1662 BCP by clergy and laity of the 1930s and 1940s and

---

521. Packer, *Evangelical Anglican Identity Problem*, 29.
522. Turnbull, *Anglican and Evangelical*, 96.
523. McGrath, *Evangelical Anglicanism*, 11.
524. McGrath, 12.
525. Chadwick, "Tradition, Fathers, and Councils," 105.
526. Turnbull, *Anglican and Evangelical*, 53–54.

comments that their piety was individualistic, paternalistic and conservative, disregarding biblical and theological scholarship and disparaging theological studies and bishops.[527]

But this negative appraisal changed in the fifties, courtesy of pastoral and theological talents inspired by the Inter-Varsity Fellowship among students, which paved the way for the Anglican Evangelical Group Movement and the Evangelical Fellowship for Theological Literature. These in turn provided the impetus for the Tyndale Fellowship for Biblical Research while liberal evangelical groups languished.[528] Many of these young people became evangelical Christians with an emphasis on the Bible, simple gospel doctrines, on a personal relationship with Jesus Christ and on Christian fellowship among themselves. It appears the faith of these young people was informed by the Anglican evangelical scholars of the day. For instance, Gills observes that Dr. Lloyd-Jones during the IFES forum in 1952 described the Church of Christ as made up of those who had experienced new birth (being born again).[529] Furthermore, Gills notes Llyod-Jones 1950s' argument that it is logically tenable for evangelicals to fellowship only with the true gospel-believing Christians who are not compromised by state church denomination.[530] No wonder young people had misgivings on the BCP and the Church of England doctrines, apart from evangelism.

The resurgence of evangelicalism was noteworthy, as expressed in the Keele and Nottingham congresses of 1967 and 1977.[531] Hitherto, McGrath and Gills describe the 1967 NEAC meeting at Keele University as the defining moment in the history of not only English evangelicalism but also of the Church of England when many clergy and laity affirmed to serve within the confines of Church traditions.[532] So, Atherstone cites Buchanan's provocative essay "Anglican Evangelicalism: The State of the Party," in which he declared that since Keele 1967 evangelicals had started to arise from the ghetto, to start careful open-ended and impartial reform in the Church of England.[533]

---

527. Packer and Wright, *Anglican Evangelical Identity*, 53.
528. Packer and Wright, 53.
529. Gills, "Forty Years on", 233.
530. Gills, 233.
531. Packer and Wright, *Anglican Evangelical Identity*, 53.
532. McGrath, *Evangelical Anglicanism*, 17; Gills, "Forty Years on", 240.
533. Atherstone, *Anglican Evangelical Identity Crisis*, 64.

MacGrath argues Anglican evangelicals who had previously emphasized morning and evening prayers as the only outstanding regular services, came to reaffirm the centrality of Holy Communion as administered in the local church.[534] This is consistent with Gills' sentiments that the NEAC meeting approved weekly communion as the center of the church's corporate service and that all in the Anglican Church are Christians, and could engage each other in ecumenical debate.[535] That being the case, Turnbull observes that historically both traditions affirm the significance of the gospel for wider society, yet there are tendencies for the Anglicans to submerge underneath society while evangelicals retreat from society.[536] Thus, the push for what appears like an indiscriminate unity would have led to discomfort for both traditions.

Nonetheless, McGrath claims that Anglican evangelicalism has inspired renewal in the Church of England today with a worship style mostly of evangelical orientation, which has been helpful and attractive, especially to the youth.[537] The presence of evangelicalism in the Anglican Church, argues McGrath, acts as a safety-belt against drawing the Anglican Christians towards American evangelicalism, completely insensitive to the Anglican tradition, on the one hand, and on the other, profit from worldwide evangelicalism.[538]

This reflects Ngugi's[539] words of welcome to the Kenyan Anglican clergy visiting the Anglican Diocese of Chelmsford, UK (26 June to 12 July 2017) to organize a *Kigoco* (vibrant songs and choruses) styled worship to enliven the entire conference. This is a distinctively practical Anglican evangelical service informed by African worship dynamics. The influence of evangelicalism cannot be ruled out of this phenomenon of change in the Church of England in the form of style, spirituality and ethics; whereas style has appealed to the instruments of worship ranging from guitar to idioms for praises of Christ and ad hoc liturgy, spirituality and ethics have respectively been invigorated by charismatics and the proper use of worldliness.[540]

---

534. McGrath, *Evangelical Anglicanism*, 17–18.
535. Gills, "Forty Years on", 240.
536. Turnbull, *Anglican and Evangelical*, 111.
537. McGrath, *Evangelical Anglicanism*, 15.
538. McGrath, 16.
539. One of the key organizers of the conference with a Kenyan descent.
540. Packer, *Evangelical Anglican Identity Problem*, 26–28.

Exclusion

In addition to the Bible, the Brethren's next most valuable possession is the BCP. Indeed, even when some have other forums outside the church service, they wait for the end of the liturgy before excusing themselves. This demonstrates their loyalty to the Prayer Book as demonstrated by the English Ordinal that appears to represent the Anglican theology of inclusion.[541] Thus the new Anglican Church of Kenya Kikuyu Prayer Book launched on 15 December 2010 by then Archbishop Dr. Eliud Wabukala has encountered resistance especially from the Brethren who are yet to rise to the new vibrant worship experience. Yet the majority of the young people and the less conservative adults have embraced the New Prayer Book. This resonates with McGrath's view that the Church of England evangelical worship style has been helpful and attractive, especially to the youth.[542]

Nonetheless, the apparent apathy towards the inclusion of the New Prayer Book in the Anglican Church of Kenya worship appears consistent with Brethren stereotyping the weekly fellowship liturgy, which is exclusive. In this regard, they "sleepeth" and need to awake to the reality of inclusive, dynamic worship in the Anglican Church of Kenya today, the Kigoco experience. The encouragement for the Brethren to arise and shine in the new dispensation of liturgical renewal reverberates with the Keele 1967 acknowledgment of renewed evangelicals open-ended relationship with the Church of England.[543]

Standing Firm

As seen earlier, McGrath indicates the BCP appears to set limits for the Church of England alongside polity and the thirty-nine articles of religion.[544] Yet, Chadwick claims that the English Ordinal expresses the Anglican theology of inclusion.[545] But this seems problematic considering Anglican tradition formularies which could to some extent inhibit an open-ended bond with evangelicals. McGrath notes that previously Anglicanism has not been bound to any set of typically exclusive doctrines; instead it has embraced some

---

541. Chadwick, "Tradition, Fathers, and Councils", 105.
542. McGrath, *Evangelical Anglicanism*, 15.
543. Atherstone, *Anglican Evangelical Identity Crisis*, 64.
544. McGrath, *Evangelical Anglicanism*, 11.
545. Chadwick, "Tradition, Fathers, and Councils", 105.

theological inclusiveness in history though not without loss.[546] For instance, Turnbull mentions Anglican replacement of a common prayer service with a weekly communion in the second half of the twentieth century signified a break from historic Reformed Anglican practice. Thus over the years the Church of England has continued to stress its boundaries in the form of new prayer books or less elegant clerical attire in a bid to be more accommodating.[547] This lack of firmness attracts more evangelical worship styles but might eventually lead to Anglican evangelicalism, which is distinctively and exclusively amorphous, without power to stand on the evil day. Certainly, scholars are yet to find a suitable definition for the Anglican evangelical identity.

The Keswick Movement referred to today as Keswick Ministry has become more of a biblical ministry that meets yearly in the Lake District town of Keswick, England.[548] But, even though the Brethren have lost the sting of the previous years, it appears to have somewhat stood the test of time. Admittedly, so far Brethren ethical codes have continued to draw inspiration from the dictums of the daily walk in the light. This, of course, is not without cost as numbers have steadily declined.

Social Convention

Turnbull maintains that charismatic renewal has impacted the Church of England in two ways. First, the liturgical form of charismatic worship has not only led to a less rigid service but a more creative variety. Second, it has resulted in the loss of form of BCP in terms of nature, theology, and content, a situation that requires reversal to enhance renewal within the framework of the Anglican evangelical tradition.[549] The call to reinstate some form in the Anglican evangelical worship services illustrates how complicated it is to erase a longstanding tradition. In other words, changing a social convention invites resistance. Certainly, the new ACK Prayer Book, *Ibuku ria Mahoya na Magongona ma Kanitha* (Book of Prayer and Church Services) has not been wholly accepted, with some congregations in the Mount Kenya region opting to continue using the Kenyan version of the BCP.

---

546. McGrath, *Evangelical Anglicanism*, 12.
547. Turnbull, *Anglican and Evangelical*, 95.
548. Porter, "Editor's Introduction," 9–10.
549. Turnbull, *Anglican and Evangelical*, 125–126.

One of the striking features of Keswick and Brethren teachings is the avoidance of BCP in their fellowships and conventions. The early Keswick had a progressive Keswick Week structure-like outline that guided the morning and evening sessions. Similarly, Brethren fellowships have taken a cue by adopting a rigid liturgical perspective which has completely relegated the BCP to obscurity. Thus Brethren stereotyping liturgy[550] like the Church of England BCP has progressively remained conventional and out of touch with the reality of the charismatic renewal. Indeed, one of the prominent stakeholder participants in this research rightly observes that in Kenya the EARM seems to be at the end of its natural life, in the sense that it has been overtaken by various forms of Pentecostalism.

A New EARM Model of the Theology of Sanctification

Having analyzed the prevailing understanding of Brethren's scriptural teachings on sanctification and holiness from the perspective of the Anglican evangelical tradition, a new model of the theology of sanctification is necessary. While this model is cognizant of the current Brethren interpretation of the scriptural verses that informs beliefs and practices of walking in the light, it suggests a preferred scenario which ought to inform a theology of inclusion rather than exclusion.

As clarified earlier, the exclusive motif is a dominant theme which has shaped the theology of exclusion in the EARM within the mainstream Anglican Church. Thus, standing firm and social convention concepts, though not necessarily subordinate themes in influencing the unfolding events of the current situation, are subsumed in the overall themes of exclusion. By doing this, a formulation of a current comprehensive theological model of sanctification and holiness is conceivable.

Prevailing Theology of Sanctification and Holiness

Brethren's lifestyle has been influenced by the way they interpret Scripture, which as observed earlier has been devotional and exclusively introverted. Arise Brethren excluded Stand, Kupaa, and other Christians from their fold

---

550. Langley and Kiggins, *Serving People*, 200.

on the basis of their interpretation of Ephesians 5:14, construed to mean they were still wallowing in sin and required to wake up. Figure 1 below explicates this scenario.

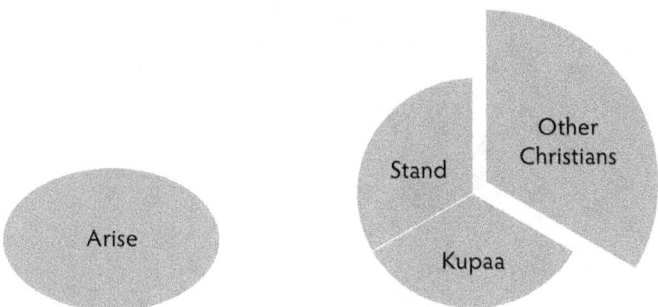

Figure 1: Factions within Brethren fellowship

On the other hand, Stand reacted by standing firm (Eph 6:13) against Arise on the one hand and against Kupaa (rising up above the earthly [Dan 1:8–15]) on the other. Eventually, the three were distinct. Although Kupaa has remained distinct it appears to have merged with Stand. Arise, though now a minority of Brethren has remained consistently distinct. However, the three groups fellowship together at the local level. 1 Corinthians 11:13–15 illustrates a social convention phenomenon in regard to head coverings which subsumes all three criteria at this point, except other Christians as shown below. The funnel (Figure 2) represents Brethren at a local fellowship which incorporates all factions. It also indicates Arise distinctiveness from Stand but tied to Kupaa in the sense of simple lifestyle. This simplicity is inferred in Stand, the largest faction, which appeared to have swallowed Kupaa. Other Christians have to some extent been influenced by Brethren spirituality, thus interlocking with the funnel (Brethren). They are the majority in the Anglican Church, Mount Kenya region. At the bottom of the funnel is the social convention code derived from the Brethren beliefs and practices of walking in the light.

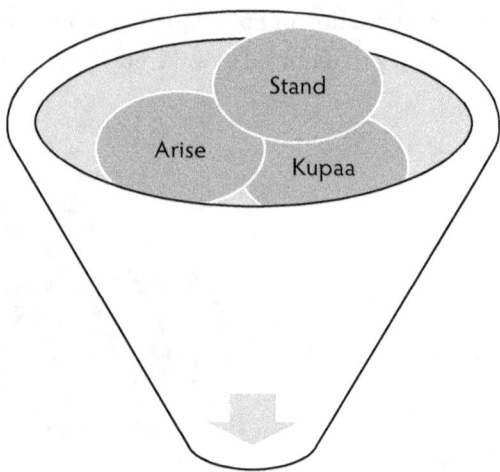

Figure 2: Brethren at local fellowship

This exclusiveness scenario seems to dictate how Brethren relate to the mainstream Anglican Church. While Stand seems more accommodative to the church polity regarding working relationship, Arise ranks a distance second orchestrated by numerous ethical codes. This is demonstrated by Figure 3 below, which also shows some relationship between Stand and Arise with respect to sharing ethical codes of walking in the light.

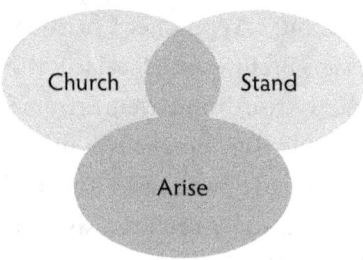

Figure 3: Sharing ethical codes

Although most of the clergy including bishops in the mainstream Anglican Church claim to have been born again, relationships with Brethren have remained strained. On the one hand, most clergy neither gives testimony nor observe daily sanctification in the form and expression that Brethren would expect. On the other hand, Brethren fail to participate in the church development projects and are keen on financial contribution towards *Mfuko wa Bwana* (the Lord's Bag) which benefits only Brethren.

Regarding engaging with the Prayer Book, Brethren possess copies of BCP for use during mainstream Anglican services but not during their fellowship in which their stereotype liturgy takes precedence.

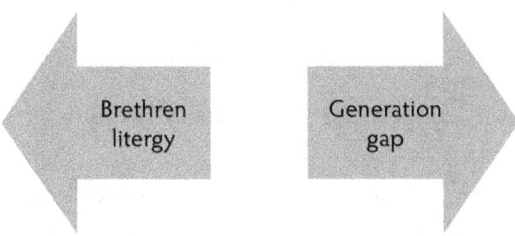

Figure 4: Generation gap dilemma

Indeed, Brethren are appalled by the charismatic and Pentecostal worship styles, and this reflects on the generation gap dilemma (Figure 4). In spite of the fact that Brethren fellowships are made of older adults, there has been little effort to address the current issues that render their worship unappealing to the youth.

Preferred Theology of Sanctification and Holiness

Since the way Brethren interpret Scripture informs their beliefs and practices of walking in the light, a transformation to a preferred scenario is critical. It is pivotal for Brethren to understand the Holy Scriptures are God-breathed and contain all things necessary to salvation, and as such are a source of hope and restoration. Therefore, since all Brethren splits share mainstream Anglican Church beliefs in the primacy of the Bible, it is possible with informed sanctification theology and exegesis to transform the apparent exclusive scriptural teachings into an inclusive viewpoint for Brethren. It is also noteworthy that Anglican tradition holds up especially the Lambeth Quadrilateral liturgical expressions and religious observance. Following this, Brethren who have been baptized and are partakers of Holy Communion ought to advocate for mutual sharing with clergy. In this way, a brother who is authentically Anglican and who not only reveres the Bible but is also versed with its interpretation dynamics will be the preferred model as illustrated by Figure 5.

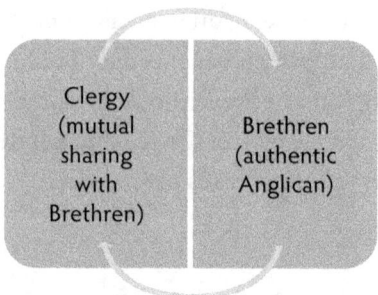

Figure 5: Mutual sharing with clergy

Further, a moderate Calvinism ecclesiology provides for the sufficiency of the cross for justified sinners, who though they may not share Brethren's legalistic code, are Christians just like Brethren. This concept is demonstrated by the interlocking shapes (gears) below (Figure 6).

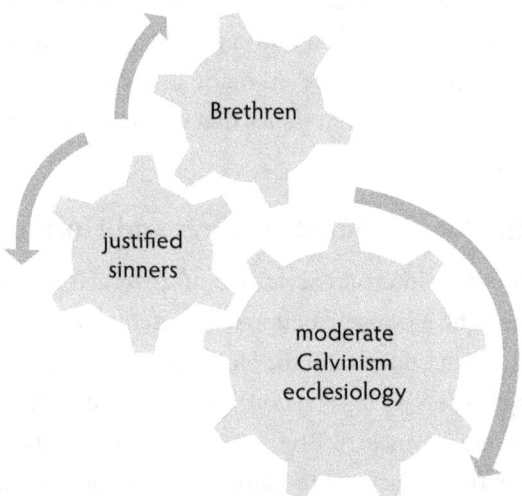

Figure 6: Sufficiency of the Cross

However, balancing between extremes is necessary and within the mainstream Anglican Church structures. This predisposition will not only benefit the Anglican Church in Kenya in terms of maintaining reasoned faith but also an avenue for demonstrating conjoint and interdependent coexistence within the Brethren, on the one hand, and on the other, within the body of Christ, the church. Such an inclusive concept would see more Anglican Brethren bishops in Kenya and a more unbiased explicated practical holiness.

As mentioned earlier, Brethren are keen observers of the BCP as opposed to the new liturgy even when it is in the vernacular. The only challenge is that the BCP is rarely used in some congregations in the Mount Kenya region, which means with time Brethren might get more uncomfortable in the church. But things should not get to that point because the new liturgy is neither too rigid not too vibrant and thus, with guidance Brethren ought to embrace this liturgy. Figure 7 below illustrates a convergent point where the Brethren embrace the new liturgy.

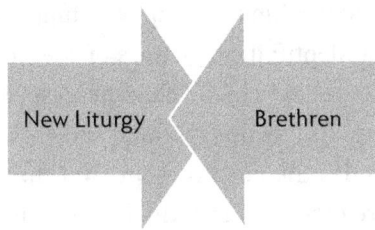

Figure 7: Convergent point

Certainly, liturgical renewal pushes the Brethren to arise from hypocritical dispositions as to allow flexibilities because not everything that is worldly is sinful. Dynamic worship, well guided, expresses the various gifts with which God has endowed the church. That being the case, biblical and theological education shouldn't be worrisome to the Brethren, though theologies should be vetted to avoid extremes.

The overall objective of the shift from the current scenario to the preferred one is to glorify God. Of course, the relationship between the factions and with the mainstream Anglican Church is not a crisis. They all appear to coexist harmoniously. However, though only suggested, moving to untested waters for some Brethren might be a worrisome but necessary endeavour.

Brethren's Lifestyle in the Anglican Evangelical Tradition; Faithful Participants in the *Missio Dei*

The central beliefs and practices of walking in the light are threefold: born again testimony (confession of sin, and daily victory or sanctification), stereotype worship style, and scripturally-based moral codes. In order to be a faithful participant in the *missio Dei*, each cluster will be analyzed from the perspective of the Anglican evangelical tradition.

Born-again Testimony

In this study, understanding a born-again testimony from the viewpoint of the Brethren cannot be overemphasized. However, to place it in the framework of the Anglican evangelical tradition, a recap will suffice. The practice of being born again is the most identifying signature of Brethren. It is important to notice that Pentecostal or charismatic churches, especially in Kenya, share born-again testimonies. But as this research shows, Brethren testimony is unique in that it includes the past, present, and the future. It also serves as a daily occurring register of a sanctified walk with Christ exemplified through confession of failures, sins and victories mostly in their weekly fellowship meetings. They attribute their daily sanctification and victory over sin to the overwhelming power of Christ's cleansing blood shed on the cross. This conviction shapes and hedge their born-again testimony to the point of shutting themselves from other Christians and people of God, for whom Christ also died.

To critique born-again testimony from the viewpoint of the Anglican evangelical tradition, a background of Reformed doctrine is necessary. Certainly, Reformed doctrine within Anglican evangelicalism does not strictly stress the benefits of the atonement of the elect but the satisfaction of the cross for all.[551] Indeed, Turnbull further observes that modern Anglican evangelical scholars like John Stott and Peter Jensen hold a moderate Calvinism view, which demonstrates a penal substitutionary understanding of atonement from the perspective of a Trinitarian God who is both the self-satisfaction and self-substitution.[552] Furthermore, Packer and Wright state that God's mission to the world is to redeem humanity through the substitutionary

---

551. Turnbull, *Anglican and Evangelical*, 94.
552. Turnbull, 94.

ministry of Jesus.⁵⁵³ So Brethren's testimony should not gratify selfish and exclusive gospel ministry but be an open door through which people enter the kingdom. Undoubtedly, the world has been subjected to bondage and condemnation, and eagerly awaits redemption through adoption as God's people (Rom 8:18–25). This is consistent with Packer and Wright who observe that the mission of God is in relation to the entire creation which is subjected to condemnation and reaffirmation.⁵⁵⁴ Brethren's confession of salvation should reach out to those living in the condemnation of sin so that together they can benefit from the covenant of grace.

Mackenzie, citing McLaren's missionary focus on Jesus as a model for Christian mission, observes that churches have elevated the concept of Jesus as Savior to the point of abandoning Jesus' life and ministry, which emphasize following him as Lord by teaching and example.⁵⁵⁵ Indeed, Brethren have pursued their mission through born-again testimony with emphasis on Jesus as Savior and Lord of their lives. This would be a great Anglican evangelical persuasion if, by way of giving testimony, Brethren are inclusive rather than exclusive. Indeed, Wabukala while commenting on the Thirty-Nine Articles of Religion maintained that real mission should be informed by clear theological principles about the gospel without a vested interest.⁵⁵⁶ In light of this conviction, self-interest on the part of Brethren should take a back seat by accommodation of different ways of expressing salvation, within the covenant of grace and faithful participation in the *missio Dei*.

Worship Styles

A distinctively Brethren element is the worship style, either in a mainstream Anglican Church service or their fellowship meetings. In respect to the former, the norm is vibrant spirit dynamism blended with either BCP or the new Prayer Book liturgies. While Brethren seems happy with the BCP liturgy and some reservation to the new Prayer Book, they appear to wear faces of holy disinterestedness to the vibrant music accompanied by electric guitars and drums. In the latter, a stereotyping liturgy is a model characterized by

---

553. Packer and Wright, *Anglican Evangelical Identity*, 95.
554. Packer and Wright, 95.
555. Mackenzie, "Mission and the Inclusive," 259.
556. Wabukala, "Thirty-Nine Articles", 55.

reverential hymns, solemnly sung without musical instruments. As a result, it is rare to find young people attending Brethren fellowships.

However, Packer and Wright are of the view that changes in worship style are inevitable if the worship is to be real and attract young people, in what has been attributed to the charismatic style mostly in British and Anglican evangelicals.[557] Also, O'Brien argues that worship as *invitation* leads to worship as *participation* within the body of Christ (the church) from which the people of God participate in God's mission.[558] This is consistent with Wright's observation that the mission of God propels the totality of creation and nations to universal worship[559] signifying an important theme of inclusiveness of Jesus' mission.[560] Thus, O'Brien states that God intends the church to exist as a *shalom* community where worship as participation centers on community rather than on individuality.[561]

This being the case, Brethren's stereotype fellowship sets itself apart from the church as a community participating in the mission of God. Thus, the Brethren philosophy of beliefs and practices of walking in the light is inconsistent with Christians' understanding of God's mission in which Christians are invited to share in the *missio Dei*.[562] In order to reflect the maxims of a worshipping community, Brethren fellowship meetings should mirror, within the Anglican evangelical structures, the very nature of God as envisioned in the *missio Dei*.

Moral Codes

Moral codes are not only a Brethren fundamental but also biblically-based and pervading all of life. Of all their beliefs and practices, codes of conduct are the most consistent feature dictating the style of giving a testimony and define the overall standing of a Brethren lifestyle of walking in the light. Langley and Kiggins term Brethren fellowship meetings liturgy as "stereotype," in the sense that they begin with singing verses of Tukutendereza, opening prayer, walking in the light, and end with saying grace together and a final

---

557. Packer and Wright, *Anglican Evangelical Identity*, 55.
558. O'Brien, "Procuring of Reverence", 339.
559. Wright, *Mission of God*, 478.
560. Bosch, *Transforming Mission*, 28.
561. O'Brien, "Procuring of Reverence", 339.
562. Turnbull, *Anglican and Evangelical*, 71.

Tukutendereza.⁵⁶³ The fellowship is punctuated with aphorisms of dos and don'ts which appear to inform certain community standards of behavior, without which the world displaces the gospel.⁵⁶⁴

Indeed, Packer and Wright maintain that separation from worldliness has been a central Christian calling that recommended abstinence from certain cinemas, alcoholic drinks, and particular types of hair styles.⁵⁶⁵ But as Packer and Wright rightly note the pendulum has swung the other way,

> Worldliness has come to be defined . . . in terms of godless motives rather than of doing this or that, and it is recognized that abuse of something does not take away its proper use, nor is the use of Christian liberty identical with lawlessness or license. In place of 1 John 2:15 ("Do not love the world") and Romans 12:2 ("Do not be conformed to this world") the guiding maxims are Genesis 1:28 ("Subdue . . . and have dominion," the so-called cultural mandate) and 1 Timothy 6:17 ("God . . . furnishes us with everything to enjoy"), and what appeared as barbarism is giving place to something more like humanism as a view of life, with corresponding entry into fields of thought and action which were previously taboo.⁵⁶⁶

This change seems to have set no limits to what extent one can indulge in godless motives without plunging into evil habits. Indeed, it appears pushing for Christian liberty away from constraining social convention has led to an amorphous scenario of freelance Christian lifestyle. No wonder some English evangelicals and many African Anglicans have expressed reservations about this trend.⁵⁶⁷ They would likely prefer to suggest to the Brethren the idea of a moderate shift in ethics as opposed to the radical swing away from limits that by all standards appear suspiciously radical.

The quotation above can become a starting point for using Scripture to justify liberalism. Thus, Wabukala observes that if Scripture is partially a human invention and is contextually interpreted, the claim to participate in

---

563. Langley and Kiggins, *Serving People,* 200.
564. Langley and Kiggins, 202.
565. Packer and Wright, *Anglican Evangelical Identity,* 56–57.
566. Packer and Wright, 57.
567. Packer and Wright, 57.

God's mission stands on a shaky foundation, in which objectivity of God's word is consequently ambiguous.[568] In addition, Wright brings to the discussion the dynamics of ethics and mission from which Christians' quality moral lives should be noticeable to the nations, as to bring them to glorify God.[569] Bosch concurs and further asserts that a missionary community should view itself as different from and yet committed to its environment in loving and challenging ways.[570] This creative tension should be the way for Brethren as faithful participants in the *missio Dei*, in the context where Anglican evangelical tradition ought to find solace. In connection with this understanding Wabukala claims that GAFCON calls upon the Anglican Communion for self-examination before God, as to remove uncertainty, so that Anglicans can wholeheartedly devote themselves to mission without confusion.[571]

Conclusion

The chapter has explicated the basic missiological tenets which provide a platform to analyze the prevailing practices of walking in the light. In order to give historical-missiological perspectives on the prevailing situation, an exegetical study has been done on some of the key biblical texts related to beliefs and practices of walking in the light. This has not only informed the researcher's theoretical framework to analyze scriptural teachings related to sanctification, and holiness but also brought to the fore new EARM models of the theology of sanctification. The study has also elucidated the evangelical Anglican tradition which hinges the missiological foundations needed to critique specific tenets of the prevailing model of walking in light in EARM.

---

568. Wabukala, "Thirty-Nine Articles", 60.
569. Wright, *Mission of God*, 389.
570. Bosch, *Transforming Mission*, 83.
571. Wabukala, "Thirty-Nine Articles", 58.

CHAPTER 5

Missiological Foundations to Critique Particular Tenets of Walking in the Light

Introduction

The chapter focuses on the missiological foundations used to critique principles of walking in the light. Whereas the scope incorporates formulations of missiological foundations, it also summarizes the prevailing situation as it is and as it should be, culminating in a viable model of *missio Dei*. The chapter is divided into five parts. First, it introduces the layout. Second, it develops missiological foundations informed by a framework of Christian history, biblical theology and Christian anthropology, which critiques particular tenets. These tenets, which are threefold, include conversion, worship, and social-ethical situation. While conversion mainly incorporates born-again testimony, worship and social ethical comprise respectively, a stereotype worship style and moral code lifestyle.

Third, it summarizes the prevailing situation as it is today using historical and empirical analyses. A comparison is carried out between the four selected dioceses and one other diocese which did not participate in the actual research to establish validity and reliability of the research instrument. To have an overall thrust into the current trend, analysis of affinity between historical and empirical trends is examined.

Fourth, it summarizes the prevailing socio-ethical situation as it should be in the perspective of the Anglican Church mission statement in Kenya. To summarize the current trend as it should be, the view of mental, physical, spiritual and social transformation is explicated. Fifth, this study suggests a viable biblically based model of *Missio Dei*. To put *missio Dei* into its rightful place succeeding models are brought to the fore culminating in the changed world example of walking in the light. Finally, a conclusion is provided.

Missiological Foundations

Missiology, argues Bosch, is a branch of the discipline of Christian theology which not only seeks to view the world in the light of commitment to the Christian faith but also subjects Christian mission to rigorous examination and assessment.[1] Thus, Kravtsev puts missiology within the framework of Christian theology from which it develops its rightful role in the study of mission.[2]

Undoubtedly, missiology is by nature a broad and somewhat fluid concept. On the one hand, its scope incorporates not only biblical, theological and historical studies but also informs social sciences and religious studies.[3] While Ott *et al.* somewhat concur with Kravtsev, he is more comprehensive by not only unpacking social sciences and religious studies but also incorporating mission strategy.[4] On the other hand, there appears to be no agreement among missiologists on the range of disciplines.[5] This apparent variance has led to a multiplicity of views as to what are missiological disciplines. Indeed, the argument for interdisciplinary actions pervades explication of missiology, but again exact delineation remains elusive.

Thus, missiologist scholars like Baker and Nehrbass sought a three-legged stool metaphor of history, theology and anthropology to delineate the discipline.[6] Even then, a multifaceted quagmire continues. So, while Baker adds a fourth leg in the name of missionary practice or mission strategy,[7] Nehrbass adds at least two more legs, demographic and strategy.[8] Thus,

---

1. Bosch, *Transforming Mission*, 9.
2. Kravtsev, "What is Missiology?", 1.
3. Kravtsev, 5–6.
4. Ott, Strauss and Tennent, *Encountering Theology of Mission*, xx.
5. Paas, *Discipline of Missiology*, 37.
6. Baker, "Missiology," 17; and Nehrbass, "Does Missiology," 51.
7. Baker, 17.
8. Nehrbass, "Does Missiology," 52.

Nehrbass observes that new legs not only weaken the significance of the stool metaphor as a heuristic device but suffers limitations, especially from scholars, as to which leg is prominent.[9]

This study will not permit discourses on the pros and cons of this metaphor; nevertheless, the three-legged concept will suffice to critique tenets of walking in the light. Thus, Christian history, biblical theology, and anthropology (social sciences) would hinge missiological foundation to critique born again testimony (conversion), stereotyping worship (worship) and moral codes (social ethical).

Historical Perspective of Missiology on Brethren Beliefs and Practices of Walking in the Light

This section constructs the scaffolding matrix of historical missiology by exploring the missiological nature of conversion, worship and social ethics from the viewpoint of Christian history.

Missiological Theory of Conversion in Christian History

To place conversion method within the history of missiology, an explication of its complex nature is critical. Indeed, Love, while conceding to the significance of conversion of sinners as a way of fulfilling the Great Commission, states that the process of conversion is a multifaceted missiological subject.[10] However, Love further notes that the terms ἐπιστρεφω (turn) and μετανοια (repentance) are the most commonly used expressions to illustrate the term conversion as a turning away from evil, idolatry and the dominion of sin, to light.[11] Rambo holds the same view but adds that these terms in the Hebrew Bible signify a change in people's thoughts, feelings, and actions as they repent, while the New Testament depicts the response to the call of God in Christ.[12] Moreover, Kerr and Mulder also assert that conversion involves a comprehensive change from one life to a more meaningful one of purity and goodness.[13]

---

9. Nehrbass, 53.
10. Love, "Conversion," 231.
11. Love, 231.
12. Rambo, "Conversion," 228.
13. Kerr and Mulder, *Famous Conversions*, ix.

Having said that, a missiological perspective on conversion seems to follow the view propounded by Bosch which associates Christian faith to an authentic faith achieved through various epochs of Christian church history.[14] Therefore, this section considers the trend of conversion faith through the early, medieval, Reformation and modern periods.

Conversions in the early church

Following the preaching of Peter in Acts 2:22ff, about three thousand people were converted leading to the birth of the church or to what Comby calls formation of a sect within many other sects.[15] But Comby asserts Christian apologists did not regard Christians as an obscure sect because they were everywhere in the empire.[16] Of note is the conversion in Armenia after Gregory the Illuminator (290 CE) preached to the king Tridates and his army leading not only to conversion of every inhabitant but as Comby observes simultaneously resulted in baptism:

> On an appointed day, after a fast, the holy man summoned the army, the king, queen Aschkhen, princess Khosrovitukhd and all the great men of the kingdom, went down to the banks of the Euphrates at sunrise, and baptized them all at the same time in the name of the Father, and of the Son, and of the Holy Spirit . . . Those who were baptized during these seven days numbered four hundred thousand.[17]

In the early fourth century a significant number of barbarians were converted to Christ through the evangelization of Ethiopia by Frumentius.[18] This epoch also witnessed many individual conversions, some construed as genuine while other were suspicious. For instance, the conversion of Constantine was hailed for declaring Christianity as the official religion of the empire and for protecting Christians who had been undergoing persecution.[19] Despite these favors to the church, Gonzalez argues that Constantine never submitted

---

14. Bosch, *Transforming Mission*, 181.
15. Comby, *How to Understand*, 3.
16. Comby, 11.
17. Comby, 14.
18. Comby, 18.
19. Kerr and Mulder, *Famous Conversions*, 4.

himself for Christian instructions, instead, he regarded himself as "bishop of bishops," and was baptized on his deathbed by the Arian Bishop Eusebius of Nicomedia.[20] Thus, Kerr and Mulder claim that Constantine's conversion in the early fourth century was more of a political strategy to unite the empire than religious.[21]

Consequently, Bosch observes that the church was calling on Constantine, the Christian emperor, to guide Christendom towards the unity of the empire informed by the Christian faith.[22] The mission was expected to be the immediate concern not just for the emperor, but also for the church because as an imitator of God the emperor held together the religious and political offices.[23] Nonetheless, Herring notes that Constantine's conversion did not trigger mass conversion, which suggests Christians were still a minority even by the time of his death in AD 337.[24]

However, some conversions like that of the Apostle Paul and St. Augustine of Hippo (one of the early church fathers) appeared prototypical. While both men experienced dramatic conversion, Paul's experience on the road to Damascus (Acts 9:3–4) demonstrates a model for transformation[25] which Corley calls a fundamental archetype of religious conversion.[26] But equally captivating is Augustine's profoundly long, painful psychological and intellectual pilgrimage recorded in his "Confessions" in which God led him to faith.[27]

Conversion in the medieval church

During the era of Christendom (fourth to eighteenth centuries) the Western church, which embodied the official religion of the state, expanded along the line of Western imperial civilization.[28] Indeed, the baptism of the king of the Franks prompted conversion of barbarians (the Germans) around AD 500 which signified conversion of their people and unity of the empire.[29]

---

20. Gonzalez, *Story of Christianity*, 121, 166.
21. Kerr and Mulder, *Famous Conversions*, 4.
22. Bosch, *Transforming Mission*, 205.
23. Bosch, 205.
24. Herring, *Introduction to the History*, 53.
25. Kerr and Mulder, *Famous Conversions*, 1, 11.
26. Corley, "History of Interpretation," 1.
27. Gonzalez, *Story of Christianity*, 215.
28. Ott, Strauss and Tennent, *Encountering Theology of Mission*, 167.
29. Comby, *How to Understand*, 21.

Further, Comby argues that evangelistic methods sought to convert countries by converting the reigning princes.[30]

Indeed, the Carolingian rulers related political conquest to conversion whereby the conquered country was divided among preachers so that baptism became a badge of loyalty on the one hand, and other, physical violence was used against pagans who resisted conversion and missionaries endorsed forced conversion.[31] Ott, Strauss and Tennent maintain use of force as a mission strategy was considered a legitimate tool for conversion to Christianity.[32] Thus, Addison claims Willibrord missionary work in the eighth century (during the Frankish-Frisian wars) sought to baptize as a way of purifying people won by the sword following the civil war after the death of Pepin in 717 CE.[33] But Raymond Lull (1235–1315), a Franciscan from Majorca opted for a new mission strategy in North Africa that aimed at preaching to the infidels through persuasion rather than sword.[34]

Conversion in the Reformation church

The discoverers and conquistadors of the new lands, like Christopher Columbus, whom Pius IX wanted to canonize, associated conversion with the destruction of heresy and trade.[35] Thus Comby notes that Columbus "wanted both to save the people and to sell them as slaves to finance a crusade and the recapture of Jerusalem. Before taking Indian women as concubines, the conquistadors had them baptized; even worse, before strangling the Indian emperors, they took care to have them baptized to ensure their eternal salvation."[36] No wonder King Afonso of Kongo complained bitterly against King Manuel of Portugal for sending him unscrupulous missionary priests, and canons, bound to ordinary life and poverty, filled their private houses with slave girls.[37] This indecent habit is consistent with Comby's claim that one of the failures of evangelization was mediocre clergy and baptism without

---

30. Comby, 26.
31. Comby, 27.
32. Ott, Strauss and Tennent, *Encountering Theology of Mission*, 167.
33. Addison, *Medieval Missionary*, 42.
34. Comby, *How to Understand*, 46.
35. Comby, 59.
36. Comby, 59.
37. Baur, *2000 Years of Christianity*, 59.

catechesis.[38] Also, Baur observes Father Gonsalo Silveira baptized Mwene Mutapa, his noble men, sub-chiefs and more than three hundred people after catechesis to Mutapa and placing a picture of "Our Lady" in his bedroom.[39] This portrait, argues Baur, made Mutapa have an inexplicable dream of a Madonna, which Gonsalo interpreted to mean the Virgin Mary wished him and his people to become Christians.[40] This psychological manipulation of the king coupled with Portuguese *Padroado* (ecclesiastical jurisdiction to evangelize all conquered countries) appeared a quick way to Christianize the newly discovered lands. However, its close link with *Conquista* – commercial interests – put missionary activity in conflict with trade and politics.[41] In this way, Christianity's persuasion for the pagans became untenable, for it was difficult to differentiate a colonialist from a priest putting mission activities in jeopardy.

But not all were scandalous. Certainly, the conversions of Luther (1483–1546), Ignatius Loyola (1491–1556) and John Calvin (1509–1564), among others, have had huge impacts on the Church since the Reformation era.

Luther was converted while lecturing on Paul's letter to the Romans 1:17 from which he became convinced that it is not a matter of good works that saves but the righteousness of God by faith. On this realization, Stepanek illustrates Luther's joy: "Here I felt that I was altogether born again and had entered paradise itself through open gates."[42] This exclamation is consistent with Marius who adds that Luther's autobiographical commentary of 1545 records his great discovery on the meaning of justification by faith.[43]

Ignatius Loyola was affected by military discipline such that when he suffered a life threatening injury (1521) went to recuperate at the castle of Loyola where he read devotional literature on the life of Christ, leading to his conversion. After recovering, he went on a pilgrimage to Montserrat where he had an all-night watch before the altar of the Virgin Mary. Consequently, he hung up his sword. He later had mystical experiences that became the basis

---

38. Comby, *How to Understand*, 73.
39. Baur, *2000 Years of Christianity*, 80.
40. Baur, 81.
41. Baur, 93.
42. Stepanek, *Luther*, 54.
43. Marius, *Martin Luther*, 105.

of his famous work, "Spiritual Exercises," which became the Jesuit's manual and is commonly used during retreats today.[44]

John Calvin was converted while studying law, thus Kerr and Mulder notes his testimony:

> First, when I was too firmly addicted to the papal superstitions to be drawn easily out of such a deep mire, by a sudden conversion, He brought my mind . . . to submission. I was so inspired by a taste of true religion, and I burned with such a desire to carry my study further, that although I did not drop other subjects, I had no zeal for them. In less than a year, all who were looking for a purer doctrine began to come to learn from me, although I was a novice and a beginner.[45]

Conversion in the early modern church

Since human rationality was viewed as a foundation to overcome superstition and solve human problems in the early modern church, Leibniz, one of the enlightenment thinkers (1697), admonished the Protestants to consider a mission as a way of civilizing the world.[46] Thus, by the time John Wesley (1703–1791) was converted on 24 May 1738, he had not only completed his university degree and entered Holy Orders but had also become a resident fellow and full-time Oxford tutor.[47] Wesley achieved this in spite of spiritual struggle informed by possible waywardness illustrated by his experience with a girl, described as an unhappy love affair.[48] Indeed, Wesley was converted before meeting with a Moravian, Peter Bohler, who mentored a saving faith in him.[49]

Likewise, George Whitefield (1714–1770) was already doing his undergraduate studies before conversion to Methodism via Wesley in 1735 at Oxford in what he termed a new birth or personal conversion to Christ, thus becoming one of the leading Reformed evangelical Anglican clergymen in

---

44. Kerr and Mulder, *Famous Conversions*, 25.
45. Kerr and Mulder, 25.
46. Ott, Strauss and Tennent, *Encountering Theology of Mission*, 121.
47. Baker, *John Wesley*, 22.
48. Kerr and Mulder, *Famous Conversions*, 54.
49. Kerr and Mulder, 55.

the eighteenth century.⁵⁰ He later briefly separated from Wesley for placing too much stress on human effort on experiential salvation but was happy with a Calvinistic understanding of the plight of humanity before God and their inability to save themselves.⁵¹ Kerr and Mulder note the confession of his arrogance and previous brutish lifestyle which despised instruction;⁵² however, his conversion inspired revivals such as the First Great Awakening in North America.

Durnford notes the despicable life of John Newton (1725–1807) preceding conversion which is described in the words of 2 Peter 2:14: "Having eyes full of adultery, and that cannot cease from sin, beguiling unstable souls."⁵³ Thus, Kerr and Mulder observe that Newton's "Amazing Grace" hymn sums up his religious experience, in addition to a self-made epitaph which depicted his conversion experience.⁵⁴ Indeed, Kerr and Mulder reckoned his salvation, thus, "John Newton, once an infidel and libertine, a servant of slaves in Africa, was, by the rich mercy of our Lord and Saviour, Jesus Christ, preserved, restored, pardoned, and appointed to preach the faith he had long laboured to destroy . . ."⁵⁵

Conversion in the modern church

Kerr and Mulder show a written conversion experience in David Livingstone's diary (1813–1873) during his 59ᵗʰ birthday, which goes thus, "19 March 1872 – Birthday. My Jesus, my King, my life, my all; I again dedicate my whole self to Thee. Accept me and grant, O gracious Father, that ere [before] this year is gone I may finish my task. In Jesus' name, I ask it. Amen, so let it be."⁵⁶ Likewise, Dorothy Day (1897–1980) was equally pious; she maintained that Christians have scarcely begun to be Christian so as to deserve the name Christian as they lived on blind and naked faith in spite of God's intimations of immortality.⁵⁷

---

50. Gatiss, *Sermons of George Whitefield*, 7.
51. Kerr and Mulder, *Famous Conversions*, 61.
52. Kerr and Mulder, 61.
53. Durnford, "Life and Works," 3.
54. Kerr and Mulder, *Famous Conversions*, 88.
55. Kerr and Mulder, 88.
56. Kerr and Mulder, 119.
57. Kerr and Mulder, 211.

But some conversions were coerced. For instance, an eleven-year-old Joseph Coen was kidnapped by a priest and taken into the house of catechumens who forcefully detained him despite his tearful plea for freedom.[58] Isser and Schwartz cite other abductions during the Second World War that reflected excessive religious fervor, and indifferent proselytization informed conspiracy.[59]

Indeed, some people like David Drach converted to Catholicism in 1827 when he became convinced that the Jews had corrupted the Hebrew Scriptures (the Enlightenment challenge) and had his children baptized and raised as Catholics following a lawsuit against his wife who upheld Judaism.[60]

Others were voluntary like Ethel Waters (1900–1977) who confessed not to be bound by denominational affiliation and stated her faith, thus: "I don't say I'm a religious person. I say I'm a born-again Christian. And that is the most important thing in my life because I've found my living Saviour."[61]

Having traced views on Christian conversion from the early church to modern, the researcher undertakes an appraisal from the viewpoint of Brethren.

Missiological appraisal of conversion theory from Brethren perspectives

Four conversion models adapted from "History of Conversion" by Issa and Schwartz are used to analyze conversion method.[62] Although Issa and Schwartz talk about three basic types of conversion,[63] a fourth has been extracted from the internalized conformity cluster of intellectual or gradual, and aggressive or sudden so that the analysis will include intellectual, aggressive, compliance and developmental (as a growing adolescence crisis). The number of clusters will not only provide a broad spectrum of analyzing conversion experiences over the centuries but also provide a robust platform to critique the Brethren tenet of conversion. Thus, these models are intertwined in expression, and one might appear to infringe the other.

---

58. Isser and Schwartz, *History of Conversion*, 50.
59. Isser and Schwartz, 52.
60. Isser and Schwartz, 76.
61. Isser and Schwartz, 220.
62. Isser and Schwartz, 25.
63. Isser and Schwartz, 25.

First, an *intellectual (gradual)* model which appeared to attract Augustine, Luther, Ignatius, and Whitefield. Thus, while Gonzalez depicts Augustine's "Confessions" informed by a painful psychological and intellectual journey that culminated in his faith,[64] Luther's conversion pilgrimage occurred when preparing lectures on Romans.[65] For Ignatius, he was converted on a pilgrimage as he read the life of Christ,[66] while Whitefield's conversion led him to brief separation from Wesley over Arminianism tendencies.[67]

Whereas the intellectual conversions appear to depict individual encounters with Christ, they seem to capture the majority of epochs. About intellectual conversions, most Brethren are uncomfortable with religious institutions which they accuse of producing *unsaved* graduates, who depict unstructured formats of giving testimony. Indeed, most graduates do not follow the threefold stereotype testimony marked with experiences of past, present and future expectations. But while not denying some graduates have questionable Christian habits, the majority are theologically and spiritually mature in the light of the informed interpretation of Scripture as opposed to Brethren's devotional approach. Indeed, one of the bishops who participated in this research has a doctorate and is a fervent member of EARM, and is frequently called upon to speak at their conventions.

Second, the *aggressive (sudden)* model finds affinity with Paul's and Calvin's dramatic conversion experiences. While Paul's encountered Christ on the road to Damascus to persecute Christians,[68] Calvin's sudden conversion inspired him to further his religious studies.[69] Most Brethren conversion testimonies depict this criterion. Indeed, some confess to getting saved in a vision, while others claim they were drunk. Truly, the majority of conversions indicate the when, how and where of salvation experience and this confirms the abruptness of the experience.

Third is the *compliance* model which *pro forma* attracts a broad range of affiliates characterized by a lukewarm conversion experience.[70] For instance,

---

64. Gonzalez, Story of Christianity, 215.
65. Stepanek, *Luther*, 54.
66. Kerr and Mulder, *Famous Conversions*, p.15.
67. Kerr and Mulder, 61.
68. Corley, History of Interpretation, 1.
69. Kerr and Mulder, *Famous Conversions*, 25.
70. Isser and Schwartz, *History of Conversion*, 25.

conversion of kings such as Mwene Mutapa[71] and Constantine[72] and the king of the Franks[73] with a single aim of the unity of the people. Others were coerced to convert before the discoverers and conquistadors of new territories killed them.[74] Still others like Joseph Coen in the last half of the nineteenth century were abducted to receive catechism.[75] Certainly, Brethren have no time for what looks like lukewarm Christianity. Indeed, they would view the Anglican Church from the perspective of compliance Christianity which is neither hot nor cold. Undeniably, they mostly use Revelation 3:15–16 to exclude other Christians from their fellowships.

Fourth, the developmental model (likened to the crisis of growth) which is neither intellectual nor traumatic. This category finds affinity with Wesley's, Newton's and Livingstone's spiritual journeys.[76] Whereas Wesley had a crisis of a saving faith, Newton's hymn of Amazing Grace sums up his conversion pilgrimage while Livingstone's rededication of the entire life illustrates his conversion experience. This model finds echoes in the sanctification crisis of consecration during early Keswick Conventions in which a Christian was ushered into the process of a victorious life of surrender and faith, or let go and let God.[77] The affinity of conversion experience is outstanding for Brethren because they believe in a born-again process that elevates them above other Christians. Although Newton and Livingstone's conversion experience for Brethren is not a prototype, Wesley's understanding of entire sanctification is behind the holiness tradition which is a precursor of Keswick theology,[78] which is believed to have influenced EARM beliefs and practices of walking in the light.

---

71. Baur, *2000 Years of Christianity*, 80–81.
72. Gonzalez, *Story of Christianity*, 166.
73. Comby, *How to Understand*, 21.
74. Comby, 59.
75. Isser and Schwartz, *History of Conversion*, 50.
76. Kerr and Mulder, *Famous Conversions*, 55, 87, 119.
77. Naselli, *Let Go and Let God*, 199–200.
78. Turnbull, *Anglican and Evangelical*, 78–79.

Missiological Theory of Liturgical Worship in Christian History

This section briefly explores how mission theory interconnects with liturgical practices in the early church, medieval church, Reformation church, Church of England and modern church

Worship in the early church

Dyrness claims that worship practices are the mutual heritage which unites Christians with God.[79] This unity echoes the worshipping community of Christians in the early church who while they viewed with suspicion, nevertheless had a strong sense of fellowship with the risen Christ and with one another.[80] Furthermore, argues Wegman, now that the church was publicly recognized, a liturgy was envisioned.[81] Although many people embraced Christianity, there was no apparent Christian practice, as most joined the church for the accruing favors from the state.

Worship in the medieval church

Dyrness claims, while commenting on the symbolism of medieval worship, that comfort for medieval people came from their understanding of the world as a unified dramatic process from birth to grave reiterated in the weekly mass, which eventually assumed liturgical form.[82] This understanding resonates with Luther's concept of Babylonian captivity which tied the medieval person from the cradle to the grave in the light of the seven sacraments which ranged from baptism to extreme unction. Dyrness argues that from around 1200 the celebration of mass started to focus on the gesture of the priest as he raises the host and signals when it has converted into the body of Christ, and all the senses are called into play.[83] Also, Wegman states that ringing of a bell indicated the moment of consecration in the context of grave silence by the faithful onlookers.[84]

Thus, Wegman illustrates the Eucharistic experience in what many believers construe a repetition of Christ's sacrifice, but theologians describe it as

---

79. Dyrness, *Primer on Christian Worship*, 5–6.
80. Hardman, *History of Christian Worship*, 3.
81. Wegman, *Christian Worship*, 53.
82. Dyrness, *Primer on Christian Worship*, 19.
83. Dyrness, 20.
84. Wegman, *Christian Worship*, 230.

re-presentation in signs of bread and wine.[85] Whatever the views of the precise form of Christ's presence in the mass, claims Dyrness, God's universal presence in worship informs a real *presence* of Christ.[86] In spite of the abuse of religious objects and images, the decisive role (*the metaphysics of worship*) concerning symbolic acts and objects played a central role in worship during this era.[87] Thus many in the churches while acknowledging the need for reform were of the view of addressing the abuses without harming the practice which nourished the worship life of medieval believers.[88]

Worship in the Reformation church

This period ushers in a concerted effort by Martin Luther to purge abuses of worship particularly the indulgences as expressed in his famous ninety-five theses, nailed to the door of the Wittenberg Castle Church on 31 October 1517.[89] Dyrness notes Luther's concern that these practices corrupted worship as they had become instruments of God's mercy instead of a means of spiritual discipline.[90] Luther's historic discovery that "the just live by faith" led him to suggest that it is the word of God that stops abuses and not outward expressions, though he was comfortable with the medieval structure of the mass.[91] However, Wegman notes some of Luther's followers were making irresponsible and radical worship reforms, as to force Luther to suggest modest liturgical revisions.[92] Indeed, John Calvin pushed away from medieval practices through his famous *Institutes*, which taught about Christian life and elaborated Luther's concept of faith in systematic form for believers.[93] However, like Luther, Calvin's conceptual framework of worship services in Geneva resonates with the medieval mass, though the relationship between believers and worship practices was theologically explicated.[94]

---

85. Wegman, 229.
86. Dyrness, *Primer on Christian Worship*, 24.
87. Dyrness, 31–32.
88. Dyrness, 32–33.
89. Nichols, *Martin Luther's Ninety-Five Theses*, 5.
90. Dyrness, *Primer on Christian Worship*, 33.
91. Dyrness, 34.
92. Wegman, *Christian Worship*, 306.
93. Dyrness, *Primer on Christian Worship*, 37.
94. Dyrness, 37.

Hence, Wegman contends that it was only Zwingli who appeared consistent in liturgical reformation.[95]

Worship in the Church of England – Reformation to modern

Reform in the Church of England began with a royal refutation of the pope's authority that led to not only the removal of medieval abuses but to the revision of liturgical forms of worship.[96] This review gave rise to a reformed Catholicism with all the trappings of Apostolic Church fundamentals, though neither Roman Catholic nor Protestant.[97] In spite of perpetuation of certain Protestant tenets the Church of England did not predispose itself to Protestant revolutionary spirit, although Protestantism continued to challenge until the restoration of the monarchy in 1660 when it aligned itself with nonconformist sects outside the Church of England.[98]

Bradshaw singles out the forms of morning and evening prayer as the most defining features of the Anglican tradition which emerged in the first Anglican Prayer Book of 1549 and have weathered successive editions of the book in the Anglican Communion.[99] Furthermore, argues Hardman, this first English prayer-book, which contained all the revised services in English was issued in 1549 and supplemented by the Ordinal in 1550 before its 1552 edition and before interruption by Mary when she succeeded Edward VI in 1553.[100] But with the reign of Elizabeth in 1558–1603, the English BCP was restored, slightly revised in line with the Church of England's Catholic position.[101] This restoration saw the Consecration of Matthew Parker as Archbishop of Canterbury (1559) as a safeguard of the apostolic succession of the ministry.[102]

The Reformation of the medieval Church of England attracted opposition from liberals and conservatives rendering Acts of Uniformity a failure with a minority laity adhering to the old order; others, Protestants and a pro-reform

---

95. Wegman, *Christian Worship*, 306.
96. Hardman, *History of Christian Worship*, 158.
97. Hardman, 159.
98. Hardman, 159.
99. Bradshaw, "Daily Prayer," 72.
100. Hardman, *History of Christian Worship*, 161.
101. Hardman, 160.
102. Hardman, 161.

majority, held a new sense of the importance of BCP.[103] However, Bradshaw observes that Anglican orders of daily prayer still require more revision alongside the traditional models in a way appropriate to those who want to associate with the church's prayer life.[104] Thus, Roberts acclaims the Church of England's *Alternative Service Book*, or ASB (1980) as the most influential liturgical example that, for instance, retains confirmation as a distinct initiation service after baptism.[105] This recommendation resonates with ACK's New English Prayer Book that tends to open the door for the baptized adult to partake of the Eucharist. However, this rubric is in practice largely ignored.

The other significant heritage from the medieval church is a threefold ministry of bishops, priests, and deacons, and while rejecting papalism, the bishops' proper status was restored, the diaconate permanent ministry status was lost, and replaced with a probationary status to the priesthood.[106] Indeed, Spinks and Tellini maintain the Chicago Lambeth Quadrilateral resolved to preserve the office of episcopacy which informed Anglican union with other churches from the perspective of episcopacy and an Ordinal with the threefold ministry.[107] Indeed, the English Ordinal corrected the notion of the almost exclusive occupation of the priesthood with the celebration of the mass, thus emphasizing pastoral and prophetic functions, as well as giving importance to the imposition of hands and prayer to the Holy Spirit as the essential elements of ordination.[108] Thus, Spinks and Tellini contend that the Ordinal is not only a hallmark of Anglicanism but a bridge church between Roman Catholicism and Protestantism.[109]

Following the above discussion on some of the heritage of the Church of England from the medieval and the Reformation, it is critical to recognize the widespread appeal of public worship regarding spontaneity of congregational singing. Stancliffe notes remarks by a four-year-old watching a televised service from Exeter Cathedral, "Now I know why the churches are true . . . The

---

103. Hardman, 164.
104. Bradshaw, "Daily Prayer," 75.
105. Roberts, "Christian Initiation," 82.
106. Hardman, *History of Christian Worship*, 165.
107. Spinks and Tellini, "Anglican Church and Holy Order," 116.
108. Hardman, *History of Christian Worship*, 165.
109. Spinks and Tellini, "Anglican Church and Holy Order," 116.

people in them enjoy singing, and walk about in patterns."[110] Indeed, this observation appears to reflect charismatic worship in the Church of England, which according to Steven, is one of the two significant developments since 1960.[111] Certainly, Steven notes that the ASB of 1980 hailed an important milestone in the history of Anglican worship since 1662 and continued with ASB's successor, *Common Worship*, which depicts new ritual structures and liturgical language for congregational worship.[112] The second development has been the proliferation of the Pentecostal worship styles related to the charismatic movement.[113]

Missiological appraisal of worship theory from Brethren perspectives
A three-forked way informs this appraisal: worship as a fellowship, worship as a renewal and worship as a spiritual discipline.

First, worship as a joint fellowship is a prominent theme throughout the Christian church worship history as supported by liturgical scholars like Hardman who portrays church as a worshipping community of Christians.[114] Furthermore, Spinks and Tellini observe the Chicago Lambeth Quadrilateral motif of the unity of Anglican and other churches.[115] Stancliffe and Steven note the spontaneity of congregational singing (charismatic worship) arising from charismatic influence and improved liturgical structures and languages since 1960.[116]

While worship dynamics in the early church may not parallel the current trend, it is centered nevertheless on a personal and corporate relationship with Christ and other Christians. In this regard, the Brethren's fellowship is a prime example of collective worship par excellence from the perspective of their meetings where among other elements of worship they sing, confess their sins and hear the word of God.[117] The challenge with this fellowship liturgy is not necessarily a tendency towards legalism but the nature of stereotyping

---

110. Stancliffe, "Is there an 'Anglican' Liturgical Style," 124.
111. Steven, *Worship in the Spirit*, 1.
112. Steven, 1.
113. Steven, 1.
114. Hardman, *History of Christian Worship*, 3.
115. Spinks and Tellini, "Anglican Church and Holy Order," 116.
116. Stancliffe, "Is there an "Anglican" Liturgical Style," 124; Steven, *Worship in the Spirit*, 1.
117. Langley and Kiggins, *Serving People*, 200.

that excludes other Christians. It appears then to be a joint fellowship for members of EARM while those Christians who neither "walk in the light" nor attend fellowship are shut out.

In a nutshell, a sectarian-like scenario of a belief system that is not only introverted but more so renders itself sanctimonious. But Nikolajsen argues that God who is triune, God the Father, God the Son and God the Holy Spirit depicts a community existence of love,[118] which is apparently lacking within the Brethren's exclusive lifestyle. Furthermore, Nikolajsen uses the biblical term *koinonia* to express not only fellowship with Christ (1 Cor 1:9) but also with other members of the local church (1 John 1:3) as part of the mission of the church.[119] Brethren fellowship may not align with this understanding of mission from the perspective of *koinonia*.

Second, worship renewal dynamics in the Church of England, while sensitive to the church tradition over the centuries continue to inform the worship style creatively. Thus, Hardman notes that worship reform in medieval Church of England faced opposition.[120] Surely, Wegman observes Luther's cautious approach that while he did not object to liturgical revisions, he nevertheless advocated for modest reforms.[121] So, Roberts cites the Church of England's ASB (1980) and ECUSA (1979) Prayer Book, their divergent approaches notwithstanding, as prime examples of liturgical renewal in the twentieth century.[122]

While one of the primary purposes of church worship is a contextual and authentic celebration of the kingdom of God on earth, it nevertheless calls for its active participation in the mission of God. Indeed, Wright states the missiological significance of worship for the people of God is to lead creation and the nations to universal worship.[123] This missiological trend is apparently consistent with worship dynamics throughout Christian history. However, Brethren as a worship community resist any form of renewal of its liturgy. This resistance has led to a static liturgy overtaken by time which has had serious consequences exemplified by the low turnout for fellowship meetings.

---

118. Nikolajsen, "Beyond Sectarianism," 463.
119. Nikolajsen, 465.
120. Hardman, *History of Christian Worship*, 164.
121. Wegman, *Christian Worship*, 306.
122. Roberts, *Christian Initiation*, 82.
123. Wright, *Mission of God*, 478.

This situation falls short of what Ott, Strauss and Tennent term "kingdom communities" that demonstrate a passion for obeying God's will not only with all their being but also live their lives as a holy sacrifice.[124] Although their calling is to a large extent clear and sacrificial, their stagnant liturgical growth does not only endanger their future survival but appear inconsistent with the principle of participation in the *missio Dei*.

Third, regarding worship as a spiritual discipline, Dyrness and Wegman observe that the celebration of mass focused on a priest who signals when the host has transformed into the body of Christ.[125] Although symbolic acts and objects informed metaphysics of worship, it was a concern for Luther that these practices would subvert spiritual discipline.[126]

The theme of spiritual discipline is considered the hallmark of Brethren lifestyle as expressed in the way they give their testimony and frequent fellowship meetings. This idea which appears to pervade the medieval and the Reformation church tends to find affinity with Brethren, albeit from a different perspective. While at one end of continuum worship dynamics in the medieval church focused reverently and exclusively on the priest during the mass, at the other end of the continuum, Brethren self-righteously and solely focus on themselves. In this way, the medieval church and Brethren appear to focus on outward practices as instruments of God's mercy instead of viewing them as means of spiritual exercises. Thus, the Brethren emphasis on beliefs and practices of walking in the light not only betrays their focus on their central tenet, the cross of Christ, but also tends to undermine the gospel for the perceived poor (in spirit), who by Brethren's legalistic discipline are locked out of fellowship.

But since the church orients itself toward the coming kingdom of God it should not isolate itself from society because being missional does not eradicate sectarianism.[127] Following this argument, if Brethren could revert their focus to Christ and the gospel, instead of self-righteous codes of conduct, a spiritual discipline informed by the inclusive embrace of other Christians will attract not only spiritual growth but also numbers. Thus argue Ott, Strauss

---

124. Ott, Strauss and Tennent, *Encountering Theology of Mission*, 159.
125. Dyrness, *Primer on Christian Worship*, 20; Wegman, *Christian Worship*, 230.
126. Dyrness, 32–33.
127. Nikolajsen, *Beyond Sectarianism*, 470.

and Tennent, the work of missions is the sending-out activity of the church to expand Christian communities among all humanity.[128] If the Brethren's informed spiritual discipline appropriates this principle of missions, they might regain their respect as a missional community.

Missiological Theory of Social Ethics in Christian History

A working description of social ethics by Carroll suffices for the understanding and perspective of this segment.[129] Carroll defines social standards generally as the shared moral values and behavior in a particular context, in which he associates identity and duty with Christian faith, tradition, and community.[130] However, this integration into the community around them ought to strike a balance between church tradition and the contextual, cultural setting.[131]

Social ethics in the early church

This age was dominated by Hellenistic-Roman civilization informed by systems of thoughts such as one model of society, one body of law and one universe of ideas, which Christianity had to permeate.[132] Nonetheless, contends Gonzalez, the majority of Christians in the first three centuries fitted into the lower strata of society.[133] Conversely, Bosch observes that by the time of Constantine the church had become the bearer of culture and a civilizing instrument in society.[134] Bosch observes for theological and cultural reasons this meant Christians were the civilized and educated, thus, mission movement was from the superior (Christian) to the inferior (non-Christian) faiths.[135] Certainly, argues Ott, Strauss and Tennent, civilization was construed to mean a deliberate attempt by missionaries to bring both the gospel and the culture of their sending church to non-Christian societies.[136] Furthermore, Bosch claims that the monastic movement which flourished during the last quarter

---

128. Ott, Strauss and Tennent, *Encountering Theology of Mission*, 160.
129. Carroll, "Ethics," 321.
130. Carroll, 321.
131. Carroll, 321.
132. Walls, *Missionary Movement*, 18.
133. Gonzalez, *Story of Christianity*, 91.
134. Bosch, *Transforming Mission*, 193.
135. Bosch, 193.
136. Ott, Strauss and Tennent, *Encountering Theology of Mission*, 20.

of the third century and the first quarter of the fourth century was essentially the real bearer of the missionary ideal and practice that saw the disintegration of rural paganism in the entire Greco-Roman world.[137] Indeed, following the Constantinian era, martyrdom was no longer required because the ascetics were seen to have replaced physical martyrdom[138] with spiritual martyrdom as a protest against worldliness.[139]

Social Ethics in the medieval church

Bosch asserts that since the fourth century the history of the church, especially in the East, was associated with the history of monasticism.[140] Whereas Eastern monasticism was a private affair (eremitic), Western monasticism was fundamentally communal (cenobitic) and prudently structured and highly regarded by the general populace.[141] For instance, Addison observes that the missionary role of monasticism in Ireland and Scotland compelled the Celtic church to organize itself virtually on monastic lines such that all the missionaries were monks and lived in monasteries.[142] However, argues Bosch, monks were not deliberately missionaries, though their conduct was that of a missionary.[143]

Addison further quotes Dowden who notes, "The monastery was everywhere the home and Seminary of Christian learning, the centre of Christian work, and everywhere, as it were, the military base of operations against the powers of heathendom."[144] Bosch notes that from the fifth to twelfth centuries the monastery was both the center of cultural civilization and mission and saved the medieval church from complacency.[145] The Irish monks, for example, are said to have contributed most to the tradition of learning and

---

137. Bosch, *Transforming Mission*, 201–202.
138. Bosch (231) notes McNally's suggestion of three types of martyrdom in the eighth-century Irish Cambrai Homily which symbolized three stages of martyrdom categorized thus: white (asceticism), green (contrition and penance), and red (total mortification for Christ's sake).
139. Bosch, 202, 231.
140. Bosch, 202.
141. Bosch, 231.
142. Addison, *Medieval Missionary*, 75.
143. Bosch, *Transforming Mission*, 233.
144. Addison, *Medieval Missionary*, 75.
145. Bosch, *Transforming Mission*, 230.

educational activities following the decline of the Byzantine Empire.[146] Bosch argues monks had resilience such that when barbarians burnt down monasteries and had them killed or driven out, the survivors would reconstitute the tradition, singing the same liturgy, reading the same books and thinking the same as their forerunners.[147]

Bosch further notes the monk's exemplary lifestyle impacted the peasants, and their conduct praised by the Celtic monk Columbanus (543–615) quoted in Baker (1970:28), "He who says he believes in Christ ought to walk as Christ walked, poor and humble and always preaching the truth."[148] Although monks were poor, they worked hard so that secular historians acknowledged their contribution to agricultural restoration in Europe.[149] Indeed, their economic lifestyle provided alms for the poor and neglected peasants, and correspondingly transformed the social values that had subjugated the empire's slave ownership society.[150]

Further, Addison claims that the Celtic monastic church was primarily a tribal institution which served as a center of family relations to the founder of the monastery, whereby the abbots typically succeeded each other from the founder's kin.[151] This is consistent with Gonzalez who adds that monks vowed obedience to succeeding abbots.[152] This family conception of the community called its members brothers and at times sons of the abbot and had categorized[153] roles.

This approach changed, as Bosch notes; during the era of Gregory the Great, the unbaptized peasant laborers were burdened with rent and slaves would be beaten and tortured while free men were jailed.[154] Indeed, pagans were harassed from every side; Markus argues that while bishops were

---

146. Bosch, 233.
147. Bosch, 232.
148. Bosch, 232.
149. Bosch, 232; Gonzalez, *Story of Christianity*, 145.
150. Bosch, 232; Addison, *Medieval Missionary*, 78.
151. Addison, 76.
152. Gonzalez, *Story of Christianity*, 145.
153. Old devoted ones conducted religious services and transcribed the Scriptures, followed by working brothers (manual labour) and finally, younger ones under instruction; no wonder all property was jointly owned and monks observed vows of poverty, celibacy and obedience (Addison, *Medieval Missionary*, 77).
154. Bosch, *Transforming Mission*, 223.

threatened with severe consequences if peasants in their estates were heathen, the local military commanders and the local governor were compelled to convert the pagans.[155] Besides, argues Bosch, international law since its origin in the late medieval ages was inclined to refuse non-Christians the same rights as Christians, leading to indirect missionary warfare and eventually direct missionary war.[156] Talbot maintains that Boniface actively enforced Christian faith to the extent that no one could choose either one way or the other as to particular elements but had to abide by the whole doctrine, authority, tradition, and discipline without question.[157]

Social ethics in the Reformation church

Bosch observes that while Western Christians in this era did not isolate cultural uplift as a mission goal, they nevertheless regarded their culture as superior to that of non-Western nations.[158] The assumption was that establishment of God's rule would civilize people's lifestyle in what Cotton Mather (1663–1728), quoted by Hutchison (1987:29) in Bosch avers, "The best thing we can do for our Indians is to anglicize them."[159] This patronizing attitude is consistent with Boxer's claim that Jesuit missionaries were prejudiced against Indian students training for ordained ministry as depicted by Hilaire Belloc's aphorism: "The Faith is Europe, and Europe is the Faith."[160] Furthermore, Boxer notes somewhat disparaging remarks made by Rector Padre Antonio Gomes to the effect that Indian people were mostly poor-spirited so that Portuguese laymen would only go for confession to a purebred Portuguese priest.[161] No wonder the humanist Desiderius Erasmus (1466–1536) associated missionary work to civilizing or taming of wild peoples.[162] Indeed, Ott, Strauss and Tennent argue that the collective practice amongst early Roman Catholics and Protestant missionaries was to put new converts in communities

---

155. Markus, "Gregory the Great," 32.
156. Bosch, *Transforming Mission*, 223.
157. Talbot, "St. Boniface," 52.
158. Bosch, *Transforming Mission*, 260.
159. Bosch, 260.
160. Boxer, "Problem of the Native Clergy," 88.
161. Boxer, 88.
162. Ott, Strauss and Tennent, *Encountering Theology of Mission*, 121.

or towns where they learned Western culture including customs, lifestyles, morals, and manners.[163]

Social-ethics in early modern church

It is hard to differentiate Western culture from Christian culture during this period because missionaries did not only bring the gospel but also the culture of the sending church as it was found moral to civilize heathen savages.[164] Indeed, claims that technological and scientific advancements that followed the Enlightenment period put the West above the rest of the world even regarding religion.[165] Thus, while heathen nations were associated with darkness, blindness, superstitions and ignorance, the West was compared to light, vision, enlightenment, and knowledge.[166] Furthermore, Ott, Strauss and Tennent note Gottfried Leibniz's (1646–1716) Enlightenment motive for mission stimulated the cultural expansion of Christianity rather than soteriology.[167]

Still, argues Bosch during the early stages of the modern mission the Christian West had the prerogative to impose its views on others.[168] Therefore, Ott, Strauss and Tennent aver, "missionaries until the twentieth century considered it an act of compassion not only spiritually but also socially to bring the savages out of their darkness and to share with them the fruits of Western civility and culture."[169] Ott, Strauss and Tennent argue that failure to civilize the natives was construed as moral negligence tantamount to debasing their humanity.[170]

In addition, Bosch in reference to Hutchison (1987:15,29,65) notes that the objective of the American Missionary Board was not only to make American Indians speak the English language and civilize their habits but also to Christianize them, a tendency that did not consider the perception of

---

163. Ott, Strauss and Tennent, 120.
164. Ott, Strauss and Tennent, 120.
165. Bosch, *Transforming Mission*, 291.
166. Bosch, 291.
167. Ott, Strauss and Tennent, *Encountering Theology of Mission*, 21.
168. Bosch, *Transforming Mission*, 292.
169. Ott, Strauss and Tennent, *Encountering Theology of Mission*, 121.
170. Ott, Strauss and Tennent, *Encountering Theology of Mission*, 121.

Indians whatsoever.[171] This ethnocentric predisposition blurred the advocates of mission so as to confuse their ideals and values with Christianity principles so that emphasis on Western standards and suppositions appeared to polarize the proprieties of traditional societies.[172]

Social ethics in the modern church

Bosch maintains that during the eighteenth and early nineteenth century the question of priorities between civilization and Christianization was not pronounced until the latter half of the nineteenth century when priorities were specified.[173] Thus, Protestant missions had sought to establish independent younger churches which were to be self-governing, self-propagating, and self-supporting. However, by the beginning of the twentieth century, this idea was shelved by the pervasive benevolent paternalism.[174] This paternalistic attitude was somewhat confirmed by the Edinburgh World Missionary Conference (1910), which directed missionary societies to treat younger churches like children not yet come of age, which needed benevolent control and guidance.[175] Indeed, Ott, Strauss and Tennent contend that missionary motifs of civilizing which was expected to prepare the way for the gospel were unfortunately mostly linked with colonialism.[176] This perspective should have raised a warning about the nineteenth-century European dominance in African missions. Baur claims missions of Abeokuta and Ibadan opted to submit to the European bishop rather than their kind (Bishop Samuel Adjai Crowther) because the authority of the mission was in the hands of the white man.[177]

Walls reckons the Christianization of Sierra Leone in West Africa blended European and African elements such that European institutions were not only adopted into an African context but were also transformed by it, as exemplified by the Krio (Creoles)[178] community.[179] Thus Walls observes:

---

171. Bosch, *Transforming Mission*, 292.
172. Bosch, 294.
173. Bosch, 296.
174. Bosch, 295.
175. Bosch, 295.
176. Ott, Strauss and Tennent, *Encountering Theology of Mission*, 123.
177. Baur, *2000 Years of Christianity*, 122.
178. Refers to liberated or emancipated slaves in Sierra Leone (Baur, 377).
179. Walls, *Missionary Movement*, 103.

> The self-conscious Christian community flocked to buildings looking like English parish churches in villages called Leicester, Gloucester, Kent, or Sussex, Wilberforce, Bathurst, Waterloo, or Wellington . . . They wore European dress, as good as they could afford . . . and lived in houses influenced by European models. They were a literate community too . . . developed their grammar schools, for boys and for girls; and their higher education institution at Fourah Bay College in which by the 1870s it was possible to take degrees in arts and theology.[180]

As a result of their spirited attempt to model European culture Krio failed to integrate into the tribal society as they appeared more inclined to the acquisition of wealth, which hindered mission to their envious poor blood-brothers in the hinterland.[181] Thus, Bosch claims that there is no room for a gospel that is indifferent to the needs of humanity because successful evangelism informs social conditions.[182]

Since Krio was also an African community, a distinctly Krio expression of Christianity emerged, though where Krio culture and church differed from that of Britain was blamed on imperfections associated with ignorance which required time and patience to correct.[183] Indeed where an African syntax developed, Englishmen called it broken English, or bad English; it never occurred to them it was a new language with an English vocabulary.[184] Thus the Krio church got a new identity, and as Walls observes, to this day, they use English for liturgy and preaching confirming their status of loss from their once coherent society.[185] Ott, Strauss and Tennent confirm the twentieth-century perspective, which censures the merger of western culture and the gospel, along with the evils of imperialism and ethnocentrism.[186]

---

180. Walls, 103.
181. Baur, *2000 Years of Christianity*, 377.
182. Bosch, *Transforming Mission*, 404.
183. Walls, *Missionary Movement*, 103.
184. Walls, 103.
185. Walls, 103.
186. Ott, Strauss and Tennent, *Encountering Theology of Mission*, 120.

Missiological appraisal of social, ethical theory from Brethren perspectives

A reflection on the social, ethical framework of mission from the standpoint of Brethren crafted into the threefold cluster of civilization, Christianization, and commerce:

First, the civilization phenomenon in the Christian church has apparently reinforced the fact that one society regards itself as more cultured than the other. This ethnocentric biased approach to mission, sometimes demonstrated by use of derogatory language such as *savage*, seems to blur mission principles of propriety with the social and ethical life of traditional societies.[187] Indeed, Christianity appears to have come to pagans clothed in Western culture so that it was difficult to differentiate Western culture from a Christian culture and yet carried the moral mandate to civilize what Ott, Strauss and Tennent refer to as the *heathen savage*.[188] Such a racist approach to social life would have most likely found resistance to penetrating the mission arena. Racism is confirmed by Bosch and Boxer who note Portuguese laymen would only go for confession to a Portuguese priest.[189]

Baur describes a situation where a section of mission in West Africa chose to stay under a white bishop reckoned to wield authority,[190] which is consistent with treating younger churches like children.[191] Of course following the Enlightenment Western culture advanced in technology as to be associated with light and vision, while *savages* were associated with darkness and ignorance.[192] This apparent disparity naturally prejudices one society over the other and brings forth a missiological challenge. While Western culture felt compelled with compassion to civilize *savages*, it never occurred to them that other worldviews matter, however retrogressively. Indeed, the Krio community suffered alienation from their culture so much so that unto this day they preach and conduct their liturgy in English.[193] Similarly, freed slaves at Freetown on the Coast of East Africa appear not only to have been uprooted

---

187. Bosch, *Transforming Mission*, 294.
188. Ott, Strauss and Tennent, *Encountering Theology of Mission*, 120.
189. Bosch, *Transforming Mission*, 260; Boxer, "Problem of the Native Clergy," 88.
190. Baur, *2000 Years of Christianity*, 122.
191. Bosch, *Transforming Mission*, 295.
192. Bosch, 291.
193. Walls, *Missionary Movement*, 103.

from their culture but were also subjected to baptism as a condition for settlement rather than the beginning of a Christian journey.[194]

Brethren's disposition depicts the grace of God. Indeed, they not only dress modestly, but are clean, smart and seemingly loving and caring. However, this is more toward their fellow Brethren than other Christians, and curtails mission. Furthermore, "walking in the light" as a motif for civilization predisposes other as Christian's inferior and are thus excluded from their fellowship. In other words, other Christians are expected to learn from Brethren cultural innovations informed by beliefs and practices of walking in the light. However, unlike Western civilization, one of the ways to culture other believers is through well-informed testimonies and inclusive evangelistic fellowships, which Brethren should cultivate.

Indeed, Brethren lifestyle depicts a superiority phenomenon which might be termed injurious to mutual societal coexistence. Their self-elevated social disposition appears not only hypocritical but is ironic considering the majority are illiterate. This disadvantages mission practices which require an informed exegesis of Scripture. Surely one of the precious companions of Brethren is a copy of Scripture which is read mostly devotionally, unlike monks who were believed not only to hold the church traditions and Scripture together during medieval ages[195] when the church was complacent, but had responsibility for enhancing cultural civilization and mission. So, if Brethren could embrace theological studies, in addition to their commitment to fellowship meetings, they would be a great source of social-ethical codes of inclusion that would inform mission.

Second, undoubtedly Christianization is a common ethical motif. Indeed Gonzalez notes the church since the early years has been a living evidence of unity in diversity, which was carried forward through monasticism,[196] reckoned to be the real bearer of the missionary ideal and practice.[197] The monks' resilience tendency during the medieval era not only safeguarded church tradition but also challenged believers to imitate the life of Christ[198] in what

---

194. Baur, *2000 Years of Christianity*, 230–231.
195. Bosch, *Transforming Mission*, 230.
196. Gonzalez, *Story of Christianity*, 18–19.
197. Bosch, *Transforming Mission*, 201–202.
198. Bosch, 232.

appears like family community comprised of brothers and sisters with the Abbot being the father figure.[199] However, overzealousness for conversion made some Christian leaders declare war against heathen peasants[200] leading to what Bosch calls indirect and direct missionary warfare.[201]

Brethren's concept of Christianization seems to some extent to mimic the early church in the sense that it depicts unity in diversity during the local fellowship meetings where they share testimonies and walk in the light with one another. This unity, also reflected by the monks during the medieval period,[202] exemplified is in the way they regard one another as brothers or sisters in the Lord. Nonetheless, while the monks' Christian ethos informed almsgiving to the needy outside their borders, Brethren appear to care mostly for their own kind.

Thus while monks' mission endeavors have received accolades,[203] Brethren's inward and exclusive social networking by all standards appears selfish and hypocritical.[204] If weighed against Christ's teaching about love (Matt 22:39), Brethren would be found wanting. Nevertheless, Brethren's exclusive love for one another is something to be admired and is a profound missiological principle based on the centrality of the cross. If this concept of brotherly-sisterly love extends to other Christians, then mission in the Anglican Church, Mount Kenya region, will not only enhance its cooperation in the *missio Dei* but also place Brethren at the very center of centripetal-centrifugal mission dynamics.

On the side of commerce, monks, as with the social ethics of Christianity and civilization seemed to control the economy of the day. The monastery was the center of Christian work, and the military base of operations against heathendom.[205] Although monks were poor, their contribution to agricultural restoration in Europe led to an economic lifestyle that transformed social values as they provided alms for the poor and neglected peasants; nonetheless

---

199. Gonzalez, *Story of Christianity*, 145.
200. Markus, "Gregory the Great," 32.
201. Bosch, *Transforming Mission*, 223.
202. Bosch, 232; Gonzalez, *Story of Christianity*, 145.
203. Bosch, *Transforming Mission*, 230–231.
204. Langley and Kiggins, *Serving People*, 202.
205. Addison, *Medieval Missionary*, 75.

under Gregory the Great, the unbaptized peasant laborers were burdened with rent to coerce their conversion.[206]

But in the modern era, the social and ethical pendulum appeared to have swung from alms and poverty informed conversion to a search for economic gain at the expense of the mission. The Krio community in West Africa failed to integrate into the tribal society as they appeared inclined to the acquisition of wealth, which hindered mission to the poor.[207] This tendency resonates with some Bombay Africans like William Jones who had interacted with the Western culture sought for socio-economic recognition leading to resignation from the Freretown mission for a better-paying job in government to the detriment of the mission.[208]

One of the identifying characteristics of Brethren is the majority are physically poor but apparently satisfied with whatever little is at their disposal. This poverty, on the one hand, is attributed to the hard economic situation in the agricultural sector, particularly in rural Kenya where rain is unreliable for commercial farming. On the other hand, some Brethren appear so entangled with the running of the Revival Fellowships and conventions that they do not have time to properly manage their farms. Nevertheless, whatever little they get, part of it goes to what has been referred to as *Mfuko wa Bwana* (Lord's Bag) to cater for needy Brethren or to use during preparation for their local and international conventions.[209] Although it does not mean monks had no flaws, they were hardworking and though poor were exceedingly generous to the needy. Truly, some Brethren would rather fail to contribute financially to church needs but not fail the Lord's Bag. This attitude raises missiological concerns about church-funded missions which require Brethren participation as partakers of the mission of God.[210]

Following this, Brethren, unlike Krio and Bombay Africans, appear so enterprising with money-making businesses. Indeed, the concept of poverty seems to a section of Brethren as destiny. The teaching of the Kupaa faction (inspired by Daniel 1:8ff) could have had a hand in some aspects of

---

206. Bosch, *Transforming Mission*, 223, 232.
207. Baur, *2000 Years of Christianity*, 377.
208. Sundkler and Steed, *History of the Church*, 554.
209. Mambo, "Revival Fellowship", 115.
210. Ott, Strauss and Tennent, *Encountering Theology of Mission*, 213.

Brethren lifestyle exemplified in their simple and cheap weddings; anything beyond that is termed worldly. Additionally, some avoid taking bank loans for reasons among others including the inability to repay and consequently embarrassing their fellowship. For the same reasons, many Brethren don't join social or economic community welfare organizations which could cushion loan repayments and improve their financial lifestyle. Certainly, while not applauding the use of money for promoting ungodly projects, mission funding by all and sundry is a noble duty for a Christian, more so Brethren, who seems superficial in social responsibility-driven evangelistic church missions.

Theological Perspective of Missiology on Brethren Beliefs and Practices of Walking in the Light

This section constructs the framework setting of mission theology by exploring the missiological theory of conversion, liturgical worship and social ethics from the viewpoint of Christian faith.

Missiological Theory of Theology of Christian Conversion

The theological basis of Christian conversion is at the very center of God's plan for the salvation of humanity. Strahler depicts conversion as a radical turning around which is derived from the Hebrew word שׁוּב *(shuv)* and Greek word ἐπιστρέφω *(epistrepho)* which means *to return* in response to God's saving activity.[211] To explain Brethren's view of conversion from a missiological theology perspective, it is necessary to explore its theological basis. Indeed, argues Morris, Christian conversion derives from the nature of the living God who is a missionary and reaches out to humanity to experience conversion.[212] This nature of God will inform the nature of theology of conversion within the framework of missiology. The nature of Christian conversion is viewed from two progressive viewpoints, which are faith and repentance. But first it is critical to distinguish conversion from regeneration.

Conversion and regeneration

Whereas in regeneration humanity are passive participants such that their part is to hear the gospel so the Spirit creates embracing faith, conversion

---

211. Strahler, Coming to Faith in Christ, 20.
212. Morris, *Mystery and Meaning*, 42.

predisposes humans as active participants.[213] Also, Frame terms regeneration as a new birth or new heart subsequent to God's call to fellowship with Christ, which is the first effect of calling that occurs in believers.[214] While Best concurs, he contests those who believe the subject is active at the achieving of the new birth.[215] Horton argues that, unlike regeneration, conversion is action oriented (Phil 2:12–13) in the sense of working out salvation in a genuine covenant relationship in Christ, which manifests through repentance and faith upon which ensues justification.[216]

This understanding is consistent with Frame who sees faith and repentance as two legs upon which conversion rests, whereby the two legs describe regeneration as a response to God's calling to turn to Christ as Lord and Savior (faith) and to turn away from sin (repentance).[217] Then follows justification, adoption, and sanctification, in which respectively God declares one's legal standing, one becomes a son or daughter of God and the Spirit develop the regenerate nature to renew the converted person in the image of Christ.[218] Implicated in this research is the trio of justification, adoption, and sanctification, but more so sanctification and holiness which hinge this study. Nevertheless, the triad will no doubt play a significant role in the reflection on the Christian conversion theory from the perspective of mission theology. Attention now turns to the two legs that depict conversion theory, namely repentance and faith, which together Frame calls conversion.[219]

Christian conversion viewed as repentance

As seen above the key Hebrew word to define repentance in the Old Testament is *shuv* שוב *to* return or to go back (2 Chr 7:14) which Strahler describes as genuine repentance of people leaving evil as a result of godly sorrow for sinful actions.[220] A good example is Numbers 21 which Best uses to illustrate Israelites' sin that led God to send fiery serpents which killed many people,

---

213. Horton, *Christian Faith*, 576.
214. Frame, *Systematic Theology*, 945.
215. Best, *Regeneration and Conversion*, 12.
216. Horton, Christian Faith, 576.
217. Frame, Systematic Theology, 998.
218. Frame, 998.
219. Frame, 951.
220. Strahler, *Coming to Faith*, 21.

and they based their salvation on looking at the brass serpent.²²¹ No wonder salvation defines God's identity, because he is the one who saves (Ps 68:200.²²²

Indeed, Strahler further claims that the word ἐπιστρέγφω (*epistrepho*), which is frequently used in the LXX to render the Hebrew *shuv*, does not only denote to return, but also to turn toward, or to convert.²²³ Other Greek words used in the New Testament for repentance are μεταμέλομαι and μετανοέω.²²⁴ On the one hand, *metamelomai* translates repentance as to have a feeling of care, concern, or regret, thus stressing the emotional aspect of repentance depicted as regret for the wrong done.²²⁵ This emotional perspective of repentance is not merely a change of mind or what Horton terms intellectual, but involves the whole person.²²⁶

On the other hand, *metanoeo* translates repentance as not only to have a change of mind but also to think differently about something, thus expressing the idea of repentance as an alteration, a conversion which influences moral conduct.²²⁷ Thus, Bosch states that Jesus did not come to call the righteous, but sinners (Mark 2:17; 5:32) to repentance (Luke 5:32).²²⁸ This is consistent with Horton but he adds that Scripture treats repentance as knowledge of sin fashioned by the law (Rom 3:20).²²⁹ Additionally Strahler, quoting Grudem, observes that conversion illustrates an inward change demonstrated in a life of love and righteousness (Matt 3:8; Luke 3:10–14).²³⁰ Still, Horton claims that the Spirit is an attorney who convicts inwardly of God's righteousness and human's unrighteousness.²³¹

Further, Strahler uses Jesus' words in Matthew 18:3 to illustrate this requirement of salvation as perceived in children receiving something as God's gift of repentance at justification, which is not a human achievement.²³²

---

221. Best, Regeneration and Conversion, 89–91.
222. Wright, *Mission of God*, 118.
223. Strahler, *Coming to Faith*, 21.
224. Strahler, 21.
225. Strahler, 21.
226. Horton, *Christian Faith*, 577.
227. Strahler, *Coming to Faith*, 21.
228. Bosch, *Transforming Mission*, 105.
229. Horton, *Christian Faith*, 577.
230. Strahler, *Coming to Faith*, 21.
231. Horton, *Christian Faith*, 577.
232. Strahler, *Coming to Faith*, 21–22.

Justification, argues Frame, is forensic, i.e., God declares humans righteous (infused[233] righteousness), which is about humans' legal status, not inner character, which means God justifies the ungodly whose inner character is evil, only because of Christ.[234] In other words, as Horton puts it, Christ came to crucify the old self and bury it within himself so that humanity may be raised with him to new life (Rom 6:1–5).[235] Thus, Wright observes that the mission of declaring repentance and forgiveness to nations in his name is written in Luke 24:45–47.[236] This appears to suggest that the Scripture finds its fulfillment not only in the life, death, and resurrection of Christ but also in a mission to all nations.

Christian conversion viewed as faith

Following the preceding discussion of repentance in conversion, the flip-side of *faith* takes center stage. Horton observes that while in repentance people confess that God's verdict against humanity is justified, in faith they receive God's justification.[237] Bosch notes the solemnness of the sinful human condition which only God can change because humanity is powerless in the hands of Satan until ransomed by God.[238] Since it required a sinless human-divine to satisfy human guilt and sin before God, Christ's vicarious death on the cross once and for all was judged necessary so that humanity could appropriate the benefits of forgiveness, redemption, and renewal by Jesus Christ.[239]

It is vital to conceptualize the word faith. Thus, Strahler observes that in the Hebrew Scriptures, the verb faith אָמַן *(aman)* translated as *to believe* or *be faithful*,[240] or to accept as a fact[241] which means to say *amen* to the work of God upon oneself. Further, Strahler notes that this verb conveys the concept of forthright confidence in someone or something or may designate assent to

---

233. God doesn't justify humanity because he likes their inner character, but justifies them for the sake of Christ (Frame, *Systematic Theology*, 966).
234. Frame, 966.
235. Horton, *Christian Faith*, 577.
236. Wright, *Mission of God*, 30.
237. Horton, *Christian Faith*, 580.
238. Bosch, *Transforming Mission*, 216.
239. Bosch, 216.
240. Strahler, *Coming to Faith*, 22.
241. Horton, *Christian Faith*, 580.

testimony, the *sola fide*.[242] However, Burkhardt and Jepsen perceive *faith* as a concept of conversion lacking in the patriarchal narratives but that to *believe* is prevalent (Gen15:6).[243] As Wright observes, prayer and confession, such as the ancient prayer *Maranatha!* (O Lord, Come) and the primal confession *Kyrios Iesous* (Jesus is Lord) embodied faith.[244]

One of the other Hebrew words used to designate faith is בָּטַח (*batach*) translated as *to trust, feel safe* or *assent*.[245] However, the use of such words as *to trust* or *committing of oneself* designates faith, and is foundational for comprehending conversion (1 Chr 5:20; Ps 22:4; 31:14; Isa 26:3). Thus, Strahler argues having faith in the OT signifies full confidence and trust in God's promises, irrespective of circumstances.[246]

The New Testament word for faith is πιστεύω (*pisteuo*) which is either *to believe what someone says* or to have *personal trust* as presupposed by the use of a preposition (in) as to *believe in the gospel* (Mark 1:15) or *believe in his name* (John 1:12).[247] This position is supported by Horton who asserts that faith is conceptualized as trust or belief in the testimony of another (Phil 1:27; 2 Cor 4:13; 2 Thess 2:13).[248] Thus, when Jesus told Nicodemus that he must be born again (John 3:3), he meant spiritual birth as a precursor to participating in the kingdom at the end of the age or to experience eternal or resurrected life.[249] Additionally, Michaels notes that one has to be born from above to perceive the kingdom of God.[250] Kostenberger observes that Nicodemus could not see (was spiritually blind) God's kingdom without a supernatural birth.[251]

The nature of faith as believing and trusting in Christ, argues Strahler, is necessary for salvation[252] and ushers in the benefits of adoption, the believer's inheritance.[253] Frame observes that it is not human efforts that entitle

---

242. Strahler, *Coming to Faith*, 22.
243. Burkhardt, *Christ Werden*, 39; Jepsen, "Aman," 305.
244. Bosch, *Transforming Mission*, 106.
245. Strahler, *Coming to Faith*, 22; Horton, *Christian Faith*, 580.
246. Strahler, 22–23.
247. Strahler, 23.
248. Horton, *Christian Faith*, 581.
249. Kostenberger, *John: Baker Exegetical Commentary*, 122.
250. Michaels, *Gospel of John*, 179.
251. Kostenberger, *John: Baker Exegetical Commentary*, 122.
252. Strahler, *Coming to Faith*, 23.
253. Frame, *Systematic Theology*, 976.

humanity to the privilege of sonship but it is given as a gift, received by reaching out with hands of faith for the blessing of adoption that places believers in a new family as sons and daughters of God.[254]

Strahler maintains that the biblical understanding of conversion brings to the fore acceptance of a new set of beliefs that propels change of religious loyalty through repentance and placing one's faith in the supreme authority, the Lord and Savior Jesus Christ.[255] This is consistent with Bosch who adds that conversion is not joining a community to secure salvation but a change of allegiance to Christ as Lord and center of one's life.[256] This change is prompted by the missional God who not only searches but also sends out to the mission field.

Missiological appraisal of theology of Christian conversion from Brethren perspective

The two-legged conversion concepts of repentance and faith will anchor this segment. Firstly, repentance.

Repentance or confessing of sins by a new believer in the Brethren Fellowship meeting is greeted with verses of *Tukutendereza* (We praise you Lord) followed with hugging by members of the same sex while the opposite sex only shakes hands. It is the Brethren's firm belief that hugging the opposite sex is carnal, and suggests a loose life and is therefore indecorous. Further, a new convert's eligibility or acceptance into the fellowship is by confessing past evil deeds before the members (this sets up the neophyte's future pattern of giving testimony) followed by restitution. On the surface, it resonates with the concept of crucifying the old self by burying it with Christ to be raised with Him in the newness of life.[257] However, the tendency to elevate the new birth through outward performance overshadows and compromises the inward change. This practice deters the form of centripetal movement of mission and becomes a challenge to the centrifugal dynamics[258] because the potential members either understands conversion life differently or are hindered by Brethren's general theological appropriation of mission strategy.

---

254. Frame, 976–977.
255. Strahler, *Coming to Faith*, 23.
256. Bosch, *Transforming Mission*, 488.
257. Horton, *Christian Faith*, 577 (comments on Rom 6:1–5).
258. Ott, Strauss and Tennent, *Encountering Theology of Mission*, 23.

Second, Brethren base its faith in the vicarious death of Christ on the cross for the forgiveness of sins.[259] Indeed, a confession that *Jesus is Lord* (Kyrios Iesous) appears to sum up their faith,[260] a declaration that may not seem complete without mentioning the blood of Christ that washed away their sins. This, for Brethren, is the typical appropriation of the saving faith described in their born-again testimonies and is, therefore, stereotyped. The apparent stereotyping of the "saving faith" by Brethren appears to disregard justification, which together with adoption are works of God in the believer subsequent to regeneration. However, they seem to confess adoption and sanctification.

While the idea of adoption into the family of God propagated during Brethren fellowship and conventions is exemplified by the use of the names "brothers and sisters in Christ," it nevertheless does not consider other Christians as members of that family. But sonship is a gift, which means it is not earned by human efforts,[261] and this discredits Brethren's family setup. Thus, as Bosch rightly observes, conversion is accepting Christ as Lord and Savior of one's life not joining a community.[262] It is this recognition of the lordship of Christ that would make Brethren participate fully in the mission of God because he is a missional God who searches and sends out to the mission field.

When it comes to sanctification, Brethren gives credence to the experiential, which by all standards appear to be achieved through practical holiness in somewhat pompous manner. Thus it looks ironical and hypocritical that while Brethren seem to exhibit a great salvation experience, they nevertheless seem to be following a *missio homo*. So, when Jesus told Nicodemus that he must be born again (John 3:3) he meant spiritual birth, not a Pharisaic superficial performance,[263] a statement that Brethren might need to reconsider if they are to be serious participants in the *missio Dei*.

---

259. Bosch, *Transforming Mission*, 216.
260. Wright, *Mission of God*, 106.
261. Frame, *Systematic Theology*, 976–977.
262. Bosch, *Transforming Mission*, 488.
263. Kostenberger, *John: Baker Exegetical Commentary*, 122.

Missiological Theory of Theology of Christian Worship

King observes that worship and mission are inseparable because God drives his mission by inviting worshipers to himself in the light of calls to worship with the strategy of response by believers.[264] This resonates with Dawn who adds that it is critical that the church maintains God as both the subject and the object of worship.[265] Thus, this section will look at worship styles from the perspective of God's call to worship and human response. A particular reference to the current Anglican worship style will tie this section before a critique of Brethren style of worship.

Christian call to worship

God's call to worship through mission reverberates in the Scripture with the first of the Ten Commandments saying, "You shall have no other gods before me" (Exod 20:3), which means he is entitled to exclusive worship shared with none other.[266] Frame notes that God declares Israel to be his people and as their God governs with supreme authority and their response is to honor him above other gods.[267] King cites the prophet Isaiah heeding the call of God in the midst of worship (Isa 6:1–8).[268] This is consistent with Frame who maintains that God comes to his people in worship as exemplified by encounters in the tabernacle and the temple (Exod 20:24), and worshipers shout with joy that Immanuel, *God with us* (Isa 7:14) is in their midst (Zeph 3:17).[269] This God, argues Frame, does not abandon his people even when they defile their worship (Gen 2:16–17; 3:1–6).[270] Additionally, Frame contends that God wants them to worship him with a consciousness of their sin and guilt, on the basis of what he has done to free them from the guilt and power of sin through the Lamb of God who takes away the sins of the world (John 1:29).[271] Wright notes that the emphasis in the Hebrew text

---

264. King, "Worship," 1034.
265. Dawn, *Reaching Out*, 76, 80.
266. Frame, *Systematic Theology*, 2.
267. Frame, 2.
268. King, "Worship," 1034.
269. Frame, *Systematic Theology*, 4.
270. Frame, 5.
271. Frame, 5.

that there is no other God apart from Yahweh (1 Sam 2:2; 1 Kings 8:60; Joel 2:27) demonstrates adoration and monotheistic worship.[272]

When Jesus met with the Samaritan woman, he discloses that God is looking for true worshipers who are in a relationship with him (John 4:24). Thus, argues King, the missionary mandate is informed by an intimate relationship with God through worship upon which the people of God join him to call worshipers to himself.[273] When Dawn encourages the church to have God as the subject of worship, it signifies that the God revealed in Jesus Christ is everything to a Christian regarding the provision, redemption and sanctification of the Lord.[274] Dawn maintains that in as much as the gathered community is important, it is critical to remember that God by his enabling gift of his grace has called Christians – those rescued from themselves through salvation in Jesus Christ – to worship and a life focused on God and what he discloses.[275] In the light of this understanding of the call to worship, King asserts that God's call to worship is spread around the world, along with openness to new forms and patterns of worship, which inform the intimate relationship between worship and mission, in a somewhat worship-propelled mission model.[276]

However, observes Dawn, while several defenders of traditional worship styles take pride in the historic liturgy, contemporary defenders attempt to control God and convert people by their power, resulting in the subsequent arrogance and presupposition to hinder God from being the center of worship.[277] Hence, while the emphasis on worship style should not replace the key issue (God as the center of worship), it is critical to question whether a style conveys the presence and the self-giving of God.

Christian response to worship

Hattori argues that the offering to Yahweh (Gen 4:1–7) which pacifies the curse of the fall (Gen 3:6–10) is a type of *proto-offering* response to God.[278]

---

272. Wright, *Mission of God*, 81.
273. King, "Worship," 1034.
274. Dawn, *Reaching Out*, 76.
275. Dawn, 76–77.
276. King, "Worship," 1034.
277. Dawn, *Reaching Out*, 93.
278. Hattori, "Theology of Worship," 48.

Indeed, when God met with people in the Old Testament the context was one of worship as exemplified by Moses at the burning bush, where he responded by not only removing his shoes because the ground was holy but also by covering his face for fear of God (Exo 3:5, 6).[279] Frame argues that when Isaiah saw God (Isa 6:1f), he was overwhelmed with the greatness of the living God and that he, Isaiah, was a sinner.[280] Therefore, argues Hattori, through the covenant of redemption the people of God responded in forms of worship informed by the redemptive-historical and historical-cultural context.[281] Indeed, Hattori observes the use of different elements of worship at various points in the history of the people of God such as *building an altar, offering sacrifice, supplication* and *praising*.[282] As Hattori puts it, worship is an active response to God, which is not only participative but is also a context whereby a human declares the worthiness of God.[283] Thus, Dawn terms entertainment evangelism mission activity indecorous, as it attracts people rather than the adoration of God.[284]

On the other hand, worship in the New Testament illustrates not only engagement with God through faith in Jesus Christ but also for what he has done for humanity.[285] Peterson states that what is done in church is expected to be consonant with that engagement with God as opposed to a traditional cultic assembly of the congregation at a certain time and place.[286] Thus, meaningful and authentic worship conveys a new mission thrust which links worship to the mission. King observes that radical separation of worship from mission dominates mission methodologies.[287] Therefore, Piper claims that "missions exist because worship doesn't," implying worship should propel missions because it is the fuel and goal of missions.[288] Moreover, Dyrness

---

279. Frame, *Systematic Theology*, 15.

280. Frame, 16.

281. While the redemptive-historical context refers to what God required of his chosen people at this point, the historical-cultural is informed by forms of corporate worship construed admissible and appropriate (Hattori, *Theology of Worship*, 49).

282. Hattori, 49.

283. Hattori, 21.

284. Dawn, *Reaching Out*, 81.

285. Peterson, "Worship," 52.

286. Peterson, 52.

287. King, "Worship," 1034.

288. Piper, *Let the Nations*, 35.

observes that worship is primary theology, and theology is in essence a secondary reflection of worship life and prayer, which means worship style demonstrates a vital Christian faith.[289]

Worship in the New Testament is best described by the verb προσκψνέιν (*proskynein*) which articulates bowing down or casting oneself on the ground, kissing feet, as a physical gesticulation of reverence before a supreme being. The Hebrew *histawah* occurs 170 times in the Hebrew Bible and translates as *bend oneself over at the waist*.[290] This is in agreement with Bosch who translates the verb *to worship* in a stronger sense as *to fall prostrate* as depicted by the disciples (in the context of the Great Commission) when they saw Jesus, "they worshipped him" (Matt 28:17).[291] Thus, *bending over to the Lord (or falling prostrate)*, in the Old Testament, argues Peterson, expressed *surrender or submission to God*.[292] Thus, Jesus' encounter with Satan in the wilderness upholds the Old Testament teaching that the response demanded by God is submission and service to him alone (Matt 4:8–10; Luke 4:5–8).[293] This is what King calls *meaningful* worship which is distinctive because worship must remain worship, must allow God to renew his original creation, and must pursue diversity within the body of Christ (1 Cor 12; Eph 2).[294]

Dawn argues that the tension between traditional and contemporary styles inhibit God from being the subject and object of worship.[295] However, it is the platform of tradition and reformation that dialectical tension would ensure godly worship as revealed in the Scriptures and the person of Christ.[296] Thus, Dawn recalls Martin Luther's explanation of the Ten Commandments which begins with the phrase, "we should fear and love God" since the human relationship with God is dialectic and alienation from him evokes fear,[297] he nevertheless, graciously invites his people to respond in love.

---

289. Dyrness, *Primer on Christian Worship*, 6.
290. Peterson, "Worship," 52–53.
291. Bosch, *Transforming Mission*, 75.
292. Peterson, "Worship," 53.
293. Peterson, 54–55.
294. King, "Worship," 1034.
295. Dawn, *Reaching Out*, 93.
296. Dawn, 93.
297. Dawn, 97.

Stancliffe states that the Anglican liturgy is comprehensive and aims at directing God's people to the very throne of God himself.[298] However, Beckwith notices the profound scriptural content and expressive style of Cranmer's 1662 BCP was apparently abandoned as the starting point on liturgical revisions in favor of patristic models, resulting in a lacking of doctrinal clarity in congregational participation.[299] Beckwith argues some Anglican churches such as that of Australia have tried to keep the doctrine of the existing liturgy in their modernization of Prayer Book services, while others in reaction to strict rubrics have allowed for lax ones putting liturgical worship in danger of giving way to impromptu worship.[300]

In Kenya, as in many other provinces in the Anglican Communion, the 1662 BCP though exceedingly useful has culturally become redundant. Thus, the ACK has put together a new Prayer Book, *Our Modern Services* which has taken excellent account of the worship needs for the Anglican Christians in Kenya today.[301] But, although lauded by the former Archbishop of Canterbury George Carey to the extent of requesting it be made available to other provinces in Africa to motivate liturgical renewal efforts,[302] it nevertheless appears to have more Old Testament sentences of Scripture that address the human response to God's call to worship than to God as the subject of worship.[303] This resonates with the BCP of 1662[304] and the Prayer Book of the Church of England in South Africa.[305] This feature might suggest that the Old Testament has a more balanced perspective of God as both the subject and object of worship than the New Testament, a fact that might be true considering various offerings and sacrifices associated with the Old Testament worship patterns.

---

298. Stancliffe, "Is there an 'Anglican' Liturgical Style," 126.
299. Beckwith, "Worship in Anglicanism," 126.
300. Beckwith, 126–127.
301. Anglican Church of Kenya, *Our Modern Services*, vii.
302. Anglican Church of Kenya, vii.
303. Anglican Church of Kenya, 1–2.
304. Church of England, *Book of Common Prayer*, 1–2.
305. Church of England in South Africa, *Prayer Book*, 1–2.

Missiological appraisal of theology of Christian worship from the perspective of Brethren

Brethren fellowship meetings revolve around worship and thus agree with King and Frame that God comes to his people in worship.[306] However, the tendency to hearken to God's intimate call to worship for all Christians as epitomized in Matthew 11:28–30 appears inconsistent with the perceived commonly-held legacy of Brethren as carriers of other people's burden. Indeed, Brethren appear interested only in bringing to their fold the ones who profess a born-again testimony while other Christians are left out. The primary distinctiveness of Israelites, argues Wright, was their exclusive loyalty to Yahweh.[307] But while Israelites were admonished to separate themselves from people of other nations who worshipped other gods, Brethren apparently separate themselves from worship with their fellow Christians only because they don't give a conversion testimony, observe a practical holiness of "walking in the light," or attend fellowship meetings.

Conversely, God does not abandon his people as demonstrated by Jesus' encounter with a Samaritan woman (John 4:7ff); we are all sinners saved by his grace, and no one is perfect.[308] Indeed, the Brethren format of giving testimony does not prove one is saved; actions do. So when Brethren despise other Christians by claiming they are not born again, they fall into the sin of sanctimoniousness. This attempt to control God as to convert and sanctify other *Christians* by their power appears to be vanity. The missionary mandate would call upon Brethren to join God in calling other Christian worshipers to himself[309] because as Dawn argues, there is a need to rescue self-righteous believers from hypocritical worship.[310]

Brethren's concept of brokenness at the cross of Christ ought to lead them to the conviction of sin, confession and restitution[311] which would have paved the way for acceptance of other believers into fellowship. If the encounter

---

306. King, "Worship," 1034; Frame, *Systematic Theology*, 4.
307. Wright, *Mission of God*, 381.
308. Frame, *Systematic Theology*, 5.
309. King, "Worship," 1034.
310. Dawn, *Reaching Out*, 76–77.
311. Church of Province of Kenya, *Rabai to Mumias*, 81.

with God overwhelms a sinner, Brethren ought to view themselves as guilty of the sin of exclusion by barring other Christians from becoming Brethren.[312]

Brethren appear to have turned Revival Fellowship into a place of stereotyping worship instead of a place to engage with God.[313] Real worship should link to the mission, and not separate worship *from* the mission.[314] It should encourage Brethren to respond to God by daily sanctification which is missional and invitational so as to avoid blocking the kingdom seekers from entering the kingdom of God.

Having said that, liturgical renewal, for example in the ACK, has taken excellent account of the needs of the Anglican Christians in Kenya though it appears more responsive to the call to worship than listening to the call of God. While this tendency is rooted in the BCP of 1662, it is pivotal to craft a liturgy that seeks to balance God as the subject and object of worship taking cognizance of public participation that is not just evangelistic entertainment but encompasses a genuine worship of God. Otherwise, it appears to buttress the Brethren response to the call more than listening to God. Thus Brethren liturgical worship has largely been reclusive rather than being directed to the worship of God.

Missiological Theory of Theology of Social Ethics

Ethics of social theology have been associated with consequences of conversion which as Strahler notes affect the whole life, whereby new sets of beliefs and a change of loyalty to Christ is expected.[315] In other words, argues Bosch, conversion or the salvation experience is not only expressed vertically as to depict love to God but also horizontally as to illustrate love to neighbor.[316] This is further elaborated by the *born again* experience informed by the gift of God at justification which leads not only to a change of individual consciousness and social belonging but also to a changed mental attitude and physical experience.[317] Having said that, a consideration of the salvation life of the converted person will hinge a missiological theology of social ethics

---

312. Frame, *Systematic Theology*, 16.
313. Peterson, "Worship," 52.
314. King, "Worship," 1034.
315. Strahler, *Coming to Faith*, 23.
316. Bosch, *Transforming Mission*, 107.
317. Strahler, *Coming to Faith*, 17, 23.

from the perspective of the Christian's moral life in general and Christian family moral values in particular.

Christian's moral life

Nkansah-Obrempong states that God's character and nature are not only at the core of Christian theological and social ethics, but also models the moral life through ethical-actions' full value systems like justice, solidarity and hospitality.[318] This resonates with Zacchaeus' announcement (Luke 19:8) that he would give back, which Bock claims signifies expression of the thank offering of a changed heart, and by any standard is generous to the poor unlike the rich ruler (Luke 18:23) who appeared less inclined to charitable actions.[319] While Green observes that Zacchaeus' conversion episode is outside the narrative, he, applauds his generosity to the service of the needy and of justice.[320] Thus, Ott, Strauss and Tennent maintain that the Lord loves righteousness and justice (Ps 11:7), further implied in the Law of Moses which requires protection of the poor, the widow, the orphan and the alien (Exod 23:1–9).[321] Hastings asserts that since mission is holistic, to evangelize without caring for the poor and improving the social infrastructure is inconceivable.[322] Ott, Strauss and Tennent observe that evangelicals excluded the social gospel for church and mission until 1928 when the IMC declared that both the proclamation of the gospel and the service of human needs are authentic and essential segments of the church's responsibility.[323]

In other words, contends Nkansah-Obrempong, the Christians' relationship with the Triune God has implications for the daily moral life following the change in a Christians' nature and its power over sin as a result of the benefits of God's grace of adoption, which enables Christians to please God.[324] Wright contends that the quality of Christians' moral lives, like the way Israel had been intended to live (but failed), should be visible to the nations so the

---

318. J. Nkansah-Obrempong, *Foundations*, 118.
319. Bock, *Luke 9:51–24:53*, 1520–1521.
320. Green, *Gospel of Luke*, 672.
321. Ott, Strauss and Tennent, *Encountering Theology of Mission*, 145.
322. Hastings, *Missional God*, 149.
323. Ott, Strauss and Tennent, *Encountering Theology of Mission*, 129.
324. Nkansah-Obrempong, *Foundations, 120.*

nations can glorify God.³²⁵ Nkansah-Obrempong claims that, to defeat an ethical system based on human effort, believers ought to walk in the Spirit (Rom 8:4) by crucifying the flesh daily through the enabling power of the Spirit (Rom 8:13).³²⁶ However, Hastings observes that when people claim to be born of the Holy Spirit and turns their backs on the needy in society, it raises a fundamental question regarding their born-again status.³²⁷

Christian family moral life

Ott, Strauss and Tennent observe the term families which translates the Hebrew *mishpaha* not only illustrates blessings through Abraham to all families of the earth but is also a vital social structure for procreation and relationship.³²⁸ But sometimes social and legal structures for the sanctity of human life are undermined, as exemplified by Pharaoh's state-sponsored genocide, which led the Israelites to suffer the extreme violence of fundamental human rights (Exo 2:1–2) that brought terror and grief to families.³²⁹

Since Jesus' ethics emphasized family moral values, Nkansah-Obrempong notes that Christians as members of God's family through repentance and faith, receive God's grace and forgiveness and by this new birth they become God's children (John 1:12–13).³³⁰ However, Strahler claims that, though this new birth is sometimes met with physical violence and breakdown in the family relationship, it sometimes improves and even wins the entire family to Christ.³³¹ The concept of belonging to God's family, says Nkansah-Obrempong has ethical implications for social life in which brothers and sisters (Matt 22:37–40) not only love and treat one another with respect but also forgive each other (Matt 18:21–35).³³²

---

325. Wright, *Mission of God*, 389.
326. Nkansah-Obrempong, *Foundations*, 121–122.
327. Hastings, *Missional God*, 149.
328. Ott, Strauss and Tennent, *Encountering Theology of Mission*, 7, 150.
329. Wright, *Mission of God*, 269.
330. Nkansah-Obrempong, *Foundations*, 95.
331. Strahler, *Coming to Faith*, 81.
332. Nkansah-Obrempong, *Foundations*, 95.

Missiological appraisal of the theology of social ethics from Brethren perspective

Brethren have been accused of dissociating themselves from social and economic activities like "merry-go-round" welfare groups for fear of being considered wealthy with material things which could lead to sin. This seems to resonate with *Kupaa* Brethren's influence associated with the literal interpretation of Daniel 1:8–15, which emphasizes a simple lifestyle away from the king's polluted diet. Brethren construe as unethical anything that can jeopardize their maxim of walking in the light. Nonetheless, as Hastings insinuates, the mission is holistic and constitutes not only evangelism but also social action.[333] Although the majority of Brethren are subsistence farmers and thus not wealthy, working together with other Christians to improve the lives of the very disenfranchised in the society is a noble Christian duty (1 John 3:17–18). Indeed, Brethren appear more inclined to evangelism and social activities for themselves but not with other Christians (such as the Lord's Bag, mentioned earlier). Truly, in this respect, Brethren's social and ethical lives appear to be based on human effort rather than what Paul terms *walking in the Spirit* (Rom 8:4).

The concept of the family seems enshrined within the Brethren ethical structure so that they refer to one another as brothers and sisters in Christ. This idea of belonging to God's family is critical for a Christian moral life because it is not only biblically based but also provides a platform on which values of forgiveness and love are upheld.[334] Indeed, the ethical response to believers being called into God's family is not just to please God, but also outsiders.[335] In other words, however much Brethren would wish to maintain their social-ethical code of "walking in the light," they should be mindful of other Christians, who due to strict moral codes have shied away from the Revival Fellowship family.

---

333. Hastings, *Missional God*, 149.
334. Nkansah-Obrempong, *Foundations*, 95.
335. Wright, *Mission of God*, 387.

Anthropological Perspective of Missiology on Brethren Beliefs and Practices of Walking in the Light

Kraft argues that anthropology has not been a part of Christian institutions' curricula[336] as it has been branded anti-Christian,[337] which Kraft observes as an overreaction to the overextension of evolutionary and ethical relativism.[338] Kraft perceives that missiological anthropology has sometimes followed the fashions of secular anthropology, in good faith, to access and understand particular anthropological insights such as the internal workings of cultures, cultural change dynamics, and the necessity of a worldview.[339]

This is consistent with Smalley, who contends that cultural anthropology is gaining relevance in the curricula of prospective missionaries and having significant impact in Christian ministry.[340] Kraft notes real insights of anthropology on Christian witness: on the one hand, a two-way influence between missiological anthropology and Bible translation, and on the other hand, influences of the cultural communication process, and a contextualization of Christianity and its worldview.[341] Additionally, Kraft understands anthropology from the perspectives of Christian ministry, in which people are not only culturally formed and constrained, but also respond to God from the viewpoint of their way of life (Mark 16:15).[342] It is within this cultural milieu that Christianity confronts culture with a radical call to change loyalty to the lordship of Jesus Christ (that is, conversion).

Missiological Theory of Anthropology of Christian Conversion

Hiebert contends that conversion to Christ encompasses behavior, beliefs, and worldview.[343] While the Lausanne Committee for World Evangelization (LCWE) concurs with Hiebert's description of conversion informed by changes in behavior and worldview, it nevertheless appears to replace beliefs

---

336. Kraft, *Anthropology for Christian Witness*, 2.

337. In ancient days cultural anthropology had been dominated by physical anthropology such as study of human fossils and the evolution of man, on the one hand, and study of primitive cultures, on the other hand (Smalley, Anthropological Study," 8).

338. Kraft, "Anthropology, Missiological Anthropology," 67.

339. Kraft, 67.

340. Smalley, "Anthropological Study," 3.

341. Kraft, "Anthropology, Missiological Anthropology," 67.

342. Kraft, *Anthropology for Christian Witness*, xiv.

343. Hiebert, *Transforming Worldviews*, 11.

with relationships.[344] Indeed, Strahler depicts the idea of conversion as a new relationship with internal (self) and external (community) ramifications for the convert.[345] Thus, the relationship seems to be a key missiological anthropological concept that overshadows conversion lifestyle. It thus appears that Hiebert, LCWE, and Strahler have similar perspectives on what comprises conversion within a cultural milieu of beliefs, and world view (behavior and relationship) which will form the conceptual framework to critique EARM's beliefs and practices of walking in the light.

Christian conversion viewed as a new mind or belief

Conversion, argues Hiebert, must not only transform personal and corporate traditional beliefs but should also reflect the change of mind because people could interpret it as a more powerful magic to harm enemies (Acts 8:14–24) resulting in syncretism, a common danger in the church.[346] Indeed, one can become a Christian after the gospel is preached, but more time is required to nurture the convert to avoid what Hiebert terms *cheap grace* and a consequently nominal church.[347] Karanja claims that at Mutira in Kirinyaga County, central Kenya, a local chief requested Herbert Butcher, the resident missionary to pray for rain following a severe famine in 1921. The missionary obliged and his prayer was instantly answered, leading to people converting to Christianity including prominent medicine men who now viewed Butcher as a superior medicine man.[348] This seemingly partial conversion could be deceiving and would require spiritual guidance to effect the real conversion.

Hiebert, arguing from Tippet's conversion model of Hindus and Muslims, observes that conversion is a multistage dynamic process that requires a period of identity negotiation.[349] Additionally, Isichei contends that productive dialogues between Christianity and African traditional religions informed by visual symbolisms as well as religious considerations should follow.[350] Such dialogues were prevalent in the *Gikuyu* traditional culture of Kenya

---

344. Lausanne Committee for World Evangelization, "Willowbank Report," 523–524.
345. Strahler, *Coming to Faith*, 79–83.
346. Hiebert, *Transforming Worldviews*, 11.
347. Hiebert, *Anthropological Reflections*, 108.
348. Karanja, "Confession and Cultural Dynamism", 150.
349. R. Y. Hibbert, "Negotiating Identity," 69.
350. Isichei, *History of Christianity*, 122.

which emphasized confession as a mark of conversion, whereby a *gutahikio* (symbolic vomiting) ritual was carried out and the person made to confess through a symbolical vomit of misdeeds of known and unknown sin.[351] As Karanja rightly observes the church's teaching on confession is grounded in Scripture (Jas 5:16; 1 John 1:9) and thus the *Gikuyu* concept of ritual cleansing through confession of evil provides a link with Christian faith.[352]

LCWE appears to contrast the contemporary church with the New Testament on the radical nature of conversion to Jesus Christ. While the former seems to trivialize it, the latter depicts it as the outward expression of regeneration by God's Spirit, a new creation, and a resurrection.[353] The concept of resurrection argues LCWE brings to the fore the eschatological dimension of Christian conversion, which God has begun and will be brought to completion when Christ comes in his glory.[354] Nevertheless, Nkansah-Obrempong warns against the emphasis on the over-realized eschatology (1 Cor 4:8) a problem Paul had to arrest in the Corinthian church.[355]

Christian conversion as a new way of life or worldview

A worldview is the most important and incorporating view of reality shared by people of one culture, which Hiebert calls the mental picture of reality or the *givens* of life that help comprehend the surrounding world.[356] Hiebert further avers, "to question worldview is to challenge the very foundation of life, and people resist such challenges with deep emotional reactions. There are few human fears greater than a loss of a sense of order and meaning. People are willing to die for their beliefs if these beliefs make their death meaningful."[357]

Following this, while making certain statements about the essence of the gospel (1 Cor 15:1–9) and the spiritual need of a sinner (Rom 3:9–18), the delivery of these truths' precise locations involves a contextualization process.[358] For instance, Kraft reflecting on cultural and worldview change, notes

---

351. Karanja, "Confession and Cultural Dynamism", 147–148.
352. Karanja, 148.
353. Lausanne Committee for World Evangelization, "Willowbank Report," 522.
354. Lausanne Committee for World Evangelization, 522.
355. Nkansah-Obrempong, *Foundations*, 123.
356. Hiebert, *Transforming Worldviews*, 84.
357. Hiebert, 84.
358. Hesselgrave, "World-view and Contextualization," 405.

that the process of change works as the process of persistence, in which, the participants in a society attempt to maintain its past alignment and configuration, while at the same time, continually changing old methods and creating new ones.[359]

Therefore, whereas conversion symbolizes death to the past, conceptualized as being crucified with Christ, dying to godlessness and putting off the old Adam, LCWE maintains that it may involve painful sacrifices (Luke 14:25ff).[360] Hiebert argues that emphasis on personal conversion recreates severing relationships with the old life and embracing the new with the significant cost of leaving the familiar life for a new one.[361] Kraft argues that Christian anthropologists are particularly concerned about worldview because whenever a conversion occurs it will affect people's worldview regarding assumptions, values, and allegiances.[362]

Missiological appraisal of anthropology of Christian conversion from Brethren's perspective

Brethren appear to demonstrate a low opinion of traditional cultural beliefs as reflected in the way they handle the conversion to Christianity. Their concern is not just mere conversion, but a change of belief achieved in a born-again testimony, which depicts a pilgrim's progress from the old self to the new self, described as putting off the old Adam and putting on Christ, often at a price.[363] The converts are not only compelled to confess their evil past (in the fellowship meetings) but also expected to change allegiance from traditional beliefs to Christ. The indoctrination is so critical to Brethren that the new convert is supposed to join *Gatia-Uki* (local fellowship) to commence the instruction process to avoid what Hiebert terms *cheap grace*.[364] Indeed, Brethren are right to avoid *cheap grace*, but their insistence on experiential sanctification mostly ends up in stereotype and a hypocritical worldview expressed through practical holiness, somewhat tantamount to over-realized eschatology.[365] This

---

359. Kraft, *Anthropology for Christian Witness*, 366
360. Lausanne Committee for World Evangelization, "Willowbank Report," 522–523.
361. Hiebert, *Anthropological Reflections*, 165.
362. Kraft, *Anthropology for Christian Witness*, 11.
363. Lausanne Committee for World Evangelization, "Willowbank Report," 522–523.
364. Hiebert, *Transforming Worldviews*, 108.
365. Nkansah-Obrempong, *Foundations*, 123.

worldview concerns missiological anthropologists because the newly acquired values tend to drive Brethren away from the community and sometimes from family members.[366]

Indeed, the change is more of enculturation than inculturation. The new Brethren worldview appears to dictate neophytes' new beliefs and practices instead of following a critical contextualization process, which, while contextualizing the gospel, remains prophetic.[367] The lack of a critical process appears to hinder appropriate adaptation and application of the gospel, because God's truth ought to be faithfully and intelligently communicated through the Spirit in all cultures,[368] including that of Brethren. Brethren's contextualization principles compare with the way in which previous Christian missionaries attempts to replace paganism with western Christianity, treating the Africans as if they had no preconceived ideas, and were thus a *tabula rasa*.[369]

Missiological Theory of Anthropology of Christian Worship

Christian worship as acquired belief

Hastings claims that the assembled worship of the church must embody both change and continuity, where the change reflects required inculturation to contextualize and communicate the gospel; continuity is derived from apostolic faith and developed by the specialists of the church.[370] Smalley, while planting the church in Alaska, attests to the fact that superstitions still exists undercover, as natives would not disclose to a white person beliefs in supernatural powers, though such information leaks to worshipers in church on Sunday mornings.[371] Isichei illustrates this further by observing that traditional beliefs and Christian beliefs sometimes exist parallel in one person as exemplified by the Nigerian radical Tai Solarin, who points out that his mother, while in danger, would call on the spirit of her grandfather more than Jesus.[372] In Kenya, argues Karanja, the pioneer missionaries preached on the

---

366. Kraft, *Anthropology for Christian Witness*, 11.
367. Hiebert, *Transforming Worldviews*, 84–86.
368. Hesselgrave, "World-view and Contextualization", 408.
369. Ott, Strauss and Tennent, *Encountering Theology of Mission*, 50.
370. Hastings, *Missional God*, 137.
371. Smalley, "Planting the Church," 110.
372. Isichei, *History of Christianity*, 6.

doctrine of original sin, which led to a sense of guilt among the Christians – as to seek services of traditional diviners to deal with illness or personal tragedy – as demonstrated by one of the pioneer African ministers in Nairobi who wore protective charms.[373] This is consistent with Kraft's concept of dual allegiance (described as the biggest problem in global Christianity) which illustrates those who pledge loyalty to both Christ and traditional powers, such as medicine men and diviners.[374]

Thus, some indigenous churches' movements in Africa find outlets for religious expression by hand-clapping and dancing and perceive the western form of worship in many mission churches as unnatural.[375] Hastings contends that church as a community that is both lively and ancient ought to express worship that is not only living and exciting but depicts continuity with redemption history and liturgy.[376] Thus, one of the prayers of intercession for the lives of those who have departed in Christ, in *Our Modern Services Prayer Book* of the Anglican Church of Kenya says "Gracious Father, we heartily thank you for our *faithful ancestors* and all who have passed through death to the new life of joy in our heavenly home. We pray that surrounded by so great a cloud of witnesses, we may walk in their footsteps and be fully united with them in your everlasting kingdom."[377] In other words, it is not all ancestors, but those who died in Christ, whose mentorship inspired and motivated a Christocentric life. Hastings further asserts that a Christocentric missional church can achieve both incarnational width and spiritual depth through cultural relevance and engagement on the one hand, and on the other hand, be confessional and ecclesial.[378]

Christian worship as acquired worldview
Kraft believes God is pro-culture as he worked with the culture of Hebrews, including their religion, except idolatry. Thus he decries Christians who trample on the traditional religion of the people they have come to win to

---

373. Karanja, "Confession and Cultural Dynamism", 148–189.
374. Kraft, *Anthropology for Christian Witness*, 201.
375. Smalley, "What Are Indigenous Churches," 159.
376. Hastings, *Missional God,* 177.
377. Anglican Church of Kenya, *Our Modern Services*, 77.
378. Hastings, *Missional God,* 146.

Christ, which ends up condemning their worldview.[379] Abrecht and Smalley observe that God appears to work with the dominant forms of culture more than missionaries would like to acknowledge, rendering them alien to the local community.[380] Abrecht and Smalley are of the view that, to lead the local community to total commitment to Christ, the missionary should motivate the people to find appropriate structures to express their new faith within their culture.[381] This resonates with Zaki's observation that worship reflects local cultural characteristics and the fact that Jesus incarnated in a distinct culture gives both a model and a mandate, for the gospel was never cultural specific, rather, the good news was to extend to the entire world positioning the church deeply into various local cultures.[382]

Further, Zaki outlines two critical approaches to contextualization of a viable worldview. At the one end of the continuum is dynamic equivalence – which tends to restate Christian worship dynamics with an appropriate local culture component, such as modelling the lordship of Jesus among "the Masai tribe in Kenya by painting a black man dressed in a red robe, since red is the colour of royalty and is always worn by the village chief." On the other end of the continuum is creative assimilation, which means enriching worship by adding relevant components of local culture, as in Egypt where an *oud* (lute) harmonic sound is used to add a fuller expression to psalms of lament.[383]

The dynamic equivalence approach is further exemplified in the Anglican Church of Kenya service of Holy Communion whereby the Turkana of Kenya tradition of casting away of sins to the setting sun is expressed in the Anglican Holy Communion service with a sweep of the arm towards the cross, to symbolize the casting of problems, difficulties and the devil's works on the cross of Christ, and setting hopes on the risen Christ.[384] Furthermore, *Nyimbo Cia Gucanjamura Ngoro* (*Gikuyu* hymn of praise) published by the Anglican Church of Kenya, captures the creative assimilation of African musical-styled rhythms that has not only revitalized the African feel of Christian music but

---

379. Kraft, *Anthropology for Christian Witness*, 210.
380. Abrecht and Smalley, "Moral Implications," 123.
381. Abrecht and Smalley, 123.
382. Zaki, *Mission Frontiers*, 17.
383. Zaki, 17–18.
384. Anglican Church of Kenya, *Our Modern Services*, 84.

has also brought jubilation to the worship due to the artistic identification with culture.

Sesi, writing on contextualization of prayer and worship among the *Digo* Christians in Kenya, observes that contextualization would enable them to devise and nurture Christian dynamics that not only make sense to them but also match their worldview.[385] Nevertheless, Zaki notes that, while it challenges anthropological missiologists to become careful readers of culture in light of biblical truths, Christian worship must resist the idolatries of a given culture that contradict the gospel.[386]

Missiological appraisal of anthropology of Christian worship from Brethren's perspective

When Brethren use the analogy of an uprooted (as of dug up) carrot to describe a change of allegiance from the traditional cultural beliefs they are essentially declaring change with discontinuity with all cultural beliefs. This drastic change in belief achieved through a born-again philosophy and expressed through selected worship style defines Brethren's worldview of Christian worship. This is in spite of the Anglican Church of Kenya thanksgiving prayer to God for the lives of those who have departed in Christ[387] which not only incorporates faithful ancestors but embodies both change and continuity,[388] and is consistent with Kraft who believes God is pro-culture.[389]

From this perspective, it appears the Brethren worldview of worship is informed by inadequate biblical and theological understanding of anthropological missiology, which as Zaki observes ought to reflect components of local culture.[390] Jesus's incarnation was in a particular culture, and appears to work with existing cultures, contradicting Brethren's worldview and suggestinh a worship style modeled and mandated by Jesus's view of cultures.[391] For Brethren to have an effective mission, it ought not only to have appropriate

---

385. Sesi, "Context and Worship,", 200–201.
386. Zaki, "Mission Frontiers", 18.
387. Anglican Church of Kenya, *Our Modern Services*, 77.
388. Hastings, *Missional God*, 137.
389. Kraft, *Anthropology for Christian Witness*, 210.
390. Zaki, "Mission Frontiers", 17.
391. Abrecht and Smalley, "Moral Implications," 123.

dynamic equivalent cultural components but also have them creatively contextualized in their fellowship meetings.

Nevertheless, Brethren antipathy towards culture should not be wholly disregarded because as Zaki observes, cultural elements (idolatries) that contradict the gospel in Christian worship is rejected.[392] Either way, an informed contextualization is required for Brethren to participate fully in the mission of God within their local communities where the complexities of dual allegiance to Christ and cultural beliefs sometimes exist in parallel in the same person.[393] The concept of dual allegiance not only appears to dishonor the second commandment (Exod 20:3) but is likely to influence Brethren private worship (opposed to dynamic equivalent and creative assimilation), unless informed structures are put in place to facilitate a responsible and viable process of change and continuity.

Missiological Theory of Anthropology of Social Ethics

In nineteenth century missions, argues Hiebert, many missionaries looked for evidence of conversion to Christ through outward features like putting on clothes and giving up alcohol, but did not change underlying beliefs.[394] People changed their behavior to win status or get jobs, until the twentieth century when transformations in people's views took center stage with missions setting up Bible schools and seminaries to teach the orthodox doctrine of Christian conversion.[395] Thus, Kraft describes transformational culture change as that which takes place in a society and its culture because of a change in worldview.[396] With that in mind, worldview-informed social and ethical beliefs and practices will hinge this segment.

Christian social-ethical life as individual beliefs and practices

A focus by anthropologists on the relationship of an individual and culture appears to have arisen from the belief that people are conceived without culture but soon find themselves encultured and socialized to a particular

---

392. Zaki, "Mission Frontiers", 18.
393. Isichei, *History of Christianity*, 6.
394. Hiebert, *Transforming Worldviews*, 10.
395. Hiebert, 11.
396. Kraft, *Anthropology for Christian Witness*, 440.

way of seeing reality, thinking and behaving.³⁹⁷ One of the profound theories of the individual appears to resonate with what Mbiti conceptualizes as "I am, because we are; and since we are, therefore I am," which depicts an individual as a social being because "only in terms of other people does the individual become conscious of his . . . responsibilities towards himself and towards other people."³⁹⁸ This concept, argues Knoetze, not only associates African identity with the *Ubuntu* principle,³⁹⁹ but also with biblical humanity and discipleship perspectives of "I am and you are, because he (God) is."⁴⁰⁰ Moreover, contends Knoetze, this viewpoint negates the individualistic understanding expounded by Descartes, "I think therefore I am," which is especially prevalent in modern South Africa.⁴⁰¹

Kraft notes enculturation is so effective that individual behavior is affected by cultural conditioning in all perspectives.⁴⁰² Nonetheless, as Grimes and Grimes observe, some cultures like the Huichol Indians in Mexico are distinctly individualistic (rather differently from Mbiti's and Ubuntu's concept) in the sense that they depict full cultural limits of acceptable variation, and consequently a low predictability of specific actions.⁴⁰³ Indeed an attempt was made to introduce congregational singing as happens in many Christian communities as a way to unify Christians but was met with resistance, and so they continued with their pattern of having one person sing⁴⁰⁴ in all gathering of Christians.⁴⁰⁵

While Mbiti's and Grimes' description of an individual relationship with culture posit differing cultural conditioning, it appears the latter would have made it easier for an individual approach to Christianization (compare Descartes' sentiments) than the former. This echoes Baur who claims that

---

397. Kraft, 150.
398. Mbiti, *African Religion and Philosophy*, 106.
399. "I am only because we are, and since we are, therefore I am" (Du Toit, "Technoscience," 33).
400. Knoetze, "Who are the disciples?," 1.
401. Knoetze, 1.
402. Kraft, *Anthropology for Christian Witness*, 150.
403. Grimes and Grimes, "Individualism," 199.
404. "One difficulty with congregational singing was that with no set form for the order of lines in a stanza and much repetition no one knew how anyone else was going to sing the same song" (Grimes and Grimes, 202)
405. Grimes, & Grimes, 202.

missionary method aimed at the individual salvation of souls as opposed to the communal concept of religion among the African peoples.[406] Consequently, Christian rites were assimilated by the African religion. Nevertheless, the individual approach, concerning later missionary Christianization efforts broke through the individual concept of the whole to form what Hiebert calls "Christian as a bounded set"[407] or what Hastings refers to the Christocentric community in which Christ is the center.[408] The African communal aspect appears to assume a new dimension of discipleship from the perspective of the *Ubuntu* principle of African identity in which God is the focus.

Indeed African culture initiation rituals appear to reinforce bounded set analogy. For example, Mbiti notes that the belief of shedding of blood into the ground during circumcision mystically bound the initiate with the living-dead (symbolically living in the ground) symbolizing new birth and a new age-set.[409] Certainly, such beliefs motivated early missionaries to forbid initiation rites, a fact that Hiebert and Meneses observe was precipitated by pagan components in the ritual and a tendency to equate it with baptism, instead of a ritual in which a Christian publicly declares transition to social and religious adulthood.[410] Hiebert and Meneses further argue that the traditional morality that connected individuals to the family, clan, and tribe is disappearing, as traditional beliefs and values are rejected as false myths.[411]

Christian social-ethical life as communal beliefs and practices
Hiebert and Meneses highlight modernity as a source of the same crisis that has led to the collapse of old ways of life and consequently to schizophrenic cultural beliefs.[412] Indeed, Langley and Kiggins contend that the symbolism of initiation rites was so profoundly expressive and meaningful that

---

406. Baur, *2000 Years of Christianity*, 94.

407. Hiebert, *Anthropological Reflections*, 115. One of the ways of classifying a person as a Christian, argues Hiebert, is by test of orthodoxy and orthopraxy (right behavior), with a verbal affirmation of belief in a specific set of doctrines, such as the deity of Christ and the virgin birth, and evidence of faith in the changed life of the Christian, such as not smoking or drinking alcohol, respectively.

408. Hastings, *Missional God*, 122.

409. Mbiti, *African Religion and Philosophy*, 120.

410. Hiebert and Meneses, *Incarnational Ministry*, 180.

411. Hiebert and Meneses, 181.

412. Hiebert and Meneses, 180–181.

anthropologists encultured it as a means of passing on to the next generation the themes of culture such as friendly relations, endurance, responsibility and orderliness in society.[413] Further, Langley and Kiggins reflect on an Anglican missionary who worked towards Christianizing initiation rites among the *Masasi* of Tanzania by retaining initiation components that inform communal identity while removing what he termed obscene or immoral aspects.[414]

About the above, Hastings argues for a contextualization which encompasses engagement with culture or what he calls inculturation without enculturation, which has both an incarnational mandate and a communal dimension of culture.[415] However, Phiri points out that an African community's collective decisions for change involve the entire society understanding the need for a change.[416] Kraft asserts that people have to be interested not only in need but also in the solution stimulated by the practical need of change, as opposed to a theoretical explanation of the value of the Christian way of life.[417] As noted earlier, Karanja argues that when the traditional rituals failed to bring down the rain following a prolonged drought that threatened animal and human life, the local chief approached Herbert Butcher (the resident missionary at CMS station) to pray for rains.[418] Butcher prayed, and heavy rain ensued immediately, encouraging not only the local diviners to renounce their practice and give up their divining paraphernalia for burning, but hundreds of people flocked into Mutira mission.[419]

Missiological appraisal of anthropology of Christian social ethic from Brethren's perspective

Brethren's social and ethical life revolves around briefs and practices encultured and nurtured in Brethren fellowships. While Brethren beliefs in individual membership are perpetuated through a personal born-again testimony and achieved through certain moral codes, they certainly value community awareness of the individual conceptualized by the exclusive nature of their

---

413. Langley and Kiggins, *Serving People*, 159.
414. Langley and Kiggins, 161.
415. Hastings, *Missional God*, 164.
416. Phiri, *Social-cultural Anthropology*, 76.
417. Kraft, *Anthropology for Christian Witness*, 388.
418. Karanja, "Confession and Cultural Dynamism", 150.
419. Karanja, 150.

spirituality tantamount to *a bounded set* of Christian phenomena[420] that desists evil practices. Nevertheless, Brethren are quick to inculturate some African cultural elements, which could boost missiological anthropology mission perspectives of African Christians who practice circumcision. One of the Brethren's fundamentals is the beliefs and practices that set apart a Christian from the old nature. Although they don't equate it to baptism, Brethren view circumcision as a symbol of marking the end of the old life which echoes African puberty rites of passage.

This resonates with Karanja's observation of a young man at St. Paul's United Theological College, today's St. Paul's University, who was jubilant that his fellow students (members of Brethren) had facilitated his circumcision so that he could reconcile his Christian faith with the cultural practices of his people.[421] This further reverberates with Langley and Kiggins' reflection of an Anglican (anthropological) missionary who Christianized useful components of initiation rites among the *Masasi* of Tanzania as a way of fostering communal identity.[422] This resonates with Brethren who expect a converted person to demonstrate clear characteristics of the new life in the same way a circumcised person is supposed to depict maturity and responsibility. This identity formation unfortunately fostered ethical codes of conduct within Brethren, yet if well guided to ensure freedom with responsibility this could motivate an informed Brethren anthropological mission.

Another aspect to note about Brethren is their beliefs and practices are communally enacted to hedge their independent lifestyle. Although change is inevitable if Brethren fellowship is to make a mark in the anthropological mission, there seems to be no general agreement across the board on what aspects need change. While some are still hesitant on hair styles, others have allowed their young members to wear a wig. This lack of unanimity on change illustrates the sensitive nature of collective decisions especially when the decision is perceived to bring loss rather than gain.[423] Nonetheless, when understood that it would add value to the Brethren community, it will be

---

420. Hiebert, *Anthropological Reflections*, 115.
421. Karanja, "Confession and Cultural Dynamism", 146.
422. Langley and Kiggins, *Serving People*, 161.
423. Phiri, *Social-cultural Anthropology*, 76.

accommodated,[424] and will no doubt translate their social and ethical beliefs and practices from being a hindrance to the anthropological mission to being faithful participants in the mission of God.

Summary of the Prevailing Situation As It is Today Using Historical and Empirical Analyses.

To dispense with the current situation, a consideration of thematic harmony regarding the historical epochs and the empirical situation of the present trend are put into their respective viewpoints as demonstrated in chapter 3.

On the one hand, the historical survey came up with six descriptive themes which seem to inform the heritage of Keswick theology in the EARM's socio-ethical life from 1935 to 2015. These themes are a *baptism of the Spirit, being born again, cross of Christ and daily victory, public confession of sins, filling of the Spirit,* and *authority of the Scripture.* On the other hand, also clustered into six key themes are the findings and analyses of nature and current trends regarding Anglicanism church scholarship today. These are, Brethren's *born again testimony, acquaintances with EARM's precursor, the daily sanctification of the new man, Scripture and moral code, effects of splits on the mission of the Anglican Church* and *synergized-diversified Anglican Church.* Most of these themes encompassed a large amount of information that made it necessary to generate subthemes.

That notwithstanding, the apparent thematic consistencies between the historical survey and the current trends appear to suggest some heritage of Keswick theology. This is in spite of the fact that a majority of the respondents could not trace EARM's antecedent. Indeed, except for themes on the baptism of the Holy Spirit which seem to have disappeared, others find affinity either in the major themes or subthemes of the current data findings. Table 6 below seeks to elucidate a possible scenario of the influence of Keswick theology on the prevailing socio-ethical trend of *walking in the light.*

---

424. Karanja, "Confession and Cultural Dynamism", 150.

Table 6: Influence of Keswick Theology

Historical Influence of Keswick Theology	Current Trend/Thematic Harmony
Baptism of the Spirit	No traits
Born again	1. Brethren's born again testimony
Public confession of sin	(a) Confession, restitution, and forgiveness of sins
The cross of Christ – daily victory	(b) Journey with the Lord Jesus 2. Daily sanctification of the new man
Filling of the Spirit	3. Synergized-diversified Anglican Church: worship (in the Spirit) dynamics 4. Effects of splits on Church mission: Pentecostal haven
Authority of Scripture	5. Scripture and moral codes
	6. Acquaintances with EARM's precursor

While the historical theme of being born again easily pervades the Brethren born-again testimony, public confession of sin and daily victory finds an affinity to some of the subthemes of the Brethren born-again testimony, like confession and the journey with Jesus respectively. This historic theme also appears to attract a current trend theme of the daily sanctification of the new man. Admittedly, this current trend theme seems to place experiential sanctification of everyday life into both Keswick and non-Keswick backgrounds.

Whereas the historical theme of filling with the Spirit finds kinship in various current situation subthemes like worship in Spirit dynamics and Pentecostal haven, it also touches on the current theme of the daily sanctification of the new man.

The authority of Scripture, is one of the themes that have consistently informed the history of the EARM, whereby members appear to conceive the idea that immediate scriptural contexts have an inherent authority of their own apart from wider contexts. Indeed some moral codes that inform the current socio-ethics seem to have sprung from literal interpretation and application of various biblical texts.

Finally, the theme on acquaintances with EARM's precursor appears to lack affinity with a historical theme. This could be attributed to the fact that it was to do with knowledge of Keswick theology which was not a concern of the historical survey.

Following this, it is pivotal from the viewpoint of the current trend to acknowledge that, despite the alleged fears that accompany EARM's socio-ethics, it has nevertheless shown a resilient lifestyle, exemplified by the number of subthemes associated with the principal themes. However, the majority of historical themes only fitted on a small proportion of the key themes which suggest a diminishing significance.

Having said that, to summarize the prevailing situation as it is today, it is critical to put the harmonized themes (current trends) into manageable clusters of conversion, worship style, and moral codes. Indeed, this triad forms the legs upon which the analytical summary of the current historical and empirical situation hinges. Thus, the conversion theme incorporates born again and daily sanctification; worship style comprises worship dynamics and Pentecostalism; and Scriptures inform moral codes.

Historical Analysis

In order to put the historical analysis of the prevailing trend into its proper perspective, a summary of the historical trends is placed within the framework of the themes of conversion, worship style, and moral codes.

Conversion

Brethren's concept of the new birth impacted Kenyan soil immediately following a visit by a team from Rwanda in 1937,[425] which led to factions (*Joremo* and *Johera*) among the revivalists in the Anglican Church in western Kenya.[426] While both *Joremo (Wahamaji)* and *Johera* claimed daily sanctification and self-righteousness, the former asserted one could be saved many times, while the latter affirmed salvation takes place once, with a provision for backsliding and restoration.[427] This pompous disposition elevated these factions above other believers, creating a two-Christian scenario.

Indeed, Brethren's sanctimonious display of the power of the cleansing blood of Christ is illustrated by the apolitical disposition during the

---

425. Church, *Quest for the Highest*, 145; MacMaster and Jacobs, *Gentle Wind of God*, 58.
426. Welbourn and Ogot, *Place to Feel*, 31, 32.
427. Welbourn and Ogot, 34, 35, 38.

state of emergency (1952–1960) and the post-election violence of 2007.[428] Furthermore, Mambo observes Brethren tribulations from both the church leadership and the African traditions over the open confession of sin and constant claim to have been born again.[429] Indeed, the concept of a new birth was misunderstood among the *Gikuyu* Christians who accused Brethren of reintroducing the traditional rite of *guciaruo ringi*[430] and they were denied fellowship in churches as heretics. Moreover, confessions of sins, especially of adultery, cost a bishop his episcopacy.[431] Thus, the 1970s came to be referred to as the generation of being born again.[432] Consequently, the 2015 Kabale Convention in Uganda exhorted Brethren to consider their call (1 Cor 1:26). Further, GAFCON 2013 recollected EARM teaching as fundamental to salvation whereby the conviction of sin was noted to be central to revival.[433]

Worship Style

The EARM's worship style appeared to conflict with that of the Anglican Church with some members, especially *Joremo* opting for a spiritual separation in 1953[434] as they felt aggrieved by the admission of nominal Christians (those who do not "walk in the light") in the fellowships. Others like *Kaggians* left physically, abandoning the Anglican Prayer Book to form a non-denominational Pentecostal church.[435]

The *Kufufuka* and *Kusimama* factions, though they observe a similar stereotyping worship style, held their local fellowships separately[436] for the better part of the second epoch. This exclusive and discriminatory attitude hinders young people from attending the revival fellowships. Nonetheless, a huge convention in 2011 of young Brethren at Lenana School in Nairobi is a welcome move. Furthermore, the reference to Brethren's maxim of *walking in the light* during the Nairobi GAFCON communique 2016 demonstrates

---

428. Gatu, "Jesus Christ," 39.
429. Mambo, "Revival Fellowship", 111–112.
430. Mambo, 112.
431. Gitari, *Troubled but not Destroyed*, 74.
432. Gathogo, "Retracing Diakonia," 8.
433. Walton, "Legacy of East African," 2.
434. Welbourn and Ogot, *Place to Feel*, 33, 34.
435. Welbourn and Ogot, 31.
436. Gitari, " Paper on East African ", 5.

its central place in Anglican spirituality. Nevertheless, Gathogo observes the majority of Brethren leaders lack theological training, and sometimes make ignorant decisions.[437]

Moral Codes

Questionable teachings by *Noo's* did not only encourage women to leave their unsaved husbands but also encouraged opposite sexes to sleep together simply because they were saved,[438] leading to sexual impropriety and other nefarious practices. Thus, Gathogo observes confessions of cheating spouses, despite hitherto appearing trustworthy.[439]

About the handling of fellowship finances, Brethren just "walk in the light."[440] Thus members of Brethren opposed to accounting procedures introduced *Mfuko wa Bwana* (The Lord's Bag) for they saw money as a source of evil and left to form *Kufufuka* (Resurrection) or the Re-awakened faction based on Ephesians 5:14–15.[441] Gathogo contends that the *Kufufuka* Brethren were discouraged from taking bank loans because Christ paid their debts on the cross.[442] Gathogo maintains the *Kufufuka* revival of 1967 witnessed people from the mainline churches convert to this faith.[443] Nevertheless, in the late 1990s, Kamau notes the *Mfuko wa Bwana* controversy within the *Kusimama* faction following an exaggerated budget for a Convention.[444]

Empirical Analyses

The empirical analysis cannot be complete without assessing the reliability of the research instruments used during the research project in the four dioceses. As suggested in chapter 1, a reliability test was to be done to establish the replication of the research findings. Therefore, a pilot study (see consent letter – annexure 9) was conducted in February 2017 in the Anglican Diocese of Mbeere (within the Mount Kenya region) which did not participate in the

---

437. Gathogo, "Retracing Diakonia," 7–8.
438. Welbourn and Ogot, *Place to Feel*, 30.
439. Gathogo, "Retracing Diakonia," 8.
440. MacMaster and Jacobs, *Gentle Wind of God*, 181.
441. Mambo, "Revival Fellowship", 115.
442. Gathogo, "Retracing Diakonia," 7.
443. Gathogo, 8.
444. Kamau, "Critical Analysis," 28.

actual study. The collected data from the four select dioceses were evaluated vis-à-vis the Diocese of Mbeere and findings were consistent, and thus the instruments were reliable and valid for generalization to other ACK Dioceses and beyond (see annexure 10).

Additionally, as a recap, it is pivotal to note the research project in the four select dioceses had six categories of research respondents or participants. These were ordinary members, leaders, theological students, clergy, bishops and prominent stakeholders. The participants' responses are adduced from the perspective of conversion, worship style, and moral codes.

Conversion

Concerning conversion, the majority of Brethren especially the ordinary people and leaders of Revival Fellowships across the four dioceses were found to give their born-again testimony regarding full disclosure of identity from the viewpoint of life in the past, present, and future expectations – demonstrating their sojourn with Christ every hour. Indeed, they repent and confess their past sins in detail, one by one followed by the restitution and forgiveness. They testify to conquer the devil with the blood of the Lamb and by the word of their testimony (Rev 12:11).

Concerning knowledge of Keswick theology, only 20 percent of all respondents have heard about its teachings. Of this percentage, the prominent stakeholders by their academic pursuit had 100 percent knowledge while all other categories depict little or no knowledge at all. Certainly some clergy mistook it for the Keswick Bookshop in Nairobi. However, while some clergy described Keswick theology as a wave of revival and renewal over East Africa, explicated by profound salvation experiences, some prominent stakeholders not only positioned it within the wider holiness movement but also emphasized conversion and personal holiness exemplified by the infilling of the Holy Spirit.

Still, other stakeholders associated it with the strict pietistic theology of being saved and daily sanctification which entrenched legalistic spirituality and prompted daily devotions and a profound sense of accountability. While some other respondents associated influence of EARM to conventions, beliefs and practices of walking in the light and overnight fellowships, some stakeholders said it was influenced by Pentecostalism and the born-again culture with the strict religious position. Additionally, other stakeholders attribute the influence to the Victorian ideals that restrain sex and depict strict moral codes. Besides, others saw a lack of theological knowledge as a prelude to the belief and practice of walking in the light. This view echoes a bishop and theological students who attribute it to a literal interpretation of Scripture.

Worship Style

Some ordinary members argue against intrusive testimony which appears not only to intrude into people's lives but also portray different standing with other Christians, which affects church witness and growth of the mission. Indeed, some claim that in the 1960s, this attitude informed strict moral codes like refraining from a bank loan and getting saved anew, which led to separate fellowship meetings and lapsed as to holiness and the witnessing Spirit. However, others argue that in the 1970s splits impacted the mission of the church positively with smart dress codes and preaching from the Bible.

But then in the 1990s youth left the church because of restrictions on hair styles, dress code, use of public address system and Pentecostal worship. This is consistent with some leaders and a bishop who say that the split within the Brethren led to new fellowships and new denominations. Some ordinary members argue this created tension between Brethren and other Christians particularly clergy who were considered not saved. Indeed, one of the prominent stakeholders said that EARM considers itself as the legislators of the church with the majority of Anglican bishops declaring themselves to be part of the revival, which is a boost for the church's mission if the declaration is not schizophrenic.

Indeed, most respondents expressed the need for an extensive and diversified church ministry and mission, especially in the areas of leadership, moral code dynamism, worship in the Spirit, and academics. Indeed, about leadership, one of the prominent stakeholders said Bishop Obadiah Kariuki, a member of EARM, in 1969 confronted Kenyatta to stop forcing church elders to take the oath. However, Bishop John Mahiani was almost chased away from the fellowship for associating with a splinter group. Thus, one of the bishops and some clergy maintain that Brethren should seek not only to coexist with other Christians but to work with the Anglican Church leadership.

Therefore, a prominent stakeholder said the Anglican Church should encourage greater flexibility and tolerance of different views. Moreover, a group of theological students and clergy expressed a need for dynamism in the fellowship with full participation of all ages. Indeed, some ordinary members suggested the sexes should hug one another. Furthermore, while one of the prominent stakeholders recommended that bishops should be transferable to share their gifts with the whole Anglican Church of Kenya, another expressed a need to look at the relationship between the older *Balokole* (saved ones in Luganda) movement and modern charismatic Pentecostalism in the light of their thoughts and practices. This is because the earlier EARM was founded within the context of the overwhelming power of the Holy Spirit, which appears to anchor the proliferation of Pentecostal churches today.

Also, one of the prominent stakeholders encouraged clergy, bishops and ACK academics like the researcher, to fellowship with East Africa Revival groups, to influence and be influenced by each other. Thus, a group of ordinary members urged St. Andrew's College lecturers not only to follow-up students during mission outreaches to offer mentorship, but also to teach them that priesthood is a calling, not a job.

Moral Codes

About moral codes, the majority of respondents observed that interpretations of various biblical texts not only appear to inform the splits but also the moral codes. The most mentioned texts were Ephesians 5:14 and Daniel 1:8ff at sixteen and fourteen times respectively. Others were 2 Corinthians 6:14–18 at six, 1 Corinthians 11:14–16 at six, Genesis 12:1 at five, Ephesians 6:14–20 at fix, Romans 13:8 at four and Psalms 127:1 at two. These texts seemed to contribute most significantly to the development of unique Brethren lifestyles.

Indeed, the majority of the respondents asserted that interpretation of various texts was understood as meaning to *leave* EARM. Certainly, the concept of leaving was espoused by some ordinary members and some leaders who argued that Ephesian 5:14 and Daniel 1:8–15 were interpreted to mean leave. The "leave" concept culminated, respectively, in the *Kufufuka* (Arise, Awake) faction in 1967 and *Mtama na Maji* (sorghum and water) in 1969 which some clergy associated with the *Kupaa* (Rising) wing in 1987. Thus, on the one hand, *Kufufuka* required the saved people to be saved again, because as a prominent stakeholder notes, those who continually confess sins after conversion were *dead* for they have no power of the Spirit to overcome sin. This signified the *Kusimama* Brethren were *dead*, which led to the standing firm (Standing/*Kusimama*) faction derived from Ephesians 6:14. The stand firm concept was used by some leaders to encourage Christians to withstand challenges. Thus the phrase *Yesu atosha* (Jesus satisfies) became *Kusimama*'s motto.

On the other hand, the *Kupaa* faction discouraged luxurious lifestyles. Consequently, as some leaders observed, *Kupaa* avoided social gatherings believed to entertain guests with a *royal diet*. Indeed, the concept of leaving is also depicted in the interpretation of 2 Corinthians 6:14–17 and Geneses 12:1. While in respect to the former, a prominent stakeholder observes that some Brethren uses this text to hedge themselves from the rest of Christian community, which is perceived to be living in sin, thus entrenching an arrogant attitude. Regarding the latter, some leaders and theological students (who referred to them as *Thama*, a Gikuyu word for leave or exodus) perceived that some Brethren sold everything and physically left their families to serve God. Certainly, some leaders said that some parents used the Genesis text to desert their unwedded pregnant daughters.

Some other texts like 1 Corinthians 11:14–16, Psalm 127:1 and Romans 13:8 were used to entrench social conventions and the dress code. Indeed, some leaders, clergy and a bishop noted that 1 Corinthians 11:14–16 was interpreted to mean men should not have beards or long hair and women should cover their heads, especially when praying. Still, other leaders used Psalms 127:1 to claim that since God is their protector, there is no need for keeping dogs or any other form of security. About Romans 13:8, one of the stakeholders said, *Tusiwe na deni* (we should not have debt) which could have contributed to avoidance of bank loans by some Brethren.

However, not all splits were a result of the interpretation of Scripture. Leadership and the public confession of sins were primarily found to have caused division. Indeed, whereas one of the prominent stakeholders said members of Brethren who were retired teachers imposed themselves too firmly, the other (prominent stakeholder) saw the question of polygamy to have brought the split between *Joremo* and *Johera*. While *Johera* argued that polygamists were honest and should be loved, the hypocritical *Joremo* pushed them away. Thus, some ordinary members said the fact that Brethren view themselves as holier-than-thou impedes the church mission.

Regarding the open confession of sin, some leaders blamed their fellow Brethren for compelling new members to publicly repent their sins as a means of admission into the fellowship. Conversely, some leaders cautioned that the

New Testament should not be used as an instruction manual for norms and overly burdensome instructions.

About other moral codes, some leaders said while Brethren instructs on dictums of ethical codes, they should engage in economic activities, encouraging welfare groups and opening saving accounts. Thus, some ordinary members and clergy expressed a need for Brethren to avoid legalistic rules and embrace change that promotes youth to join the fellowship. On the one hand, theological students said Brethren should learn exegesis and interpretation of the Bible. On the other hand, some leaders argued that the church should refocus on strengthening biblical knowledge and Christian witness to attract the younger generation.

Analysis of Affinity Between Historical and Empirical Trends

In order to have a full thrust into the current trend, it is necessary to consider a synopsis of historical and empirical harmony from the perspective of conversion, worship style, and moral codes.

Conversion

The *Joremo* and *Johera* factions which infiltrated the church in Western Kenya in the early years of revival in Kenya, appear to echo the current trend of *Kufufuka* and *Kusimama* factions in the Mount Kenya region today. While *Joremo,* Welbourn and Ogot felt aggrieved by the admission of nominal Christians into the fellowships, a prominent stakeholder argued that *Kufufuka* used Ephesian 5:14 to claim other Brethren are dead and should be saved again.[445] Nonetheless, *Johera* severed its ties with the Anglican Church in 1958 to form the Church of Christ in Africa.[446] However, some leaders assert that *Kusimama* used Ephesians 6:14 to encourage itself to stand firm against challenges because of *Yesu atosha* (Jesus satisfies), and works in close cooperation with the Anglican Church today, a disposition upheld by *Kufufuka*.

But as Mambo observes, Brethren's tribulations by the church leadership over the open confession of sin and constant claim to have been born again

---

445. Welbourn and Ogot, *Place to Feel*, 33–34.
446. Welbourn and Ogot, 57.

is yet to be resolved.⁴⁴⁷ Thus, some ordinary members argue Brethren's reference to other Christians, particularly clergy, as not saved, just because they neither attend fellowship nor "walk in the light," creates a disturbing tension. Indeed, Brethren's sanctimonious display is further illustrated in the confession of sins especially of adultery, which for instance led a bishop to lose his episcopacy.⁴⁴⁸ Although Karanja claims public confession of sins has been discouraged, it seems to continue unabated.⁴⁴⁹ Indeed, some leaders observe that new members are compelled to publicly repent their sins as a means of admission into the fellowship.

Worship Style

Separate fellowship meetings by *Kusimama* and *Kufufuka* until the 1980s disillusioned the youth as to hinder their attendance of revival fellowships.⁴⁵⁰ Even though the two factions sometimes meet in local fellowships, young people still feel excluded due to stereotyping liturgical worship. Thus, some leaders argue that in 1990s youth left the church over hair styles, dress code, use of public address system and Pentecostal worship. Furthermore, other leaders and a bishop say that the impact of the split within the Brethren led to new fellowships and new denominations.

Nonetheless, a huge convention of young Brethren at Lenana School in 2011 illustrates a new dawn to narrow the generation gap. This is consistent with a group of theological students and clergy who expressed a need for dynamism in the fellowship with full participation of all ages. Furthermore, the reference to Brethren's maxim of walking in the light during the 2016 Nairobi GAFCON communique appears to demonstrate its defining spirituality in the Anglican Church of Kenya. Indeed, one of the prominent stakeholders maintains that EARM was founded within the context of the overwhelming power of the Holy Spirit, which appears to anchor the proliferation of Pentecostal churches today, something that Brethren should consider exploring.

---

447. Mambo, "Revival Fellowship", 111–112.
448. Gitari, *Troubled but not Destroyed*, 74.
449. Karanja, *Confession and Cultural Dynamism*, 146.
450. Gitari, "A Paper on East African," 5.

Moral Codes

Issues of morality which are foundational to the current trend came to the fore right after revival entered Kenya. A good example is the teachings by Noo's who in his ignorance claimed opposite sexes could sleep together simply because they were saved because *to the pure all things are pure*.[451] Even though the majority of Brethren leaders lack theological training, and sometimes make ignorant decisions, this unorthodox teaching is unacceptable to Brethren today.[452] Indeed, a group of ordinary members emphasized the importance of moral teachings at St. Andrew's College to curb what they perceive as questionable behavior among some young people enrolled for ministerial qualifications.

Another element buttressed in the Brethren's ethical behavior is what has been noted by Langley and Kiggins as the strict legalistic prohibitions such as do not drink, do not smoke, do not part your hair, and do not wear short skirts.[453] Surely this sort of admonition persists to date and alienates many admirers. Thus, some ordinary members attribute the failure of growth of Brethren fellowship to the fact that they view themselves as the self-righteous, which impedes the church's mission. Besides some leaders argue that some parents treat as outcast their daughters who get pregnant before marriage.

Finally, *Mfuko wa Bwana* (The Lord's Bag) initially started by the *Kufufuka* who did not approve accounting and auditing procedures as they believed in walking in the light.[454] However, Kamau highlights a controversy in 1998 within the *Kusimama* associated with the *Mfuko wa Bwana*, occasioned by an exaggerated budget for a convention.[455] Undoubtedly, although *Mfuko wa Bwana* appears to substitute accounting and banking procedures as a recourse to avoid one of the stakeholder's terms, *tusiwe na deni* (we should not have debt), it has nevertheless bolstered their inclusive tenets and shut out options for welfare economic activities.

---

451. Welbourn and Ogot, *Place to Feel*, 30.
452. Gathogo, "Retracing Diakonia," 7–8.
453. Langley and Kiggins, *Serving People*, 202.
454. Mambo, "Revival Fellowship", 115.
455. Kamau, "Critical Analysis," 41.

Anglican Church Mission Statement Perspective to Summarize the Current Situation As It Should Be

The Church Diary and Lectionary of the Anglican Church of Kenya (2017) states the mission of ACK as "To equip God's people to transform the society with the Gospel", which is driven by the vision, "a growing, caring Anglican Church boldly proclaiming Christ." Therefore, to summarize the current situation from the perspective of the Anglican Church mission statement, it is critical to bring to the fore Luke's description of the growth of Jesus from the viewpoint of increase in wisdom, in stature and favor with God and man (Luke 2:52). This concept of growth, in a nutshell, appears to demonstrate the Anglican Church mission. So, to put this text into its rightful place, it is necessary to debunk it (the growth concept).

Bock claims that the mention of both God and humans in Luke's text illustrates the fact that the growth of Jesus could not be hidden.[456] The increase in wisdom (σοφία) refers to Jesus' increase in insight described in Greek as συνέσει (*synesei*) which signifies understanding that penetrates the crux of the matter.[457] Lenski states that Jesus kept growing in wisdom.[458] This growth is consistent with Bovon who introduces προκόπτω translated *to make progress*.[459] While ἡλικια (*hēlikia*) explains stature as a physical growth,[460] Bovon terms it a stage in life,[461] as to designate the physical size and not age.[462] Concerning χάριτι (*chariti*) Bock interprets grace or favor as moral growth and favorable nature[463] which Bovon understands it as depicting relationship, in this case of the divine and human,[464] which Lenski affirms, and adds that this progress continues in the three noun datives of relations (in wisdom, in stature and favor).[465]

---

456. Bock, *Luke 1:1–9:50*, 274.
457. Bock, 268.
458. Lenski, *Interpretation of St. Luke's Gospel*, 170.
459. Bovon, *Luke 1*, 115.
460. Bock, 274.
461. Bovon, *Luke 1*, 115.
462. Lenski, Interpretation of St. Luke's Gospel, 170.
463. Bock, *Luke 1:1–9:50*, 274.
464. Bovon, *Luke 1*, 15.
465. Lenski, Interpretation of St. Luke's Gospel, 170.

Indeed, the ACK mission not only seeks to equip but also to transform society with the gospel of Jesus Christ which could be viewed from at least four dimensions: mental (wisdom), physical (stature), spiritual (favor with God) and social (favor with man). This means that ACK mission cannot be seen to be complete without engaging the four dimensions of growth which is pivotal to the transformative gospel. As seen in chapter 1, the gospel is not only evangelistic but is also a social responsibility[466] which means due justice should be equally apportioned to both spiritual and non-spiritual tasks. This echoes the Lausanne Covenant (attended by David Gitari, Archbishop of ACK from 1997 – 2002) during *The International Congress on World Evangelization* at Lausanne in July 1974 which expressed penitence for neglect and sometimes regarding evangelism and social concern as exclusive.[467] Indeed, the 1982 Grand Rapids Report on *Evangelism and Social Responsibility: An Evangelical Commitment* stated that Christian social concern could be not only a consequence of evangelism but also a bridge to evangelism and a partner of evangelism.[468] This interlocking relationship appears to inform the ACK transformative mission from the perspective of the four dimensions of growth summarized below. Eventually, this relationship lays the foundation for the prevailing situation as it should be, via the overarching triad of conversion, worship, and moral codes.

Mental Transformation

Mental change is brought to the fore by the progressive training and education through ACK academic institutes like SPU,[469] its affiliate's colleges, and industrial institutions. On the one hand, SPU's mission appears consistent with ACK in that it champions the development of servant leaders by imparting knowledge, skills and values, and Christian spiritual formation.[470] Among the faculties are theology[471] and social sciences[472] with programs ranging from certificate to Ph.D. Graduates from theology are passionate about their calling

---

466. Bosch, *Transforming Mission*, 418.
467. Gitari, *Troubled but not Destroyed*, 27.
468. Gitari, 130.
469. St. Paul's University, 2010–2017.
470. St. Paul's University, 2016c.
471. St. Paul's University, *Faculty of Theology*, 2016b.
472. St. Paul's University, *Faculty of Social Sciences, 2016a*.

and find work in community transformation, chaplaincy and lay ministry. Likewise, social sciences graduates confront developmental challenges such as poverty and persistent conflicts at various levels. No wonder in the first section of this chapter, we saw that Kraft conceptualized a Christian ministry which is not only culturally formed, but also responds to gospel confrontation of culture from the vantage point of people's lifestyle.[473] Thus, SPU seeks not only to equip graduates with mental tools for life but also to influence community with the gospel of Christ positively.

On the other hand, the ACK mission incorporates equipment for technical and vocational training appropriate for entrepreneurship and self-propelled income generating projects as a way of providing self-employment. Indeed, church involvement with industrial training has been a key pillar to training for social, economic and political development as opposed to the pietistic approach to education.[474] Furthermore, Church of the Province of Kenya captures George David's (a freed slave from Bombay) sentiments concerning industrial training:

> Missionaries should concentrate more on industrial training which would enable Africans to provide for themselves: this would make the Christian life more meaningful and attract people to the faith, whereas the ascetic life of self-denial and indifference to all worldly enjoyments and employments emphasized by Rebmann only aroused people's admiration without converting them to Christianity.[475]

Industrial training echoes the *Lausanne Covenant* document on Christian social responsibility[476] discussed earlier. It informs CICT which not only provide quality vocational and commercial training to the less privileged youth today but also empower them to compete in the job market or start and run fruitful businesses.[477] Equally significant to positive mental growth is bible translation and literacy, which again is a fundamental tenet of ACK mission emphasis. The church has been keen to translate the Bible into the vernacular

---

473. Kraft, *Anthropology for Christian Witness*, xiv.
474. Church of Province of Kenya, *Rabai to Mumias*, 48.
475. Church of Province of Kenya, 48.
476. Gitari, *Troubled but not Destroyed*, 27.
477. Kenplex, *Christian Industrial Training Centre Details, 2008–2017*.

for all Christians, which resonates with *missio logoi* tenets discussed in chapter 4, and points to the fact that spiritual ministry must take flesh in human languages and cultures. Thus, BTL facilitates Bible translation, sustainable literacy and language development programs amongst marginalized language groups in Kenya and beyond, isolated by the harsh climate and rough terrain.[478] In 1972 Rev. David Gitari, in his role as Executive Secretary of the Bible Society of Kenya undertook a three-day rough journey to Turkana in northern Kenya, to deliver the Gospel of Mark in the Turkana language.[479]

Physical Transformation

As regards physical change, the equipping aspect of the ACK mission informs physical growth, which could be translated to numerical expansion across the current thirty-four dioceses as shown in the 2017 Anglican Church Diary and Lectionary.[480] Indeed, by 1960 the diocese of Mombasa under Bishop L. J. Beecher was one massive area covering the whole province of Kenya,[481] and had a membership of less than 500,000.[482] However, today ACK has a population of about five million[483] which indicate ten times growth over the last fifty years. The relatively large population has seen widespread infrastructural growth in church buildings and related church sponsored facilities like the ADS which is a development arm of the church.

As the church remains a place of comfort, hope, and renewal, especially for the vulnerable, it is critical for ADS to facilitate the transformative mandate of the gospel of Jesus Christ (Luke 4:18–19) to alleviate all forms of poverty, injustices, and ignorance.[484] Indeed, as Gitari observes, evangelism and pastoral responsibilities are significant concerns for the mission, but not at the expense of community health, agricultural projects and social work.[485] The ADS mission mandate has led to general transformative structures like Mount Kenya Hospital and *Utugi* (Grace) Children Home, which respectively attend

---

478. BTL, *Bible Translation and Literacy (E.A)*.
479. Langley and Kiggins, *Serving People*, 16–17.
480. Anglican Church of Kenya, *Church Diary and Lectionary 2017*.
481. Church of Province of Kenya, *Rabai to Mumias*, 114.
482. Barrett, "Expansion of Christianity," 184.
483. Anglican Church of Kenya, *World Council of Churches*.
484. *Anglican Church of Kenya: Development and Community Services*.
485. Gitari, *Troubled but not Destroyed*, 115.

human physical and social needs. Thus, while these structures complement the mental development above, they also provide an appropriate nurturing environment for spiritual and social strands of transformation with the gospel of Christ as demonstrated below.

Spiritual Transformation

The forms of worship in the Anglican Church appear to have changed dramatically since the beginning of the twenty-first century in the light of contextual worship dynamics. The ACK new prayer book, *Our Modern Services*, cited earlier in this chapter, incorporates cultural and spiritual dynamics demonstrated by a prayer of thanksgiving for faithful ancestors and throwing problems to the cross of Christ. Similarly, the new hymn book,[486] *Nyimbo Cia Gucanjamura Ngoro* (songs of praise) has brought back the traditional rhythmic expressions that allow for vibrant worship. ACK has not only invested its resources in the ministerial formation of clergy and church leaders but also in the music industry.

Young people are encouraged to compose important Christian music to help lead Christians to respond to God in their context. The majority of research respondents (chapter 3) recommended dynamic worship style as a strategy of worshipping God in Spirit and truth. Thus, while worship style aims at retaining young people in the church, it also seeks to woo back those who had left to join Pentecostal churches. Accordingly, while mission strategies informed by talented Christian musicians and vibrant modern public address systems have led to somewhat entertaining worship and open air crusades, the ACK mission statement reminds worshippers that it is all about a holistic Christian family response to God's gift of adoption following justification. Surely, charismatic fervor in the ACK has brought outstanding liturgical renewal that allows for corporate and personal prayers, mostly within the Anglican tradition.

Indeed, this spiritual development seems to have been occasioned not only by corporate liturgical worship but also by church organized quiet places for reflection like *Safari ya Biblia* (Walk Through the Bible) in the ACK Diocese of Kirinyaga. A trip to the Holy Land in July 2017 saw Kirinyaga Diocese join

---

486. Anglican Church of Kenya, *Nyimbo cia Gucanjamura Ngoro*.

many others in retracing the nativity of Jesus, which brings to life a profound biblical understanding of the life of Christ and spiritual transformation.

However, the events of the post-election violence (2007 and 2017) put a dent in Anglican spirituality and in other denominations at large. This is illustrated by a high level of dichotomy about believers associating with one political party as opposed to the other, with consequent spates of post-election violence. This dichotomy echoes political alignment in Uganda in the 1960s, when the Roman Catholic Church identified with the Democratic Party and the Protestant church associated with Uganda's People's Congress.[487] Certainly, such dichotomy spells doom to a well-phrased mission statement. Nonetheless, when the church adheres to this transformative mission which pervades cultural, ethnic and political boundaries, it is the light and the salt of the earth (Matt 5:13–16) in which brothers and sisters love and encourage one another (Heb 10:24–25).

Social Transformation

As a response to God's favor expressed in spiritual equipping, social change should be the obvious outcome. Indeed some social growth centers like CICT and *Utugi* Children Home mentioned above are essential to development even at the basic level. For instance, CICT Nairobi equips vulnerable children from the nearby *Majengo* slums with not only vocational skills like mechanical engineering, electrical installation and food and beverage but also with good morals as a way of enhancing a secure and honest livelihood.[488]

Furthermore, ACK Kirinyaga Diocese in the rural Kenya, through Utugi Children Centre, provides solace for the orphans and vulnerable children from the street and less privileged families' holistic education and vocational training founded on sound Christian morals.[489] This wholesome concept depicts what Gitari terms a holistic gospel (Luke 4:18–19; Matt 9:35) of body and spirit (psychosomatic unit), which not only evangelizes and responds to spiritual needs but also attends to the physical needs of God's people.[490]

---

487. Anderson, *Church in East Africa*, 135–136.
488. Kenyaplex, *Christian Industrial Training Centre Details, 2008–2017*.
489. ACK - Kirinyaga Diocese, *Anglican Church of Kenya Kirinyaga Diocese: Utugi Children Home, 2016*.
490. Gitari, *Troubled but not Destroyed*, 40–41.

A Summary of the Situation (of Walking In the Light) as It Should Be

A summary of the current trend as it should be in the ACK Mount Kenya region is informed by the above critiqued ACK mission statement, which equips and transforms the community with the gospel of Christ. Thus, while Brethren should view other Christians as truly converted, they should also embrace a vibrant spirituality which informs beliefs and practices of walking in the light. To craft a new concept of walking in the light from the perspective of the ACK mission statement, it is critical for Brethren to accommodate change. The change should not only address the way they understand their conversion (born again) experiences but also their worship style and moral codes.

Conversion Experience As It Should Be

In regard to the conversion experience, the ACK mission of a transformative gospel not only incorporates all Christians but leaves the door open for the gospel to influence non-Christians. The fundamental goal of the mission is not just Christian conversion, but responsible coexistence with one's neighbor. The manifesto of Jesus, expressed particularly in Luke 4:18–19, which Gitari says had a profound impact on his conception of the holistic mission of the church, echoes *The Lausanne Covenant* sentiments to the effect that evangelism and social concern are flipsides of one coin.[491] Indeed, earlier in this chapter, Nikolajsen uses the word *koinonia* to express fellowship with Christ (1 Cor 1:9) and with one another (1 John 1:3) as part of the mission of the church.[492] Certainly, this is the way forward for Brethren's born again testimony, which should inform the whole lifestyle that depicts Christians as a family that has received the Spirit of adoption so as to call God, *Abba Father* (Rom 8:15–16).

In essence, sonship is a gift and has nothing to do with human efforts; it is subsequent to justification (the ground of forgiveness and acceptance) and should inform the lifestyle of those who have received new birth.[493] Thus, Brethren's born again behavior should be consistent with the fact that salvation

---

491. Gitari, 27, 40.
492. Nikolajsen, "Beyond Sectarianism," 465.
493. Frame, *Systematic Theology*, 976–977.

is a gift of God, endowed to believers, not by merit, but because of what God did for humanity at the cross. This means sanctification, which is evidence of justification, should be understood as the achieving of God's renewing spirit that informs believers' growth in holiness as they humbly respond by loving God and neighbor. A daily walk with God and experiential sanctification should express a mutual relationship with God reflected in the holistic mission which equips and transforms society with the gospel. Conversely, conversion is accepting the Lordship of Christ and not just joining a family,[494] which ACK mission affirms both in its evangelism and social action roles in the society.

Certainly, an experiential sanctification as expressed by Brethren is not a means to enroll with Christian Industrial Training Centre or *Utugi* Children's Home, but expressions of love for the vulnerable in society (Matt 25:34–40). Inevitably, social responsibility expresses tenets of the kingdom and demonstrates actual conversion. Indeed, judging from Jesus' teaching, the saved or righteous person before God is the one who takes care of the sick and suffering (physical needs) as opposed to Pharisaic hypocrisy destined to damnation (Matt 25:41–46). Thus, the pilgrimage method of sharing a testimony regarding past, present and future which is hypocritical should change to incorporate not only social action to the needy neighbor but also to fellowship with other Christians and enquirers.

Worship style As It Should Be

The order of service in *Our Modern Services* ACK new prayer book boasts of a relaxed liturgy that not only reserves time for prayerful choruses and hymns but also provides for extemporaneous prayers.[495] This freedom appears to have led more people, especially youth, to return to the Anglican Church. Furthermore, in chapter 3 a research respondent argues for the importance of teaching the value of worship and practices of the Anglican Church to inform new forms of spirituality among young people. Therefore, it is pivotal for the Brethren to adopt new ways of spirituality within the Anglican Church mission as a way of embracing change cognizant of the gospel. Also, in chapter 4 worship dynamics were alluded to by Ngugi as he welcomed a

---

494. Bosch, *Transforming Mission*, 488.
495. Anglican Church of Kenya, *Our Modern Services*, 14.

delegation of the Kenyan Anglican clergy visiting the Anglican Diocese of Chelmsford, UK to bring to the conference vibrant ACK worship informed by African dynamics.

These worship dynamics capture the ACK's mission of equipping God's people to transform society with the gospel. In other words, it is not just worship, but one which is consonant with an African rhythmic style, of worshipping God in truth and the Spirit. That being the case, it is vital to agree with O'Brien that worship as invitation leads to worship as participation within the church from which the people of God participate in the *missio Dei*.[496] Since the mission of ACK is to equip and change people to take part in the church mission within *missio Dei*, it is pivotal that Brethren should allow a worship style that does not only inform inclusive participation but is also compliant with *missio Dei*.

Moral codes As They Should Be

As regards moral codes, the human being is a psychosomatic unit comprising of body and spirit. Hence, social responsibility and spiritual formation are twin doors of one house, in this case, one community or family of God. Therefore, religious and social dynamics should equally define human development from the vertical and horizontal perspective, in the sense of loving God and neighbor. Indeed, St. Paul's University's slogan, "Servants of God and Humanity"[497] resonates with the ACK mission statement of equipping humanity to change society with the good news of the Lord Jesus Christ. Brethren, if they have a good theological education, should be at the forefront of transforming society. Unfortunately, codes of ethics have to a large extent been informed by the Brethren's overly literal interpretation of the Bible. It will, therefore, take ingenuity of the church through BTL and theological education by extension programs, to encourage and motivate Brethren literacy in theology to inform acceptable Christian moral codes.

The two case scenarios about CICT and Utugi Children's Home provide holistic education to the vulnerable children who combine vocational skills with sound Christian morals. Brethren are not left behind regarding strict

---

496. O'Brian, "Procuring of Reverence", 339.

497. St. Paul's University, https://www.spu.ac.ke/old/attachments/media/The-Voice-Magazine-2020-Edition.pdf.

ethical morals but fall short of social responsibility. Consequently, the *Mfuko wa Bwana* (The Lord's Bag) aspect should not only follow accounting and auditing procedures but also support other Christians and church activities. The most efficient way to walk in the light is not necessarily via moral codes of dos and don'ts but through reaching out to the needy in the community. Indeed, dress codes and hair styles should not be the means to an end. While it is critical to observe acceptable Christian social conventions, social welfare activities should take precedence because of their concern for the entire community, not a supercilious minority group. When ACK mission speaks about societal change, the point of reference is a gospel influencing community as to participate in the mission of God. The Brethren should overhaul their dictum of walking in the light to conform to the real light of Christ in society. Indeed, society influenced by the gospel of transformation within *missio Dei* which is not only inclusive but also participates in self-help social and economic projects that include access to bank loans.

Viable Biblically Based Model of *Missio Dei*

A biblical model of *missio Dei* is one that demonstrates a walk with God in both the OT and the NT. Indeed, chapter 2 of this study shows that the two Testaments are *prima facie* examples of walking in the light in the *missio Dei*, whereby the biblical concept of walking in the light is identical to walking with God. Indeed, the Hebrew word which translates "walk" is הָלַךְ (*halakh*) which means *to go* or *to walk*. Genesis 5:21–24 and 6:9 indicate Enoch and Noah had a righteous walk with God. The writer of Hebrews credits this habitual walk with God to faith, and Enoch was reckoned to have pleased God (Heb 11:5–6). Abraham walked in the way of the Lord, and is a model for God's people (Gen 18:19). To walk in the way of the Lord is associated with doing righteousness and justice which implies that Israel was to mirror divine activity, a visible exemplar to the nations as to the nature and character of their God.[498]

Wright contends that to walk in the way of the Lord means doing for others what God has already done for us, which suggests right human actions and relationships tantamount to social justice – with powerful ethical and

---

498. Wright, *Mission of God*, 363.

missiological impact.[499] The moral quality of the Israelites in the form of ethical obedience links their calling to mission, for there is no biblical mission without biblical ethics.[500] The ACK mission statement, observed earlier, depicts the gospel of Jesus Christ as the good news of the transformation of humanity, particularly for the vulnerable (Matt 25:34–46). Consequently, the interface of ethical living, social responsibility and Christian witness are viewed as two sides of the same coin. But as seen throughout this study, Brethren appear to have missed this very point as they tend to conform to legalism leading to exclusive self-righteousness and a hypocritical lifestyle of "walking in the light."

Following this, it is the mandate of this research to attempt to construct a viable biblical model of *missio Dei*. The existing model appears to have been driven by moral codes with Christ seemingly relegated to the periphery in what looks like a self-directed lifestyle. It is therefore critical that a viable biblical model should demonstrate a Christ-directed lifestyle tantamount to changed world model informed by the Great Commission.

Nonetheless, Brethren passionately preach Christ crucified, though their stringent beliefs and practices of walking in the light appear to overshadow the good news of salvation following justification of sinners. The fact that the act of justification declares the regenerate righteous before God overtakes Brethren's self-righteousness that creates two categories of Christians, the born again (those who walk in the light and attend fellowship), and ordinary Christians. So, an examination of a self-directed model is vital to a *new* understanding of "walking in the light."

Self-directed Lifestyle (Brethren's Old Model)

The Brethren's old model is a self-directed way of life in which self-interests are enthroned in place of Christ and there are myriads of interests purported to be informed by Christ. These viewpoints inform the aspirations of members of EARM (Brethren) into the mission field. Thus, Mackenzie observes that while using Jesus as a model for Christian mission, churches have elevated the concept of Jesus as Savior to the point of abandoning Jesus' life and

---

499. Wright, 365, 367, 368.
500. Wright, 369.

ministry.[501] The consequence has been disastrous, leading to discord and frustration within the Brethren fellowship, on the one hand, and with other Christians, on the other.

Viewpoints in connection with stereotyping testimonies and legalistic worship style and the subsequent moral codes appear to blur walking in the light. This is consistent with chapter 3 and 4, which demonstrate various biblical passages that led not only to discord and frustrations among the Brethren but also to strict moral codes that hinder the growth of the fellowship. Therefore, whereas Ephesians 5:14 led to dissension between *Kufufuka* and *Kusimama*, Daniel 1:8–15 and Ephesians 6:13 respectively resulted in a simple lifestyle and strict hair styles and dress codes. Still, *Ngwataniro ya utheri* (fellowship of the light) based on Matthew 5:14, an offshoot of *Kupaa* ironically accept greetings of "praise the Lord" yet do not recognize weddings of expectant girls. Therefore, divisions, hypocrisy, and the quest for propriety have maintained the status quo which informs an sanctimonious exclusiveness that distorts missiological dynamics within the fellowship and has negative impacts on the ACK mission.

Indeed, the admirers of Brethren are barred from attending the fellowship just because their conversion testimony lacks a pilgrimage perspective. Ordinary members who participated in this research says that Brethren repent and confess their past sins one by one followed by restitution and forgiveness. Where it was necessary to repay back stolen properties, they did so, which resonates with Zacchaeus' announcement (Luke 19:8) to give back what he could have acquired by fraud.

Perspectives of Brethren's literal interpretation of Scripture has been propounded in this study and inform their interests (moral codes). Literal interpretation is not exceptional, though in this case, it appears to have further pushed ways of giving testimony. This has been demonstrated by way of disclosure of the past sins and restitution, which depending on nature and magnitude could be disastrous not only to the born again person but also to the fact that it entrenches the two-Christian scenario: that is, the born again (the ones who undertakes this rigorous process of becoming a member of Brethren) and the ordinary Christian (who disregards the process). This idea of achieving born again testimony hinders Brethren's participation in the

---

501. Mackenzie, "Mission and the Inclusive Kingdom," 259.

missio Dei. If Brethren would shelve their self-interest as to express salvation within the covenant of grace, their faithful participation in the *missio Dei* is conceivable. It is elucidated below.

Christ Directed Lifestyle (Brethren's New Model)

The self-directed model of *breathing out* legalistic moral codes ought to be replaced by a Christ- directed model of fruitfulness and abundance. In this model Christ is on the throne and the self-life yields to the lordship of Christ. The interests are not only Christ-centered but also Christ-directed so as to inform individual actions in harmony with God's plan for salvation. The holier-than-thou predisposition of Brethren is replaced with the self-effacing or modest conceptualization of conversion and worship style which informs beliefs and practices of walking in the light.

Christ-directed Conversion Model of Fruitful Abundance

The fact that regeneration or new birth is an activity of God in which believers are passive informs the new conversion model of the Brethren. Additionally, unlike regeneration, conversion is action oriented (Phil 2:12–13), achieved through repentance and faith in a genuine covenant relationship in Christ.[502] So, when Jesus told Nicodemus that he must be born again (John 3:3), he meant a new birth which is spiritual and is by faith because it is an action of God as an antecedent to participating in the kingdom. Genuine conversion illustrates an inward change that must be demonstrated in a life of love and righteousness (Matt 3:8; Luke 3:10–14). While the new model suggests a conversion experience consonant with a mutual covenant relationship with Christ, informed by repentance and faith, the necessary response is a lifestyle of genuine love and righteousness. Undoubtedly, the missionary mandate calls upon Brethren to participate in the mission of God including calling other Christian worshipers to fellowship with God.

Indeed, a real conversion testimony arises from what God through Christ has done in the life of the believer at justification. It has nothing to do with the believers' efforts. All believers are made righteous by what God did on the cross of Christ, and none is more saved than the other. All have received the gift of sonship through adoption not only as children who call God,

---

502. Horton, *Christian Faith*, 576.

Abba, Father, but also as co-heirs with Christ (Rom 8:15–17). Surely, then, sanctifying faith is within the limits of Brethren's covenant relationship that renders Christians a family of God bound by the love of Christ on the cross. This sanctifying faith suggests a Christ-directed lifestyle that shuns the sanctimonious tendencies of the old model.

Christ-directed Worship Style Model of Fruitful Abundance

In addition to a new conversion model informed by the fruitful abundance arising from the enthroned Christ, is a new worship style among the Brethren. When Jesus is on the throne, self-interest dies, and the Holy Spirit takes over worship style dynamics in harmony with God's plan for his church in *missio Dei*. Surely, fruits in abundance are the due outcome of the new model informed by worship in Spirit dynamics (Gal 5:22–23). The abundance of the fruit of the Spirit makes the worship not only lively, in the sense of achieving love, joy, and peace of the Lord but also informs patience, kindness, goodness, faithfulness, gentleness, and self-control. Truly, when the fruit of the Spirit takes center stage in the believers' life, there is neither hypocrisy nor legalistic rules of conduct in worship, but openness and responsible freedom of praise and worship of the Lord.

In this way, as illustrated before, a reminiscence of God who encounters his people in the tabernacle and the temple (Exod 20:24) is brought to the fore, so that worshippers shout with joy that *Immanuel, God with us* (Isa 7:14) is in their midst (Zeph 3:17). As demonstrated earlier in this chapter worship is an active response to God[503] which is not only participative but i a contextual human declaration of the worthiness of God. However, self-control, which is one of the fruits of the Holy Spirit must guard against show-business like evangelistic mission activity, which could attract all and sundry but not participate in the *missio Dei*. Since ACK is keen on liturgical renewal as shown in the *Our Modern Services* prayer book, Brethren's fellowship liturgy should take cognizance of diverse public participation as a new model. The new model should depict a response to God's call to worship in the Spirit and truth in fruitful abundance within the confines of the Great Commission.

---

503. Hattori, *Theology of Worship*, 21.

The Great Commission: The Basis for the Changed World Model of Walking in the Light

The theme of Christ on the throne continues to pervade the new model that demonstrates yielding of the believer's (Brethren) interests to the lordship of Christ. The enthroned Christ directs the life of the believer in relation to the Godhead (vertical dimension), the Great Commission (horizontal dimension) resulting in the changed world of walking in the light which is then informed by changed perspectives of Brethren Christian witness and social responsibility. Fundamentally, the relationship between the Trinity and the Great Commission puts Trinitarian mission into perspective.

It was noted in chapter 2 that following the Willingen Conference of 1952, mission came to be understood as flowing from the very nature of God, as God the Father sending the Son, and the Father and the Son sending the Spirit, and the Father, the Son and the Holy Spirit sending the church into the world.[504] The Trinitarian focus appears to have evaded Brethren's mission appeal for they tended to avoid preaching on members of Trinity except for the second person. Whereas there is no doubt that God affirmed His supremacy in missions by confirming the supremacy of his Son Jesus Christ as the conscious center of the Church,[505] there is a need in the new model, to strike a balance, so that Brethren accommodate worship in dynamic of the Spirit. Indeed, the baptizing formula in the making of disciples for all nations demonstrates the Trinity.

Wright argues that Matthew 28:18–20 places the Great Commission as the biblical basis of mission in which Jesus commands his disciples to make disciples of the nations. Having hitherto been restricted to Israel's borders, now the boundaries are extended wherever the gospel is proclaimed.[506] This resonates with Ott, Strauss and Tennent who observes the launch of the centrifugal movement of a mission to the nations as opposed to the centripetal mission of the OT.[507] Indeed, Ott, Strauss and Tennent regard *go, baptize*

---

504. Bosch, *Transforming Mission*, 390.
505. Piper, *Let the Nations*, 133.
506. Wright, *Mission of God*, 35, 354.
507. Ott, Strauss, and Tennent, *Encountering Theology of Mission*, 37.

and *teach* as participles describing the imperative verb, *make disciples*,[508] a fact observed by Wright.[509]

Following this, it is critical to clarify the mandate of the Great Commission. To dispense its mandate from the viewpoint of new Brethren fellowship, the concepts of *go*, *baptizing* and *teaching* as outlined by Ott, Strauss and Tennent[510] are vital. Therefore, while the term *go* suggests an intention to bring the message to the nations and *baptism* (repentance and faith) a public initiation into the new kingdom community, *teaching* encompasses obedience to Jesus' commands.

"Go" Mandate of the Great Commission

Concerning the *go* mandate, Ott, Strauss and Tennent embrace the centrifugal dimension,[511] which is consistent with Wright who further links the Great Commission with the Abrahamic commission, *go* and be a blessing to all nations, which is covenantal and ethical, as to extend to others beside Abraham and his descendants.[512] If this model is to work for Brethren, a complete transformation is necessary, whereby centrifugal dynamics inform the perspective of mission as opposed to the old model of discipling only their own as shown in chapter 4. Furthermore, being a blessing to other Christians and the general public is a covenantal command to go out with the gospel of Christ that engages the life as a whole – both spiritual concerns and social responsibility within the confines of the new model. Ss Hastings observes the Great Commission facilitates reconciliation of humans with God to enhance achieving the cultural mandate in relational participation with God which informs Christian mission.[513] Concerning this view, exclusiveness characteristics of the old model's beliefs and practices of walking in the light should give way to the inclusiveness of the new paradigm. In other words, the command is applicable to all places and social occasions that require the genuine gospel of Jesus Christ.

---

508. Ott, Strauss, and Tennent, 36.
509. Wright, *Mission of God*, 35.
510. Ott, Strauss, and Tennent, *Encountering Theology of Mission*, 36.
511. Ott, Strauss, and Tennent, 36.
512. Wright, *Mission of God*, 213–214.
513. Hastings, *Missional God*, 155.

"Baptizing" Mandate of the Great Commission

As for baptism, this is essentially the Christian answer to the call of God into the body of Christ to become a child of God and heir to the kingdom of heaven.[514] It resonates with Paul's concept of crucifying the old self by burying it with Christ to be raised with Him in the newness of life (Rom 6:1–5). This explicit public declaration of conversion presupposes repentance and henceforth holding fast to the Christian faith. Early in this chapter repentance and faith were viewed as two legs on which conversion rests. While repentance has been seen as a change of mind, a conversion which influences moral conduct,[515] faith embodies the primal confession *Kyrios Iesous* [Jesus is Lord].[516] For that reason, the new moral conduct lifestyle should confess the lordship of Jesus informed by love of God and neighbor, and not by a legalistic stringent stereotyping born-again testimony which is exclusive and apparently depicts disparaging moral codes.

Therefore, it is vital for Brethren in the new model to acknowledge that the new life in Christ is built on repentance and forgiveness of sins and in faith. It is not based on exclusive moral codes, but on a lifestyle that aspires informed growth in holiness. Indeed, the good news of salvation exhorts that Jesus did not come to call the righteous, but sinners (Mark 2:17; 5:32) to repentance (Luke 5:32). The new model is of the view that neither Brethren nor any Christian should regard himself or herself as more righteous than the other. It is a judicial act of God through Christ that Christians are made righteous. In other words, righteousness is a gift of God imputed in the regenerate's new life of faith at justification. Thus, baptism in the new model is a full disclosure of the new birth and sanctification work of the renewing Spirit of God by faith, appropriated to the Brethren's changed world within the mission mandate of the Great Commission.

"Teaching" Mandate of the Great Commission

Finally, the *concept of instruction* of the Great Commission is anchored in obedience to Jesus' teaching which is not only transformative but also binding on the disciples as they call people to acknowledge and submit their lives

---

514. Anglican Church of Kenya, *Our Modern Services*, 47.
515. Strahler, *Coming to Faith*, 21.
516. Wright, *Mission of God*, 106.

to the lordship of Christ.[517] The Great Commission text seems to echo the Abrahamic commission to go and be a blessing (Gen 12:1–3).[518] Furthermore, Abraham (Gen 22:16–18) serves as a model for the continuing education of his descendants who must walk in the way of the Lord in righteousness and justice so that God can accomplish the missional purpose of Abraham's election.[519] Therefore, the Great Commission illustrates the command of the universal promulgation of the new covenant by the resurrected Christ[520] and has Deuteronomic undertones, "to observe everything that I have commanded you." This corresponding teaching mandate appears to link the covenant presence of God among his people in the OT with the presence of Jesus among his disciples as they carry out the mission order.

The new model of the changed world within the Great Commission mandate embodies ethical teaching which transcends the confines of the covenant.[521] Concerning the new lifestyle informed by actual new moral codes, the transformative teaching of disciples goes beyond the boundaries of the Brethren's weekly fellowship meetings. These teachings which are reckoned to be a blessings to all are an integrated whole. At the one end of the continuum is the proper interpretation of Scripture to avoid inappropriate application of biblically-informed ethical codes of dos and don'ts. The other end of the continuum teaches good conceptualization of salvation as to point out genuine born-again testimonies and a daily walk in the light. Still, within the continuum is the inclusive and united fellowship that not only embrace Spirit dynamism in worship but also engages social responsibility functions with other Christians as brothers and sisters in the Lord. This new model of the changed world of walking in the light is informed by knowing God and doing God's will within the confines of the Great Commission and faithful participation in the *missio Dei*.

Thus, the teaching concept of the Great Commission in the changed world from the viewpoint of walking in the light gives a picture of real life journey of knowing and doing God's will. On the one hand, walking in the light depicts

---

517. Ott, Strauss, and Tennent, *Encountering Theology of Mission*, 36.
518. Wright, *Mission of God*, 213.
519. Wright, 358.
520. Wright, 355.
521. Wright, 214.

the changed world within the confines of the enthroned Christ, while on the other hand, it demonstrate challenges that the disciple needs to negotiate in the course of training in righteousness (cf. 2 Timothy 4316–17). Thus, while knowing God informs proper handling of scripture and the doctrine of salvation, doing God's will addresses holistic Christian witness/making disciples' and informed real social-ethical response to the needs of the neighbor. Therefore, in the changed world Brethren are exhorted not only to learn to walk in the light of God's love but also to live out the teaching (1 John 1:7).

Conclusion

This chapter focused on the missiological foundations used to critique tenets of walking in the light. It was divided into five parts. While the first part introduced the chapter, the second developed missiological foundations informed by a framework of Christian history, biblical theology, and Christian anthropology, which critiqued specific tenets: conversion, worship, and social-ethical responses. Whereas conversion mainly incorporated a born-again testimony, worship and social-ethical responses comprised, respectively, stereotyped worship style and moral codes.

Third, it summarized the situation as it is today using historical and empirical analyses. This brought to the fore the validity and reliability of the research instrument used to conduct this study by comparing findings of the four select dioceses *vis-à-vis* the Diocese of Mbeere which had not participated in the research. Also, analysis of affinity between historical and empirical trends was examined to establish the status of the current trend.

Fourth, the chapter summarized the prevailing socio-ethical situation as it should be in the perspective of the Anglican Church mission statement in Kenya, by demonstrating the gospel of transformation of society mentally, physically, spiritually and socially. Fifth, this study suggested a viable, biblically-based model of *Missio Dei*, illustrated through sequential models which summarized the prevailing situation as it was and as it should be.

CHAPTER 6

Conclusion and Way Forward

This chapter provides a summary of the viewpoints that arose from the study. It identifies the crux of the investigation from which the researcher's own insights are clearly quantified. The chapter shows that the gaps in the literature have been filled, and the research objectives accomplished. Recommendations on further research are also made.

Summary of Viewpoints

The researcher has shown how qualitative research could be used to document information from primary and secondary sources. This method was not only necessary to analyze historical and empirical data of the present situation but also to work out a synopsis of relevant biblical and theological resources to recommend a preferred scenario. This could not have been possible without a feasible thesis statement which stated that Keswick teaching on sanctification theology had been the catalyst behind the dominant socio-ethical influence of "walking in the light" in EARM. The thesis statement anchored the following viewpoints:

First, socio-historical circumstances provided affinity for the Keswick theology of sanctification in the East African context. To explore the affinity between sociological circumstances and Keswick theology, an exploration of a historical view of Keswick theology was critical. Indeed, to elucidate the concept of walking in the light, it was placed within the framework of *missio Dei*. Therefore, EARM seems to have not only contextualized much of its inheritance from Keswick theology expressed through practical holiness but also taken a contextual perspective fashioning a theology with an African face.

Second, Anglican Church scholarship on Keswick theology brought to the fore the influence of Keswick theology on EARM socio-ethical beliefs and practices of walking in the light in the Anglican Church Mount Kenya region. The task incorporated an overview of the Anglican Church scholarship from the perspective of historical literature and documents on the one hand, and the findings and the analysis of the current situation on the other. A summary of the prevailing situation as it is today using historical and empirical analyses were necessary to show the validity and reliability of the research instrument used for this study. This was done by comparing findings of the four selected dioceses *vis-à-vis* the Diocese of Mbeere which had not participated in the actual research.

Third, the core missiological tenets provided a platform to analyze the prevailing practices of walking in the light. Thus, to give historical-missiological perspective on the current situation, an exegetical study was done on some of the key biblical texts related to beliefs and practices of walking in the light. Further, evangelical Anglican tradition not only informed the researcher's theoretical framework to analyze scriptural teachings related to sanctification but also emphasized new EARM's models of the theology of sanctification.

Fourth, the missiological foundations informed by a framework of Christian history, biblical theology, and Christian anthropology were essential features to critique particular tenets of walking in the light – conversion, worship, and social-ethical responses. This viewpoint not only summarized the prevailing socio-ethical situation as it should be from the perspective of the Anglican Church mission statement in Kenya, but also suggested a viable, biblically-based model of *missio Dei*.

Synthesis of Own Insights of Moving from the Current to Preferred Scenario

In order to draw a final synthesis, it is critical to bring out viewpoints that inform undertakings from the current to the preferred trend of walking in the light in EARM. The aspects of the prevailing trend of walking in the light have by and large been both contentious and exclusive. This is cognizant of the fact that Brethren seem to focus more on outward conformity informed by experiential sanctification than an inward renewal of the regenerate achieved through the power of the Holy Spirit. A focus on justification as evidence of sanctification permits a mutual inclusive lifestyle within Brethren but also with other Christians. Thus, to accurately synthesize insights gleaned from this study, an integrated framework of beliefs and practices of walking in the light would suffice to move from the current situation to the preferred scenario.

The argument of this study has been that Keswick theology of sanctification was the catalyst behind the prevailing socio-ethical influence of walking in the light in EARM which appeared to some extent to inform both the historical and empirical viewpoints of the current trend. This trend, which seems to embody beliefs and practices of walking in the light from the perspectives of a born-again testimony, exclusive worship, and consequent moral codes seem to incorporate Brethren's whole existence from conversion to the end of earthly life.

The fact that some defining features of early Keswick teachings like exclusive lifestyle and devotional reading of the Bible find affinity with EARM's lifestyle suggests not only a favorable socio-historical environment but also a somewhat dry orthodoxy propounded by the mainstream Protestant churches in East Africa. Thus, while the daily life circumstances and experiences in the East Africa milieu led to the accommodation of Keswick teachings of two types of Christians – the born again and the ordinary – the maxim of walking in the light was the consequence. These dictums appear to be reinforced by consistent trends of exclusive rather than inclusive coexistence.

Synthesis of Insights on Current Scenarios; Exclusive Beliefs and Practices of Walking in the Light

Public confession of sin as taught by the Keswick movement found familiar ground in the East African setting of vomiting out the evil spirits. The need to walk in the light could have made sense as a way to achieve a not guilty verdict as to sin. This bonding of Keswick theology with East African sociological circumstances no doubt led to the emergence and growth of EARM with remarkable higher life undertones. Thus, while Brethren appear to put their trust in a panoply of God's righteousness informed by daily sanctification as a defense against adversaries, they nonetheless segregate themselves from other Christians. This tendency seems to entrench perspectives prone to exclusiveness even within the Brethren fellowship. As a consequence,

Kufufuka's pompous viewpoint that other members of EARM are sleeping and needed to arise formalized a formidable split within EARM in Kenya.

Jesus' inclusive mission model appears impossible for *Kufufuka*, who seems to exclude not only other Christians but other Brethren as well. While Jesus' mission design brings all to the fold, *Kufufuka* sanctimoniousness appears to blur missiological dynamics in the church. *Kufufuka,* as well as other members of the Brethren, seems to have radically downplayed justification as the basis of salvation and elevated experiential sanctification, rendering the noncompliant ineligible for Brethren membership. The Brethren's practical social convention has strengthened a rigid mindset that sets boundaries for Brethren's code of conduct, without which indecorum arises. Following this disposition Brethren's exponential growth has continued to dwindle as they seem old-fashioned and out of touch with the Anglican Church of Kenya's worship dynamism. In this regard, Brethren are sleeping and need to awake to the reality of inclusive, dynamic worship in the Anglican Church of Kenya today, the Kigoco experience.

Exclusive dissensions with the power to set norms of inclusion and exclusion from the fellowship have rendered Brethren a community living on the edge looking over their shoulders at the ones excluded while marking the boundaries for the included. This superciliousness has not only tended to put some members of Brethren on a collision course with clergy but has also denied themselves chances of being frontrunners in the evangelism activities of the Anglican Church of Kenya. Furthermore, the acclaimed perception that the majority of Kenyan Anglican bishops are Brethren might be superficial, considering that they do not attend the Brethren fellowship regularly.

Moreover, most Brethren are uncomfortable with religious institutions which they accuse of producing graduates who they perceive are unsaved, who depict an unstructured format of giving testimony. Furthermore, Brethren view the Anglican Church from the perspective of compliant Christianity or as lukewarm – neither hot nor cold. The affinity of conversion experience is outstanding for Brethren because they believe in a born-again process and development that elevates them above other Christians.

This sectarian-like scenario of a belief system is not only introverted but also arrogant as they consider their lifestyle better than for those outside their fellowship. Although Brethren's calling is to a large extent clear and sacrificial, their stagnant liturgical growth not only endangers their future survival but appears inconsistent with the principle of participation in the *missio Dei*. Moreover, Brethren's emphasis on beliefs and practices of walking in the light not only betrays their focus on their central tenet, the cross of Christ, but also tends to undermine the gospel for the perceived poor (in spirit), who by Brethren's legalistic discipline are locked out of fellowship. Thus, Brethren's lifestyle depicts a superiority phenomenon which is injurious to mutual societal coexistence. Indeed, *Mfuko wa Bwana* has not only bolstered their inclusive tenets but also shut out options for welfare economic activities. Therefore, self-elevated social disposition appears not only hypocritical but also ironic considering the majority are illiterate.

Furthermore, the tendency to elevate the new birth through outward performances overshadows and compromises the inward change. Thus it looks satirical and insincere that while Brethren seems to exhibit a great salvation experience, they nevertheless seem *missio homo*. The apparent stereotyping of the "saving faith" by Brethren appears to disregard justification, which together with adoption are works of God in the believer after regeneration. The BCP inclination to response rather than listening to God seems to buttress Brethren response to the call more than listening to God. Brethren's liturgy has largely been reclusive rather than being directed to the worship of God. However many Brethren would wish to maintain their social-ethical codes of walking in the light it should be mindful of other Christians, who due to strict moral codes have shied away from the Revival Fellowship family.

Following this, it would be an exercise in futility if Brethren's practical holiness achieved through the dictums of walking in the light were not faithful participants in *missio Dei*. Therefore, it is critical for Brethren to work towards godly driven missionary tasks because the mission of God does not follow Brethren, but Brethren should follow or participate in the mission of God. The preferred scenario ought to be Brethren *missio logoi* – a mission achieved from the viewpoints of the centrifugal and centripetal mission.

Synthesis of Insights on Preferred Scenario; Inclusive Beliefs and Practices of Walking in the Light

Brethren ought to advocate for mutual sharing with clergy. In this way, a Brethren member who is authentically Anglican who not only reveres the Bible but is also versed in its interpretation dynamics will be the preferred model. Indeed, moderate Calvinism ecclesiology provides for the sufficiency of the cross for the justified sinners, who though they may not share Brethren's legalistic code, are Christians just like them. Such an inclusive concept would see more Anglican Brethren bishops in Kenya and a more unbiased practical holiness.

Also, liturgical renewal would encourage Brethren to arise from hypocritical dispositions so as to allow flexibilities because not everything that is worldly is sinful. Dynamic worship, well guided, becomes a pointer of expressing the various gifts with which God has endowed the church. That being the case, biblical and theological education should not be worrisome to the Brethren, though theologies should be vetted to avoid extremes.

In light of this conviction, self-interest on the part of Brethren should take a back seat by accommodation of different ways of expressing salvation, within the covenant of grace and faithful participation in the *missio Dei*. In order to reflect the maxims of a worshipping community, Brethren fellowship meetings should mirror, within the Anglican evangelical structures, the very nature of God as envisioned in the *missio Dei*.

Indeed, one of the ways to culture other believers is through well-informed testimonies and inclusive evangelistic fellowships, which Brethren should cultivate. If Brethren could embrace theological studies, in addition to their commitment to fellowship meetings, they could be an excellent source of social-ethical codes of inclusion that would inform mission. Indeed, Brethren's exclusive love for one another is something to be cherished and is a profound missiological principle based on the centrality of the cross. If this concept of brotherly-sisterly love extends to other Christians, then mission in the Anglican Church, Mount Kenya region, will not only enhance its participation in the *missio Dei* but also place Brethren at the very center of centripetal-centrifugal mission dynamics.

For Brethren to have an active mission, it ought not only appropriate dynamic equivalent cultural components but also have them creatively contextualized in their fellowship meetings. Certainly, Brethren are quick to enculturate some African cultural elements, which could boost missiological anthropology mission perspectives of African Christians who practice circumcision. Furthermore, the Brethren expect a converted person to demonstrate clear characteristics of the new life in the same way a circumcised person is supposed to depict maturity and responsibility. This identity formation unfortunately fostered ethical codes of conduct within Brethren, yet if well guided to ensure freedom with responsibility could surely motivate an informed Brethren anthropological mission in the *missio Dei*.

Furthermore, mission strategies informed by talented Christian musicians and vibrant modern public address systems have led to somewhat entertaining worship and open-air crusades. Indeed, the ACK mission statement reminds worshippers that it is all about a holistic Christian family response to God's gift of adoption following justification. Charismatic fervor in the ACK has brought outstanding liturgical renewal that allows for corporate and personal prayers, mostly within the Anglican tradition. However, there is a challenge in spiritual growth illustrated by a high level of dichotomy about believers associating with one political party as opposed to the other, with consequent spates of post-election violence in the recent past.

The ACK mission of transformative gospel incorporates all Christians but also leaves the door open for the gospel to influence non-Christians. The fundamental goal of the mission is not just Christian conversion, but also responsible coexistence with one's neighbor. Sanctification, which is evidence of justification, should be understood as the achieving of God's renewing spirit that informs believers' growth in holiness as they humbly respond by loving God and neighbor. So, experiential sanctification should express a mutual relationship with God reflected in the holistic mission which equips and transforms society with the gospel. Indeed, the pilgrimage method of sharing a testimony regarding past, present and future which is hypocritical should change to incorporate not only social action toward the needy neighbor but also fellowship with other Christians and inquirers. Since the mission of ACK is to equip and change people to take part in the church mission within *missio Dei*, it is pivotal that Brethren should allow a worship style that not only informs inclusive participation but is also compliant with *missio Dei*. While it is critical to observe acceptable Christian social convention, social welfare activities should take precedence because of their concern for the entire community, not a supercilious minority group.

Undoubtedly, if the Brethren would shelve their self-interest as to express salvation within the covenant of grace, then their faithful participation in the *missio Dei* is conceivable. The new model should depict response to God's call to worship in truth and the Spirit in fruitfulness abundance within the confines of the Great Commission. The holier-than-thou predisposition of Brethren is replaced with the self-effacing, modest conceptualization of conversion and worship style which informs beliefs and practices of walking in the light. Thus, the maxims of the born-again testimony in the new model is a full disclosure of the new birth and sanctifying work of the renewing Spirit of God by faith, appropriated to the Brethren's changed world within the mission's mandate of the Great Commission.

Gaps in the Literature

Keswick theology as rightly put is scarcely known by the majority of the research respondents which may confirm Ward's assertion that Keswick teaching did not influence EARM. Nonetheless, the outcome of the historical and empirical research proves that there are some outstanding consistencies between Keswick teachings and EARM beliefs and practices of walking in the light. The following features suffice to indicate the gaps in the literature.

EARM Convention

Scholars appear to have failed to notice the apparent influence of the Keswick Convention on the EARM concept of a yearly meeting. While it is clear that the typical Keswick weeklong form of assembly has been replicated in East Africa as it had been done in Keswick England since 1875, it appears no scholar has documented this influence. Though the seven-day Keswick week has been reduced to three, and the topics profoundly changed to focus more on evangelism than hitherto countering the sin principle, the yearly convention has endured. Indeed a document by Mutembei[1] demonstrates the consistency of EARM's annual conventions over the years. Despite the obvious frequency of the convention epochs on East African soil, no scholars to the best of the researcher's knowledge have documented this historical development, in which experiential theology is entrenched, and from the viewpoint of *missio Dei*. This study has brought to the fore sanctification theology as taught and applied by the Brethren to the detriment of the mission in the Anglican Church of Kenya.

---

1. Mutembei, Historia Fupi ya Ushirika, 38.

Doctrine of Justification

Scholars such as Andrew Naselli have written on the doctrine of justification concerning Keswick theology,[2] but no scholars have looked at this doctrine about EARM in the *missio Dei*. Consequently, the subject of the doctrine of justification which is God's work in the believer following regeneration has led to Brethren's perverse neglect, albeit ignorantly, of its primary role in salvation. Thus, Brethren have continued to drum for sanctification theology, as they understand it, oblivious to the fact that it is the evidence of justification. As a consequence, experiential sanctification or practical holiness pervades Brethren fellowships unabated from local convention to the East African level. This study has bridged this gap by showing the primacy of justification in the daily life of sanctification of the members of the Brethren. Attendance to this gap is pivotal to Brethren unity amongst themselves and with other Christians as they achieve the tenets of the Great Commission as faithful participants in the mission of God.

Born-again Testimony

The born-again concept is central to the belief and practice of "walking in the light," which unlike the convention and justification factors above, appears to have been fashioned by factors on East African soil. The fact that scholars have not investigated the various components that comprise a born-again testimony have entrenched Brethren beliefs and practices of walking in the light culminating in dissension among Christians. This is in spite of scholars like John Karanja who have researched widely the socio-cultural concept of public confession of evil deeds,[3] which could have influenced public confession of sin within Brethren circles. Indeed, the born-again testimony informed by public confession of sin and consequent daily walk with the Lord or practical holiness have been reinforced through the threefold method of giving testimony. The ensuing format of past, present, and future characterize typically born-again testimony which not only sets boundaries between Brethren and non-Brethren but also sets out dictums of futuristic undertones. This study has dispensed with the born-again concept and adequately bridged

---

2. Naselli, *Let Go and Let God*, 224–229.
3. Karanja, Confession and Cultural Dynamism, 145–148.

the gap in the literature which had severely affected Brethren participation in the *missio Dei*.

Eschatological Undertones

The apparent doctrine of last things has been propounded by scholars of early Keswick theology and appears to have some bearing on EARM's inclination towards futuristic comfort. However, this discourse is strikingly missing from EARM academics, in spite of its significant influence on the born-again testimony. Indeed, the *Stand firm* concept derived from Ephesians 6:13 which has been translated by Brethren to mean standing firm against perceived evil forces now or in the future, appears to inform what could be termed a moderate eschatological view. Nonetheless, though one of the commonest songs in the fellowship meetings, *kaza mwendo, ndugu yangu, Yesu yuaja kutusukua* (be steadfast, my friend, Jesus is coming back to take us home) appears to confirm the eschatological trend, Brethren seem to envisage a future within their lifetime. Thus, the preceding insinuates Christ's second coming and is the engine behind Brethren's struggle to maintain the stereotyping and holier-than-thou stand in the guise that they are destined to face persecution then and in the indefinite future. Although, this theological narrative has been missing in the existing literature on EARM, it has nevertheless been brought to the fore in this study within the context of the mission of God.

Research Objectives

The research objective of this study was to investigate the contribution of the Keswick theology of sanctification to the socio-ethical understanding of walking in the light in the EARM, which to a large extent influenced the mission of the Anglican Church in the Mount Kenya region. In order to achieve this, specific objectives were used to evaluate the impact of the ensuing beliefs and practices of walking in the light. But while Keswick theology appears to have been the catalyst behind the beliefs and practices of walking in the light, other factors seem to have influenced the current situation. Therefore, the research objective appears to have accomplished its task as depicted by the following deductions derived from the specific objectives outlined in chapter 1.

The first objective, to determine the socio-historical circumstances that led to the influence of Keswick theology on the current trend, has been demonstrated in chapter 2. The study has established that the Keswick theology of sanctification found affinity with East African socio-historical circumstances which enabled Keswick theology and East Africa sociological worldview to have some significant exchange of concepts and meanings. While most external and internal conditions and experiences of the socio-historical situation in East Africa were attracted to Keswick teachings of exclusion and inclusion, some aspects like a public confession of sins have been distinctively African. Certainly, the African tradition of public confession of evil has been peculiarly African and could only have been adopted in the dictums of walking in the light in EARM.

The second objective concerned investigation of the current Anglican Church scholarship with reference to Keswick theology of sanctification and walking in the light. The study found that Anglican Church scholarship has mainly explored EARM from historical, cultural and theological perspectives. Some scholars like Kevin Ward and Joe Church have scarcely linked EARM with Keswick theology, while John Karanja and Esther Mombo have not documented any scholarship on its influence on the walking in the light, particularly in the Mount Kenya region.[4] This propensity is consistent with the majority of respondents (see chapter 3) depicting ignorance of Keswick theology. Consequently, other factors like classical evangelical revivalism of the late nineteenth century, Pentecostalism and the born-again culture with the strict religious position, have been cited.

The third objective examined the basic missiological tenets and practices of walking in the light in which it was established that the missiological principles explicated in chapter 4 had positively impacted these beliefs and practices in EARM. As a consequence, the missiological principles were found to challenge the walking in the light fundamentals of a born-again testimony, spirit dynamics, and moral codes to inspire Brethren's participation in the mission of God.

Concerning the fourth objective, to explore the missiological foundations required to critique particular tenets of walking in the light in EARM, a three-legged concept of church history, biblical theology, and anthropology

---

4. Ward, *The East African Revival: History and Legacies,* 4; Church, *The quest for the Highest,* 157–159; Karanja, *Confession and Cultural Dynamism,* 143–151; Mombo, *The Revival Testimony of Second Wives,* 153–161.

illustrated in chapter 5 was used. The analysis was done through the scaffolding matrix of a born-again testimony, stereotyping worship, and moral codes. Indeed, these elements of walking in the light when critiqued against the missiological foundations undeniably fell short of the mission mandate of participation in the *missio Dei* due to hypocrisy, legalism and exclusive disposition.

Concerning the fifth objective that explored how Keswick theology influenced walking in the light in the Anglican Church, the following inference was observed. While it is true that Keswick theology appears to have affected walking in the light in the Anglican Church, the majority of respondents except prominent stakeholders seemed ignorant of Keswick teachings. Nevertheless, the apparent thematic consistencies between the historical survey and the current trends (chapter 5) support prominent stakeholders' viewpoints and thus appear to suggest some heritage of Keswick theology. Furthermore, to some extent devotional reading of Scripture which seems to inform splits and a two-Christian scenario, displays Keswick distinctives.

Relating to the final objective, to determine significant consequences of walking in the light for the mission in the Anglican Church of Kenya, the ACK mission statement anchored the discourse. Indeed, the ACK mission statement was found to equip and transform the community with the gospel of Christ. Consequently, when the current trend was placed against the mission statement, it was noted that the prevailing situation of walking in the light had hindered mission in the Anglican Church of Kenya. Chapter 5 shows that the ACK mission demonstrates the preferred scenario that embraces both evangelism and social responsibility as a single unit and informs holistic Christian life. This suggests a change on the part of Brethren from exclusive to the inclusive predisposition of mutual Christian's coexistence.

Recommendations for Further Research

There are five areas in particular where it would be useful to do further research.

1. The conceptual similarity between the Keswick theology of sanctification and Pentecostalism.

2. The apparent disconnection between scholarship on Keswick theology and the EARM, though there are compelling conceptual similarities.
3. The historical and theological foundations of the Arise and Stand factions within East African Revival Movement.
4. The reasons behind the apathy shown by scholarship within the Anglican Church toward East African Revival Movement beliefs and practices related to walking in the light.
5. Anglican evangelicalism and mission praxis in the ACK.

Bibliography

Aagaard, J. "Trends in Missionary Thinking During the Sixties." *International Review of Mission* 62, no. 245 (1973): 8–25.

Abbott, J. J. "Boardman's Higher Christian Life." *Bibliotheca Sacra* (July 1860).

Abrecht, P. and Smalley, W. A. "The Moral Implications of Social Structure." In *Readings in Missionary Anthropology*, edited by W. A. Smalley, 119–123. Pasadena: William Carey Library, 1974.

ACK - Kirinyaga Diocese. "Anglican Church of Kenya Kirinyaga Diocese: Utugi Children Home." 14 August 2017. http://ackirinyaga.org/index.php/departments/utugi-children-s-home.

Addison, J. T. *The Medieval Missionary: A Study of the Conversion of Northern Europe A.D. 500–1300*. New York & London: International Missionary Council, 1936.

Ambrosiaster. "The Metaphors of Sleeping and Death." In *Ancient Christian Commentary on Scripture: New Testament VIII; Galatians, Ephesians, Philippians*, edited by M.J. Edwards, 179. Downers Grove: Inter-Varsity Press, 1999.

Ambrosiaster. "The Whole Armour of God." In *Ancient Christian Commentary on Scripture: New Testament VIII; Galatians, Ephesians, Philippians*, edited by M.J. Edwards, 179. Downers Grove: Inter-Varsity Press, 1999.

Anderson, W. B. *The Church in East Africa: 1840–1974*, 2nd edition. Dodoma: Central Tanganyika Press, 1977.

Anglican Church of Kenya. *Nyimbo cia Gucanjamura Ngoro*. Nairobi: Uzima Publishing House, 1994.

———. *Our Modern Services: Anglican Church of Kenya*. Nairobi: Uzima Publishing House, 2003.

———. "Anglican Church of Kenya: Development and Community Services." 2 August 2017. http://www.ackenya.org/provincial_office/development.html.

———. *Church Diary and Lectionary 2017*. Nairobi: Uzima Publishing House, 2016.

———. "World Council of Churches: A worldwide fellowship of churches seeking unity, a common witness and Christian service." 1 August 2017. https://www.oikoumene.org/en/member-churches/anglican-church-of-Kenya.

Anglican Diocese of Melbourne. "What do Anglicans Believe?" 13 June 2017. https://www.melbourneanglican.org.au/faith/AnglicanTradition/pages/anglicantradition.aspx.

Anonymous. *The 8th abale Revival Convention 20th August 2015*. Kampala: Kigezi Diocesan Printery, 2015.

Anonymous, "Lenana School convention: Ushirika wa Vijana Wangofu-Kenya." Unpublished document, Kenya Fellowship of Young Brethren-Kenya, 4–7 August 2011.

Aquinas, T. *Commentary on Saint Paul's Epistle to the Ephesians, Vol. 2*. 1st edition, translated by Matthew Lamb. Albany: Magi Books, Inc. 1966.

Arnold, C. E. "Ephesians." In *Zondervan Illustrated Bible Backgrounds Commentary: Romans to Philemon (Vol. 3)*, edited by C.E. Arnold, 300–301. Grand Rapids: Zondervan, 2002.

———. *Ephesians: Exegetical Commentary on the New Testament*, 1st edition. Grand Rapids: Zondervan, 2010.

Athanasius. *On the Incarnation*, 4th edition. Crestwood: St. Vladimir's Seminary Press, 1977.

Atherstone, A. *Latimer Studies, Vol. 70: An Anglican Evangelical Identity Crisis: The Churchman-Anvil Affair of 1981–1984*. London: The Latimer Trust, 2008.

———. "Evangelicals exit their Ghetto." *Church Times*. 6 July 2017. https://www.churchtimes.co.uk/articles/2017/31-march/features/features/evangelicals-exit-their-ghetto.

Augustine. "Why Such Long Hair?" In *Ancient Christian Commentary on Scripture: New Testament VII; 1–2 Corinthians*, edited by G. Bray, 107. Downers Grove: Inter-Varsity Press, 1999.

Aune, D.E. "Religion, Graeco-roman." In *Dictionary of New Testament Background*, edited by C.A. Evans, and S.E. Porter, 917–926. Downers Grove: Inter-Varsity Press, 2000.

Baker, D. P., 2014. "Missiology as an Interested Discipline-and Where Is It Happening." *International Bulletin* 38, no. 1 (2014): 17–20.

Baker, F. *John Wesley and the Church of England*, 2nd edition. London: Epworth Press, 2000.

Barabas, S. *So Great Salvation: The History and Message of the Keswick Convention*. London & Edinburgh: Marshall & Scott, 1952.

Barrett, C.K. *A Commentary on the First Epistle to the Corinthians*. London: Adam & Charles Black, 1968.

Barrett, D. B. "The Expansion of Christianity in Kenya AD 1900–2000." In *Kenya Churches Handbook: The Development of Kenyan Christianity 1498–1973*, edited by D. B. Barrett, G. K. Mambo, J. McLaughlin and M. J. McVeigh, 157–191. Kisumu, Kenya: Evangel Publishing House, 1973.

Barrington-Ward, S. "The Revival Through CMS Eyes." In *The East African Revival: History and Legacies*, edited by K. Ward & E. Wild-Wood, 53–60. Farnham; and Burlington: Ashgate Publishing Limited, 2012.

Barth, M. *Ephesians: Introduction, Translation and Commentary on Chapters 4–6*. New York: The Anchor Bible Doubleday, 1960.

———. *Ephesians 4–6: A New Translation with Introduction and Commentary*. New York: The Anchor Bible Doubleday, 1974.

Baur, J. *2000 Years of Christianity in Africa: An African History AD 62–1992*. Nairobi: Paulines, 1994.

Beckwith, R. "Worship in Anglicanism." In *Worship: Adoration and Action* edited by D. A. Carson, 123–127. Grand Rapids: Baker Book House; Carlisle: The Paternoster Press, 1993.

Beet, J. A. *A Commentary on St. Paul's Epistles to the Corinthians*, 7th edition. London: Hodder & Stoughton, 1902.

———. *A Commentary on St. Paul's Epistles to the Ephesians, Philippians, Colossians, and Philemon*, 3rd edition. London: Hodder & Stoughton, 1902.

Beidelmann, T. O. *Colonial Evangelism: A Socio-Historical Study of an East African Mission at the Grassroots*. Bloomington: Indiana University Press, 1982.

Best, W. E. *Regeneration and Conversion*. Houston: South Belt Grace Church, 1981.

Blauw, J. *The Missionary Nature of the Church: A Survey of Biblical Theology of Mission*. New York: McGraw-Hill, 1962.

Boardman, H., A. *The Higher Life Doctrine of Sanctification Tried by the Word of God*. Harrisburg: Sprinkle Publications, 1966.

Bock, D. L. *Luke 1:1–9:50: Baker Exegetical Commentary of the New Testament*. Grand Rapids: Baker Books, 1994.

———. *Luke 9:51–24:53: Baker Exegetical Commentary of the New Testament*. Grand Rapids: Baker Books, 1996.

Bosch, D. J. *Witness to the World: The Christian Mission in theological Perspective*. Atlanta: John Knox, 1980.

———. *Transforming Mission: Paradigm Shifts in Theology of Mission*, 7th edition. Maryknoll: Orbis Books, 1991.

———. *Transforming Mission: Paradigm Shifts in Theology of Mission*, 20th edition. Maryknoll: Orbis Books, 2011.

Bovon, F. *Luke 1: A Commentary on the Gospel of Luke 1:1–9:50*. Minneapolis: Fortress Press, 2002.

Boxer, C. R. "The Problem of the Native Clergy in the Portuguese and Spanish Empires from the 16th to 18th Centuries." In *The Mission of the Church and the Propagation of the Faith* edited by G. J. Cuming, 85–105. London: Cambridge University Press, 1970.

Bradshaw, P. F. "Daily Prayer." In *The Identity of Anglican Worship*, edited by K. Stevenson and S. Bryan, 69–79. Harrisburg: Morehouse Publishing, 1991.

Brenz, J. "We Must Resist Temptations." In *Reformation Commentary on Scripture: New Testament X; Galatians, Ephesians*, edited by G.L. Bray, 401. Downers Grove: IVP Academics, 2011.

Bright, B. "*Walk in the Spirit.*" 7 August 2017. https://www.cru.org/train-and-grow/transferable-concepts/walk-in-the-spirit.1.htm.

Brooke, R. "The Message: Its Methods and Presentations." In *The Keswick Convention: Its Message, its Method and its Men*, edited by C. F. Harford, ed. London: Marshall Brothers, 1907.

Brown, D. "Defective Consecration." In *The Keswick Authentic Voice: Sixty-five dynamic addresses delivered at the Keswick Convention 1875–1957*, edited by H. F. Stevenson, 124–134. London: Marshall, Morgan and Scott, Ltd., 1959.

Brown, R. "Higher Life Theology." In *New Dictionary of Theology*, edited by S. B. Ferguson, 301. Downers Grove: Inter-Varsity Press, 1988.

Bruner, J. "Public Confession and the Moral Universe of the East African Revival." *Studies in World Christianity* 18, no. 3 (2012): 254–268.

BTL. "Bible Translation and Literacy (E.A)." 9 August 2017. http://www.btlkenya.org/.

Bucer, M. "Call Evil by its Name." In *Reformation Commentary on Scripture: New Testament X; Galatians, Ephesians*, edited by G.L. Bray, 372–373. Downers, Grove: IVP Academic, 2011.

Bundy, D. "Keswick Higher Life Movement." In *Dictionary of Pentecostal/Charismatic Movements*, edited by S. Burgess and G. McGee, 518–519. Grand Rapids: Zondervan, 1988.

Burkhardt, H. *Christ Werden: Bekehrung and Wiedergerburt-Anfang des Christlichen Lebens*. Giessen: Brunnen, 1999.

Calvin, J. *A Commentary on Daniel*. 3rd edition, translated by T. Meyers. London: The Banner of Truth Trust, n.d.

Calvin, J. *Commentaries on the Epistles of Paul to the Galatians and Ephesians*. Translated by W. Pringle. Grand Rapids: Baker Book House, n.d.

Calvin, J. *Commentary on the Epistles of Paul to the Corinthians, Vol. 1*, edited by W. Pringle. Grand Rapids: William B. Eerdmans Publishing Company, 1948.

Calvin, J. "Paul's Exhortation Contains the Promise of Victory." In *Reformation Commentary on Scripture: New Testament X; Galatians, Ephesians*, edited by G. L. Bray. Downers Grove: IVP Academic, 2011.

Carroll, M. D. "Ethics." In *Evangelical Dictionary of World Missions*, edited by A. S. Moreau, 319–322. Grand Rapids: Baker Books; Carlisle: Paternoster Press, 2000.

Chadwick, H. "Tradition, Fathers, and Councils." In *The Study of Anglicanism.* 2nd edition, edited by S. Sykes, J. Booty and J. Knight, 110–115. London: SPCK and Minneapolis: Fortress Press, 1988.

Chandran, E. *Research Methods: A Quantitative Approach with Illustrations from Christian Ministries.* Nairobi: Daystar University, 2004.

Chrysostom. "Addressed Also to Believers who Sleep in Sin." In *Ancient Christian Commentary on Scripture: New Testament VIII; Galatians, Ephesians, Philippians*, edited by M. J. Edwards, 179. Downers Grove: Inter Varsity Press, 1999.

Chrysostom. "Judge for Yourself." In *Ancient Christian commentary on Scripture: New Testament VII; 1–2 Corinthians*, edited by G. Bray, 106. Downers Grove: Intervarsity Press, 1999.

Church of England in South Africa. *Prayer Book of the Church of England in South Africa: Alternative to the Book of Common Prayer 1662*, 1st edition. Gillitts, R.S.A: Church of England in South Africa, 1992.

Church of England. *The Book of Common Prayer: The Church of England.* London: Cambridge University Press, 1968.

Church of Province of Kenya. *Rabai to Mumias: A Short History of the Church of Province of Kenya 1844 to 1994.* Nairobi: Uzima, 1994.

Church, J. C. T. "A Personal Experience of the Revival." In *The East African Revival: History and Legacies*, edited by K. Ward and E. Wild-Wood, 41–51. Farnham; Burlington: Ashgate Publishing Company, 2012.

Church, J. E. "Needs Spiritual and Temporal at Gahini." *Ruanda Notes* 37, no. 18 (July 1931).

Church, J. E., 1976. *Every Man a Bible Student.* Exeter: Paternoster Press, 1976.

Church, J. E. *Quest for the Highest: An Autobiographical Account of the East African Revival.* Exeter: Paternoster Press, 1981.

Church, J. E. "Church, John Edward (1899–1989) – School of Theology: History of Missiology." 9 September 2017. http://www.bu.edu/missiology/missionary-biography/c-d/church-john-edward-1899-1989/.

Clement of Alexandria. "Long Hair a Woman's Pride." In *Ancient Christian commentary on Scripture: New Testament VII; 1–2 Corinthians*, edited by G. Bray, 107. Downers Grove: Inter-Varsity Press, 1999.

Collins, J. J. *Daniel: A Commentary on the Book of Daniel.* Minneapolis: Augsburg Fortress, 1993.

Comby, J. *How to Understand the History of Christian Mission.* London: SCM Press Ltd., 1996

Coomes, A. *The Authorized Biography of Festo Kivengere.* Eastbourne: Monarch Publications, 1990.

Corley, B. "History of Interpretation: Interpreting Paul's Conversion - Then and Now." In *The Road from Damascus: The Impact of Pau's Conversion on His*

Life, Thought, and Ministry, edited by R. N. Longenecker, 1–17. Grand Rapids; Cambridge, UK: William B. Eedmans Publishing Company, 1997.

Cross, F. L. and Livingstone, E. A., editors. *Dictionary of the Christian Church.* Peabody: Hendrikson Publishers, Inc., 1977.

Curiosmith. "The Eclectic Society." 6 September 2017. http://curiosmith.com/index.php/who-were-the-eclectic-society.

Dale, R. W. *The Epistle to the Ephesians: Its Doctrine and Ethics.* 11th edition. London: Hodder & Stoughton, 1900.

Daugherty, K., 2007, "Mission Dei: The Trinity and Christian Missions." *Evangelical Review of Theology* 31 (2007): 151–168.

Dawn, M. J. *Reaching Out without Dumbing Down: A Theology of Worship for the Turn-of-the-Century Culture.* Grand Rapids: William B. Eerdmans, 1995.

Dayton, D. W. *American Holiness Movement: A Bibliographic Introduction.* Wilmore: B.L. Fisher Library, Asbury Theological Seminary, 1971.

De Young, K. "Andy Naselli on Why 'Let Go and Let God' Is a Bad Idea." 1 September 2017. https://blogs.thegospelcoalition.org/kevindeyoung/2010/06/03/why-let-go-and-let-god-is-a-bad-idea/.

DeMarrais, K. "Qualitative interview studies: Learning through experience." In *Foundations for Research*, edited by K. DeMarrais and S. Lapan, 51–68. Mahwah: Erlbaum, 2004.

Dickson, D. "The Children Must Preach the Gospel." In *Reformation Commentary on Scripture: New Testament X; Galatians, Ephesians*, edited by G. L. Bray, 373. Downers Grove: IVP Academic, 2011.

Diodati, J. "Everyone is Called to Conversion." In *Reformation Commentary on Scripture: New Testament X; Galatians, Ephesians*, edited by G. L. Bray, 373. Downers Grove: IVP Academic, 2011.

Dunaetz, D. R. "Missio-Logoi and Faith: Factors that Influence Attitude Certainty." *Missiology: An International Review* 44, no. 1 (2016): 66–67.

Dunlop, P. "A Critique of the Higher Life Movement." 4 November 2014 http://gospelforlife.org/articles/2012/4/23/a-critique-of-the-higher-life-movement.html.

Du Toit, C. W. "Technoscience and the integrity of personhood in Africa and the West: Facing our technoscientific environment." In *The integrity of the human person in an African context: Perspectives from science and religion*, edited by C. W. Du Toit, 1–46. Pretoria: Research Institute for Theology and Religion, University of South Africa, 2004.

Durnford, F. H. "The Life and Works of John Newton (1725–1807): A Study in Five Parts." *Churchman* 56, no. 1 (1942): 1–7.

Dyrness, W. A. *A Primer on Christian Worship: Where We've Been, Where We Are, Where We Can Go.* Grand Rapids; Cambridge, UK: William B. Eerdmans, 2009.

Edie, J. *A Commentary on the Greek Text of the Epistle to the Ephesians*. 2nd edition. London: Griffin Bohn & Co., 1861.

Edmond, E. "Notions of Sanctification: A Survey of Sanctification Theories, With Reference to Roman Catholic, Eastern Orthodox, Progressive and Holiness Traditions." A paper submitted as part of a master's degree in Applied Theology. 24 September 2013 http://www.enterhisrest.org/doorway/notions_sanctification.pdf.

Edwards, M. J., editor. *Ancient Christian Commentary on Scripture: New Testament, Vol. VIII; Galatians, Ephesians, Philippians*, 1st edition. Downers Grove: Inter-Varsity Press, 1999.

Edwards, T. C. *A Commentary on the First Epistle to the Corinthians*, 2nd edition. London: Hodder and Stoughton, 1885.

Egnell, H. "A Minority Community of Equality and Difference." In *Walk Humbly with the Lord: Church and Mission Engaging Plurality*, edited by V. Mortensen & A. Q. Nielsen, 184–190. Grand Rapids; Cambridge: William B. Eerdmans Publishing Company, 2010.

Ellicott, C. J. *St. Paul's Epistle to the Corinthians: With a Critical and Grammatical Commentary*. London: Longmans, Green & Co., 1887.

Farrar, F. W. *The Expositor's Bible*. London: Hodder and Stoughton, 1895.

Figgs, J. B. "Some Characteristics of the Message." In *The Keswick Convention: Its Message, Its Method, and Its Men*, edited by C. F. Harford, 99–109. London: Marshall Brothers, 1907.

Findlay, G. G. *The Epistle to the Ephesians*. London, Hodder and Stoughton, 1892.

Fitzmyer, J. A. *First Corinthians: A New Translation and Commentary*. New Haven; London: Yale University Press, 2008.

Frame, J. M. *Worship in Spirit and Truth*. Phillipsburg: Presbyterian and Reformed Publishing Company, 1996.

———. *Systematic Theology: An Introduction to Christian Belief*. Phillipsburg: P & R Publishing Company, 2013.

Franklin, D. E. "TRUTH: You were Dead in Your Trespasses and Sins." 2 September 2017
https://defranklin.wordpress.com/2017/08/11/truth-you-were-dead-in-your-trespasses-and-sins/.

Gaebelein, A. C. *The Prophet Daniel: A Key to the Visions and Prophecies of the Book of Daniel*, 17th edition. New York: Publication Office "Our Hope," 1911.

GAFCON 2013. "GAFCON Global Anglicans: Guarding and proclaiming the unchanging truth in a changing world: The Nairobi Communique and commitment." Downloaded from www.gafcon.org

Galgalo, J. *African Christianity: The Stranger Within*, 1st edition. Limuru: Zaph Chancery, 2012.

Garland, D. E. *1 Corinthians: Baker Exegetical Commentary on the New Testament.* Grand Rapids: Baker Academic, 2003.

Gatiss, L., editor. *The Sermons of George Whitefield.* Wheaton, Illinois: IL, 2012.

Gathogo, J. "Article on East African Revival Movement." 17 June 2016. https://mail.google.com/mail/u/0/#all/15534a375895b3d0?projector=1.

———. "Retracing Diakonia in East African Revival Movement." In: *Evangelism and Diakonia in Context*, edited by J. Knud, Jørgensen et al, 10–11. Regnuum Books International, 2016.

Gatu, G. G. "Jesus Christ, The 'Truthful Mirror.'" In *The East African Revival: History and Legacies*, edited by K. Ward and E. Wild-Wood, 33–40. Farnham: Ashgate Publishing Limited, 2012.

Gatumu, K. *The Pauline Concept of Supernatural Powers: A Reading from the African Worldview.* Milton Keynes, Colorado Springs, Hyderabad: Paternoster, 2008.

Gill, D. W. J. "1 Corinthians." In *Zondervan Illustrated Bible Backgrounds Commentary: Romans to Philemon*, edited by C. E. Arnold, 101–193. Grand Rapids: Zondervan, 2002.

Gills, A. "Forty Years On: An Evangelical Divide Revisited." 6 May 2017. http://archive.churchsociety.org/churchman/documents/cman_120_3_grills.pdf.

Gitari. D. M. "A Paper on East African Revival." Unpublished Research Paper: Bishop's Office, Embu, Kenya, n.d.

Gitari, D. M. *Troubled but not Destroyed: The Autobiography of Archbishop David Gitari.* McLean: Isaac Publishing, 2014.

Godet, F. *Commentary on St. Paul's First Letter to the Corinthians.* Edinburgh: T & T Clark, 1889.

Goldingay, J. E. *Word Biblical Commentary: Daniel.* Milton Keynes: Word Publishing, 1987.

Goldsworthy, Graeme. *According to Plan: The Unfolding Revelation of God in the Bible.* Downers Grove: Intervarsity Press, 1991.

Gombis, T. G. *A Triumph of God in Christ: Divine Warfare in the Argument of Ephesians.* S.l. Ph.D. The University of St. Andrews, 2005.

Gonzalez, J. L. *The Story of Christianity, Vol. 1: The Early Church to the Dawn of the Reformation.* New York: Harper Collins Publishers, 1984.

Gore, C. *St. Paul's Epistle to the Ephesians: A Practical Exposition.* London: John Murray, 1923.

Green, J. B. *The Gospel of Luke.* Grand Rapids; Cambridge: William B. Eerdmans Publishing Company, 1997.

Grimes, J. E. and Grimes, B. "Individualism and the Huichol Church." In *Readings in Missiology Anthropology*, edited by W. A. Smalley, 199–203. Pasadena: William Carey Library, 1974.

Guder, D. *Mission Church: A Vision for the Sending of the Church in North America.* Grand Rapids: Eerdmans, 1998.

Guder, D. L. "Defining and describing mission: A response to Charlse Van Engen, Keith Eitel, and Enoch Wan." In *Missionshift: Global mission issues in the third millennium*, 51–61. Nashville: B & H Publishing Group, 2010.

Guillebaud, L. *A Grain of Mustard Seed: The Growth of Ruanda Mission of CMS.* London: Ruanda Mission CMS, 1959.

Guillebaud, M. *Rwanda: The Land God Forgot; Revival Genocide and Hope*, 1st edition. London: Mid-Africa Ministry (CMS), 2002.

Harford-Battersby, C. F. *Pilkington of Uganda.* New York: Fleming H. Revell, 1899.

Hafford-Battersby, T. D. "How to walk more closely with God." In *Keswick's Authentic Voice: Sixty-five dynamic addresses delivered at the Keswick Convention 1875–1957*, edited by H. F. Stevenson, 265–273. London: Marshall, Morgan and Scott, Ltd., 1959.

Hardman, O. *A History of Christian Worship.* London: University of London Press, Ltd. and Hodder & Stoughton, Ltd., 1937.

Harper, S. "Walking in the Light: Knowing and Doing God's Will." 25 August 2017. http://bookstore.upperroom.org/Products/1344/walking-in-the-light.aspx.

Hastings, A. *A History of Christianity 1950–1975.* Cambridge: Cambridge University Press, 1979.

Hastings, R. *Missional God, Missional Church: Hope for Re-evangelizing the West.* Downers Grove: IVP Academic, 2012.

Hattori, Y. "Theology of Worship in the Old Testament." In *Worship: Adoration and Action*, edited by D. A. Carson, 21–50. Grand Rapids: Baker Book House; Carlisle: The Paternoster Press, 1993.

Head, A. "The Watchword of the Convention." In *The Keswick Convention: Its Message, its Method, and its Men*, edited by C. F. Harford, 113–119. London: Marshall Brothers, 1907.

Heading, J. *First and Second Corinthians.* Kilmarnock: John Ritchie Ltd., 1995.

Henriksen, J. O. "Mission: Invitation to the Community." In *Walk Humbly with the Lord: Church and Mission Engaging Plurality*, edited by V. Mortensen and A. Q. Nielsen, 70–73. Grand Rapids; Cambridge: William B. Eerdmans Publishing Company, 2010.

Herring, G. *An Introduction to the History of Christianity: From the Early Church to the Englightenment.* London: Continuum, 2006.

Hesselgrave, D. J. "World-view and Contextualization." In *Perspectives on the World Christian Movement: A Reader*, edited by R. D. Winter and S. C. Hawthorne, 398–410. Pasadena: William Carey Library, 1981.

Hibbert, R. Y. "Negotiating Identity: Extending and Applying Alan Tippert's Model of Conversion to Believers from Muslim and Hindu Backgrounds." *Missiology: An International Review* 43, no. 1 (2015): 59–72.

Hiebert, P. G. *Anthropological reflections on Missiological Issues.* Grand Rapids: Baker Books, 1994.

———. *Transforming Worldviews: An Anthropological Understanding of How People Change.* Grand Rapids: Baker Academic, 2008.

Hiebert, P. G. and Meneses, E. H. *Incarnational Ministry: Planting Churches in Band, Tribal, Peasant, and Urban Societies*, 4th edition. Grand Rapids: Baker Books, 1995.

Hoehner, H. W. *Ephesians: An Exegetical Commentary.* Grand Rapids: Baker Academic, 2002.

Hoekema, A. A. "The Reformed Perspective." In *Five Views on Sanctification*, edited by Donald L. Alexander, 61–90. Grand Rapids: Zondervan, 1987.

Hofstee, E. *Constructing a good dissertation: a practical guide to finishing a Masters, MBA or Ph.D. on schedule.* Sandton: EPE, 2006.

Holden, J. S. "Abiding with God." In *The Keswick Week 1911: Thirty-Seventh Convention*, 186–192. London: Marshall Brothers, 1911.

———. "The Gospel of the Second Chance." In *The Keswick Week 1911: Thirty-Seventh Convention*, 153–157. London: Marshall Brothers, 1911.

Hooper, E. "The Theology of Trans-Atlantic Evangelicalism and Its Impacts on the East African Revival." *Evangelical Review of Theology* 31, no. 1 (2007) 71–89.

Hopkins, E. H. "Deliverance from the Law of Sin." In *Keswick Authentic Voice: Sixty-five dynamic addresses delivered at the Keswick Convention 1875–1957*, edited by H. F. Stevenson, 157–167. London: Marshall, Morgan and Scott, Ltd., 1959.

Horton, M. *The Christian Faith: A Systematic Theology for Pilgrims On the Way.* Grand Rapids: Zondervan, 2011.

Inwood, C. "The Missionary Passion." In *The Keswick Week 1911: Thirty-Seventh Convention*, 133–138. London: Marshall Brothers, 1911.

———. "Counterfeit Consecration." In: *Keswick Authentic Voice: Sixty-five dynamic addresses delivered at the Keswick Convention 1875–1957*, edited by H. F. Stevenson, 117. London: Marshall, Morgan and Scott Ltd, 1959.

———. "The Unveiling of the Carnal. In *Keswick Authentic Voice: Sixty-five dynamic addresses delivered at the Keswick Convention 1875–1957*, edited by H. F. Stevenson, 71–79. London: Marshall, Morgan and Scott, Ltd., 1959.

Isichei, E. *A History of Christianity in Africa: From Antiquity to the Present.* Grand Rapids: William B. Eerdmans Publishing Company; Lawrenceville: Africa World Press, 1995.

Isser, N. and Schwartz, L. L. *The History of Conversion and Contemporary Cults.* New York: Peter Lang Publishing, 1988.

Iversen, H. R. "Pro me in the Age of Authenticity: The Missiological Significance of 'Christ in Us' and 'We in Christ.'" In *Walk Humbly with the Lord: Church and Mission Engaging Plurality*, edited by V. Mortensen and A. Q. Nielsen, 191–204. Grand Rapids; Cambridge: William B. Eerdmans Publishing Company, 2010.

Jepsen, A. "Aman." In *Theological Dictionary of the Old Testament, Vol. 1*, edited by G.J. Botterweck, and H. Ringgren, 292–309. Grand Rapids; Cambridge: William B. Eerdmans Publishing Company, 1977.

Jerome. "Being Able to Stand." In: *Ancient Christian Commentary on Scripture: New Testament VIII; Galatians, Ephesians, Philippians*, edited by M. J. Edwards, 198–199. Downers Grove: Inter-Varsity Press, 1999.

Jerome. "God Gave Daniel Favor." In *Ancient Christian Commentary on Scripture: Old Testament XIII; Ezekiel, Daniel*, edited by K. Stevenson and M. Glerup, 159. Downers Grove: Inter-Varsity Press, 2008.

Kamau, R. K. "A Critical Analysis of the East African Revival Movement with Special Emphasis to ACK Diocese of Kirinyaga." Unpublished research paper, St. Paul's University, 2001.

Karanja, J. *Founding the African Faith: Kikuyu Anglican Christianity 1900–1945*. Nairobi: Uzima Press, 1999.

———. "Confession and Cultural Dynamism in the Revival." In *The East African Revival: History and Legacies*, edited by K. Ward & E. Wild-Wood, 143–151. Farnham: Ashgate Publishing Limited, 2012.

Kariuki, O. *A Bishop Facing Mount Kenya: An Autobiography 1902–1978*. Nairobi: Uzima Press, 1985.

Kenplex. "Christian Industrial Training Centre Details." 10 August 2017. https://www.kenyaplex.com/colleges/1534-christian-industrial-training-centre.aspx.

Kenyatta, J. *Facing Mount Kenya*. New York: Vintage Books, 1965.

Kerr, H. T. & Mulder, J. M., editors. *Famous Conversions*. Grand Rapids: William B. Eerdmans Publishing Company, 1983.

Keswick Week. *The Keswick Week 1911: Thirty-Seventh Convention*. London: Marshall Brothers, 1911.

King, R. R. "Worship." In *Evangelical Dictionary of World Missions*, edited by A. S. Moreau, 1034–1035. Grand Rapids: Baker Books, 2000.

Kisembo, B., Magesa, L. and Shorter, A. *African Christian Marriage*. London: Geoffrey Chapman, 1977.

Klein, W.W. "Ephesians." In *The Expositor's Bible Commentary: Ephesians - Philemon* (Vol. 12), edited by D. E. Garland and T. Longman III, 21–173. Grand Rapids: Zondervan, 2006.

Knoetze, J. J. "Who are the disciples? Identity perceptions about millennials and the church." *Verbum et Ecclesia* 38, no. 1 (2017): 1–7.

Kostenberger, A. J. *John: Baker Exegetical Commentary on the New Testament.* Grand Rapids: Baker Academic, 2004.

Kraft, C. H. *Anthropology for Christian Witness.* Maryknoll: Orbis Books, 1996.

Kraft, C. H. "Anthropology, Missiological Anthropology." In *Evangelical Dictionary of World Missions*, edited by A. S. Moreau, 66–68. Grand Rapids: Baker Books, 2000.

Kravtsev, A. "What is Missiology? An Introductory Paper." 4 July 2017. http://www.academia.edu/4809782/What_is_Missiology_An_Introductory_Paper.

Kunhiyop, S. W. *African Christian Ethics.* Carlisle: HippoBooks, 2008.

Langley, M. & Kiggins, T. *A Serving people: A Textbook on the Church in East Africa for the East African Certificate of Education.* Nairobi: Oxford University Press, 1974.

Lausanne Committee for World Evangelization. "The Willowbank Report." In *Perspectives on the World Christian Movement: A Reader*, edited by R. D. Winter and S. C. Hawthorne, 507–538. Pasadena: William Carey Library, 1981.

Lecompte, M. D. *Ethnography and Qualitative Design in Educational research*, 2nd edition. Orlando: Academic Press, 1993.

Lean, Garth. *Frank Buchman: a Life.* London: Constable, 1985.

Lees, H. C. "The Ministry of Conscience." In *Keswick Authentic Voice: Sixty-five dynamic addresses delivered at the Keswick Convention 1875–1957*, edited by H. F. Stevenson, 80–90. London: Marshall, Morgan and Scott, Ltd., 1959.

Lenana School Document. Kenya, 4–7 August 2011.

Lincoln, A. T. *Word Biblical Commentary, Vol. 42: Ephesians.* Dallas: Word Books, Publisher, 1990.

Lenski, R. C. *The Interpretation of St. Luke's Gospel.* Minneapolis: Augsburg Publishing House, 1946.

Livingston, J. K. *A Missiology of the Road: Early Perspectives in David Bosch's Theology of Mission and Evangelism.* Eugene: Pickwick Publications, 2013.

Longman III, T. Daniel: *The NIV Application Commentary; from biblical . . . to contemporary life.* Grand Rapids: Zondervan, 1999.

Louw, J. P., and Nida, E. A., editors. *Greek-English Lexicon on the New Testament Based on Semantic Domains, Vol. 1.* Roggebaai, Cape Town: The Bible Society of South Africa, 1989.

Love, R. D. "Conversion." In *Evangelical Dictionary of World Missions*, edited by A. S. Moreau, 231–232. Grand Rapids: Baker Books, 2000.

Lucas, E. *Apollos Old Testament Commentary: Daniel.* Leicester: Apollos, 2002.

Mackenzie, E. "Mission and the Inclusive Kingdom of Jesus: Assessing the Missiological Approach of Brian McLaren." *Missiology: An International review* 43, no. 3 (2015): 259–269.

Mackinnon, H. "The Christian Growth in Grace." In *The Keswick Week 1911: Thirty-Seventh Convention*, 121–125. London: Marshall Brothers, 1911.

MacMaster, R. K. and Jacobs, D. R. *A Gentle Wind of God: The Influence of the East Africa Revival*. Waterloo: Herald Press, 2006.

Magesa, L. *African Religion*. Nairobi: Paulines Publications Africa, 1997.

Makower, K. *The Coming of the Rain: The Life of Dr. Joe Church; A Personal Account of Revival in Rwanda*. Carlisle: Paternoster Press, 1999.

Mambo, G.K. "The Revival Fellowship (Brethren) in Kenya." In *Kenya Churches Handbook: The Development of Kenyan Christianity, 1498–1973*, edited by D.B. Barrett et al., 110- 117. Kisumu: Evangel, 1973.

Mantle, J. G. "The Victorious Life." In *The Keswick Week 1911: Thirty-Seventh Convention*, 161–165. London: Marshall Brothers, 1911.

Mare, W. H. "1 Corinthians." In *The Expositor's Bible Commentary: Romans to Galatians*, edited by F. E. Gaebelein, 175–297. Grand Rapids: Zondervan Publishing House, 1976.

Marius, R. *Martin Luther: The Christian between God and Death*. London: The Belknap Press of Harvard University Press, 1999.

Markus, R. A. "Gregory the Great and a Papal Missionary Strategy." In *The Mission of the Church and the Propagation of the Faith* edited by G. J. Cuming, 29–38. London: Cambridge University Press, 1970.

Marshall, H. I. "Evangelicalism and Biblical Interpretation." In *The Futures of Evangelicalism: Issues and Prospects*, edited by C. Bartholomew, R. Parry and A. West, 100–123. Leicester: Inter-Varsity Press, 2003.

Martin, T. W. "Paul's Argument from Nature for the Veil in First Corinthians 11:13–15: A Testicle instead of a Head Covering." *JBL* 123 (2004), 75–84

Mbiti, J. *African Religion and Philosophy*, 2nd edition. Oxford: Heinemann Educational Publishers, 1969.

———. *Introduction to African Religion*. Nairobi: Heinemann, 1975.

———. *African Religion and Philosophy*. London: Heinemann, 1982.

———. *Introduction to African Religion*, 2nd edition. London: Heinemann, 1991.

McCollough, C. T. "Introduction to Daniel." In *Ancient Christian Commentary on Scripture*, edited by K. Stevenson and M. Glerup, 149–154. Downers Grove: Inter-Varsity Press, 2008.

MacCulloch, D. *Christianity: The First Three Thousand Years*. New York: Penguin Group (Viking), 2009.

McGavran, D. *The Bridges of God*. New York: Friendship/World Dominion, 1955.

McGrath, A. "Evangelical Anglicanism: A Contradiction in Terms." In *Evangelical Anglicans: The Role and Influence in the Church Today*, edited by R. T. France and A. E. McGrath, 10–21. London: Society for Promoting Christian Knowledge (SPCK), 1993.

McQuilkin, J. R. "The Keswick Perspective." In *Five Views on Sanctification*, 151–183. Grand Rapids: Zondervan, 1987.

Merriam, S. B. *Qualitative Research: A Guide to Design and Implementation*. San Francisco: Jossey-Bass, 2009.

Michaels, J. R. *The Gospel of John: The New International Commentary on the New Testament*. Grand Rapids; Cambridge: William B Eerdmans Publishing Company, 2010.

Miller, P. M. *Equipping for Ministry*. Tanzania: Central Tanzania, 1974.

Miller, S. R. *The New American Commentary: Daniel*. Nashville: Broadman & Holman Publishers, 1994.

Mombo, E. "The Revival Testimony of Second Wives." In *The East African Revival: History and Legacies*, edited by Kevin Ward and Emma Wild-Wood, 153–161. Farnham: Ashgate Publishing Limited, 2012.

Montgomery, J. A. *A Critical and Exegetical Commentary on the Book of Daniel*. Edinburgh: T & T Clark, George Street, 1927.

Moreau, A. S., Corwin, R. G. and McGee, B. G. *Introducing World Missions: A Biblical, Historical, and Practical Survey*. Grand Rapids: Baker Academic, 2004.

Morgan, G. C. "The Secrets of Power." In *The Keswick Week 1911: Thirty-Seventh Convention*, 178–186. London: Marshall Brothers, 1911.

Morris, G. E. *The Mystery and Meaning of Christian Conversion*. Nashville: World Methodist Council, 1981.

Moule, H. C. G. *Ephesian Studies*. London: Hodder & Stoughton, 1902.

Muck, T. C. "Missio-logoi, interreligious dialogue, and the parable of the Good Samaritan." *Missiology* 44, no. 1 (2016): 5–19.

Muita, I. W. *Hewn from the Quarry: The Presbyterian Church of East Africa 100 Years and Beyond*. Nairobi: The Presbyterian Church of East Africa, 2003.

Murray, A. *The Full Blessings of Pentecost*. New York: Fleming H. Revell, 1908.

Mutembei, D., 2012. *Historia Fupi ya Ushirika wa Wangovu katika Yesu wa Africa ya Mahsariki [A Short History of Brethren Fellowship in Christ in East Africa]*. Meru, Kenya: Unpublished document.

Naselli, A. D. *Keswick Theology: A Survey of the Doctrine of Sanctification in the Early Keswick Movement*, Detroit: Detroit Theological Seminary, 2008.

———. *Let Go and Let God? A Survey and Analysis of Keswick Theology*. Bellingham: Lexham Press, 2010.

———. *How to Understand and Apply the New Testament: Twelve Steps from Exegesis to Theology*. 1st edition. Phillipsburg: P & R Publishing Co, 2017.

Neely, A. "Missiology." In *Evangelical Dictionary of World Missions*, edited by A. S. Moreau, 633–635. Grand Rapids: Baker Books; Carlisle: Paternoster Press, 2000.

Nehrbass, K. "Does missiology have three legs to stand on? The upsurge on interdisciplinary." *Missiology: An International Review* 44, no. 1 (2016): 50–65.

Neil, S. *Creative Tension*. London: Edinburgh House, 1959.

Nichols, S. J., editor. *Martin Luther's Ninety-Five Theses*. Phillipsburg: P & R Publishing Co., 2002.

Nikolajsen, J. B. "Beyond Sectarianism: The Missional Church in a Post-Christendom Society." *Missiology* 41, no. 4 (2013): 462–475.

Njoku, C. A. "The Missionary Factor in African Christianity 1884–1914." In *African Christianity: An African Story*, edited by O. U. Kalu, 191–225. Trenton: Africa World Press, 2007.

Nkansah-Obrempong, J. *Foundations for African Theological Ethics*. Carlisle: Langham Monographs, 2013.

North-West University. *Manual for Postgraduate Studies,* Potchefstroom: Institutional Office, NWU, 2010.

Nthamburi, Z. *From Mission to Church: A Handbook of Christianity in East Africa*. Nairobi: Uzima, 1991.

Nyaga, D. *Customs and Traditions of the Meru*. Nairobi: East African Educational Publishers, 1997.

O'Brien, P. T., editor. *God's Mission and Ours: The Challenge of Telling the Nations*. Sydney: Church Missionary Society, 1999.

O'Brian, G. J. "The Procuring of Reverence, Piety, and Devotion: Determined Worship for a Determined Church." *Churchman* 127, no. 4 (2013): 337–346.

Odhiambo, E. S. *A History of East Africa*. London: Longman Group Ltd., 1977.

Ogot, B. A. "The Church of Christ in Africa." In *A Place to Feel at Home: A Case of Two Independent Churches in Western Kenya*, edited by F. B. Welbourn and B. A. Ogot. London: Oxford Press, 1966.

Osborn, H. H. *Pioneers in the East African Revival*. Winchester: Apologia Publications, 2000.

Ott, C., Strauss, S. J. and Tennent, T. C. *Encountering Theology of Mission: Biblical Foundations, Historical Developments, and Contemporary Issues*. Grand Rapids: Baker Academic, 2010.

Ott, C. "Globalization and contextualization: Reframing the task of contextualization in the twenty-first century." *Missiology: An International Review* 43, no. 1 (2015): 43–58.

Paas, S. "The Discipline of Missiology in 2016: Concerning the Place and Meaning of Missiology in the Theological Curriculum." 11 July 2017. http://www.godgeleerdheid.vu.nl/nl/Images/The_Discipline_of_Missiology_in_2016_CTJ_51.1_Paas_%28printer_ready%29_offprint_%281%29_tcm238-787272.pdf.

Packer, J. I. *Latimer Studies, Vol. 1: The Evangelical Anglican Identity Problem: An Analysis*. Oxford: Latimer House, 1978.

———. *Keep in Step with the Spirit.* Old Tappan: Fleming H Revell Company, 1984.

———. "Theology of Revival." In *New Dictionary of Theology*, edited by S. B. Ferguson and D. F. Wright, 588–589. Bath: IVP, 1988.

———. *A Passion for Holiness.* Leicester: Crossway Books, 1992.

———. *The Collected Shorter Writings of J.I. Packer, Vol. 4: Honouring the People of God:* Carlisle: Paternoster, 1999.

Packer, J. I. and Wright, N. T. *Anglican Evangelical Identity: Yesterday and Today.* Vancouver: Regent College, 2008.

Pahls, M. "Born of Revival and Genocide: The Mission of Province de l'Église Épiscopale au Rwanda and the New Evangelization." 9 September 2017. https://www.academia.edu/386084/Born_of_Revival_and_Genocide_The_Mission_of_Province_de_l%C3%89glise_%C3%89piscopale_au_Rwanda_and_the_New_Evangelization.

Paul, T. "Integrated Research Institute." 19 April 2017. https://iriucbc.org/2016/03/02/a-review-of-christianity-and-genocide-in-rwanda/.

Pearce, T. P. "An Examination of the Higher Life Concept of Sanctification with respect to its Dependence and upon the Trychotomous Views of Man." ThD diss., Mid-America Baptist Theological Seminary, 1994.

Perkins, P. "The Letter to the Ephesians: Introduction, Commentary, and Reflections." In *The New Interpreter's Bible: General Articles & Introduction, Commentary, & Reflections for Each Book of the Bible*, edited by E. Keck, 351–367. Nashville: Abingdon Press, 2000.

Peterson, D. "Worship in the New Testament." In *Worship: Adoration and Action*, edited by D. A. Carson, 51–94. Grand Rapids: Baker Book House; Carlisle: Paternoster Press, 1993.

———. *Possessed by God: A New Testament Theology of Sanctification and Holiness.* Leicester: Apollos, 1995.

Phiri, G. A. *Social-cultural Anthropology: Christian Communication and the African Culture.* Eugene: Wipf & Stock Publishers, 2008.

Pierson, A. T. "The message: its practical application." In *The Keswick Convention: Its Message, its Method, and its Men,* edited by C. F. Harford, 89–96. London: Marshall Brothers, 1907.

Piper, John. *Let the Nations Be Glad! The Supremacy of God in Missions*, 3rd edition. Nottingham: Inter-Varsity Press, 2010.

Pollock, J. C. *The Keswick Story: The Authorized History of the Keswick Convention.* London: Hodder & Stoughton, 1964.

Porter, D. "Editor's Introduction." In *Truth on Fire: 1998 Keswick Ministry*, edited by D. Porter, 9–10. Carlisle: OM Publishing, 1998.

Pratte, D. E. "Gospel Way." 27 August 2016. http://www.gospelway.com/topics/salvation/baptism-who-performs.php.

Price, J. R. "Bible Answers." 9 September 2017. http://www.bibleanswer.com/confssin.htm.
Rambo, L. "Conversion." In *Dictionary of Pastoral Care and Counseling*, edited by R. J. Hunter, 228–230. Nashville: Abingdon Press, 1990.
Reed, Colin. *Walking in the Light: Reflections on the East African Revival and its link with Australia*. Brunswick East: Acorn Press, 2007.
Richebächer, W. "*Missio Dei:* The Basis of Mission Theology or a Wrong Path?" *International Review of Mission* 92 (2003): 588–605.
Roberts, P. J. "Christian Initiation." In *The Identity of Anglican Worship*, edited by K. Stevenson and B. Spinks, 80–87. Harrisburg: Morehouse Publishing, 1991.
Roberts, V. "J.C. Ryle: 'Evangelical Churchman.'" *Churchman* 128, no. 1 (2014): 25–38.
Rodgers, J. H. *Essential Truths for Christians: A Commentary on the Anglican Thirty-Nine Articles and Introduction to Systematic Theology*. Blue Bell: Classical Anglican Press, 2011.
Ryle, J. C. "Thoughts on the Prayer Book: The Usefulness of Liturgy." *Anglican Way: The Magazine of the Prayer Book Society* 38, no. 3 (2015): 18–19.
Sagay, J. O. and Wilson, D. A. *Africa: A Modern History (1800–1975)*. London: Evans Brothers Ltd., 1978.
Sampley, J. P. "The First Letter to the Corinthians: Introduction, Commentary, and Reflections." In *The New Interpreter's Bible: General Articles & Introduction, Commentary, & Reflections for Each Book of the Bible*, edited by L. E. Keck, 773–795. Nashville: Abingdon Press, 2002.
Sarcerius, E. "Repentance Brings Light." In *Reformation Commentary on Scripture: New Testament X: Galatians, Ephesians*, edited by G. L. Bray, 372. Downers Grove: IVP Academic, 2011.
Schaff, P. "The Lambeth Quadrilateral: The Creeds of the Evangelical Protestant Churches."
http://biblehub.com/library/schaff/the_creeds_of_the_evangelical_protestant_churches/i_the_lambeth_quadrilateral_.htm.
Senyonyi, J. "GAFCON EA Revival Distinctives." 6 June 2017. https://www.gafcon.org/sites/gafcon.org/files/news/pdfs/East_African_Revival_Talk_Senyonyi.pdf.
Sesi, S. M. "Context and Worship Among Digo Muslims in Kenya." In *African Missiology: Contribution of Contemporary Thought*, 200–224. Nairobi: Uzima Publishing House, 2009.
Shipley, M. "The Dependence of Faith." In *Keswick's Authentic Voice: Sixty-Five Dynamic Addresses Delivered at the Keswick Convention 1875–1957*, edited by H. F. Stevenson, 258–260. London: Marshall, Morgan and Scott, Ltd., 1959.
Silverman, D. *Doing Qualitative Research*. London: SAGE Publishers, 2005.

Smalley, W. A. "Anthropological Study and Missionary Scholarship." In *Readings in Missionary Anthropology* edited by W. A. Smalley, 3–13. South Pasadena: William Carey Library, 1974.

———. "Planting the Church in a Disintegrating Society." In *Readings in Missionary Anthropology*, edited by W. A. Smalley, 107–118. Pasadena: William Carey Library, 1974.

———. "What Are Indigenous Churches Like? In: *Readings in Missionary Anthropology,* edited by W. A. Smalley, 157–161. Pasadena: William Carey Library, 1974.

Smith, K. G. *Academic Writing and Theological Research: A Guide for Students.* Johannesburg: South African Theological Seminary Press, 2008.

Smith, T. L. *Called Unto Holiness: The Story of the Nazarenes.* Kansas City: Nazarene, 1962.

Smith, Uriah. *Daniel and the Revelation.* Battle Creek: Review and Herald Publishing Co., 1897.

Snodgrass, K., *Ephesians: The NIV Application Commentary*, 1st edition. Grand Rapids: Zondervan Publishing House, 1996.

Spinks, B. D. and Tellini, G. "The Anglican Church and Holy Order." In *The Identity of Anglican Worship*, edited by K. Stevenson and B. Spinks, 116–123. Harrisburg: Morehouse Publishing, 1991.

St. John, P. *Breath of Life: The History of the Ruanda Mission.* London: Norfolk Press, 1971.

St. Paul's University. "St. Paul's University." 18 August 2017. https://www.universities.com/kenya/st-pauls-university/.

———. "Faculty of Social Sciences." 18 August 2017. http://www.spu.ac.ke/spu-academics/faculties.html.

———. "Faculty of Theology." 18 August 2017. http://www.spu.ac.ke/spu-academics/faculties.html.

———. "St. Paul's University." 18 August 2017. http://www.spu.ac.ke/spu/vision-mission.html.

Stancliffe, D. S. "Is there an 'Anglican' Liturgical Style?" In *The Identity of Anglican Worship*, edited by K. Stevenson and B. Spinks, 124–134. Harrisburg: Morehouse Publishing, 1991.

Stanley, B. "The East Africa Revival: African Initiative within a European Tradition." (Paper presented to a meeting of the Historians' Study Group of the UCCF Associates, 26 March 1977)

Stepanek, S. *Luther.* New York: Chelsea House Publishers, 1986.

Steven, J. H. *Worship in the Spirit: Charismatic Worship in the Church of England.* Milton Keynes: Paternoster, 2002.

Stevenson, H. F., editor. *Keswick's Authentic Voice: Sixty-five Dynamic Addresses Delivered at the Keswick Convention 1875–1957*. London: Marhall, Morgan and Scott, Ltd., 1959.

Stock, E. "The Missionary Element." In: *The Keswick Convention: Its Message, Its Method and Its Men*, edited by C. F. Harford, 131–141. London: Marshall Brothers, 1907.

Stockmayer, O. "The Sufficiency of Grace." In *Keswick's Authentic Voice: Sixty-Five Dynamic Addresses Delivered at the Keswick Convention 1875–1957*, edited by H. F. Stevenson, 183–188. London: Marshall, Morgan and Stott, Ltd., 1959.

Stott, John. *The Message of Ephesians*, 2nd edition. Leicester: Inter-Varsity Press, 1979.

Strahler, R. *Coming to Faith in Christ: Understanding Conversion*. Nairobi: SIM - Life Challenge Assistance, 2010.

Sundkler, B. & Steed, C. *A History of the Church in Africa*. Cambridge: Cambridge University Press, 2000.

Talbot, C. H. "St. Boniface and the German Mission." In *The Mission of the Church and the Propagation of the Faith*, edited by G. J. Cuming, 45–57. London: Cambridge University Press, 1970.

Tertullian. "The Value of Partial Fasts." In *Ancient Christian Commentary on Scripture: Old Testament XIII; Ezekiel, Daniel*, edited by K. Stevenson & M. Glerup, 159. Downers Grove: Inter-Varsity Press, 2008.

Theodoret of Cyr. "The Youths Reject the Kings Food." In *Ancient Christian Commentary on Scripture: Old Testament XIII; Ezekiel, Daniel*, edited by K. Stevenson & M. Glerup, 158–159. Downers Grove: Inter-Varsity Press, pp. 2008.

Thielman, F. *Ephesians: Baker Exegetical Commentary on the New Testament*, 1st edition. Grand Rapids: Baker Academic, 2010.

Thompson, W. R. "An Appraisal of the Keswick and Wesleyan Contemporary Positions." 9 September 2017. https://www.lcoggt.org/Articles/an_appraisal_of_the_keswick_and_.Htm.

Thornton, G. R. "Trust and Obey." In: *Keswick's Authentic Voice: Sixty-Five Dynamic Addresses Delivered at the Keswick Convention 1875–1957*, edited by H. F. Stevenson, 261–264. London: Marshall, Morgan and Stott, Ltd. 1959.

Tizon, A. *Transformation After Lausanne: Radical Evangelical Mission in Global-Local Perspective*. Eugene: Wipf & Stock, 2008.

Trumbull, C.G. *Victory in Christ: Messages on Victorious Life*. Fort Washington: Christian Literature Crusade, 1984.

Tufford, L. and Newman, P. "Qualitative Social Work: Bracketing in Qualitative Research. *SAGE Journals* 1 (2010): 80–96.

Turnbull, R. *Anglican and Evangelical?* London: Continuum International Publishing Group, 2007.

Verbrugge, V. D. "1 Corinthians." In *The Expositor's Bible Commentary: Romans to Galatians*, edited by T. Longman III and D. E. Garland, 241–414. Grand Rapids: Zondervan, 2008.

Wabukala, E. "The Thirty-Nine Articles of Religion: The Church and its Mission." *Churchman* 128, no. 1 (2014); 51–64.

Walls, A. F. *The Missionary Movement in Christian History: Studies in the Transmission of Faith*, 12th edition. Maryknoll: Orbis Books, 1996.

———. *The Cross-Cultural Process in Christian History.* Maryknoll: Orbis Books; Edinburgh: T & T Clark, 2002.

Walton, J. "Legacy of East African Revival Frames GAFCON Opening Night." 17 August 2017. https://www.gafcon.org/news/legacy-of-east-african-revival-frames-gafcon-opening-night.

Wambugu, H., Ngarariga, J. M. and Kariuki, P. M. *The Agikuyu: Their Customs, Traditions & Folklore.* Nairobi: Wisdom Graphics Place, 2006.

Ward, K. "The Balokole Revival in Uganda." In *From Mission to Church: A Handbook of Christianity in East Africa*, edited by Z. Nthamburi. Nairobi: Uzima Press, 1995.

———. *A History of Global Anglicanism.* Cambridge: Cambridge University Press, 2006.

———. "Introduction." In *The East African Revival: History and Legacies*, edited by K. Ward and E. Wild-Wood, 3–10. Farnham; Burlington: Ashgate Publishing Company, 2012.

———. "Revival, Mission, and Church in Kigezi, Rwanda, and Burundi." In *The East African Revival: History and Legacies*, edited by K. Ward and E. Wild-Wood, 11–30. Farnham: Ashgate Publishing Company, 2012.

Ward, K. & Wild-Wood, E., editors. *The East African Revival: History and Legacies.* Kampala: Fountain Publishers, 2010.

———. *The East African Revival: History and Legacies.* Farnham: Ashgate Publishing Limited, 2012.

Warfield, B. B. *Perfectionism.* Philadelphia: The Presbyterian and Reformed Publishing Company, 1958.

Warren, M. A. *Revival: an Enquiry.* London: SCM Press, 1954.

Webb-Peploe, H. W. "The Christian Walk." In *Keswick's Authentic Voice: Sixty-Five Dynamic Addresses Delivered at the Keswick Convention 1875–1957*, edited by H. F. Stevenson, 254–257. London: Marshall, Morgan and Scott, Ltd., 1959.

Webster, J. *The Holiness of the Christian.* London: SCM Press, 2003.

Wegman, H. A. *Christian Worship in East and West: A Study Guide to Liturgical History*, 2nd edition. New York: Pueblo Publishing Company, 1985.

Welbourn, F. B., and Ogot, B. A. *A Place to Feel at Home: A Study of Two Independent Churches in Western Kenya.* London: Oxford University Press, 1966.

Westcott, B. F. *St. Paul's Epistle to the Ephesians: The Greek Text with Notes and Addenda*. London: Macmillan & Co., Limited, 1906.

Wild-Wood, E. "The East African Revival in the Study of African Christianity." In *The East African Revival: History and Legacies*, edited by K. Ward and E. Wild-Wood, 201–212. Farnham: Ashgate Publishing Company, 2012.

Willard, Dallas. *Renovation of the Heart: Putting on the Character of Christ*. Colorado Springs: NavPress, 2002.

Winter, B. W. *After Paul Left Corinth: The Influence of Secular Ethics and Social Change*. Grand Rapids; Cambridge: William B Eerdmans Publishing Company, 2001.

Winter, R. D. "The Future of Evangelicals in Mission." In *MissionShift: Global Mission Issues in the Third Millennium*, edited by D. J. Hesselgrave and E. Stetzer, 164–191. Nashville: B & H Publishing Group, 2010.

Wright, C. J. H. *The Mission of God: Unlocking the Bible's Grand Narrative*. Nottingham: Inter-Varsity Press, 2006.

Wright, N. T. *Latimer Studies, Vol. 8: Evangelical Anglican Identity: The Connection between Bible, Gospel & Church*. Oxford: Latimer House, 1980.

Yamamori, T. *Penetrating Missions' Final Frontier: A New Strategy for Unreached Peoples*. Downers Grove: Inter-Varsity Press, 1993.

Zaki, A. "Mission Frontiers." 10 August 2017. http://www.missionfrontiers.org/pdfs/36-5-Four-Ways-Culture-Worship-Relate.pdf.

Appendices

Appendix 1

Factions in the EARM

Arahuka (Arise): This group is popularly known in Kiswahili as *Kufufuka* or *Kuzuzuka* which Nthamburi argues originated in 1935 from Blasio Kigozi who challenged the sleeping church of Uganda to wake up.[1] The concept of "wake up" was derived from a text in Ephesians 5:14, "Wake up O sleeper, rise from the dead and Christ will shine upon you." The members understood this text to mean the spirituality of the mission church was dead and thus to wake up meant to rise from the dead and consequently to associate with the Arise group. So members of this movement detached themselves from the mission church and social activities claiming that getting involved meant one is spiritually dead. Their interpretation of the text led to their distinctive beliefs and practices. For instance, members are forbidden to obtain loans from banks, take items from the shop on credit, receive or give a bride price, adopt children, take life insurance or keep dogs. Being involved in such activities means that one is spiritually dead. Group members are serious in tithing within the movement in support of their operations.

Simama (Stand): *Simama* is a Swahili word meaning "stand" and refers to members who have stood firm in the revival in the wake of the split. This is the biggest group and is actively involved in evangelism in the church. Its adherents argue that they have stood firm in their faith in Christ in the sense of being the original revival members, i.e., they call themselves *Simama na*

---

1. Nthamburi, From mission to Church, p.117.

Yesu (stand firm in Jesus). They cooperate with the church and appear to emphasize their theology rather than an interpretation of Scripture. They have no particular biblical text for reference.

Mtama na Maji (Sorghum and water): The origin of *Mtama na Maji* is traced from a convention held at Taita, Kenya in 1960 whose theme was "give us nothing but vegetables to eat and water to drink" (Dan 1:8). The members sought to live like Daniel and the young men in the king's palace. So, they emphasized a simple lifestyle by wearing simple clothing and eating simple food. To them, high living is defilement from the king's devilish palace. As a result, they do not take part in church leadership, Holy Communion or church functions like fundraising. These are the king's foodstuff and should be avoided. Other elements to avoid are expensive gowns, cakes, cars, bridal attires, flowers and any decorations in their wedding venues. Outward performances appear to inform their spirituality.

Thama (Leave): The origin of this schism finds its origin from a convention held at Murang'a in central Kenya in 1957, whose theme was "to leave," derived from Genesis 12:1. At the end of the convention, the idea of leaving was misunderstood to mean leaving their unsaved family members, clans and friends. This split the EARM with one group emphasizing leaving one's sinful life and the other insisting on physically leaving their relatives and property because, to them, they were a hindrance to salvation. This group has died, and little is heard of it. However, its teaching has not died away completely.

Kupaa (Rising Up): This small group split from Arise and claimed to be more saved than merely *Kufufuka*. They were so completely detached from the world and its affairs and were in the glory train to heaven. Due to their small membership in Kirinyaga County, they have joined the *Simama* (Stand) group, the largest in the county. Their teachings are similar to those of *Arahuka* (Arise) and are active particularly in Embu, Kenya.

Appendix 2

Interview Guide for the Focus Groups and the One-on-One, EARM's Leaders

(i) Describe the way you give testimony.
(ii) Have you ever heard about Keswick teachings?
   If yes, in what way have they influenced the current socio-ethical life in EARM?
   If no, what influenced beliefs and practices are apparent in the EARM?
(iii) Describe the aspects of walking in the light in EARM showing how they could have brought division in the revival?
(iv) What is the dominant text (s) used by members that could have led to the split?
(v) Briefly, describe the history of the split in EARM, showing how it has affected the mission of the church?
(vi) What change would you recommend for the current socio-ethical life?
(vii) Is there anything you would wish to share which has not been covered above?

Appendix 3

Interview Guide for Theological Students, Clergy, Bishops and the Main Stakeholders

(i) Have you ever heard about Keswick theology?
   If yes, in what way has it influenced the prevailing socio-ethical life in EARM?
   If no, what influenced beliefs and practices apparent in EARM?
(ii) Describe the aspects of walking in the light in EARM showing how they could have brought division in the revival?
(iii) What is the dominant text(s) used by members EARM that could have led to the split?
(iv) Briefly, describe the history of the split in EARM, showing how it has affected the mission of the church?
(v) What change would you recommend for the current socio-ethical life?
(vi) Is there anything you would wish to share which has not been covered above?

Appendix 4

Inductive and Comparative Data Analysis in the Seven Centers in the ACK Diocese of Mbeere

The data accruing from each question was analyzed and observations made in the form of notations, which were gleaned to construct themes for comparison with the four selected dioceses.

Focused group interview for ordinary members
Question 1: Describe the way you give a testimony

Gara: They say is a journey of salvation.

Ngca: They begin with Tukutendereza greetings, mention past sins by name, and then describe daily life with God.

Kare: One says the date of receiving Christ, quote the Scripture that was read, outline all sins of the past, and testify about the current status of salvation.

Kiri: Saying how Jesus saved them.

Notations: Begins with Tukutendereza greetings followed by a sequence of salvation journey since getting saved - mention date and what sin one had committed, current status and daily walk with God.

Question 2: Asked whether the respondents have ever heard about Keswick teachings, they replied:

Gara: Never

Ngca: Never

Kare: Never, but acknowledged other influences from an unknown source which challenged people to holiness.

Kiri: Never

Notations: They have never heard about Keswick teachings, though one center acknowledged influence from unknown people.

Question 3: Describe walking in the light showing how it could have brought division in EARM

Gara: It is legalistic codes of conduct.

Ngca: It talks about public confession of sins.

Kare: It is about testimony – declaring of sins, such that people shy away.

Kiri: Sin leads to separation.

Notations: They termed it legalistic especially testimony that depicts public confessions of sin, thus exclusive.

Question 4: What is the dominant text used by members of EARM that could have led to the split?

Gara: Matt 5:13–14, you are light and salt.

Ngca: Matt 5:14

Kare: Rev 3:15–17, be hot or cold

Kiri: Theological and religious differences led to split.

Notations: Matt 5:13–14 and Rev 3:15–17, theological differences led to division.

Question 5: Briefly describe the history of the split in EARM, showing how it has affected the mission of the church?

Gara: Don't know, but says it belongs to the elderly people.

Ngca: Don't know, but pointing at people's sin led to split.

Kare: Don't know, but mention leadership squabbles and difference with other Christians.

Kiri: Don't know, but talk about journey to heaven in their fellowships.

Notations: They have no knowledge of the history of division but appear to blame generation gap, hypocrisy (terming other Christians as sinners) and leadership.

Question 6: What change would you recommend for the current social-ethical life?

Gara: Change manner of worship to attract youth.
Ngca: Accept change, freedom of expression and dressing.
Kare: Inclusive fellowship.
Kiri: Equality among Christians.
Notations: Inclusive worship that allows free speech and dressing especially by youth.

Question 7: Is there anything you would wish to share which has not been covered above?

Gara: No.
Ngca: Students should not go for theological education so that they can earn a salary. Young people should be allowed to attend Kenya team preserved only for the saved people (Brethren).
Kare: Avoid holier-than-thou attitude and extremes.
Kiri: People should get saved.
Notations: They expressed disappointment with clergy who appear to go for ministerial formation training not as calling but a source of money. They also expressed reservations for Brethren's self-righteous disposition.

One-on-one interview for EARM's leaders

Question 1: Describe the way you give testimony.

Gara: Someone acknowledges his sin, saying that Jesus died for our justification and that testimony includes time and venue – can take 10 – 20 minutes.
Mama: Tukutendereza, greetings, Pilgrim testimony beginning with past sins.
Njge: They start by disclosure of identity, date of salvation and what prompted salvation or text that was read, and pilgrim progress regarding the past, present and pressing on to the future.

Kiri: Tukutendereza, disclosure of identity, date of salvation, current status of salvation and future prospects.

Notations: They begin with Tukutendereza, the disclosure of identity, Pilgrim testimony starting with past sins and pushing on.

Question 2: Have you ever heard about Keswick teachings?

Gara: Never heard about Keswick teachings and attributed the prevailing social, ethical life to Brethren Fellowship meetings and conferences.

Mama: Never heard, and have no idea what brought the influence, but feels fellowships and conventions influenced beliefs.

Njge: Never heard, no idea what brought the influences but feels Kupaa faction informed by teachings of Mtama na Maji (Sorghum and water) influenced the practices. Another leader said it was influenced by peer pressure and the church leadership.

Kiri: No comment, said that beliefs and practices of walking in the light were influenced by sin.

Notations: They have never heard about Keswick theology and suggests splinter groups influenced belief and practices, Brethren stereotyping fellowships, peer pressure, sin and church hierarchy.

Question 3: Describe walking in the light showing how it could have brought division in EARM?

Gara: Brethren's self-righteous attitude and shameful public testimonies.

Mama: Transparent and open confessions.

Njge: Sharing public confessions and extreme lifestyles, self-righteousness, and exaggerations.

Kiri: Following the teachings of Jesus, avoiding evil.

Notations: An open and transparent (public confessions) lifestyle, turned hypocritical and legalistic.

Question 4: What is the dominant text that could have led to the split?

Gara: Matt 5:13

Mama: Matt 5:14–16

Njge: Luke 9:23, leave your people; Matt 16:25

Kiri: Dan 1:8ff

Notations: Matt 5:14–16; Luke 9:23; Matt 16:25; Dan 1:8ff

Question 5: Briefly describe the history of the split, showing how it has affected church mission.

Gara: It was brought by leadership squabbles, dress code, and hypocrisy.

Mama: EARM were bearers of the doctrine of walking in the light without which one is not saved.

Njge: leadership squabbles.

Kiri: Interpretation of the Bible leads to legalism.

Notations: Majority associated it with leadership disputes, dress code and hypocritical walking in the light.

Question 6: What change would you recommend for the current socio-ethical life?

Gara: Love for one another and understand all are equal before God.

Mama: Avoid conservativeness, embrace change and accommodate youth.

Njge: Observe dressing according to the code because it is biblical; let status quo remain, change will kill the church but give opportunities for change driven testimonies.

Kiri: Brethren to embrace others, including young people.

Notations: Majority respondents indicated that Brethren should embrace change, by loving other Christians including youth while some felt status quo should remain.

Question 7: Is there anything you would wish to share which has not been covered above?

Gara: Need for brotherly love without discrimination – genuine walk in the light.

Mama: EARM is interdenominational, which challenges relationship with ACK. If EARM has to grow, it should understand current generation.

Njge: ACK should initiate fellowship of youth and Brethren, and seminars on role models.

Kiri: Always confess sins so that the Holy Spirit will help us defeat Satan.

Notations: EARM is an interdenominational fellowship which should engage youth and exercises brotherly love by genuinely walking in the light.

Interview for clergy

Question 1 Have you ever heard about Keswick teachings?

Gara: Never, not aware of what influenced EARM.

Kaa: Never, but feel public confession and fellowship meetings influenced EARM.

Ngce/Kare: Never, but think it originated from Rwanda.

Kiri: No comment.

Notations: Clergy have never heard about Keswick teachings, but while some said it was influenced by fellowship meetings and public confessions, others felt the teachings originated from Rwanda, while still others were not aware of the impact.

Question 2: Describe walking in the light and how it brought division in EARM.

Gara: It is a public confession of sin.

Kaa: It has to do with a public confession of sin.

Ngce/Kare: It is public disclosures – traumatizing, some issues should be personal.

Kiri: Believers continued to commit sin.

Notations: It is a public confession of sin, which could be traumatizing.

Question 3: What is the dominant text used by members of EARM that could have led to the split?

Gara: Matt 13:14, light of the world.

Kaa: John 8:12; Matt 5:14

Ngce/Kare: Rev 3:15–17; Luke 9:23

Kiri: Dan 1:8ff; Deut 14:8

Notations: Matt 5:14, 13:14; John 8:12; Luke 9:23; Rev 3:15–17; Dan 1:8ff; and Deut 14:8

Question 4: Briefly describe the history of the split showing how it has affected the mission of the church?

Gara: It was brought to strict dress code and boring liturgy – Tukutendereza.

Kaa: Dress code and sitting arrangement in the fellowship.

Ngce/Kare: It has raised the standard of spirituality in the church. Factions like Kupaa and Kufufuka, concentrates on issues of sin and heaven, thus no time for the church mission.

Kiri: Scripture inform splits and affects the whole church mission, not just Brethren.

Notations: Majority associate the split with dress code while others link it to preaching about sin and heaven, forgetting about the task of the church.

Question 5: What change would you recommend for the current socio-ethical life?

Gara: Male and female to mix during conferences to enhance plenary discussions.

Kaa: Avoid over-spirituality.

Ngce/Kare: Encourage flexibility on dress code and hairdos.

Kiri: All believers to embrace one another other.

Notations: Gender mix in plenary discussions, balanced spirituality and valid moral codes.

Question 6: Is there anything you would wish to share which has not been covered above?

Gara: To be taught Keswick theology; Brethren should lead by example, not just talk about walking in the light.

Kaa: Avoid strict dress code, give necessary advice; clergy to go for theological education, not for money but to acquire knowledge to fight heresy.

Ngce: EARM to be custodians of informed spirituality.

Kiri: Brethren to be consulting one another to unify the fellowship.

Notations: Need for theological education for Brethren that address dress code and genuine spirituality. That theological education is a calling and not a money making adventure for clergy.

Evaluation of the collected data from the four select dioceses against the Diocese of Mbeere

The above data from Mbeere Diocese (MD) is collated along with the perspectives of the notations and is compared with constructed themes (see chapter 3) accruing from the four Select Dioceses (SD). Surely, the themes ensuing from MD resonates with those from SD which suggest that the research instrument was valid and reliable. These themes are outlined below.

On the theme of born-again testimony the SD put forward a threefold way which echoes that of MD. While the beginning of a testimony encompasses full disclosure of identity, the middle comprises confession of past sins followed by the restitution and forgiveness, and the ending illustrates a journey with the Lord Jesus.

As regards acquaintances with EARM's precursor, whereas the majority of Brethren in the SD except prominent stakeholders were not aware of Keswick theology, MD reported 100 percent ignorance. Thus, some respondents from the SD and MD associated influences of the prevailing situation to other sources.

Concerning scriptural verses believed to have caused a split, while both SD and MD displayed texts from both testaments, MD relied only on the New Testament, specifically from the gospels. However, biblical texts propounded by both SD and MD inform the split and subsequent moral code.

On the subject of other causes of the split, while some SD and MD respondents had no idea, others linked it to leadership squabbles and to open confession of sin.

About splits, SD and MD are in agreement that the ensuing moral codes have had adverse effects on the mission of the Anglican Church in Kenya.

Regarding what change they would recommend to the current trend, most respondents in both SD and MD expressed the need for an all-inclusive and diversified church that allows balanced reciprocating social, ethical dynamics of mission and ministry.

Appendix 5

Nature and Current Trends Regarding Anglican Church Scholarship on Keswick Theology's Influence on EARM's Walking in the Light: Findings and Analyses of the Prevailing Situation

Data Construction

This section gives vivid responses to research questions as they were put to the respondents. Some answers were recorded verbatim while others due to length were diligently summarized to reflect the actual text, mostly in the third person. This was done across the categories of respondents for each of the interview questions. The answer to each research question was collated in terms of comment or a note at the end of each category. This was done in all the subsequent categories. Finally, these notations were put together to glean the most recurrent elements, which became the themes or findings of this research.

Merriam calls this process of making appropriate notations of bits of data that looks potentially useful in answering the research questions as coding.[1] This process is different from coding as a way of de-identifying sources of data, which also accompanied this analysis. Thus the interview centers and identifying personal information have been de-identified.

Describe the Way You Give a Testimony

This question was answered by only the ordinary members and the leaders of the EARM because of their unique way of giving testimony which is not common among theologians. The research will start with sets of data from ordinary members.

Ordinary members of EARM
Diocese of Kirinyaga

Kini: They begin with saying *Tenderezza*[2] and what God has done in the sense of deliverance from sins.

Muri: starts with the full name, where they came from and when one was born again. They also seek to know what prompted conviction, whether it was the Word that was preached or a song that was sung. They complete their testimony with affirming their growth in Christ every hour.

Kigu: "I should say my name and place of residence. Where I was when I got saved. What I was saved from and to return what I had stolen. After that, I say what God has done in my life since I got saved. I finish with future expectations from God."

Kama: Somebody starts with saying his name, then the date he met with Christ and sought Brethren to give his testimony. He realized his sin and corrected the sin by returning all acquired illegal properties. Then he realized forgiveness of Jesus, and he was cleansed of his sins. He then started following the Brethren way of life.

Baho: Someone starts by saying his name and his home place. Then the year of accepting Christ and that Jesus is Lord.

---

1. Merriam, *Qualitative Research*, 178.
2. Denotes "praise God."

Diocese of Mt. Kenya West

Caal: in giving testimony, they repent and confess in details all the sins they had committed before accepting salvation. Secondly, where it was necessary to repay what was stolen, they did so. Those who had avoided paying taxes go to the government officials to say he had not paid. Even if he had committed adultery he would go back to repent and *guthondeka* (make amends). He said he lives within the fellowship by repenting his sins. He mentions all the sins that he had previously committed.

Kaba: "I was born again on July 26, 1981. I don't forget that day. *Uria utakanyumbura guku ndikamumbura iguru* ("whoever will not acknowledge my name before men, I will not acknowledge him before my Father in heaven," Matt10:33). I used to see the evil ways of other people's lives, though were confessing Christ. I decided to witness so that Jesus will say he knows me."

Kiya: they start by indicating the full name, date of salvation in full and the text that led to salvation. They also give the light of their past dark practices without hypocrisy.

Diocese of Embu

Kagu: They start with where you come from, date of salvation, details of sins you were saved from, the progress of salvation by Jesus, future hope.

Kima: They start with *Tukutenderezza* because it is their universal greeting. They realized their sin and found the light.

Caal: What God has done in your life beginning with the time you encountered God. Through testimony, one should ask God for forgiveness.

Kigi: The time and year you got saved. How it happened, was it as a result of hearing the Word, dream or hearing other peoples' testimonies?

Diocese of Mount Kenya Central

Kigi: They begin by saying their names, where they came from when they got saved (time, date, day, month and year) where they were and what they were doing. They confess their past sins one by one.

Mugu: Through the experience of life in Jesus Christ being your Savior and Lord.

Kadu: You start with the year you got saved, then you proceed with the sins you were doing before and finally what the Lord has done in your life.

Kiro: "I start with my name, and then say how I have interacted with the Lord and finally how I have experienced His power."

Kaia: While introducing yourself, you should say "my name" but not "my names," openly confess sins; repentance and forgiveness. You should also mention the date you got saved and your present walk with God. Say what brought you to repentance and describe your walk with God thereafter.

Notations

The majority of ordinary members across the four dioceses give their testimony in a threefold way. First, they disclose their full identity, where and when they met with the Lord, what led to their conviction; second, they repent and confess their past sins, then restitution and forgiveness of sins. Third their journey of salvation with Jesus, walk in light or with God. A few mentioned a fourth aspect, which is future hope.

Leaders of EARM
Diocese of Mount Kenya Central

Kaia: While introducing yourself, you should say "my name" but not 'my names," openly confess sins; repentance and forgiveness. You should also mention the date you got saved and your present walk with God. Say what brought you to repentance and describe your later walk with God.

Kiro: A born-again person gives testimony. It gives Brethren identity. "We start with saying the day, month, year and "the place Jesus met with me, we meet weekly for fellowship . . . we confess how God has journeyed with us and it climaxes with the victory of Jesus in the trials we might be going through."

Kiui: Testimony is given by anyone born again and starts from before getting saved. It details the prosperity you have gained after getting saved. It brings fellowship among believers as they open up to each other. They testify about challenges in life and how the Lord helps them to overcome. In this way, they encourage each other.

Mugu: ". . . you start by mentioning your name, stating the year you got saved, and then you continue with how you met your savior. You have to say the evil things or sins you committed before you were saved, and how you walk with the Lord since then."

Kigi: start by giving his name, where he had come from when he got saved: dates, month, year, day, and time, confession of sins God saved him from, mentioning those sins one by one.

Kini: start by saying the year you got saved and testify to the sins you were saved from. You tell your local fellowship up to the district level. You testify how you have been walking with God.

Diocese of Mount Kenya West

Guse: Mention of name and dates in full, what drove you to salvation, tell how your Savior has walked with you, finally what you yearn to achieve in your salvation life.

Otya: Tell how the Lord is good, how he has sustained you, what he has done for you and how you have daily walked with God.

Diocese of Embu

Kahs: ". . . it is based on my conversion experience when Christ saved me on April 29, 1967, at 3. 00 A.M in a beer bar when drunk with alcohol . . . The particular sins that the Lord convicted me of I confessed and asked for his forgiveness . . ." Another leader said his testimony is about how he met with Christ, and the words that convicted him in August 1979 were from John 21:15–19.

Kima: An old man of ninety-six years said he gives testimony this way to defeat the devil as is written in Revelation that they overcame by the word of their testimony. In the same center, a woman of eighty-three years said she gives her testimony because of what God has done for her, creating miracles for her. She tells how God saved her from sin. So when she sees sin, she points them out to the sinners. She feels her burdens were taken away; she claims to withstand trials and temptations. She hopes to receive everlasting life.

Caal: Starts from the time you received Christ in your heart. Mention the sins that you had committed before getting saved. Confess them.

Kagu: You start by saying your name when you got saved. "I was touched by the word that was preached . . . [which says] if we say we have no sins . . ." (1 John 1:8–10). You then confess sins and journey with the Lord on a daily basis.

Kigi: Start by indicating the time and the year you got saved, say how you felt. Also, provide information on whether it was a Bible verse or somebody's testimony that led you to salvation.

Diocese of Kirinyaga

Baho: The day one was saved, month, year, what God has done for you then and now. They also say what things they were saved from. Another respondent said it begins with mentioning the past life followed by day-to-day sanctification.

Kini: Testifying about what God has done in one's life, having hope in the journey of salvation, trusting God through the temptations until one wins the crown of glory. Another person said that testimony begins with mentioning of the name, then what you were saved from and finally mention the daily walk with God.

Kigu: "I got saved on 26 February 1967 as a young girl while knitting. I was saved from lies." She relates to Joseph's victorious life and derives strength from reading the word of God. The other respondent said he begins by addressing the fellowship, Tukutenderezza meaning praise the Lord. "Then I mention my name, when and how I got saved. The word of God that touched my soul, then I briefly narrate what my Lord Jesus Christ has done for me so far. However, the way (of saying testimony) may vary with situations."

Muri: You start with the name, where he or she comes from, then says his or her present spiritual status and when he or she got saved. Also mention past life, public confession, restitution and battles with evil, daily walk with Christ, future expectations. The other respondent said that testimony begins from the first encounter with God, the exact date and what one was saved from followed by a daily walk with God. This involves public confession of sin and restitution (returning stolen items).

Kama: Start with saying, "I am one of you Brethren, I met with Christ at midnight, when I was asleep. I saw the light in the house, and I cried Lord, and I got saved. In the morning I sought the Brethren to give the testimony. In July 1991 there was a Convention at Kiini; I got a chance to give my testimony on how I met Christ." Also, you have to say which area you come from and your church.

Notations

The majority of the respondents begin their testimony by declaring their full identity. Then the context of an encounter with the Lord (what led to a conviction [lesson from the Bible], what one was saved from), confession and restitution. This was followed by stating your sojourn or walk with the

Lord. The ordinary members and leaders of EARM started their testimony by saying *Tukutenderezza*.

Have You Ever Heard of Keswick Teachings? If Yes, in What Way Have They Influenced the Prevailing Socio-ethical life in EARM? If No, What Influenced Beliefs and Practices Apparent in the EARM?

Concerning whether the respondents have ever heard of Keswick teachings, the reply was as follows across the categories:

Ordinary members
Diocese of Mount Kenya central
Kiro: Never
Kadu: Never
Mugu: Yes
Kigi: Never
Kaia: Never

Diocese of Kirinyaga
Kini: Never
Muri: Never
Kigu: Never
Kama: Never
Baho: Never

Diocese of Mount Kenya West
Kiya: Never
Kaba: Never
Caal: Yes

Diocese of Embu
Kigi: Never
Caal: Never
Kima: Never
Kagu: Yes

Notations
Three centers across the four dioceses have heard but none in Kirinyaga.

Leaders of EARM

Diocese of Kirinyaga
    Kama: Never
    Muri: Never
    Kigu: Never
    Kini: Never
    Baho: Yes

Diocese of Embu
    Kagu: Never
    Caral: Never
    Kima: Never
    Kahs: Yes
    Kigi: Never

Diocese of Mount Kenya West
    Otya: Never
    Guse: Never

Diocese of Mount Kenya Central
    Kini: Never
    Kigi: Never
    Mugu: Yes
    Kitu: Never
    Kiro: Yes
    Kaia: Never

Notations

Four centers across the four dioceses have heard, but none in the Mount Kenya West.

Theological students
    Never

Clergy

Diocese of Mount Kenya Central
    Mugu: Never

Kitu: Yes
Caral: Yes

Diocese of Mount Kenya West
Caal: yes
Thuri: never
Otya: never

Diocese of Embu
Mugu: never
Kahs: never
Caal: never
Kagu: yes

Diocese of Kirinyaga
Kini: yes
Dok: yes
Muri: never
Kama: never

Notations
At least one center in every diocese has heard.

Bishops

Embu
Never

Mount Kenya Central
Never

Mount Kenya West
Yes

Notations
Only one bishop has heard.

Prominent stakeholders

Mobo: Yes

Kaja: Yes
Mwda: Yes
Hald: Yes
Wad: Yes
Gago: Yes

Notations

All have heard.

The second part of the question concerned affirmative responses and was answered across the categories as followers:

Ordinary Members

Diocese of Mount Kenya Central

Mugu: "It enabled me to maintain my identity in Christianity by observing decrees from the Bible."

Diocese of Kirinyaga

No knowledge.

Diocese of Mount Kenya West

Caal: Keswick as a movement was there but did not influence Revival Fellowship.

Diocese of Embu

Kagu: "Their way of salvation is similar."

Notations

Out of the four dioceses, the Kirinyaga ordinary leaders had no knowledge of Keswick's influence on EARM. Others reported some awareness of its impact. Its influence on Christian identity, Bible decrees and salvation procedure was noteworthy.

Leaders of Revival

Diocese of Kirinyaga

Baho: "They have brought a renewal in spiritual life and have given Christianity a real meaning."

Diocese of Embu

Kahs: "Yes, once in August 1969, not specifically in any way but it confirmed my biblical belief as taught by the revival movement."

Diocese of Mount Kenya West

No knowledge

Diocese of Mount Kenya Central

Mugu: "This is the Higher Life Movement originated in England nineteenth century." Yes, it made one know about conventions.

Kiro: "Have heard about it but never involved in any of their meetings. So I have nothing to say about it."

Notations

There was some knowledge of Keswick teachings in Mount Kenya Central, Kirinyaga and Embu, but not in Mount Kenya West. A mention of the Higher Life Movement, biblical beliefs, renewal and convention show some significant elements of Keswick influence.

Theological students

They showed unawareness of Keswick theology.

Clergy

Diocese of Mount Kenya Central

Kitu: "Yes, sanctification is one of the greatest doctrines the EARM holds dearly."

Caal: It has molded EARM's piety, setting themselves apart from other Christians.

Diocese of Mount Kenya West

Caal: Yes, "not in any connection with EARM, but the internet associates it with the Fellowship."

Diocese of Embu

Kagu: Yes, "this wave of revival and renewal has spread all over East Africa. This has resulted to those converted to have deeper experiences of salvation." It is almost similar to today's view of salvation.

Diocese of Kirinyaga

Kini: Yes, introducing strict rules to members.

Dok: Yes, giving testimony of when and how one got saved.

Notations

There were indications of influence exemplified by the use of such terms as sanctification, piety, setting apart, renewal, and deeper experiences of salvation, legalism and the way of saying testimonies.

Bishops

Bishop of Embu

Not aware.

Bishop of Mount Kenya Central

Not aware.

Bishop of Mount Kenya West

Yes, but cannot remember its influence.

Notations

They were not aware of its influence.

Prominent stakeholders

Mobo: The Keswick theology influenced some of the missionaries to Africa, especially CMS. The theology influenced some of the first converts, but Aldo laid some of the foundation for the East Africa Revival. The revival influenced the second generation Christians but entrenched a form of spirituality that became legalistic and hence created hypocritical Christians.

Kaja: Yes, it prompts Brethren daily devotion, it encourages profound sense of accountability.

Mwda: Yes, "I attended it in England, Great Lakes District. The Bible studies that went on continued to inflame my East Africa Revival Spirit in me."

Hald: Yes "based on my knowledge and observations, I would say that it has contributed to the strong commitment to the moral life in East Africans, and especially personal holiness."

Wad: Yes, "I think that the spirituality of the Keswick movement, and of the wider Holiness movement, has been very influential in putting a priority on personal holiness, defined as purity of heart and body, an emphasis on conversion and on the infilling of the Holy Spirit, a strict sexual morality, a lack of interest in overtly political issues."

Gago: Yes, the theology of being saved and daily sanctification (Phil 1:6). It is pietistic theology, nearly legalistic evangelical theology. It's a replica of Wesleyan or Keswick theology, quite close to salvation by works rather than by grace and faith in the resurrected Christ.

Notations

The stakeholders were aware of the influence exemplified by activities of the pioneer missionaries and first converts who entrenched legalistic evangelical theology and hypocritical spirituality. They noted an emphasis on daily devotion and accountability and a moral life with strict sexual morality and personal holiness. They stressed the importance of Bible study, Spirit revival, conversion theology of being saved and infilling of the Holy Spirit and daily sanctification, close to salvation by works.

The final responses to Question 2 dealt with alternative sources of influence of the socio-ethical practices of walking in the light apart from Keswick theology. This question was put to the participants in their categories and was mostly answered by those who had not heard about Keswick movement.

Ordinary members

Diocese of Mount Kenya Central

Kiro: Different forms of spirituality.

Kadu: Salvation which one must confess.

Kigi: Biblical teachings and leader's mentorship.

Diocese of Kirinyaga

Kini: influenced by the word of God to grow spiritually through confessing Christ and through church conventions. Other influences are the mode of dressing, hairstyle, forgiveness of each other and humbleness.

Muri: EARM maintains gender separation and dignity as was taught by their forefathers. Brethren's teachings from Rwanda and Uganda influenced Kenyans. It shows separation from the congregation accusing it of being worldly.

Kigu: they said they were influenced by the Bible, open confession of sin and testimony, cleansing by the blood of Christ, legalistic life of dos and don'ts.

Kama: they were influenced by different teams' fellowships' (ranging from local fellowship to East Africa Revival convention) that dictate certain teachings.

Baho: Brethren love for one another and humbleness.

Diocese of Mount Kenya West

Kiya: lack of knowledge to many on the meaning of the movement leading to setting themselves apart from others to strictly follow Jesus' teachings.

Kaba: kimitugo ni thamiri yaningiriirie, kimaundu ni kurora ndikwenda maya, na maya ni ningwenda. Ndungituira mundu uge ni mwihia – no gutiga (regarding the socio-ethical beliefs and practices my conscience influenced me, as a person you decide to hate one practice and to like the other. You cannot judge a person and say he or she is a sinner – I will just stop).

Diocese of Embu

Caal: knowing the truth through reading the word of God and being faithful to it.

Kima: "salvation came to us through Rwanda..."

Notations

Influences came through Rwanda and other spiritualities. Stress on Bible reading, mentorship, hearing confession about Christ and forgiveness and humility. Also, the emphasis on love for one another, terms like legalism and setting apart, fellowships and conventions.

Leaders of EARM

Diocese of Kirinyaga

Kama: the beliefs and practices were first taught at Kiini church around 1933 by people like Kaggia. He taught wearing of long dresses and also believed in dreams to get a marriage partner. They instill strong faith in their fellowships called *Gatia-uki,* overnight fellowships, etc. Also, teaches the importance of reading the Bible every day and arranges a convention of three days per year. Teachings by the central team and East African revival fellowship teams have impacted the beliefs and practices.

Muri: beliefs in the teachings handed down by East African leaders who traced their beliefs and practices from Uganda.

Kigu: Revival's lifestyle, zeal and love for one another, conservative faith, staunch beliefs, dress and moral code, stand on the Bible.

Kini: they were influenced by teachings from previous revival leaders. Beliefs and practices, the teachings of St. Paul on how to live the Christian life.

Baho: Brethren's behavior; they hate sin; they love God and look for help at the cross.

Diocese of Embu

Kagu: "origin is Rwanda."

Caal: dressing style where women were supposed to cover their heads and eating habits where women were served first.

Kima: they were able to identify and move away from sins.

Kahs: "the Bible is the source of all that we believe in and also do."

Kigi: before one was admitted as a member of EARM, one was required to stand in front of the congregation to denounce sin publicly and promise before God and those assembled that one would not live in sin. Norms of conduct were set by the East Africa Revivalists like polygamy, female initiation, snuff-taking, etc. Anyone who would get involved in sin would be excommunicated, and that was humiliating.

Diocese of Mount Kenya West

Otya: many fellowship meetings especially on Wednesdays where testimonies and the word of God are shared.

Diocese of Mount Kenya Central

Kigi: Biblical teachings.

Notations

Embu and Kirinyaga seem to have received indirect influences of Keswick theology and possibly from other spiritualities. The main components of responses from the perspectives of other purported forces apart from Keswick theology were as follows: the teachings of Rwanda and from the previous revival leaders, fellowships (convention) and Bible reading and instruction. The cross of Christ, confession of sin, love for one another, strict norms of dressing and conduct.

Theological students

They have never heard of Keswick theology. They said the influence was from a literal interpretation of the Scripture which leads to legalism.

Notations

Socio-ethical life was influenced by the literal interpretation of Scripture.

Clergy

Diocese of Mount Kenya Central

They were not aware of any alternative influence.

Diocese of Mount Kenya West

Caal: a life-changing personal encounter with the Lord Jesus Christ. They have uncompromising faith, accepting the plaiting of hair but condemning sin.

Otya: Conventions based on one major theme of walking in the light and fellowships within the districts of its jurisdiction.

Diocese of Embu

Mugu: Scripture and other practices of EARM.
Kahs: influenced by biblical teachings and other EARM norms.
Caal: they read Scripture non-selectively and love one another.

Diocese of Kirinyaga

Kini: " elders of my church including my grandfather . . . could camp at our home, the so-called Kesha (overnight) meetings and fellowships, preaching, sharing testimonies and encouraging one another. I was much attracted to this."

Kama: their conservative teaching, a way of giving testimony and selective contact with other members of society.

Notations

Mount Kenya Central seems unaware of any other alternative influences to the current socio-ethical life except Keswick theology. Other dioceses were aware of alternative influences like Scripture reading and teaching (conservative), sharing testimonies, separate life from society, strong faith, walking in the light and love for and fellowship with each other.

Bishops

Bishop of Embu
Other influences were literal interpretation of the Scripture and influence of modernity.

Bishop of Mount Kenya Central
Not aware.

Bishop of Mount Kenya West
Influence of Church growth.
Notations
Interpretation of Scripture and challenges of modernity could inform church growth influenced by the revival.

Prominent stakeholders

Mobo: Little or no theological knowledge, Victorian ideals from Europe and repression of Christian teachings on being human.

Wad: Born-again culture, strict moral discipline, the entrenchment of Pentecostalism and other forms of evangelical Christianity.

Gago: Strict religious position, moral, ethical conduct, legalistic theology, walking in the light, condemning social evils and peaceful coexistence by repentance and forgiveness. "Jomo Kenyatta was influenced by their teachings in 1963 when he told the young nation, 'forget the past, build the nation.' He also said let us forgive both the former collaborators who took us to Colonial jails plus the colonialists, though we shall never forget."

Notations
Other alternative influenced people with little or no theological knowledge. The impact of Victorian ideals, born-again culture, other forms of evangelical Christianity and the strict moral discipline (legalistic theology) of walking in the light, repentance, and forgiveness.

Describe Walking in the Light, Showing How It Could Have Brought Division in the Revival?

Ordinary members
Diocese of Kirinyaga

Kini: it means saying where they are going. *Utheri ware* (lets the light shine). They use this phrase when they go to the diocesan conventions. The group agrees that walking in the light has brought division.

Muri: it is telling others what one intends to do – walking in righteousness. Failure to walk in light brings division. New revelation or enlightenment has brought division in the forms of *Kufufuka* (reawakened), *Kupaa* (rising), *Mtama na maji* (millet and water), etc.

Kigu: it is scriptural; we are the light of the world, openness and keeping fellowship and acceptance among the Brethren. Division occurs due to leadership's *ngarari* (arguments), lack of brokenness and hypocrisy.

Kama: it is openness. This has brought division due to hypocrisy, long testimony – sometimes ridiculing the church especially youth, valuing testimonies more than the word of God.

Baho: it is accepting Jesus as a personal savior, walking with Jesus, walking in righteousness. The Kufufuka (reawakened) group and others split but returned later.

Diocese of Mount Kenya West

Caal: *Kumaniria ngoro* (reveals all, openness, even family issues); testimony is a part of walking in the light. In God, there is no darkness (John 1:5). They said walking in the light has not brought division except for those walking in darkness.

Kaba: "share with you, we are supposed to put in the light within ourselves everything good or bad. You are expected to know my stand from me not hearing from others. If I am out on a safari (journey), I am supposed to tell the Brethren I am away for prayer and that they don't wait for me."

Kiya: "without hypocrisy. Some followers were not truthful to the movement yet claiming they belong."

Diocese of Embu

Kagu Archdeaconry: talking about sins and the truth.

Kima: Being honest. It brought division in their way of greeting, introducing themselves and sharing a testimony. Nowadays some Brethren are not honest, and when something is not brought to light it causes divisions.

Caal: this is about talking the truth. In 1942 some pastors confused EARM's walking in the light for another denominations.

Kigi: this is confessing sins publicly to be saved by Jesus. Hence walk in the light under new birth. The text about Nicodemus (John 3:1–21) has been popular with Brethren as it emphasizes public declaration of faith. *Tuketenderezza Yesu* has become an identification tune of the EARM's fellowship.

Diocese of Mount Kenya Central

Kigi: It is putting the program of their daily activities on the table for the members to know.

Mugu: "the phrase has a meaning of testifying the bad and good things you do, used to do and asking for forgiveness. This causes disunity among Christians and even to the society at large."

Kadu: it is to say all about yourself. This brought division because some of the wrongs were done to the members of the fellowship.

Kiro: having a closer walk with the Lord.

Kaia: it is openness, no hypocrisy. Others forsake those perceived to be not walking in the light.

Notations

Openness, i.e., no hypocrisy and a daily walk with the Lord. But the open confession of sin and hypocrisy brought division.

Leaders of EARM

Diocese of Mount Kenya Central

Kaia: Open confession, repentance, forgiveness, date of salvation, and daily walk with God.

Kiro: it is openness, shedding the light of activities and events. However, Luke 19:8, returning stolen goods, asking for forgiveness regardless of whether the other party has accepted Christ or not, caused friction.

Kiui: sharing with the Brethren what you are doing or going through. Exposing lights outside the fellowship and derogatory statements "straight to heaven" has caused divisions.

Mugu: Sharing within Brethren right or bad experiences you are going through. This brings differences because the ones who confess without hiding blame those who don't share openly.

Kigi: it is shedding light about your program to the Brethren. It brought rift because some people were not open to some issues.

Kini: this is walking closely with the Lord, giving details of your testimony. But some testimonies confuse especially young people. For instance, when "one testifies that he was adulterous or a thief, it is like telling the young you can start like me and at my age, you get saved."

Diocese of Mount Kenya West

Guse: testifying without hypocrisy. Lack of transparency brings division.

Otya: doing everything truthfully among the brothers. If somebody is accused of not walking in the light on some known sins he or she is chased from the fellowship and told *thii ugethe Jesu* (search for Jesus).

Diocese of Embu

Kahs: saved person shares forthcoming activities like marriage, buying land or putting up a stone building. It is shedding light on daily matters, more so to the Brethren.

Kima: this is speaking of our sins in repentance; it also means telling the truth of our whereabouts, openness. It became divisive after the church accused it of "naughty" statements before children during testimonies.

Caal: to be transparent, and truthfulness. It led to a split after one's sin has been exposed.

Kagu: it is information to Brethren about your intentions, no darkness but openness. It brings division when one ignores walking in the light, or there is perceived darkness in your walk; one leaves the group or does not attend fellowship.

Kigi: this is a public confession of sins to be saved by Jesus Christ. It has contributed to division because a member could publicly confess sins that are touching the other group members. Due to shame, one could leave the fellowship. The other cause has been a holier than thou attitude among some members.

Nature and Current Trends Regarding Anglican Church Scholarship 431

Diocese of Kirinyaga

Baho: notifications of your intentions and activities, public confession of aspects of life. Those who oppose the light quit, or backslide.

Kini: sharing your personal life and regular testimony. Without testimony and walking in the light, one backslides and is forsaken by others.

Kigu: being open about yourself. If one is not open he ceases to be a member and may form another group.

Muri: it is openness within Brethren, repenting the long done sins. This caused division because of lack of trust, hypocrisy, exposing personal matters to outsiders and show of wealth. Those who fail to repent do it personally.

Kama: this is a confession of all sins. It has caused division due to its stress on purity thus keeps others away. It is long and tedious, and exposes the person.

Notations

The majority saw "walk in the light" as a daily walk with the Lord, a daily testimony, public confession and openness to God and humanity or sharing your personal life. The division came when one failed to share a testimony with other people. Thus, hypocritical holiness and exposure of one's secrets brought splits. That is, those who were perceived as not walking in the light were forsaken.

Theological students

EARM teaches public confession of sin, walking in the light, stress on salvation, emphasis on the Bible and sanctification. The beliefs and practices concern all Christians; modesty dressing like covering of hair by women and shaving beard by all men. Testimonies sometimes lead to social problems like family violence and breakups.

Notations

They noted public confession of sin, Bible teaching, and stress on sanctification. Strict dress code and damaging testimonies were obvious influences.

Clergy

Diocese of Kirinyaga

Kama: how to give testimony, fellowship, and visitations among the Brethren. It influences dress code – no beard, no miniskirts, and ladies cover their heads, ways of giving testimonies (sometimes long and exaggerated), repetition of repented sins, strict morals and ways of reading the Scripture.

Muri: it emphasis distinct lifestyle, righteousness, cleanliness, and shares your whereabouts. But dress code hinders many mostly youth.

Dok: it teaches confession of sin, about testimony. It influences lifestyle, commitment to Christians and morality, but has corrupted the theology of justification and sanctification, believes in "other salvation" (Spirit-filled or second blessing) apart from baptism.

Kini: it teaches confession of sins, Jesus as Lord and Savior, purity, brotherly love, prayer life, and daily Bible study. It influences concern for one another, checks on daily relationships, role models of Brethren clergy – walk in the light of God, but can be judgmental on non-Brethren, personalizing salvation, its theology molds many priests.

Diocese of Embu

Kagu: Teaches salvation, fellowships, Christian discipleship, deeper salvation experience (*kurikiria*) – 1 John 1:1–10, Christ is the light, no darkness, regenerates Christians' daily walk in the light. It influences Gospel incarnation into Africans' thought pattern and expressions, though mentioning of sins and hypocrisy kept many people away.

Caal: it teaches walking righteously with God, repentance, forgiveness, and humility. It influences social, ethical discipline – moral uprightness, but its focus on heaven slows economic activities. Also categorizing Christians affects social cohesion as some people feel they are not in the same ministry unless they follow their teachings and practices.

Kama Secondary: Teaches repentance, sanctification, openness and transparency and influences dress codes.

Mugu: illustrates sanctification, renewal, and openness among Brethren. It influences morality of the church in weekly fellowships, enhancing mission and evangelism.

Diocese of Mount Kenya West

Otya: It teaches the salvation message, that people might see Jesus and offers proper mentorship – gendered seating in the church. It influences antisocial attitude with non-Brethren and self-reliance; no bank loans. It also encourages modest dressing, disciplined worship, challenges charismatic lifestyle – public address system and clapping of hands.

Thuri: it teaches walking with God but fails to understand the meaning of walking in the light. It is seen as a church within a church and thus is not quite integrated because of its ensuing regulations.

Caal: Teaches Bible, Jesus, salvation, open repentance and confession, and firm faith. It is a biblical principle to walk in the light. "You are the light of the world." The late Bishop Obadiah Kariuki, a keen Brethren influenced Anglicans socially.

Diocese of Mount Kenya Central

Caal: it teaches about repentance, confession of sins and God's righteousness to inform our beliefs and practices like integrity and honesty reflected in our actions and behavior. However, there is no unity in church activities.

Kiui: it teaches attending fellowships, public confession of sins, restitution, and the Bible (John 3:21f). It influences walking in the light – transparency, and accountability.

Mugu: teaches public confession of sin and leaving a sinful lifestyle. However, it does not accept church census since their citizenship is in heaven. Ways of saying testimony differs from general Anglicans who only like to testify of what God has done for them.

Kiro: Sharing with Brethren every aspect of life. However, shedding some light brought divisions in the EARM. For example, a man shed light that he slept with a lay reader (woman). Another said he killed a man in the presence of children. Also holier-than-thou attitude brings division.

Notations

EARM teaches confession of sins, restitution, daily Bible study, sanctification and renewal, Christian discipleship, deeper salvation experience, walking righteously with God, Jesus is Lord and Savior, purity, brotherly love, prayer life and about fellowship with one another. It influences legalism; dress code, corrupted theology and is judgmental, leading to a church within the church or categorizing Christians, hypocrisy, and shedding of deep lights.

Bishops

Bishop of Mount Kenya West

Church growth and spirituality is founded on these teachings; an open-hearted ethical life which is biblically based. Jesus was against hypocrisy (not in the light). Walking in the light emphasizes the new man, family stability, and modest dressing.

Bishop of Mount Kenya Central

Walking in the light teaches repentance, forgiveness, restitution, fellowship with God and each other, self-examination, how to be right with God and other people. It influences transparency and accountability in Christian life and particularly in church leadership.

Bishop of Embu

Walking in the light teaches centrality of Scripture, confession of sins and focus on heaven. It influences leaders to be a light to the world – provides social and spiritual direction. Most senior clergy are the product of EARM; affirms anti-alcoholism, dressing ethics, walking in the light.

Notations

Walking in the light teaches centrality of Scripture, repentance, forgiveness and restitution, open-hearted ethical life, being right with God and other people. It influences renewal and the new man, family life, moral code and openness in Christian life and leadership.

Prominent stakeholders

Gago: it teaches confession before preaching, as friends meet, singing its anthem and encouraging public officers to be open and speak up against injustice. It is legalistic, *ribia ritwo ribia* (sin be called sin), too open to the extent of hurting them socially. Second or third wives viewed as a sin, no bank loans or keeping dogs or security officers. It fails to document their theology by publication, hence getting overtaken by the Pentecostal wave; no budgets, no bureaucracy, no membership lists, no subscription fees, no minutes, no officials, no salaries, no headquarters, etc. However, EARM's approach could help Kenyans overcome tribalism, corruption, hypocrisy, xenophobia or hatred for Somalis, who are seen as terrorists.

Wad: it teaches the need to be born again, to be broken at the cross, to be saved by the blood of Jesus, the need to testify to this salvation, confess sinful life before getting saved (testimony); discipline of conversion and walking in the light – strong disincentive to committing sin after salvation – can lead to hypocrisy; critique of the worldly church; need to preach to Christians and non-Christians to get saved, even clergy, it refrains from politics and owns up to shortcomings. It upholds honesty and openness but can be judgmental, holier than thou attitude – hypocritical – opposite of walking in the light.

EARM is "ideal" for evangelical churches, though the majority might not conform to the model. The Anglican, Methodist, and Presbyterian churches have been profoundly influenced but have many "unsaved" members. Pentecostal churches often claim to consist of the saved, but this is not true for the mainline churches. Sexual ethics – emphasis on abstinence, monogamy, and faithfulness within marriage, though not exemplified in the life of the church. These ethical standards justify hostility against homosexuality, but criminalization of gay relations by state suggests lapse from the ethics of earlier *Balokole* which thought the government could not enforce morality.

Hald: it teaches Keswick moral values, the evangelical doctrine of salvation – emphasis on renewal and personal conversion. However the focus on moral issues can become moralism – can diminish the gospel of grace and forgiveness, but when the practice of repentance is within the economy of grace it can be a vibrant life in Christ and witness to the power of transformed living in the world. It has a strict legacy: a strong emphasis on moral rectitude, the holiness of life, a genuine conversion.

Mwda: it teaches receiving Christ into your life as Savior and Lord, repentance and faith; testify publicly, restitution, walk in the light, Bible study and constant prayer, firm testimony, attend fellowship and conventions, wait with zeal for the coming of our Lord Jesus Christ and His kingdom, discipline of accountability. Most clergy and Bishops are influenced; candidates selected for theological training are often expected to give testimony.

Mobo: it acknowledges the sinful status of humanity, confession of sin, walking in the light, commitment to lead a perfect life, "I was influenced by a Quaker ethos in terms of recognizing that [the image] of God in all people and living the teachings of Jesus in the way I treat people." Its theology does not impact on life, only on most of the leaders as far as the doctrine of salvation is concerned but not reflected in the socio-ethical life. Anglican lifestyle has been influenced by the society around. The leadership has no particular theology but appears schizophrenic in faith. For survival's sake, they rely on who has power and manipulate the power to survive. There is a disconnect between the theology and lifestyle of the members.

Kaja: it teaches confession, repentance, and radical moral transformation. Although it is biblically based, it can at times be intrusive. As late as the 1990s, all candidates for ordained ministry were expected to have been actively involved in the EARM; Kiambu district revival fellowship still meets once a year at St. Paul's University, a practice that began in 1930s when Bishop Obadiah Kariuki and Canon Elijah Gachanja taught at the school.

Notations

Bishops noted significance of confession of sinful life, born again, holiness, moral rectitude, genuine conversion, walking in the light, the blood of Jesus, restitution, Bible study, prayer and firm testimony. Many were influenced including clergy, though some are hypocritical. Walking in the light teaches a strong disincentive to sin and repentance within the economy of grace.

What's the Dominant Text(s) Used by Members That Could Have Led to the Split

Ordinary members

Diocese of Mount Kenya Central

Kigi: Not aware.

Mugu: Isaiah 1:18 "Come now, let us reason together, says the Lord. Though your sins are like scarlet, they shall be as white as snow; though they are red as crimson, they shall be as wool." There are also other biblical texts given during their meetings.

Kadu: 2 Cor 6:14–18; they emphasize verse 17, "Therefore come out from them and be separate."

Kiro: "Do not put off the Spirit's fire" (1 Thess 5:19).

Kaia: "Therefore, if anyone is in Christ, he is a new creation; the old has gone, the new has come!" (2 Cor 5:17)

Diocese of Embu

Kagu: "Come to me all you who are weary and burdened and I will give you rest . . ." (Matt 11:28–30). Also, Matt 5:13–14, "you are the salt of the earth . . . you are the light of the world . . ." and Mark 1:15 ("Repent for the Kingdom of God is near"). This text was used to challenge those who were not in fellowship with the Brethren. Also, see Matthew 13:30 (wheat and tares to grow together until the harvest).

Kima: there is no particular text, mostly use Acts 9 which demonstrates change from Saul to Paul.

Caal: Jeremiah 7:3 "This is what the Lord Almighty, the God of Israel, says: Reform your ways and your actions, and I will let you live in this place."

Kigi: Not aware.

Diocese of Kirinyaga

Baho: Romans 12:17–21 (don't revenge) and other texts as God would reveal.

Kini: no dominant texts: but texts that teach against sin.

Muri: depends on season and revelation from God.

Kigu: Philippians 3:1–12 (no confidence in the flesh) but monthly readings and context are given prominence.

Kama: Exodus 10:27–29 (The Lord hardened Pharaoh's heart); Numbers 21:4–9 (people complained; look at the bronze snake, and you shall live); 1 Corinthians 1:9 "God, who has called you into fellowship with his Son Jesus Christ our Lord, is faithful"; Revelation 3:1–2 "He who has an ear, let him hear what the Spirit says to the churches"; Isaiah 43:1 ("Fear not, for I have redeemed you").

Diocese of Mount Kenya West

Kiya: no dominant text; they believe all Scripture is God-breathed.

Caal: No single verse is given dominance in the Bible.

Kaba: Hebrews 10:25 (not forfeit fellowship).

Notations

There was no dominant biblical text.

Leaders of EARM

Diocese of Mount Kenya Central

Kiro: Luke 19:8, Zacchaeus returned illegal possessions has been used to justify returning stolen goods, seeking forgiveness from accomplices in crime. The interpretation of Genesis 12:1 led parents to desert their unwedded pregnant daughters and would not even attend their weddings. Also, Daniel 1:8ff led some Brethren to refuse kingly food and to shun social gatherings.

Kaia: Lack of *walk in light* leads to being sidelined.

Kitu: dress code 1 Corinthians 11:13–15 Brethren took this text literally, and many youths left the church in the 1990s over hair and clothing.

Mugu: notes about three groups: firstly, *Simama* has been noted for the use of the phrase *Yesu atosha* (Jesus satisfies); secondly, Kufufuka says they have been raised from sins. Members share two testimonies, one about being born again (saved) and the other about when one was raised or revived (Eph 5:14). Thirdly, *Mtama na maji* (sorghum and water) led to Kupaa faction, that lays its foundation on Daniel 1:8–15 (Daniel refused kingly food).

Kigi: Not sure of the text.

Kini: Genesis 12:1ff, some Brethren interpreted it to mean saved people should leave their unsaved families.

Diocese of Mount Kenya West

Guse: No dominant text.

Otya: 1 Timothy 5:23, St. Paul's challenge to drink a little alcohol led to some members keeping a little wine in their houses. Some saw it a sinful and left the fellowship.

Diocese of Embu

Kahs: in the 1970s there were social and economic problems; borrowing loans became a challenge to the borrowers. Interpretation of Daniel 1:8–21 led to *Kupaa* group and which was against earthy influence. Others argued that leadership struggles were another cause of splits.

Kima: text on confession with your mouth (Rom 10:9), some Brethren confessed by mentioning their sins while others refused. But try to live well with all men (Rom 12:18).

Caal: Isaiah 60:1 "Arise, Shine for your light has come." EARM is about walking in the light but many walk in darkness.

Kagu: issues of repenting and confessing; forced to repent sins you don't know, you leave the group for not repenting (repent for the kingdom of God is near); keeping of dogs made Brethren not visit *Matofu* in Uganda. Some were killed because they were regarded as a sin.

Kigi: interpretation of Ephesian 5:14 meant that the saved should be saved anew. But Ephesians 6:13–20 was used by *Kusimama* (standing up) group to encourage Christians to withstand challenges.

Diocese of Kirinyaga

Baho: some said it was an individual decision, not a biblical text. Others cited text like Daniel 1:12 (give us nothing but vegetables to eat and water to drink). This led to *Mtama na Maji,* which means millet and water. This formed *Kupaa* (rising) group that set itself for simple life, e.g., no wedding cake or expensive wedding dress, etc. Also, Genesis 12:1 ("Leave your country and your people . . ."). Some sold everything and "physically" left their families for distant places to serve God.

Kini: texts related to filling of the Holy Spirit (Pentecostalism), Kaggia brought speaking in tongues in 1946 leading to a split.

Kigu: Ephesians 5:14, "Wake up O sleeper, rise from the dead, and Christ will shine on you." This led to *Kufufuka* (reawakening) that accused other members who were not awakened as dead. Other texts include those against sin and thus call for confession, repentance, and forgiveness, e.g., Ezekiel 18:4 ("the soul that sins shall surely die"); Romans 10:9 (confession); John 3:16 (God's love for the world).

Muri: John 11:25 "I am the resurrection and the life" is a pleasant verse for Kufufuka who claim to follow the resurrected Christ; Ephesians 5:14 led to Kufufuka in 1967 – "Arise" was to leave EARM; Daniel 1:8f to live like Daniel, shun the royal meal at king's table for water and vegetables. Thus, applied as *Mtama na Maji* (see above) which was understood in 1969 as leaving EARM to form another group.

Kama: Hebrews 10:24–25 regular fellowship and meetings; James 1:19–21 giving of testimony; 2 Corinthians 6:14–16 separation from unbelievers; 2 Corinthians 3:2–3 demonstration of purity; 1 Corinthians 11:15–16 men should not keep beards and women should cover their heads.

Notations

There were a couple of recurring texts: Daniel 1: 8ff; Genesis 12:1ff; Ephesians 5:14; 1 Corinthians 11:15–16; Romans 10:9; and 2 Corinthians 6:14–18 were also mentioned by the ordinary members.

Theological students

Genesis 12:1–3 *Thama;* Ephesians 5:14 *Kufufuka;* Daniel 1:12 *Mtama na Maji*

Clergy

Diocese of Kirinyaga
Kama: Not aware.
Muri: No particular text, except the one circulated by the leaders.
Dok: Not aware.
Kini: 1 Corinthians 11:1–7, particularly verse 5 "And every woman who prays or prophesies with her head uncovered dishonors her head" – it is as though her head were shaved. 2 Corinthians 6:14 says, "Do not be yoked together with unbelievers. For what do righteousness and wickedness have in common? Or what fellowship can light have with darkness?"

Diocese of Embu
Kagu: Ephesians 5:14, some believers claim to have *ufufuo* (resurrection) while others do not. Also, biblical teachings of Romans 7 as opposed to Romans 8.
Caal: 2 Timothy 2:9 "God's word is not chained."
Kahs: Not aware.
Mugu: Female circumcision controversy led to split.

Diocese of Mount Kenya West
Otya: Mark 10:21 "Sell everything you have and give to the poor, then follow me"; Isaiah 3:16 haughty women . . . adornment with rings; Acts 2:45 selling everything; 1 Corinthians 11:14 dress code; issues of long and short hair.
Thri: no idea.
Caal: Daniel 1:8ff in Kiambu 1987 led to a split from EARM known as *Mtama na Maji*. They referred to Daniel's story and refused to eat the king's delicacies. In Murag'a the split became the people of the light and based their belief on 1 John 2:9–11, saying *ithui nituonete utheri* (we have seen the light). It thus came to be called *Ngwataniro ya utheri* (fellowship of the light) based on Matthew 5:14. They accept "praise the Lord" greetings, do not accept

weddings of expectant girls nor renewal marriages; the third group came to be called "revival fellowship" which believes in walking in the light.

Diocese of Mount Kenya Central

Caal: Revelation 18:4–8; 2 Corinthians 6:14–18; Matthew 8:10–12; Matthew 15:1–2; Romans 4:10–12.

Kitu: Daniel 1:8ff, Daniel, and his friends refused to eat good food from the king's table.

Mugu: 1 Corinthians 11:14 women to cover their heads while praying.

Notations

Some repeated texts: 1 Corinthians 11:14; 2 Corinthians 6:14–18; Ephesians 5:14; Daniel 1:8ff.

Bishops

Mount Kenya West

There were no particular texts, but a social lifestyle; dress code, shaving of the hair leads to walking in the light (Utheri) faction.

Mount Kenya Central

Ephesians 5:14; Daniel 1:12

Embu

No particular text. Splits caused by personal differences; old clergy wanted to take up leadership of EARM. There were also social life differences leading (2005–2008) to different fellowships, i.e., Nembure and Kiangima (worked with the church).

Notations

Bishop of Mount Kenya central indicated Ephesians 5:14; Daniel 1:12 as the cause of split.

Prominent stakeholders

Gago: Proverbs 13:20; John 15:13; Proverbs 27:6; Amos 3:3; 2 Corinthians 6:14, 17.

Wad: Ephesians 5:14 is basic to the Reawakened, *Abazukufu*; those who constantly confess sins after conversion are dead, they have no power of the Spirit to overcome sin. Ordinary *Balokole* is dead, *abafu*. The split was formalized in 1972.

Hald: Not sure.

Mwda: Daniel 1:8ff; Romans 13:8 (let no debt remain outstanding); 2 Corinthians 6:17 (come out from them and be separate).

Mobo: resurrection stories of Jesus; interpretation of the meaning of the death of Jesus based on love or the blood of Jesus – thus love for Christ's church in Africa, and mainstream stressed the blood of Jesus.

Kaja: Biblical interpretation not solely responsible; each faction used their favorite biblical texts to support positions that they already held. Also, strong personalities and divergent attitudes to cultural practices could have led to splits.

Notations

The most recurring texts were Daniel 1:8ff, 2 Corinthians 6:17; 2 Corinthians 6:14; Ephesians 5:14.

Briefly Describe the History of the Split in EARM, Showing How It Has Affected the Mission of the Church

Ordinary members of EARM

Diocese of Mount Kenya Central

Kiro: the holier-than-thou attitude has hampered the church mission.

Mugu: division came due to misinterpretation and understanding of testimony. This affected the growth of the church mission.

Kadu: division affects church growth and financial base.

Kigi: division brought by some people advocating to be governed by cultural beliefs and practices while others sought biblical teachings. Also, public confession of sins brought tensions.

Kaia: division brought by lack of openness and doubt of others' salvation. This brought enmity and mistrust among Brethren and with other Christians, weakening their mission.

Diocese of Kirinyaga

Kama: interpretation of various biblical passages and leadership wrangles brought division. This affected the church's mission: deprived of leadership who had good testimonies, young people declined to join the fellowships, no motivation in the church to accede to the fellowship, no Brethren support of church activities, no church support for Brethren activities.

Kigu: disagreement with the vicar, damaging testimony. This has led to hypocrisy and lack of brokenness in the church.

Muri: took place in 1967 between reawakening (resurrected) and the dead (born again) in 1967. There were confusing testimonies some saying they were resurrected and accusing others of deadness. Apart from reawakened (*uriukio, kufufuka*), other splits were *Mtama na Maji* (sorghum and water), *ona Yesu* (see Jesus) and Kusimama (Stand). This led to separation among the Brethren.

Kini: division started in 1970. It impacted the mission of the church positively particularly with a smart dress code and preaching from the Bible.

Baho: took place in 1980 when Kufufuka (Arise or Awakening) split from East Africa Revival Movement.

Diocese of Embu

Kigi: in the 1960s, Brethren's initial enthusiasm and holiness had lapsed in terms of dress, fashion and aggressive witnessing. This split originated from a leading lay evangelist from Baganda, Mr. William Nagenda. In his sermons, he emphasized that revived Christians should avoid worldly involvement, particularly to refrain from bank loans. This was guided by Ephesians 5:14 which required those who were saved to be saved again leading to the *Awake* (Kwarahuka or Kuriuka) group. Some Brethren disagreed with this campaign and saw nothing wrong with taking bank loans to improve their welfare. This led to separate meetings. In 1956 the *Nthama* (Exodus) faction sprang up in Nairobi. They regarded traditional nicknames to be a sin. They identified themselves with the *Kuhama* (Exodus) group. The other faction is *Kusimama* (Standing) emphasizing Christians to stand firm to withstand challenges (Eph 6:13–15). Finally came *Kupaa/Mtama na Maji* (Sorghum and water) which came to be known as ascension/rising up. However, there hasn't been a serious disagreement within Revival Fellowship in Embu and Mbeere. They remain united but not uniform.

Caal: it was due to a leadership misunderstanding which led to beginning some new denominations.

Kima: division began in 1960s when "two lights" arose, one had an open confession of sins, and the other was not open. After the 1970s "deep lights" (personal testimonial lights) were discouraged because of mistrust within the members. There were "lights" that acted as rules or codes of ethics, e.g., dress and hair codes.

Kagu: it came when the team members stopped walking together. The ensuing different views and ideas affected the mission.

Diocese of Mount Kenya West

Kaba: rebuke to the revivalist for not giving money for mission.
Caal: not aware.
Kiya: conflict with church leadership.

Notations

It was noted that division began in 1956; later *Nthama* in Nairobi became *Kuhama,* then became *Kusimama* (Eph 6:14–20) and 1967 Re-awakening (Eph 5:14) which was led by William Nagenda. Another faction was *Kupaa.* There were other internal splits of "lights" in 1969. Others claimed the 1970s and 1980s. But most of them noted the 1967 date. Leadership and legalistic codes of conduct, and devastating testimonies were also blamed for the split. This caused disharmony in the mission field which affected church growth.

Leaders of EARM

Diocese of Kirinyaga

Kama: split has led to new fellowships, new denominations, backsliding and desertion by young people. The fellowship is not involved in church activities.

Muri: it began with conventions in Uganda. The preaching from Psalm 127:1ff encouraged people to trust God for protection, no need for dogs for security. Also, interpretation of Ephesians 5:14 led to "reawakening" group claiming they have resurrected. This confused the members, leading to separation.

Kigu: By 1967 fellowship was one: but different beliefs and practices like not to keep dogs, not to tolerate pregnant daughters and not have debts. For example, *Ufufuo, mtama na maji* (kupaa) and the quest for leadership have brought harm to the mission of the church.

Kini: history began in Nairobi; leaders had a meeting and refused to accept the new movement but some accepted.

Baho: Not aware.

Diocese of Embu

Kagu: there were divisions in the fellowship; some held meetings at home, others left the church, weakness of clergy versus fellowship. Thus, no effective mission, as each justified its positions leading to different missions from either group.

Caal: fighting for leadership positions. Some members started their own churches.

Kima: people sought a salvation (saved) that does not mention sin.

Kahs: division weakened EARM's unity, slowed its witness spirit, with each defending its theological stand and thus failed witness to the church.

Kigi: beginning 1960s following a lapse in holiness (Eph 5:14) and witnessing, refrain from a bank loan, being saved anew for the saved leading to awake group and separate meetings. They separated from culture due to beliefs and practices. In 1956 there emerged *Nthama* faction, then *Kusimama* (Eph 6:14–20) and *Kupaa/Mtama na Maji*.

Diocese of Mount Kenya West

Otya: leadership; some fellowship leaders were leaders in the church. So they had followers, and their division caused wrangles.

Guse: Not aware.

Mount Kenya Central

Kini: EARM separates from others (sinners), and this affects the mission, Jesus came for such not the righteous.

Kigi: due to the unequal recognition of members.

Mugu: revival arrived in Kenya in 1930s as one block, like a church within church, different fellowship meetings leading to unbiblical founded mission.

Kitu: the 1969 oath-taking led to the split. Some went to Pentecostal churches; dress code (1 Cor 11:14–16), youth left the church in the 1990s over hair and clothing, public address system and Pentecostal worship. Parents abandoned daughters who become pregnant before marriage (father refused to attend such weddings). Also, dowry payment in terms of beer caused the split.

Kiro: division came when confessing Christians were excommunicated from mainstream churches. Some members took an oath (during Kenya's struggle for independence) and others never claiming they had drunk the blood of Jesus. This brought serious split with some members joining other churches.

Another cause of division was conservatism whereby some members stressed issues like dressing, plaiting of hair (1 Cor 11:14–16). Thus youth left the church in 1997 – 1998 in Kimathi region (accused of not being born again). Also, public address system was not appreciated as Brethren claimed to pray loudly is a sin. Those who pray loudly and in tongues were seen as sinners.

Genesis 12:1ff led to some people in Murang'a to desert their daughters who gave birth at home or refuse to attend weddings of such daughters. Deriving from Daniel 1:8ff many Brethren did not go to gatherings because the food was worldly.

Kaia: division was due to lack of openness, doubt of others' salvation, enmity and mistrust among Brethren and with other Christians.

Notations

The Uganda Convention, and Psalm 127:1ff encouraged people to rely on God's protection, not on dogs. Also, interpretation of Ephesians 5:14 led to reawakening. Some note that the fellowship was one before 1967. Some think in Kenya split began in Nairobi; there is mention of *Nthama* 1956 and another meeting in Nairobi that confirmed the split. Ephesians 6:14–20 was applied by *Kusimama* group to stand against Kufufuka group. 1969 oath-taking also led to divisions. Some left for Pentecostal churches due to the interpretation of 1 Corinthians 11:14–16 that oppressed the youth. In 1990s lots of youth left Anglican for Pentecostal churches. Genesis 12:1ff led to some parents abandoning their unwedded pregnant daughters. This has affected the mission of the church due to mistrust within the church, separation, inequality, excommunication and a poorly-biblically founded mission.

Theological students

Not aware.

Clergy

Diocese of Kirinyaga

Kama: splits have led to liberalism in the church exemplified by women becoming clergy. However, youth left the fellowship leading to declining morals in the church and society.

Muri: Too much shedding of light brings division.

Dok: not sure.

Kini: Holier-than-thou attitude that differed with youth. EARM seemed like a church within a church.

Diocese of Embu

Kagu: EARM opposed hierarchy structures of the church and conflicted with bishops. Also, poor interpretation and application of biblical texts brought splits.

Caal: avoid reading the Scripture selectively and embrace all believers.

Kama Secondary: theological differences brought a split. It slowed down evangelism.

Mugu: Not sure.

Diocese of Mount Kenya West

Otya: observes doctrinal issues and financial management as the primary cause of splits.

Guse: aware of splits but notes competing interests of different groups affect the mission.

Caal: the split affected the church negatively especially central Kenya where *Utheri* Fellowship was strongly led by the late Bishop Obadiah Kariuki. This resulted in controversy in central Kenya. Some clergy opposed open confession of sins and recommended disclosure should be made secretly to God.

Diocese of Mount Kenya Central

Caal: a cloud of confusion particularly to the young generation, lack of synergy for church growth and development.

Kitu: The movement has lost virtues like holiness, love, no longer carry burdens or support its members. This has led to weakening the mission because others lose confidence in the fellowship.

Mugu: EARM exemplifies hypocritical holiness which leads to separation affecting mission because EARM is a key part of the Anglican Church.

Notations

Most respondents avoided the history part of the question but were comfortable with effects. For example, they noted liberalism as women became clergy, declining morals as the youth left the fellowship, church hierarchy conflicts with fellowship, poor biblical teaching and theological differences, open confession of sins and hypocritical holiness. Some observe a declining evangelism and apathy.

Bishops

Mount Kenya West

He noted a congregation split into two, bought a plot and build a church.

Mount Kenya Central

Not aware.

Bishop of Embu

Split in Embu (2005–2008) affected conventions because Brethren are both members of the church and fellowship. This led to decline in spirituality.

Notations

They were not quite aware of the earlier splits but impacts were construction of a new church, effects on conventions and a drop in spirituality.

Prominent stakeholders

Gago: splits have weakened EARM. They were brought on by lack of theological training and versions of being saved. He noted that revival has no leader but the Holy Spirit, but some retired teachers imposed themselves, isolating others. The habit of attacking clergy as not saved weakened their bargaining power. They dismissed Canon Johana Njumbi as not saved for using tobacco.

It dates from 1937. In 1967 *Arahuka*, basing its position on Ephesians 5:14, remained like an opposition party within a church assassinating one another while hiding under walking in the light. Thus its mission weakened, with youths joining Pentecostal churches.

Wad: noted earlier as a result of Ephesians 5:14 leading to the formalization of the split in 1972. *Balokole* movement has always been at loggerheads with the "nominal" church. Recently revival saw itself as the legislators of the church with the majority of Anglican bishops claiming to be part of the revival. Evangelical Revivalists are often at the heart of church-sponsored mission activities and on a personal level in evangelism.

Hald: only general knowledge.

Mwda: splits compromised real witness of the Brethren all over East Africa.

Mobo: *Joremo* vs. *Johera* splits; Johera loved polygamists but Joremo (the True Anglicans) were hypocritical, not wanting them near. Sexuality issues challenges the Anglican Church today, for example, lesbian, gay, bisexual, transgender and intersex (LGBTI). Some church leaders have accepted criminalization of LGBTI people.

Kaja: it was 1970s, not sure of details.

Notations

Splits in revival began in 1937; *Joremo* vs. *Johera*. Some mention 1967; the *Abafu* (dead) and *Bazukufu* (reawakened). Brethren attacked clergy saying they were not saved. The youth were joining Pentecostal churches. This compromised witness though the majority of Anglican bishops claimed to be part of the revival, some accepting to criminalize LGBTI.

What Change Would You Recommend for the Current Socio-ethical Life?

Ordinary members' responses
Diocese of Mount Kenya West

Kaba: no change; it's an individual conscience between you and God.

Caal: All, not just EARM to repent and turn to God (Rom 10:1), to be saved not just repentance to avoid nominal Christians.

Kiya: it's good to know the motive of EARM. It is a vehicle to help people grow spiritually and not a faction.

Diocese of Kirinyaga

Kama: to stick to God's word and not our beliefs and knowledge. Testimonies should not be a measure of personal salvation, rather it should glorify God.

Kigu: to have a biblical foundation; modest dress code and friendly testimonies.

Muri: should attract young people and avoid rigid fellowship or laws. Brethren should be incorporated in the preaching program and priests should provide mentorship.

Kini: advocated status quo: that people should dress well; respect gender dress and observe teaching about the hairstyle.

Baho: encouraged a proper handling of the neophytes.

Diocese of Embu

Kagu: to obey the Bible, have one faith, understand God's law and change revival leadership.

Kigi: to accommodate fashion norms, reach out to all languages and avoid micromanaging youth.

Caal: allow hugging of opposite sex particularly by the young people.

Kima: Encouraged to revert to former Brethren ways, to be good mentors for youth and clergy, allow Christ headship of our lives and to be honest new creations.

Diocese of Mount Kenya Central

Kigi: Brethren to be role models, doing as the Bible teaches, embrace church economic activities and be sensitive to what they say at social gatherings to avoid vices.

Kiro: to embrace changes in the twenty-first century in the church.

Mugu: Brethren encouraged to adopt improved social life.

Kadu: EARM to embrace change and to avoid legalistic rules that hinder youth to join fellowship.

Kaia: to shy away from hypocrisy, theft, drunkenness, laziness and strict dress code.

Notations

Embrace a changed social life (modesty), return to old Brethren lifestyle, and good mentors for youth and clergy, church to use Brethren, proper use of the Bible and practice constructive testimonies.

Leaders of EARM

Diocese of Kirinyaga

Kama: to sensitize people on the word of God, proper nurture of converts and encourage conventions.

Muri: word of God should guide the converts, not socio-ethical rules. Avoid self-centerdness, wealthy and poor should coexist (equality). Help the less fortunate to harness unity.

Kigu: Address the dress code (my dress my choice), dowry price and secularism. Engage youth. Avoid other activities during Brethren Sunday and clergy to provide proper mentorship for youth.

Kini: Encourage modest dressing – avoid fashions and makeup that show nakedness. Makeup fosters inequality.

Baho: to relax dress code and allow makeup; girls should not go near men (behave like animals), respect gender roles; men should not wear earrings and necklace, short hair or headscarf for women and no decoration.

Diocese of Embu

Kagu: Encourage unity of clergy and Brethren, provide one fellowship Sunday per month, and walk in the light and clergy to teach salvation.

Caal: to relax dressing style; women should be allowed to preach with or without a headscarf.

Kima: "we should identify and repent our sins, 'sins' have returned to the church. We should state sins in our testimonies and speak the truth."

Kahs: focus on the spiritual renaissance in the church and respond to negative socio-ethical issues like corruption in Kenya.

Kigi: Address the generation gap; should not condemn youth, appreciate African heritage's positive values – circular sitting during fellowship meetings is African. New Testament should not be used as an instruction manual for norms; overly burdensome teaching and preaching. Encouraged to use lectionary readings because not all saved people can preach. Need preaching lessons.

Diocese of Mount Kenya West

Otya: avoid holier-than-thou attitude.

Guse: accept the transformation.

Diocese of Mount Kenya Central

Kini: EARM to accept the ministry of the Holy Spirit and allow change.

Kigi: to address dress code, uphold morality and engage in economic activities.

Mugu: should join self-help social groups and avoid being conservative, should not compare 1930s or 1950s salvation standards with today, and accommodate young people who confess Christ and have good morals.

Kitu: to address dress code, to embrace twenty-first century culture and Brethren to embrace healthy African culture and norms.

Kiro: teaching about dress code, embrace good morals, good cultural activities and all accept Christ.

Kaia: shy away from hypocrisy, theft, drunkenness, laziness and dress code.

Notations

They emphasized moderate dress code, encouraged fellowship to join social groups, good mentorship for youth, clergy to include Brethren in the Sunday Church program, proper use of the Bible and embracing healthy cultural norms and activities.

Theological students

Brethren should learn interpretation of the Bible, appreciate dynamism in fellowship and accommodate other people, especially youth.

Notations

Bible should be used correctly and fellowship to be inclusive.

Clergy

Diocese of Mount Kenya Central

Mugu: EARM and the Anglican Church should work together to fight the devil than fight each other. EARM should be less strict on morals.

Kigu: EARM to be less conservative, embrace change as most Brethren are old people.

Caal: to preach and teach the unity of purpose based on Ephesians 4, one God, one Spirit and one hope.

Diocese of Mount Kenya West

Caal: everyone should be saved but confess sins to God alone.

Thuri: Emphasis on the oneness of God.

Otya: Allow interaction between both sexes and enrich all church departments.

Diocese of Embu

Mugu: revisit public relations, dress code and morality, and handling marriage conflict.

Kama Secondary: to dress decently and believers walk as per their confession.

Caal: there should be freedom to worship in the truth and in the Spirit.

Kagu: Fellowships should carefully handle the Scripture in the Spirit to bring harmony and growth of the church. Should provide for conflict resolution and not just condemn without enough information.

Diocese of Kirinyaga

Kini: Encourage salvation for all, a special workshop for believers on spirituality and Brethren to embrace change.

Dok: to strike a balance between nominalism and holier-than-thou attitude.

Muri: to give room for change and avoid rigidity.

Kama: teach the actual Word of God, encourage worship dynamics and recognize Brethren in the church.

Notations

To balance between nominalism and holier-than-thou hypocrisy, allow dynamism in worship, recognize Brethren in church, proper exegesis of the Bible, embrace change, a workshop on spirituality, allow interaction of young people of both sexes and unity as per Ephesians 4, oneness of God.

Bishops

Embu

Uphold EARM's heritage of addressing sin but allow change. The church should mediate between Brethren and other Christians.

Mount Kenya Central

Encourage Christians on repentance and transparency.

Mount Kenya West

The church should imitate EARM's way (strict ethics – e.g. no beards) and bring people to church.

Notations

They encouraged the church to address sin; allow change, repentance, and transparency. Others felt the church should embrace EARM (heritage) moral conduct.

Prominent stakeholders

Kaja: Not aware.

Mobo: socio-ethical life should be led by the life and ministry of Jesus, more re-reading of the Bible in the light of the scientific discoveries of today. The leaders should be visionary and imaginative.

Mwda: Bishops should be transferrable to share their gifts with the whole Anglican Church of Kenya.

Hald: Anglican tradition concerns for the entire life should foster holistic discipleship and define whole life as Christ's followers.

Ward: The Anglican Church should value its revival heritage, encourage new forms of spirituality among young people, while teaching the importance of worship and practices of the Anglican Church, and promote great flexibility and tolerance of different views. Church leaders should learn from Anglicans in other parts of the world to value sexual minorities.

Gago: this is a challenge because there is no true Anglican Church in Kenya. It combines elements of African culture, Pentecostalism, EARM but the mode of confession and testimony remains EARM. In the Kenyan ecclesiology, it remains rainbow spirituality.

Notations

They emphasized revival heritage, new forms of spirituality, encouraged flexibility and tolerance, value sexual minorities, holistic discipleship, re-reading the Bible from the perspectives of scientific discoveries, visionary leaders, socio-ethics led by life and ministry of Jesus. They noted there is no pure Anglican Church in Kenya. Indeed the Anglican Church mode of confession and testimony is EARM and Pentecostalism with some elements of African culture.

Is There Anything You Would Wish to Share Which Has Not Been Covered Above?

Ordinary members' responses

Diocese of Mount Kenya Central

Mugu: Brethren should set good moral examples

Kadu: A social-economic gathering is not sinful. Some Brethren are wealthy, yet advocate for a strict dress code and hairstyle. This confuses people.

Kiro: no comment.

Kigi: that a convention theme trickles down to the local fellowship level.

Kaia: no leadership in the fellowship, all are equal, and Christ is the chief priest. Marriage renewal is accepted.

Diocese of Embu

Kima: we should avoid dishonesty; ask people to join fellowships and church should embrace Brethren. People should seek forgiveness before partaking of Holy Communion. Brethren should command respect as it was before.

Caal: EARM has relaxed legalism; ladies could attend fellowship without headscarf but does not allow dancing for the Lord in their forums.

Kigi: No comment.

Kagu: they follow a stereotypical fellowship liturgy in their meetings.

Diocese of Mount Kenya West

Kiya: everyone is welcome to the fellowship but must abide by its rules.

Caal: East Africa is not a movement but a fellowship. It is a fellowship of all Christians who confess Christ not just for Anglican. It has no registration list for its members.

Kaba: the fellowship is between you and God. You live well and you are blessed. You go to God; he goes for you.

Diocese of Kirinyaga

Baho: Brethren wishes clergy and youth would join them, should have a revival week, and respect EARM's forums. Ministerial formation for clergy is not acceptable.

Kini: Brethren shouldn't sacrifice their families for the convention. Their testimony should be reconciliatory. Brethren show God's righteousness and should be smartly dressed. The fellowship is united in Christ.

Muri: emphasis on righteousness and cleanliness. The clergy should support the EARM. Youth should return to the fellowship.

Kigu: the clergy and theological students should join the fellowship. Lecturers should follow-up students during mission outreaches. The students training for ministry should know it is a calling and not a job. The church should recognize fellowships.

Kama: No Comment.

Notations

Brethren encouraged clergy and students to join the fellowship and that the Brethren should be recognized in the church (allow a revival week). However, Brethren were challenged to join social-economic groups while proper ministerial formation of clergy was encouraged.

Brethren never recognize church leaders but Christ. They have stereotypical fellowship liturgy. They need to emphasize constructive testimony. Indeed some Brethren have relaxed moral codes. But fellowship has no denominational boundary and is not a movement and accepts marriage renewal. They have no membership list. They encourage preaching themes to trickle down from convention level.

Leaders of EARM

Diocese of Mount Kenya Central

Kaia: the fellowship has a guiding text every month from District to local church level. They encourage gendered sitting arrangements. They have conventions every April for senior Brethren and youth, and mission at Lodwar every August. Monetary contribution (*Gicunji kia Mwathani*) in local churches caters for fellowships up to East Africa level. Every fellowship has its leaders or burden bearers (*Akui a Murigo*). They support dowry payment and weddings. Light is given from Kenya team down to the local church.

Kiro: leadership; no elections or age limit, leaders are referred to as burden bearers. At team meetings, they sit in a circle. Youth are encouraged to join the fellowship. Fellowship should be handled carefully because it can become a church within a church. EARM is the backbone of the Anglican Church in Kenya.

Kitu: EARM is the backbone of the Anglican Church, Convention monies comes from Brethren. It can be a church within a church. Vicars and youth should be members.

Mugu: everyone needs a revival of heart. The only difference is what sin is and what isn't. Brethren are encouraged to socialize.

Kigi: None.

Kini: to harmonize EARM with the church to avoid what looks like a church within a church.

Diocese of Mount Kenya West

Guse: Revival is not a faction within the church.

Otya: youth should be permitted to preach in the fellowship. Also, allow dynamism in praising God.

Diocese of Embu

Kahs: EARM should refocus on strengthening biblical knowledge and Christian witness to attract the younger generation.

Kima: to read a book by Dorothy Smoker called "Salvation Concept then and now in EARM." St. Andrew's College should address sin in its ministerial formation.

Caal: EARM encourages the same gender sitting arrangement and hugging.

Kagu: love everyone; St. Andrew's to teach clergy to be role models of salvation. The Spirit of God should lead Brethren.

Kigi: None.

Diocese of Kirinyaga

Baho: St. Andrew's student should join fellowship; God calls His people, including youth. There is need of the Holy Spirit's guidance in the mission of the church.

Kini: there is need to encourage welfare groups where people contribute money to help each other, clergy to attend and support fellowship and allow them to participate in the Sunday services. People are encouraged to save in the bank and get loans.

Kigu: Avoid jumble sales during fellowship as it hinders mission and encourage parents to counsel children against social evils.

Muri: Encourage local church fellowship and regional fellowships and conventions. Clergy should publicly confess sin to be relevant as God's watchman.

Kama: Brethren to be members of church councils.

Notations

They emphasize a gender-separated sitting arrangement, a monthly guiding text, harmony between EARM and the Anglican Church. EARM is the backbone of the Anglican Church, and the Brethren contributes *Gicunji kia Mwathani* (portion of God's money [convention money]). EARM is not a faction and should welcome clergy and youth. The concept of sin should be taught at St. Andrew's College Kabare.

Theological students

Allow accountability, change, socialization of different gender and age, and allow full participation in church activities.

Notations

Brethren should accept change, acceptance of others and accountability.

Clergy

Diocese of Kirinyaga

Kama: Nothing.
Muri: Emphasize righteous salvation and cleanliness in the church.
Dok: Revive the dying movement and entrench sound theology.
Kini: Clergy should support Brethren. The former Archbishop Eliud Wabukala was a product of it. Factions like *Kupaa* (Rising Up) still cause division. Brethren abhor socio-economic projects such as loans. They have segregated themselves.

Diocese of Embu

Kagu: Involve bishops and clergy to end these divisions in the church.
Caal: Brethren search for marriage partners for their members.
Kahs: Anglican Church should support EARM and include them in church programs.
Mugu: None

Diocese of Mount Kenya West

Otya: Give youth opportunities to preach in fellowships, accommodate them in the leadership of EARM and remove some radical stands like prohibiting the plaiting of hair.

Thuri: Many join the fellowship. It is not a movement.

Caal: EARM is scholar's terminology. It is a fellowship of the saved across denominations.

Diocese of Mount Kenya Central

Caal: Exploits the principle of Isaiah 1:18 to develop effective communication for an understanding of one another, sentimental values for the Christian faith, salvation, and service.

Kitu: Allow integration of membership in the fellowship with other people.

Mugu: Brethren should allow jumping, singing and dancing for the Lord (like David). It is biblical and not evil.

Notations

They should allow integrated fellowship and dynamic worship, and emphasis on proper communication (Isaiah 1:18). EARM is a fellowship (not a movement) across denominations. Clergy should incorporate Brethren in the preaching program. Brethren should include youth in EARM's leadership. Church leadership should end these divisions. Brethren assists eligible members in getting a marriage partner. They emphasize cleanliness and sound theology.

Bishops

Mount Kenya West

Brethren should not behave like a politician by attacking other Christians. Bishop Mahiani was almost chased away for associating with *Uther* (Light). You should say the time when you got saved and teach clergy to appreciate Brethren. Clergy should avoid being bearded. There should be oneness in Christ.

Diocese of Mount Kenya Central

The EARM has its way of dealing with marriage issues. This should be considered and well-polished by the church.

Diocese of Embu

Address ethical issues such as daughters cannot give birth at home, nurture those saved in school and appreciate youth. Work towards the informed interpretation of the Scripture.

Notations

Brethren should be tolerant with other people (oneness in Christ). Clergy should appreciate Brethren and avoid having a beard. The church should refine Brethren's ways of conducting marriages, understand youth, address ethical issues and improve interpretation of Scripture.

Prominent stakeholders

Gago: Revival is critical in reshaping post-colonial Kenya, Jomo Kenyatta a friend of Bishop Obadiah Kariuki, used his "forgive they don't know what they do," an echo from Christ, which is well propounded by EARM. In 1969 Bishop Kariuki confronted Kenyatta to stop humiliating church elders who were being stripped naked and forced to take the oath.

Wad: Need to look at the relationship between the older *Balokole* movement and modern charismatic Pentecostalism in the light of their thought and practice.

Hald: Great for African Anglican clergy interested in their history; this knowledge should strengthen the church and its witness to the nations of Africa and the wider world.

Mwda: Clergy, bishops, and ACK academics should devote time for fellowship with EARM groups in their areas, to influence and be influenced by real spiritual and theological growth in the church and EARM fellowship.

Mobo: Not Applicable.

Kaja: Not Applicable.

Notations

Revival re-shaped post-colonial Kenya; compare thought and practice of the old *Balokole* and modern charismatic movements and Pentecostalism. This knowledge should strengthen the church and its witness. The church leadership and scholars should influence and be influenced by the revival.

The notations that accrued from the recurrent responses across the categories were compared to get the most consistent bits or units of data from which the following themes were sorted. On the construction and analysis of these themes hinge the remaining section of this chapter, which begins with demographical information about the respondents.

Langham Literature, with its publishing work, is a ministry of Langham Partnership.

Langham Partnership is a global fellowship working in pursuit of the vision God entrusted to its founder John Stott –

> *to facilitate the growth of the church in maturity and Christ-likeness through raising the standards of biblical preaching and teaching.*

Our vision is to see churches in the Majority World equipped for mission and growing to maturity in Christ through the ministry of pastors and leaders who believe, teach and live by the word of God.

Our mission is to strengthen the ministry of the word of God through:
- nurturing national movements for biblical preaching
- fostering the creation and distribution of evangelical literature
- enhancing evangelical theological education

especially in countries where churches are under-resourced.

Our ministry

Langham Preaching partners with national leaders to nurture indigenous biblical preaching movements for pastors and lay preachers all around the world. With the support of a team of trainers from many countries, a multi-level programme of seminars provides practical training, and is followed by a programme for training local facilitators. Local preachers' groups and national and regional networks ensure continuity and ongoing development, seeking to build vigorous movements committed to Bible exposition.

Langham Literature provides Majority World preachers, scholars and seminary libraries with evangelical books and electronic resources through publishing and distribution, grants and discounts. The programme also fosters the creation of indigenous evangelical books in many languages, through writer's grants, strengthening local evangelical publishing houses, and investment in major regional literature projects, such as one volume Bible commentaries like the Africa Bible Commentary and the South Asia Bible Commentary.

Langham Scholars provides financial support for evangelical doctoral students from the Majority World so that, when they return home, they may train pastors and other Christian leaders with sound, biblical and theological teaching. This programme equips those who equip others. Langham Scholars also works in partnership with Majority World seminaries in strengthening evangelical theological education. A growing number of Langham Scholars study in high quality doctoral programmes in the Majority World itself. As well as teaching the next generation of pastors, graduated Langham Scholars exercise significant influence through their writing and leadership.

To learn more about Langham Partnership and the work we do visit langham.org

www.ingramcontent.com/pod-product-compliance
Lightning Source LLC
Chambersburg PA
CBHW050524300426
44113CB00012B/1942